D1094610

FOUNDERS OF
MODERN PSYCHOLOGY

EDUARD ZELLER
1814–1908

FOUNDERS OF
MODERN PSYCHOLOGY

BY

G. STANLEY HALL, Ph.D., LL.D.

PRESIDENT OF CLARK UNIVERSITY AND PROFESSOR
OF PSYCHOLOGY AND PEDAGOGY

NEW YORK AND LONDON
D. APPLETON AND COMPANY
MCMXII

Published July, 1912

2834

Printed in the United States of America

INTRODUCTION

This book is an amplification of six lectures given early in 1912 at Columbia University to an audience composed of students and a wider public. They were not addressed to experts and were only designed to give those who heard them some general idea of the personality, standpoint, and achievements of each of the men described. The chapters are therefore for the most part light and untechnical. They can make no claim to completeness or originality.

Of the twelve years from 1870 to 1882, the author spent nearly six as a student in Germany. The first triennium, ending with the year 1873, was devoted to philosophy, and it was at this period that I came under the influence of those men characterized in the first four chapters. After coming home and teaching what I had learned from these masters and others for six years, during which my interest in more scientific methods and modes of approach grew, especially after the first edition of Wundt's *Psychologie* in 1874 and as a pupil of James and Bowditch, I passed a second triennium in Germany, to which period Wundt and Helmholtz belong. Since then empirical and scientific interests have been so dominant, and many of the results of the first stage so neglected or forgotten, that the re-reading of my own old lecture notes and of works more lately written by the authors treated has proven a pleasant recreation. I do not know of any other American student of these subjects who came into even the slight personal contact it was my fortune to enjoy with Hartmann and Fechner, nor of any psychologist who had the experience of attempting experimental work with Helmholtz, and I think I was the first American pupil of Wundt. The twelve years included in this span, more than any other equal period, marked and gave direction to modern psychology, even though they lie in what has been called the blind-spot of history, *i. e.*, between the memory of the best men in their prime and the point where most standard histories end. I have been told, too, by representatives of several other sciences that it was epochal for them as well. It was also about this time that German science generally began to be recognized as dominant the world over. The years just following the Franco-Prussian war were marked by an almost marvelous outburst of intellectual energy in Teutonic lands.

The diversity of the field of work of these six men suggests that the period of my stay abroad was one when academic traditions in Germany favored more general and less acutely special studies than now. Indeed, in these delightful years, there was almost no limit to the field over which a curious student, especially if he was not working for a degree, might roam. He could indulge his most desultory intellectual inclinations, taste at any spring, and touch any topic in the most superficial way in his effort to orient himself. He could take the widest periscope, and, especially if an American, he was allowed to drop into almost anything to his heart's content, so that there were others besides myself who yielded to the charm of spending much of each day in the lecture rooms, hearing often very elaborate experimental and demonstrational introductory courses, most of them five hours a week. Fresh from the narrow, formal, rather dry curriculum of a denominational American college, the stimulus and exhilaration of this liberty of hearing was great. During the first triennium, besides the more stated work, I took the complete course of Dorner in theology, translating my notes afterward,[1] attended Trendelenburg's seminary on Aristotle, heard De-

[1] Outlines of Dr. J. A. Dorner's System of Theology. Presbyterian Quarterly Review, Oct., 1872, Apr., 1873; N. S., Vol. I, pp. 720-747; Vol. II, pp. 60-93; 261-273.

INTRODUCTION

litzsch's biblical psychology, logical courses by Lasson,
recent psychology by Pfleiderer, comparative religions by
Lazarus. I even tried to follow the venerable Hegelian
Michelet, Drobitsch, the Nestor, and Strümpell, the more
poetic expositor of Herbartianism, and took Kirschmann's
courses. I heard much more of these men in the weekly
philosophical club, and dropped in occasionally to about
all the courses that my friends among the students were
taking. Even in the second triennium this *Wanderlust*
was not extinct. I attended full courses each in chemistry by Kolbe, biology by Leuekhardt, physiology by Du
Bois-Reymond at Berlin, and Ludwig at Leipzig, anatomy
by His, neurology by Flechsig, Westphal's clinic at the
Charité, running over later to Paris for a month to get a
glimpse of Charcot's work there, and to Vienna to sample
Meynert and Exner. Virchow and Bastian were both lecturing in anthropology. Indeed, we students "dropped
in" to almost everything—clinics, seminary, laboratory,
lecture—and if we had a goodly number of registrations in
our book, we were practically unmolested wherever we
went. Perhaps all this meant more distraction than concentration, but if it was mental dissipation, it at any rate
left a certain charm in memory and brought a great and
sudden revelation of the magnitude of the field of science.

It is these considerations that have induced me to yield,
not without some hesitation, to the advice of pupils and
friends to print these sketches, the preparation of which
has been a work of renewing my philosophical and psychological youth.

I am much indebted to my assistant, Dr. Amy E. Tan-
ner, who has borne the burden of revising and correcting
the entire manuscript of the book, and seeing it through
the press. I am also indebted to Miss Helen Cashman for
the preparation of the bibliographies, under my general
direction.

CONTENTS

EDUARD ZELLER

EDUARD ZELLER

1814-1908

Eduard Zeller was born in 1814 in a small Wittenburg town, of humble but respectable parents, who were just able to educate him. The influences of his early life were wholesome and strongly religious. He was from the first a diligent and promising student, and at eighteen passed from the local gymnasium to the University of Tübingen as a student of theology, expecting to become a Lutheran pastor. Dilthy [1] says that his entrance there was at the most stimulating moment of that inspiring movement in which more scholarly and emancipated minds were devoting themselves to new insights into both the historical and the psychological nature of Christianity than had perhaps ever before been focused upon this subject. Zeller immediately fell under the influence of the great author of the so-called Tübingen movement, Christian Ferdinand Baur, a man of great learning and liberality, who, despite his emphasis on the mythic influences that he thought so largely constituted Christianity, always preached, and with great edification, for the *Gemüth*. Thus he and his associates made an almost ideal environment for a young man to pass the stages of the religious *Aufklärung* in.

We know almost nothing of Zeller's student life, for his biography has never been written, but at the age of twenty-six he became *Privatdocent* in theology at Tübingen, and soon after married Baur's brilliant daughter. There he lectured nine years, but in 1847 he was called

[1] Aus Eduard Zellers Jugendjähren. Deutsche Rundschau, 1897, pp. 280.

to Berne as *Professor extraordinarius,* and two years later, in 1849, to Marburg as full Professor of Theology. Here he was bitterly opposed by the Pietists, the only enemies he ever made, whose influence had from the beginning of his career retarded his advancement, and when, in 1862, he was called to Heidelberg, he became a professor of philosophy beside Kuno Fischer, although he had for years before this devoted most of his activity to this field. In 1872 he was called to Berlin as the successor of the great Aristotelian, Trendelenburg (whose seminary I had attended with Paulsen). In 1880 his influence brought Lotze to Berlin, where he died the next year. He was the founder and for many years the editor of *Die theologische Zeitschrift,* and wrote many articles that are to be found only in its pages. In 1887 he was elected Rector of the University of Berlin, receiving thereafter, according to German custom, a generous fraction of all examination fees. And in 1894, at the age of eighty, and twenty-two years after his appointment, he retired and spent the rest of his life at Stuttgart with his son, a physician and surgeon, where he died March 19, 1908, at the patriarchal age of ninety-four. Upon his retirement he was made Privy Councillor with the title of *Excellenz.* The University honored the fifty-year *Jubilatum* of his doctorate and his ninetieth birthday. His life-size portrait now hangs in the *Aula* at Berlin, and his bust stands near the Brandenburg Gate in the Tiergarten beside that of the free-thinking Empress Frederick, the mother of the present Kaiser, whose confidential religious adviser he was for many years.

In the fourteen years of his retirement, which was at first very bitter to him and still more so to his society-loving wife, whom he survived, he was active to the end in revising various editions of his works and in composing articles, the last of which was written when he was nearly ninety. He was the Nestor of the philosophic world, and

4

his place, when he died, like that of his colleagues, Helmholtz, Virchow, and Mommsen, could not be filled. W. Lang [1] describes his personality and his later years, and says that his career was marked by the "supreme blessedness of moral unity, harmony, and repose, and is itself the best illustration of the last problem he discussed, viz., is Eudæmonism blessedness or the highest good?"

In person Zeller was almost alarmingly sallow and lean; small but lithe and erect; sprightly and animated, yet with precise and formal manners, like many small men. His lectures when I heard him were marked by a deliberateness that verged on monotonousness, as well as by directness and by the absence of most of the vast erudition which marks his printed works. He was prematurely bald and gray, and his features have been variously compared to those of Pope Leo XIII, Kant, and Spinoza. His face always wore a slight, agreeable smile. One writer compares his large and lustrous eyes to those of Schleiermacher. He traveled very little, and his life was almost as quiet and uneventful as that of Kant.

Zeller's first years of teaching were largely devoted to the digest, history, defense, and amplifications of the Tübingen School, to giving it cohesion and a proper setting, so that his digest of what it is and means is now the best we have. Thus, he was first its historian and its spirit and method made probably the deepest of all impressions upon his soul and had most to do with shaping his later career.

Nearly half of the first volume of the "Essays" is devoted to a critical digest of the Tübingen school of theology, of which Zeller is by far the ablest and most philosophical as well as the most moderate representative. The middle, half-orthodox party which rested upon Hegel's and Schleiermacher's attempts to reconcile reason and faith, and which never had any logical basis, had been broken up

[1] Eduard Zeller. Deutsche Rundschau, 1908, pp. 173-191.

by Strauss, Bruno, and Feuerbach, and all its ambitious and domineering or its weak and despondent members betook themselves to the confessional hyper-orthodoxy which was then favored by the reactionary German courts. Church and state fell largely under the leadership of dogmatic fanatics or impatient hierarchs, though later a tidal wave of reaction strongly set in. The desolation thus wrought in the head and heart may still be seen in the fact that, while other sciences have progressed, theology was till lately stationary or retrogressive. On the one hand were the free religionists, shallow, tasteless, unscholarly, without thoroughness or method, negative and eminently unprogressive; and on the other an ultra-orthodoxy of the Hengstenberg type, ever elaborating its uncritical gospel harmonies; or an exegesis of the patristic type, which can put any meaning into or out of the Scripture text, and which is well content with working out practical unionistic platforms for evangelical coöperation between trivially diverging sects. Both are alike unsusceptible, Zeller says, to the great pressing needs of scientific theology, viz., the explanation of religion itself from its psychologic and of Christianity from its historical grounds.

The latter problem is by no means finally solved by the Tübingen school. Baur, its coryphæus, held that the last result of the criticism of the New Testament and other early Christian writers should and would be a noble and at the same time historical picture of Jesus himself. This, however, far from being given by the negative residual methods of Strauss, could only be reached after the bias of each evangelist and apocryphist, the authenticity of every text, as well as its historical validity, and every personal, dogmatic, or philosophical party influence of the age had been weighed and tested. It was to this, in some sense preliminary, work (which Strauss, by destroying the foundation of dogmatic supernaturalism, made seem possible) that Baur mainly devoted himself; and the goal which in-

spired him, but which he did not attain, must be striven for
and reached by his method if Christian theology is to
maintain a respectable position in the modern intellectual
world. Man's desire for happiness is oppressed by a sense
of his finitude, but the true religious consciousness reveals
a higher and compensating happiness attained by the cultivation of purity of moral disposition. Man's elevation
through the religious consciousness above the finitude of
his nature, expressed as poverty of spirit, humility, simplicity, unselfishness, and the inwardness and absoluteness
of religious life characterized by the doctrine of the father-
hood of God—something like this Baur thought would be
ultimately found to be the fundamental idea of Jesus, conceived with intense realistic ethical genius, and made a
pressing and practical question by being boldly and saga-
ciously interpreted as the bottom meaning of a coming
messianic reconstruction of the Jewish state. In his earlier
Hegelian ˙period Baur regarded Christianity as mainly a
philosophical but in his later as a purely moral, problem.
The incomparable influence which Jesus started in history
consisted not so much in any novelty of his conceptions—
these are now traced to earlier sources—but in the nobility
of his character and the force and purity of his personality, which were so great that a new moral and religious
type of life was inevitable. He *was* the Messiah in his own
inspiring sense, and not merely claimed to be. This, as
every such conception must now be (in the absence of reliable or detailed historical information respecting Jesus),
is as yet too general and vague, and must be, on the one
hand, elaborated by a sound and vigorous ethical philosophy into a wealth of needed moral power too long unutilized (somewhat as Pfleiderer has since attempted, although the ethical genius of a Fichte is more adequate to
such a work than that of Baur); and on the other it must
be verified and corrected by a deeper and stricter critico-
historical study than even the Tübingen school has made.

2   7

One of Zeller's best essays is devoted to a characterization of his teacher, F. C. Baur, who, in his uneventful, home-staying life, his slowly ripening nature, his amazing industry and perseverance, in his philosophic, critical tact and vigor, in the growing importance and initiative power of his work, is aptly compared with Kant. His temperate mind could hold an important question open for years, sifting and weighing evidence with respect for every suggestion of fact, and so honestly and *con anima candida,* so without hyper-self-consciousness, that he seemed like the noblest of the old reformers, while his moral sensitiveness was so acute that he was more grieved by lack of thoroughness or honesty in the work of his pupils than by the bitterest attacks of his opponents. He lived in and for his work, but could always preach edifyingly to the *Gemüth,* and his nature was profoundly religious and pastoral.

His school, which has revolutionized religious opinions throughout Germany, Holland, Switzerland, and even in protestant France, and has found many points of access even to English and American thought, is unlike the liberalism of deists, encyclopedists, Schiller, Strauss, and Feuerbach, in that it was founded by professional theologians and by men of deep personal piety. It simply drew conclusions which hovered in the intellectual air and which every one who thought logically must infer. It showed the time its own image and in urging that the New Testament was not pure history and not supernatural it only applied the critical methods which had almost revolutionized our knowledge of antiquity and its literature.

Every one has smiled over the forcing, torturing, and tasteless methods of the old German rationalism which explained away the miracle of Cana as a wedding jest, the fiery tongues of Pentecost as electricity, the resurrection of Jesus as the recovery from a trance; which declared that Paul at his conversion was blinded by lightning and was cured by the natural effect of the shock of an old man's cold hands, that the fetters were shaken from the hands of the imprisoned Paul and Silas by an earthquake; that Jesus, though seeming to walk on the water, really walked at its edge on the shore, etc. In short, this rationalism, by interpreting Oriental imagery and referring natural processes immediately to God, though exorcising the supernatural, yet makes Scripture none the less credible, though in an altered sense, and it had its effect upon the then current method of orthodox interpretation because this orthodoxy was no less tortuous and tasteless. This is perhaps best seen in the church history of Neander, who, without abandoning a single miracle or wavering on the doctrine of inspiration, which makes all biblical criticism impossible, yet loves to break off the points of the strongest miracles and is constantly conceding to the rationalistic methods and capitulating to the *Zeit-geist;* also in Bruno Baur, who later declared the Tübingen school too conservative and was removed from his professorship, and who deduced Messiahship, resurrection, and other evangelical motifs from abstract dialectic principles ignoring or denying, like Drews, the existence of an historic Jesus; and also in Marheinike, who made Bible texts into many-sided scholastic formulæ; and in Göschel, who all but identified philosophy and Scripture. All these men were alike unable to see the necessity or accept the results of such minute and painstaking researches as those of Baur.

First of all, Zeller continues, it must be borne in mind that the sense of literary property during the early Christian centuries was as undeveloped as any socialist could desire. Plato and Xenophanes put their sentences into the mouth of Socrates (perhaps somewhat as a modern theologian states the "true Bible doctrine," although in quite other than scriptural terms). To present or develop the views of another, to win attention, to produce immediate effect, to seek shelter from criticism behind a great name, on account of personal modesty, or piety to a beloved teacher to whom nowadays a volume would be dedicated— all these motives of apocryphal fabrication were so common that a moralist must be as naïve and devoid of historic sense to raise the scruples of a modern conscience here as to apply the laws in a modern statute book against stealing to the constitution of Sparta. The well-proven cases of pseudonymous authorship in ancient times, many of which Zeller instances, are extremely numerous. Baur's conclusion that the Gospels and the greater number of the Epistles are unauthentic, of later origin, and mainly records of violent partisan controversies which rent early Christianity from its beginning opens the most interesting and classic of all ancient literature to the use of scholars, and elevates and frees the intellectual life of the age to a degree to which only the work of modern science can be in any degree compared. It was his special endeavor to discover the bias or tendencies of the early Christian writers. In an age when men believed what pleased, interested, or edified them, whether it was that Homer argued for the Jewish Sabbath, that Orpheus sang of Abraham, Moses, and the ten commandments, that an old or hardened heathen was converted by a relic stealthily laid under his pillow, that chiliasm is true, or that new records of the life of Jesus, written by apostles, were suddenly discovered at opportune polemic moments, and when credentials and criticism were all but unknown—under such conditions the chief task of the historian is to seek and define the tides of party feeling and prejudice, the currents of men's wishes, ambitions, and hopes, and occasionally their political relations and the ground traits of individual character. These, together with traditions and sagas as material for a mythopœic fantasy in a most agitated age of persecution and millenial expectations, must be controlled before the objective history of that time can be reconstructed.

It was hard for the personal disciples of Jesus and

EDUARD ZELLER

the Ebionite party gathered about them to uphold his
tenets against the dominant Pharisaic sect after their leader
had been executed as a seditious agitator, but it was still
harder for them to see Paul, who had never known Jesus
personally, so successfully propagating his teachings, as
not only independent of, but actually irreconcilable with,
Judaism, among Gentile races and even declaring that
by his doctrine Jews were freed from their own laws. The
conservative wing of the early Christian party, which held
that Jesus could be the Messiah of the Jews only, and that
the Mosaic rites and laws were still binding as a propæ-
deutic of Christianity, regarded Paul as an interloper who
really designed to use the large collections he was making
ostensibly for the church at Rome in order to buy the gift
of apostleship. He is again even described as a conjurer
who represented himself as inspired till Peter exposed him.
To define and defend his universalistic view, viz., that
Christianity simply set men in right relations to God, Paul
composed the Letters to the Galatians, the Corinthians,
and especially that to the promising and hitherto neutral
church at Rome. Meanwhile, hard pressed and perplexed
by the vast discrepancy between the actual low-born Jesus
and the splendors of the messianic kingdom of popular
and patriotic hopes, the disciples had come to expect that
he would appear again—an event by no means unparalleled
in Jewish story—and inaugurate a new kingdom of inde-
scribable magnificence. Nero, too, the anti-Christ, it was
rumored, was not dead but had escaped and would come
again with Oriental armies, and new wars and persecu-
tions would most severely test the fidelity of the faithful.
In this condition of things the book of Revelations
was written by John as a manifesto before the decisive
struggle, after which the millenial new Jerusalem, with
Jesus as king, would fill the earth. Thus read, it is no
longer a puzzling riddle book, but most historical and authentic, in fact the only book in the New Testament writ-

11

ten by an apostle-disciple. The old Israelitic expectations are all to be fulfilled in the wonder-world of the reappearing Messiah. Those who claim to be apostles but are not, together with the hated doctrines of the Nicolaitans—a bitter allusion to Paul and his teachings—are to have no place in the new theocracy, with its walls of jasper, its streets of gold, and its tree of life. Thus, too, the most phantasmagorical dream of Jewish patriotism is successfully used to save the forlorn hope of a leaderless and losing cause. The controversy between the Pauline and the Jewish Christians was long and bitter, and colored, if it did not inspire, most of the books of the New Testament. The twelve apostles are paralleled by the seventy co-workers of Paul. The Petrine party elaborated the Samaritan and Judean, the Pauline party the Galilean activity of Jesus. Peter is even represented as the founder of the first church at Antioch, and is made to go to Rome because Paul had been there. James repudiates Paul's doctrine of justification by faith, urges that even devils may believe, and represents Jesus, perhaps his own brother, as an ascetic Essene with long hair, and as abstaining from flesh and wine. In a word, Paulinism, which dispensed with offerings and with circumcision, and denied that the only way to the new faith was through Judaism, stands for the freedom of wisdom and mature manhood, while the Jewish Christians argued for the status and moral regimen of adolescence.

Meanwhile both parties were persecuted alike; both were represented in nearly every church, and so gradually a practical and administrative unity became more essential as the church began its immense organization, while old passions and prejudices only faintly survived in a new generation. In the second century a conciliatory desire to save the effects of the work of both wings is manifest by accommodating, and often even transforming, their destructive tenets. Thus the Acts, written in the second century and based perhaps on the notes of Paul's traveling companion, and Luke, though both written with an unmistakable Pauline drift, are very conciliatory; Colossians ends with a complimentary mention of a list of Petrine worthies, while, like Ephesians, its Paulinism is very tempered. The first Epistle of Peter makes surprising concessions to Paulinism. On the one hand it was apparently granted that Paul was too intricate and speculative, and that faith alone was not enough for salvation, and on the other it was necessarily acknowledged that the wall of partition between Jews and Gentiles was broken down, in fact, and the vast numbers of non-Jewish Christians were taken into fellowship. Thenceforth all traces of primitive discord were carefully scored away, and the energies of the church were free for the work of practical and dogmatic development and defense.

As the church grew, all parties united to elevate the conception of the person of Christ still higher, as a convenient point for dogmatic zeal in which old discords might be forgotten, until at last even the Messiah idea, with which it had become identified in the first century, was not exalted enough for the head of a church that had its stronghold in the capital city of the world and was destined to become universal, and of a hierarchy so rapidly growing in influence and self-conscious dignity. The Son of David gradually became, with the growing influence of the ultra-Pauline Gentile element and the Alexandrian gnostic philosophy, not merely the heavenly pneumatic man, the new Adam, but the preëxistent, creative Word. The gospel of John (A. D. 170-180), which is not historical, but represents the maturest and best points of the work and teaching of Christianity up to the period of its composition, which quietly appropriates the serviceable elements of the dangerous heresies of Gnosticism and Montanism, and shows no trace of hierarchism in the church, marks the point where the history of primitive Christian-

13

ity ends and that of Catholicism begins. The charm of the Johannean image of Jesus, so pure, so exalted, and almost femininely delicate, so harmonious that his inward peace was undisturbed by conflict and sorrow, and so free from all earthly limitations, is unprecedented among all the ideal personalities hitherto offered to human contemplation. The Johannean gospel not only reconstructs the previous Christian history from its new and tranquil standpoint, but represents the highest theological development of the first period of Christian history.

In an essay entitled "Greek and Roman Prejudices against Christianity" Zeller shows that, while Alexander and the Roman Empire had prepared the way for the outward spread of Christianity, the popular Stoic philosophy, which taught that all men were brothers, with equal rights and duties, and subject to the same moral law, which, instead of faith, made ethical temper the saving principle, which divided mankind into the two great classes of the fools and the wise, instead of the redeemed and the lost, and which longed for the "birthday of eternity," an entrance into the "great eternal peace," prepared the mental soil for the reception of Christian doctrine. The popular heathen notion still was that the Christians, if not all Syrian barbarians, were atheists, or criminals, who perhaps cooked and ate children, and prayed to a god with an ass's head, were the worst and most unpatriotic citizens, and, in fact, enemies of the human race, so that Nero found no difficulty in circulating the report that it was they who had fired Rome. Pliny thought their creed in itself a harmless superstition, but believed that their stiff-neckedness in refusing to adore images of the gods and the Emperor, and in violating the laws against making proselytes, should be punished. The mild M. Aurelius persecuted them because he deemed the pertinacity of their creed—so unlike his all-sided toleration and uncritical eclecticism—dangerous to the discipline of the state. Lu-

cian said that the sect was composed of the pitiable and
deluded disciples of an arch-sophist. The platonic Celsus
argued that Jesus had stolen and disseminated philosophic
doctrines which he could not understand, was of illegitimate birth, and a conjurer. Greek joyousness and Roman
pride had only contempt for a religion designed for the
sorrowing, oppressed, weak, and guilty. The neo-Platon-
ists revered Jesus, but inquired, like Reimarus, why, if
salvation was through him, he appeared so late, and urged
that if Peter and Paul could disagree about fundamental
tenets his doctrine must be very uncertain. Others thought
that Jesus did too few miracles to be really a god, and
proved that Apollonius did far more, while Julian, believing that it was impossible for all men to have the same
religion, argued that all noble men and great deeds in the
world had come from heathendom and forbade Christians
to teach the ancient literature.

In the saga of ''Peter as Roman Bishop '' the ground
motive is the ultra-Ebionite view of Paul, which described
him under the name of Simon, the gnostic Samaritan sor-
cerer, who, after he had been exposed by Peter in Palestine,
came to Rome, where, by his arts and by the aid of demons,
he won great honors and many followers. Later when Rom-
ish canonists sought to derive the power of the popes directly through Peter it is said that the latter followed
Simon—Paul—to Rome. The Jewish legend dishonored
Paul, whom the catholic party would honor, hence he is
now distinguished from his double and made to join Peter
in opposing Simon, and both Paul and Peter, it was said,
died in Rome. Later Peter alone is made the first Bishop
of Rome, and thus the greatest work of Paul's life is ac-
credited to the hostile apostle of the circumcision.

Much importance is ascribed to Schwegler's work on
''Montanism and the Post-apostolic Age,'' wherein it is
concluded that Christianity assumed at first to be nothing but a more complete form of Essenic Judaism, and that

the autonomy and universality which Paul attempted to give it transformed and de-Judaized it materially less than had been generally supposed.

In the platonic republic Zeller sees not only a significant ideal and prophecy impossible of realization, despite Plato's unreserved belief in it, and not only a product of the time, when, after the Peloponnesian war, the dangers of individualism, the greed of riches, and party strife seemed to show that men could not be trusted with their own development, but he saw in it especially a type of society which has been the germ and norm for the organization of the mediæval church. Instead of the philosophers who were to rule absolutely in the platonic republic are the priests; instead of the warrior caste, the temporal powers; instead of community of goods, which was an early Christian ideal, voluntary poverty of goods or of spirit and the mendicant orders. Community of wives, which was recommended to restrain, not to satisfy desire, is paralleled by celibacy, that monks may live all for the church. Both the ideal and the actual system rest upon ethical dualism and teach that suffering here will be compensated in a future life, and both assert a divine leadership of the state. The Republic, like Augustine's City of God, is an institution for training men in virtue. The church on the other hand does not so absolutely subordinate the individual to the community and the spirit of universal fraternity is widely contrasted with the castes and the national exclusiveness of the Republic. While Plato would class modern theology, so far as it does not coincide with philosophy, as mythology, and would be able to find in modern universities no suitable philosophers for rulers, and would be incensed at the modern political romances, wherein private interest is satisfied instead of annihilated, he must nevertheless be counted as one of the most important predecessors of organized Christianity. Much space is devoted to showing that this was not the result of mere analogy, but was history, and that Plato's conception, at first too spiritualistic to be popular, passed into the general culture of the day.

This matured and moderated digest of the Tübingen school, so briefly and imperfectly epitomized and digested above, records, we believe, despite its many errors which subsequent criticism has shown in it, and which it would be out of place to point out here, the most important achievement of the historic critical method. It affords the general terms of a suggestive and edifying solution of the most intricate and also the most obscured of all historical problems—a problem not of one sect and race or century but of commingled nationalities and of contending political, philosophical, religious, partisan, and personal interests. The facts were so inaccessible and so metamorphosed in this long contest that only the most patient and conscientious research, coupled with amazing psychologic insight and tact, was able to reconstruct them at last after ages of misconception, with so high a degree of verisimilitude that the most distinguished of Roman historians, Mommsen, whose essential impartiality cannot be denied, declared that thirty years ago no German scholar under forty-five had thoroughly studied the Tübingen writers without being in the main convinced by them. There will long be many to fear that moral restraints may be practically weakened if Scripture is proven uninspired in the old sense, or if miracles are disallowed, just as the Emperor Julian feared that classical literature would be ignored and perhaps lost if faith in the ancient gods was destroyed. For now not a soul believes in Jove, father of gods and men. This is, without doubt, sometimes the case among the young and the undiscriminating. But on the other hand it is only thus now made possible for men of thorough modern culture and moral self-respect to call themselves Christians if they will, and to be so in mind and heart in a sense deeper and larger than many conventional churchmen comprehend, even though these liberal thinkers see fit and hopeful occasion to urge friendly, even though misconstrued, aid in ameliorating too narrow a severity in faith and life, and in sustaining and reforming church organization, as a right by no means invalidated by stricter modern definitions of the Christian name but rather new vested by the supreme sanction of a positive and adult moral understanding. Myth is a deeper and broader expression of humanity's common nature and needs than reason or philosophy itself has yet attained. It is never the utterance of the mere individual, but is the *logos,* or oversoul, or the half-unconscious moral instinct of a race or an age. It is never bound too closely to details of place or time. These only hinder or embarrass its rare and strange moving and edifying power. In its noblest scriptural form—Biblical in the classic sense wherever found—it comes most clearly and directly home to the *Gemüth,* takes men out of their own selfish personal lives, and raises, purifies, and broadens their motives and feelings and purposes as does nothing else. How to make it most effective for good is a problem which homiletic art has perhaps not yet finally solved.

The "Tübingen men" in Germany later grew inactive and retrospective, and even Zeller was somewhat prolix and boastful in some of his recapitulations, and yet not only is their critical work incomplete, but its practical deductions (the last consideration of a German savant), because left to be drawn in a negative, popular, and superficial way, have been often sadly injurious instead of helpful, as they should be, to the cause of religion and morality, and "the German capital, Berlin, has grown perhaps more unconscious of the existence of religion and its institutions than any city in Christendom." Far from assenting to any ultra theories as, *e. g.,* that of Rothe—that the modern state, more than the church, expresses the essence of Christianity—we cannot deny that Christianity has grown

18

far too consubstantial with our social, moral, intellectual, and æsthetic life and development to be eradicated by any violence, or even to be intellectually distinguished and traced through all the long and subtle associations by which it has become ingrained in our inmost psychic character. By being proven the oldest of all historic categories, and rooted in the earliest written records, instead of a supernatural graft upon an old and decaying trunk, it challenges the reverence of science itself as the most important problem of folk (Völker) psychology, by contributing to the experimental solution of which all known civilized races and ages have become in a noble philosophic sense organically united. As the modern musical scale and the masterpieces composed in it are not endangered by the proof of its mathematical inaccuracy, its rude empirical origin, or by the suggestions of improvement; as the modern state is not lost to socialism by the demonstration that all values originated in the ten fingers of the working man, or that the rights of bequest and of absolute private ownership are, so to speak, recent habits, resting upon a series of accidents and misconceptions, so the Christian church is by no means essentially or permanently weakened by being compelled to relinquish its belief in miracles, inspiration, and an incarnate deity for more historical conceptions of its origin. It is only another reformation that impends, as radical, possibly, to the more assumptive and unreasoning of modern Pharisees as was the new dispensation of Jesus itself, but only salutary to every true religious interest. This was Zeller's attitude.

In the above we have seen that a leading trait favored by Zeller's home life, his theological studies, and his Tübingen relations, and one which pervaded all his mature work, was its religious motivation. His conception of Greek philosophy, if not entirely theodician, was at any rate such as to make him at first chiefly interested in it where and so far as it was religious. From Kant he had learned that re-

ligious belief was chiefly valuable as it influenced men for
virtue and the supremacy of the practical over the pure
reason; in a word, that belief was for the sake of conduct
and character. From Schleiermacher he had learned the
inwardness of things and that doctrines had worth only as
they met the needs of the heart, while from Baur he had
learned that creeds are only the personal faith of dominant
groups of men, so that theologies must ever be made over
anew. From this point of view he naturally passed on to
the insight that philosophies are only the changing formulation of the choicest wishes of cultured souls, and also
that the historic conceptions of the past, even those most
inveterate and sacred, must be forever analyzed, criticized,
and gone back of, and what they say interpreted in terms
of what they mean. Thus he came to regard philosophy
as very largely a sublimation of religion and its creeds,
and from this view he gradually passed to that which gave
to it its own independent worth as the highest expression
of the culture of the day.

We shall next epitomize for our readers his remarkable
summary of the then recent investigations in the field of
comparative religions and the psychology of religion in
the "Vorträge und Abhandlungen," which contain his
most personal as well as, perhaps, his most original views.
In a laboriously compacted essay on the "Origin and Essence of Religion" he premises that philosophy, or psychology, is the closest and most indispensable friend of religion. Doubt, which marks the important moment when
we question or seek explanation about the things which
have surrounded us from childhood, is sure to lead to a
deeper and purer faith if it is manfully faced. The notion of God is not innate, but is given perhaps necessarily,
although always mediately, through experience, and thus
rests upon the same sort of grounds and inferences as does
the notion of atoms, and is as scientific. In fact, all intellectual possessions whatever are self-won; we make all

which comes into our minds out of experience. All men irresistibly infer that there are laws and that things are connected, not merely in time and space, but inwardly; they not merely are, but hang together, and do so not only in our ideas objectively carried over into experience but in themselves by the law of causation. Like all things else, causality itself must have a cause. Thus at first as many substances are postulated as there are forces observed; later these forces are found so closely connected, their actions and reactions so poised and equipolated, the one by the other, that they must be thought as one. But this unity is, of course, as hyper-sensuous and immaterial as force itself. Consciousness in its essence is a union of the manifold, and hence, by the very form of its knowing, its every object, whether cosmic or microscopic, must be a unity of the composite or the simple. Hence the necessity of inferring a primitive unitary force. In illustration of these principles, Zeller proceeds to group a great number of facts gathered from folk psychology and mythology.

From just such feelings as arise vividly in our own consciousness when we take the first spring ramble in the country, by the sea, or under the stars, from just such instinctive needs as we now feel in thunder storms, floods, battle, famine, or sickness, and from the experiences of family and social life, not only all poetry and mythology, but all religion have taken their origin. These are the feelings and needs which they interpret. The strongest or most unwonted impressions drive us irresistibly beyond the limits of our own ability or knowledge to supernatural causes. General forces are not deified. There are no gods of space or gravity. There was no interest in the beautiful, but only in the pleasant and the fearful; and what was more fearful than night, before man was possessed of fire? Because most of his instincts are satisfied, man assumes that somehow his wishes also must be, and so, when thought asks, fancy answers, though the answers are but changed facts. Thus the first religions are polytheistic and preserve a faithful record of the wishes, fears, and hopes of prehistoric peoples whose spirits were wrought upon by nature and history with an intensity inversely as their knowledge of them. As long as no one dreamed that, *e. g.*, the sun and fire might be the same, no one thought of ordering this crowding and increasing throng of deities. But as men saw unity in the world and later as they learned to concentrate their own efforts upon some one paramount object, then first some group of gods became paramount, and later some one god was made king or president in the council of the others. Sometimes a tribe who had developed a national deity like that of the Jews induced others by argument or by the sword to accept it as their own. Perhaps monotheism was first the result of a philosophical critique, as among the disciples of Xenophanes, or again unity may have been favored or suggested by the all-inclosing arch of heaven and the apparent limits of the horizon and the visible universe. The visible always precede the invisible gods, and monotheism is always developed from polytheism. The personification of active forces is in fact the natural form under which the idea of cause is first represented. It is impossible to follow all the subtle associations of ideas by which the wind was represented as a breath, the lightning as God's spear, every bright or smooth stone as an amulet, the stars as living beings; by which a stick was thought to reveal hidden treasure, or a backward look to the left to cure sickness. Whether it was at first some fancied analogy or a rare but opportune chance sequence in time to which they owe their origin, such beliefs have possessed the mind of man for unnumbered ages, and hence, and because they minister, however unworthily, to a real need, they are very hard to eradicate. As long as there is no postulate that all things are connected by laws, and in proportion as man is uncertain of his own position in an unexplored world where the most unexpected thing may happen to him at any moment, so long and so far is he anxious to get the unknown powers on his side by presents, wounds self-inflicted, the offering of animals and finally of human beings and especially of innocent persons. Sometimes the deity is small and weak, or perhaps the priest, who even in the Catholic church holds a sort of conjuring power, has found some magic liturgy or ceremony of mighty and constraining cogency, and the god may even be whipped or imprisoned till the wish is gratified or the fear allayed.

But religions must ever become more rational, *i. e.*, immaterial. This process begins before all known languages developed, in the inference that soul and body are distinct, and that the ego is not a whole, made up of soul and body as subordinate unities. In the dreams about a dead acquaintance this distinction begins. The souls of men are at first located in the heart, head, bowels, liver, diaphragm, etc., and are weak and shadowy. The "he himself" is the body, as in Homer. Shades led an unreal life under the earth, affecting the fruits of the fields, were figured as ghosts, manes, elves, and finally, in German mythology, survived as dwarfs, till the conception took more definite form in the idea of Hades. At first only chiefs and leaders had souls and these are invoked along with the sun and moon as in the worship of ancestors.

As long as their favor could be bought deities had, of course, no moral character. As hospitality, agriculture, commercial and family life, conceptions of regularity in nature, etc., were developed, the gods ceased to be awe- or fear-inspiring (*unheimisch*) and influenced more directly the life of men. Religion now began to grow in importance with the worth of the moral life. The lowest form of prophecy is the interpretation of signs. Faith is first only the child of the wish; then an audible voice must speak from the clouds; then men are inspired by a daimon, which is the inner oracle of conviction below distinct consciousness. They are suddenly and perhaps violently possessed by ideas, which wrap them in a dream, revery, or vision, so new and so absorbing that the poet or musician dare not claim his work as his own. They did not know the inner process but were sure of its results, and thus inspiration was the best form which creative genius knew to give itself.

From the above principles of its growth we may infer why religion sometimes became largely political, as among the Jews; why ancient systems lay great weight upon the cultus, or worship, and modern upon dogmatic orthodoxies; why religions must change; why the tension between the old and the new is proportional to the rapidity of this change; why all that cannot be harmonized to the new standpoints should, as Schleiermacher said, be allowed to lapse quietly from the Christian consciousness; and above all we can see that, as we should not study the Bible to know what Jesus believed but what we ourselves must—so the worth of religion does not depend on how it originated but on what it does, just as the dignity of man and of science is not impaired by the conviction that one was developed from the ape and the other from astrology, alchemy, etc.; or as the cogency of a man's logic is not prejudiced by the fact that a few decades before he could use only baby language. Not the first form but the historic principle is the essential thing. No man loses esteem for the German people of to-day by reading Tacitus or studying the life of the mediæval Teutonic tribes.

A poetic race will emphasize the mythological element, a speculative people the dogmatic, and a practical the active side of religious life, but Schleiermacher was right in seeking a deeper common principle. We must always reason from what the religious consciousness says to what it means. Dogma ignores scientific interests. Knowledge is no measure of the worth of religious life, and is value-

EDUARD ZELLER

less for its own sake. Morality, very far from being the
natural and implacable enemy of religion, as Feuerbach
argued, is its chief, though not only, constituent. As well
argue against the use of fire on account of conflagration
or against civic life because of corruption, or against judicial tribunals because they sanctioned the torture chamber,
as to reject religion because of the selfishness, fanaticism,
and superstition which are ever found to attend it. Religion is not merely recognition of our duties as divine commands, any more than the notion of God originated in the
moral sense, but it includes everything which concerns the
well-being of man. It rests upon and is determined by the
needs of social and individual life, and especially of the
Gemüth. Its cultus is the natural expression of a natural
feeling, and must evoke worthy frames of mind and all
noble resolves. Does it bring joy and certainty into the
life of the soul, does it increase the sense of personal happiness, rest, peace, etc., and not does it make us work successfully for the rewards of a future pay day, are the
questions. Can we dispense with the sense of our universal relationship and give up the postulate of a unity of
all things?

Again, the germ of the Roman religion Zeller finds in
the Latin-Sabine veneration of invisible spiritual beings in
nature. The solitude of woods, the gurgling of springs,
the crackling of flames, the gloom of forests, the phenomena
of the sky, the change of the seasons, suggested to the old
Romans three classes of natural forces, heavenly, terres-
trial, and subterranean, which were poetically personified
as gods instead of scientifically interpreted. The transition from a fanciful conception to a natural ethical religion can be nowhere so fully studied as among the Romans,
whose fundamental characteristic was awe of unknown
forces and constraint before supernatural influences.
Hence their reverence for tradition, their extreme care not
to offend the gods by inauspicious chance words, or by the

neglect of the innumerable formalities which hallowed
nearly every act of life. For centuries, like the Germanic
races, the Romans had no or few images of the gods, but
later there were throngs of protective deities, *e. g.*, one for
gates, another for hinges, one for doors, another for thresholds, or again one for the cry of a new-born babe, another
for the father's acknowledgment of it, a goddess of the
cradle, another who presided over the ceremony of naming,
another as protectress from witches. There was one each
for the child's food and drink, and one which brought it
from the cradle to the bed. Sacrifice was made to appro-
priate deities respectively that the boy's bones might grow
rightly when he first stood, walked, went to and came from
school; to others that he might reckon, sing, be strong in
body and in mind, etc. In the third and fourth century
B. C. the influence of the religions of the north and south,
especially that of Greece, began to be felt. First the mythology and rites, then the literature, and later the Greek
philosophy radically changed the popular faith and at last
prepared the way for an easy transition to Christianity.
First the shallow Euhemerus taught that the gods were
our ancestors and Jove was the head of an old regnant
house. His doctrines were long influential. The Epicu-
rean deist Lucretius described the world as set free from
the heavy oppression of superstition by philosophy. The
gods were far off and cared not for men. They could have
no sex or age, the story of Iphigenia was an unmitigated
horror. Scævola declared that the religion of the poets
was childish and often immoral, and that of the philosopher abstruse and powerless, and held that religion was
chiefly an art of the statesman, who must and ought to
use it for political ends. That the *pontifex maximus* could
thus hold dogma as nothing besides religious cultus without exciting antagonism is significant. Varro, the authority
for most modern knowledge of the religion of ancient
Rome, declared God to be the universe, especially the soul

and reason. The public religion should be allegorized philosophy rather than the myths of the poets. Seneca's conception of a world-ruling wisdom, beneficent goodness, pious disposition, his description of deity as near, about, in us, was the highest form of Stoicism, in which it most nearly coincided with Christianity. Epictetus and especially M. Aurelius, to whom Zeller devotes a laborious essay, were far less emancipated from the popular faith. The former believed in Demeter and Persephone because men enjoyed their fruits, and because they restrained from wrong, and apparently never reflected that there is no error which may not do good at times, while the latter, too practical for the Stoic allegorization of myths, believed not only in dreams and oracles, but apparently in many foreign rites himself, and excused many other superstitions because they satisfied man's religious needs. Cicero held that faith in deity is deeply implanted in all men and is taught by the beauty and wisdom of the world, that a pure heart is the best worship, and that, whether or not the existence of the gods can be scientifically proved, natural religion must be strenuously upheld as the chief bond of human society. After the Republic the split between the doctrines of philosophy and the old Roman faith grew wider till the ancient gods lost their distinct individuality in the popular consciousness and the Oriental monotheism of a denationalized Christianity readily absorbed all the purer and better elements of moral and religious culture into itself.

In discussing the teleological and mechanical explanation of nature, which is perhaps the most fundamental question of religious philosophy, Zeller urges that it is equally senseless and tasteless to conceive animals as machines, the world as a huge timepiece, the mind as a body, attraction as caused by hooked atoms, and to banish all notion of final causes as barren vestals on the one hand, and to explain trifles teleologically on the other. Neither can he agree with Plato and Aristotle that nature is to be explained in part mechanically and in part teleologically; nor with Leibniz that the world as a whole is teleological and single phenomena mechanical. While the latter satisfies science it grants too much to metaphysics. All possible worlds had no struggle for existence in God's mind, but the world as it is is the only possible form of his revelation, and is hence necessary. In a perfect nature the divine will and ability coincide with action. The world has no beginning and will have no end in time. It was never without life and reason in some form. Because necessity is perfect and absolute it is best conceived as immanently teleological, and the antithesis between the two applies only to its elements and not to the world as a whole. The need of teleology is only felt after man's acts have become planful, and if assumed would require an infinite series of reasons, which at bottom would be, like the conclusions from logical premises, rather more mechanical than otherwise. Before matter, as space-filling, moving, etc., can become an adequate logical cause of all things it must be conceived in a radically new way, while teleology is at most only one heuristic presupposition, and not a scientifically grounded constitutive principle.

The development of monotheism Zeller considers as the most important of moral-theoretical problems, and among the Greeks, the most gifted of all races, it is especially suggestive. The poesy of Homer and Hesiod depicts Zeus, the God-king, as subject to fate, surrounded by a turbulent and tricky aristocracy of deities, and, although the protector of rights, as yet possessing no very moral character. His rule is far milder than was the shadowy old dispensation of the Eumenides. The poets were the first theologians, and it was they who reformed the crudities of the early faith. Philosophy did not grow up, as since the Christian era, in the service of theology. Xenophanes contributed the first monotheistic conception in describing men and gods as having one origin, and the Infinite One as being all eye, ear, thought, etc. From his keen irony, *e. g.*, in saying that the Thacian gods have blue eyes and red hair, and that horses and oxen, could they think and speak, would have quadruped gods like themselves, anthropomorphic polytheism never entirely recovered. The teachings of the Sophists, which pervaded all ranks of society, that we cannot tell whether the gods exist or not, that religion was the invention of shrewd legislators who sought in an appeal to fear the strongest sanction for their laws, and that the gods represent those natural objects found to be the most useful, was followed by Socrates' conception of a unitary plan in nature and an all-wise and good principle overruling all things. Yet Socrates was by no means hostile to the popular religion, but believed in many gods, who do all for the good of man, who must submit to and obey them. The Eleatics believed in one only God, not in human form; the Cynics ridiculed the popular faith; the Skeptics declared it not proven; the Epicureans thought that chance and necessity ruled the universe and that the gods led a life of placid repose, far off between the worlds, and were worthy of unselfish veneration. Over Plato's eternal, changeless, ideal world, the Good rules supreme. It is the ground of all thought and being, giving to things reality and to thought truth. It is essential Deity, toward which we strive in every act and thought, yet is hard to know. It created and rules the world, is approached by purity of life, is not jealous of human happiness, is beyond feeling pleasure or pain in human acts. To this conception Christian theology is immensely indebted. Yet Plato does not give up the idea of other visible gods. Stars, like the world, are incorporate deities. Men must be trained by mythic lies to abandon figured and poetic for true thinking. Aristotle reasserts most of the same notions, but adds that God must be a personal, active, first-moving cause, etc., and his providence immanent. The Aristotelian conception requires polytheism only for political ends. The Stoic pantheism, which held that creative fire, reason, and law could all be worshiped, also granted that myths were indispensable allegoric representations of eternal elements. But the reaction of Skepticism which, from its extreme distrust of reason, came to long for revelation, and which, even among the Jews, after the Babylonian exile, admitted the doctrine of angels and devils to gratify man's polytheistic cravings, led, among the Greeks, to the notion of daimons, which were only the old deities of polytheism, as the servants and tools of the Supreme Being. The commingling of races led to the conception of the later Stoics that all men are children of the same father, to the belief in the unity of God, and to dissatisfaction with any merely national god or messiah. The last stand of polytheism was made in the neo-platonic philosophy in its long but ineffective struggle with Christianity, which, refuting its central conception of a descending series of beings emanating from the one perfect light, which was at last extinguished in inert matter, adopted it as a form of speculation. Thus, Zeller argues, Greek philosophy prepared the way, though somewhat esoterically at first, for Christianity, and supplied the elements for its subsequent rational development to an extent hitherto unsuspected.

The relations of church and state in the past and present and the discipline, cultus, orders, property and influence on education of the former are discussed from an abstract, moral standpoint in a readable little volume, which space fails us to epitomize.[1] In other essays the trial of Galileo, studied in part from original sources, is described, Schwegler, Waitz, and Lessing as theologians are characterized, the relations of policy and justice and of nationality and humanity are discussed, and the condition and

[1] Staat u. Kirche; Vorlesungen an der Universität zu Berlin, gehalten von Eduard Zeller, 1873, p. 250.

problems of German philosophy and of the theory of knowledge (*Erkenntniss-theorie*) are explained.

The latter has been the central question in German philosophy since Kant brought into flux the question of the origin and truth of our notion of things. Based upon special solutions of it, the great idealistic systems were wrought out. The cry "back to Kant," and the general abandonment of the foundations upon which Fichte, Schelling, and Hegel built, which in many quarters have degenerated to an uncritical cultus of Kantian orthodoxy, were at first matured by the conviction that he alone had fairly examined and justly estimated the importance of the theory of knowledge, while later the experimental psychology of the physiologists and the studies of Helmholtz have only more especially elaborated this theory and more critically answered Kant's problem. We must not infer from the study of Kant that experience can give unordered matter, or that all form is innate, still less can we agree with him that because we apprehend things by means of subjective forms we must necessarily be ignorant of things as they are in themselves. There is another case. Perhaps the forms are adapted by nature to give us the *right* view of things. Subjective and objective belong to one nature. True, if we isolate one phenomenon we cannot distinguish its elements, but every new observation applies the method of differences. We prefer to say that, with the increasing compass and accuracy of our knowledge, it approaches practically— though not theoretically in the sense of Fichte and Hegel— to absoluteness. It necessarily grows certain as it grows wide. It is reflection which sifts out the a priori elements from experience and thus brings knowledge of things. Hence logic is grounded on the theory of knowledge, which must in turn be completed by it. Number, time, and space Zeller makes the most general forms of connecting objects. Properties are causal ideas which are not innate in the old historic sense—so intimately connected with the doctrine of preëxistence—but are hypotheses to satisfy the unifying impulse of the mind. Space, however, unlike the other two, which are objectively real, at the basis of being and change, may be only the general way in which things impress us, or a general form of reaction of our organism in its habit of connecting sensations. Different hypotheses of the external cause of sensation may supersede it; or again tridimensional space may be only a special case of another relation, embracing other cases also.

Here at last we glimpse a limit to Zeller's remarkably wide critical horizon, which is particularly manifest throughout his courses of psychological lectures. The hypothesis of a fourth dimension of space in no way destroys the validity of the old geometrical three. Mathematical physics has elaborated equations containing functions which might be true in a space of x dimensions and forthwith metaphysical psychologists, reasserting old idealistic traditions, or perhaps too easily bullied by scientific authorities, stultify science by talking of an absolutely spaceless universe, and a nonextended matter. To Zeller this is only a logical possibility which must not be forgotten. Like many of the older German professors of philosophy he did not deem it all too unworthy the dignity of his department to interest a curious class by recounting some of the more striking results and methods of the physiological study of sensation, but too often only to disparage their philosophical importance and to limit to the narrowest the impressions deduced from them in detail while roundly acknowledging the general importance of such investigations for the theory of knowledge. The fundamental importance and the immense scope of these, centering as they do about the transforming psychological conception of reflex action modified by specific nervous functions and inhibition, Zeller failed adequately to appreciate. We will pause here only to observe that the whole drift of German physiology is now strongly and almost without exception against the possibility of such materialistic deductions as Zeller feared therefrom.

Philosophical truths to Zeller were not coins stamped and weighed to pass unchanged from hand to hand, but historical products deeply rooted in personal, national, and religious character. As such they must first be approached and studied if we would add our own individual thinking as a contribution however trivial to the thoughts of the race, instead of reviving old issues, re-solving old problems, and thrice slaying the slain. The history of philosophy is thus a labor-saving department of study most economic of mental effort, and prepares men for the problems of to-day. It should aim in the first place simply to present and not to criticize or estimate its subject matter. It should teach us how our consciousness became what it is. It should show that all practical sciences and institutions of human life and society presuppose a theoretical foundation which is deep and broad, in proportion as they are high or important. Not only do the roots of all things go back to philosophy, but it is an unnatural condition of things if philosophy is suspected or degraded. As Cavour said that the state should be occasionally led back to first principles, even by revolution, if need be, so it is well not to allow men entirely to forget how law and every political and social institution were at first and still are at bottom only devices to establish simple morality as an individual habit, and between man and man, and that all religions are but formulations of man's relations to the universe as a whole. Moreover the special branches of knowledge are able to act and react fruitfully upon each other only as it is seen how organically they are connected. The effect of science upon philosophy may be in some sense compared to its effect upon poetry. Since it became impossible to believe longer in myths, poetry, instead of being crippled or suffering any limitation of her domain, as many predicted, has found new sources of inspiration deeper and stronger than ever before, while even historic myths exert undiminished magic charm over the imagination of men. So likewise the metaphysical myths, platonic ideas and ideals, innate intuitions, an absolute ego, a dialectic, world-developing reason, a universal will, and scores more, are no less quickening now than before, while the observational and exact experimental study of the psychic powers is opening a radically new conception of the human soul, reason, and conscience. With this is suggested, at least to those whose supreme passion of life it is to conceive it, however faintly, the possibility again of one organized intellectual world manifestly monistic, without unscientific, hyper-logical guesswork, in which idealism and realism, instead of being absolute even in their opposition, are simply two cardinal points of direction of which philosophic thought must not lose sight.

In his somewhat popular history of German philosophy since Leibniz [1] written as the thirteenth volume of the "History of Science in Germany," under the auspices of the Saxon commission, somewhat monographic, and mainly devoted to the seven great names from Leibniz to Schopenhauer (both inclusive), and not to be compared with Kuno Fischer's exhaustive work on the history of modern philosophy, Zeller urges that the Reformation made Germany introspective. The deepest roots of her power in the world's history he finds in her philosophy and more especially in her idealism—at once her weakness and her strength. Germany will be false to all her traditions if she forgets the power of subjective reflection. Her philosophy was developed in a period of peace unbroken save by the inspiring war of liberation, and even now, with all her political, military, and material successes, her growing love of money, and devotion to business, this philosophy

[1] Geschichte der deutschen Philosophie seit Leibniz, von E. Zeller, 1873, pp. 917.

must be guarded with pious patriotic care as yet full of saving and guiding power.

Perhaps one trait that withheld Zeller from making the history of philosophy merely the play of impersonal ideas was his keen sense of character and the pathos and humor of individualities. Before our differential psychologizing or conscious methods of estimating men he would labor long and exhaust every resource to delineate a personality and divest it of all mythic ravelings or pretenses or shams and to seek the fundamental motives that control life. This is seen in his "History," but still more so in his "Essays." To be sure, he does not go as far as a few would now have us and regard a man's system of philosophy as a set of organized symptoms by the aid of which to diagnose his diathesis. Of Zeller's happy way of hitting off traits with critical acumen a few epitomes must suffice.

In his "Pythagoras," after premising that the stronger the impression made by any person or event the greater will be the mythopœic reaction, he infers that the sage of Crotona must have been a many-sided, earnest, and sagacious ethical reformer. He came from his native Samos to southern Italy in a time peculiarly fitted for his work. The central doctrine of the society of which he became the center was that of future rewards and punishments and the transmigration of souls, or that moral purification was the highest end of life. This and his asceticism were perhaps learned in the Orphic mysteries. He taught music— or the art of the muses—and gymnastics, and that all things might be expressed in numerical relations. His followers refused to eat the heart of animals because it was the seat of life, and were buried in linen garments that the suffering of wool-bearing animals might be mitigated. They held their goods in common, made fidelity the chief virtue, and taught that the best should rule. Such are probably the facts. Within four centuries after the master's death his followers described him as a prophet, whose head was constantly surrounded by a nimbus, who called up storms, healed the insane, arrested plagues, called down an eagle from the sky, ordered a bear to cease eating flesh and was obeyed, was seen at two distinct places at the same time, was called by name by a river god, remembered his preceding life, in which he was the son of Hermes, as in this of Apollo, heard and taught the harmony of the spheres, had made a visit to Hades, etc. Nearly all distinguished men in Egypt and the East, it was said, had been his teachers. The older his school became the more his young disciples were able to tell of him. He left no writings, but in the first century B. C. many ascribed their writings to him partly as a compliment and partly to win consideration for them, till several scores of volumes now bear his name.

In his defense of Xanthippe, Zeller reminds us that the young wife of an old man—who could humorously boast of the advantage of ugliness like his over the classic Greek type of beauty; that the bridge of his nose was so low that with one of his prominent eyes he could look directly into the other, favoring introspection; that his mouth was so large that he could save much time by eating faster than others; his lips so thick and soft that he could give and receive the sweetest kisses, and that his ponderous body was of the type of Silenus—might be excused for not being proud among all the handsome Greeks of having this monster for a husband. Moreover, Socrates would seek no office, lounged all day on the streets and in the public marts talking with tailors, shoemakers, and even *heterai,* about the dialectic conception of their professions, and, although so poor that wife and husband had but one outer garment between them, so that one must stay at home when the other was out, he would sometimes stand all day in one spot lost in revery, ridiculed by boys and comedians, and at last come home, old and fat as he was, to practice a dancing lesson for which, perhaps, he had paid his last *heller*. Moreover, the suspicion that he had married her as a discipline in patience would hardly have been delicate and flattering to a woman's nature. When she came sobbing with their child in her arms to see him for the last time in prison before the fatal draught of hemlock, severely looking at her he ordered Krito to take her home; and when she had been removed, screaming, he calmly began a philosophic discourse. Possibly Xanthippe did throw dirty water over him, attempted to tear off his garments in the market place, overthrew his table, and trod upon a cake that had just been sent in, no one knows from whom, and perhaps Socrates consoled himself that she never kicked or bit him, but more probably these are unsalted inventions of lively Greek gossips or chronicles to make the name of Socrates brighter by contrast. She was probably no worse than many a modern woman would have been with her provocation.

Very readable is Zeller's characterization of Alexander the Paphlagonian impostor, and Peregrinus, the enthusiast. The former was famous for his beauty, and lived in the time of Trajan. Planning to found a new oracle at Abonouteichos, he buried and caused to be found brazen tablets, like the plates of Joseph Smith, the founder of Mormonism, announcing that Asklepios and his father, Apollo, were about to remove thither, caused it to be proclaimed that he was the grandson of the former, and later appeared himself in a feigned ecstasy, clad in purple, with the sword of Perseus, and with artificial foam flowing from his mouth. Throwing aside all his garments he showed the assembled multitude a young serpent in a broken egg shell, and a few days later an immense artificial snake with a human face, with eyes and mouth worked by invisible hairs, which he declared had grown from the little one and was a new god, Glycon, from whom he would receive divine messages. Sealed letters were sent, and if they could be opened and re-sealed without suspicion they were returned with answers written beneath every question. He hired a *claque* in distant cities and finally in Rome, who reported the most astonishing miracles—hidden treasures, and thieves discovered, the sick healed, and even the dead raised. Messengers were bribed, difficult questions generously referred to the priests of other oracles, until at last Rutilinus, a man of high standing in the Roman court, like another Zöllner, fell completely into his net, and he became the fashion in the Imperial City to which he graciously offered his protection against pest, conflagration, and earthquake. He became immensely rich and made it dangerous for rationalistic Epicureans or for Christians to attempt to expose him, and died at the age of seventy with undiminished fame.

Peregrinus of Pazium gave his fortune to his townsmen and traveled in the East, where he learned the "rare wisdom" of the Christians, who, it was said, made him a bishop. Later he appeared in Rome as a Cynic, anathematizing all the world, and especially the Roman emperor Antoninus Pius, who banished him from the city limits, beyond which he lived in a hut and attracted many young men by his philosophical discourses. He afterward went to Greece, and when no one took further notice of him announced at the end of the Olympic games that at the end of the next festival he would burn himself alive. When the time came he had an immense pile erected, made a long harangue to the curious crowd, enumerating all the privations and sufferings which he had borne in the service of philosophy, declared he would die, like Herakles, to teach men to despise death. As, contrary to his hopes, no one interfered, but rather, when a single voice cried "save thyself to the Greeks," the crowd vociferously exhorted him to courage and the speedy accomplishment of his purpose, after adjourning the act till another night "that the moon might also see it," clad in the Cynic uniform, casting a handful of incense into the flames and commending himself to the spirits of his ancestors, he walked, trembling and pale, into the flames and was seen no more.

In "A Strike in Rome" Zeller discusses the variously recorded story of the origin of the Roman festival Quinguatrus. The pipers, it is said, vexed by certain restrictions of their prerogatives, withdrew to a man to Tiburnum and occasioned thereby great distress in Rome. There could be no festive sacrifices to the gods, no religious processions, no marriages, no burials. The Senate in vain tried to induce the irate musicians to return, and only after they had been made drunk at a feast given in Tiburnum and brought home in wagons did they consent, if all their ancient rites were restored, to resume their duties as before. This is compared with the legend of the origin of festivals of *Carmenta*. The Roman matrons of old had the right to ride in carriages, of which they were deprived by the Senate. They all swore to bear no more children till the privilege was restored, which the Senate hastened to do. Both these tales, the former of which has been hitherto undoubted, Zeller argues, with great ingenuity, are instances of the etiological sagas so common among the Romans and utterly without historical foundation.

In Wolff's expulsion from Halle Zeller sees the epitome of a contest which is not yet ended. At the close of the Thirty Years' War Germany had grown barbarous, ignorant, schismatic, sensuous in taste and life to a degree which German patriotism now finds it hard to admit. Protestantism had fallen into the hands of men whose rule was scarcely less fruitless, formal, and unprogressive than that of the Jesuits, then dominant in the Catholic church. It had no understanding of the religious needs of the people, and had driven edification from the church, learning from the schools, and freedom and thoroughness from the universities and from literature. At this period pietism and philosophy first took their rise in Germany. Spener, reacting against the dry and dead intellectualism of theology, urged at first a most salutary form of emotional and practical religious living, and argued the necessity of a definite and typical change of inner life, which found wide acceptance and has founded the Lutheran church deep in the *Gemüth,* giving it its peculiar freedom and independence of scientific reason. Wolff, whose methods affected mathematical form and certainty, who used the vernacular tongue in his thronged philosophical lecture room, who had argued that even an atheist might lead a moral life, and that even if no divine revelation had been made reason would incline men to virtuous lives, was violently attacked by the pietists and obliged to enter into tedious and profitless disputations. He saw his students and followers and even his friends gradually alienated from him until at length the king of Prussia, induced by a plump lie of an enemy of Wolff, ordered him to leave his domains within forty-eight hours on penalty of being hung, and made it a crime to circulate or read his writings. This his pietistic colleagues declared was in answer to their prayers. He was recalled later, but not until his vigor and his influence were forever impaired.

In characterizing Fichte as a politician we are told that he possessed the very rare combination of great scientific acumen and culture with immense vigor and sensitiveness of moral character. It was the substance of his philosophy that the will of the individual created not only his own character but his own world, and that individual action and development might be free and unhindered was the ground motive of his life. The true state itself is only a threefold compact of the sovereign people who can therefore never rebel. Its business is solely to protect men in their rights. To this end it must oversee all departments of work in every detail, and cause every one to be remunerated according to his services. This view has made Fichte a favorite with modern socialists. The state alone controls intercourse with foreign states, and its citizens should have only its money and never that of other countries. So long as the state is anything other than the spontaneous organization of the people the latter are not free. An absolutely free people would need no state. The fate of true freedom rests with regenerated Germany. Her language, which has been developed indigenously, without obscured etymologies, from a primitive kindred people and not adopted or borrowed, or adumbrated by change, like that of other European nations, makes true mental freedom possible only for her people. Fichte's philosophy and political theories, Zeller concludes, are both superseded by later and better views, but will yet long remain, even where most contradicted, very instructive and elevating.

In his religious views Zeller was greatly influenced by Schleiermacher, whom he very justly terms "the greatest of all Protestant theologians, a many-sided, platonic mind, a true ethical genius who *must* preach," and who is best understood not by his avowed pupils but by those who, refuting his letter by his spirit, his later by his earlier works, have passed beyond his standpoint. His great object was to mediate between supernaturalism and rationalism, mysticism and empiricism, docetism and Ebionitism, Manicheism and Pelagianism; to test the true value of all knowledge by the religious consciousness; to bring the culture of his time back to piety. In his earlier writings, Schleiermacher argued that Scripture became Bible solely by force of its own inward excellence, by the natural law of survival, in short that Christianity does not insist upon being the only form of religion, but would prefer at any time to yield to a better should it appear. Not only all dogma, but even Jesus himself, to whose person he attached such central importance later, but who never claimed to be the only mediator, are not indispensable to the Christianity characterized in the religious *Reden*. His philosophy was always for the sake of his theology, of which it was only a broader form. God and the world, he says, are different expressions for the same worth, each unthinkable without the other. God is the essence of the world and not a will over it; hence there is no difference between his will and knowledge, between the possible and actual, between ability to do and performance. As providence is the law of Nature, there can be no miracles, no origin of the world, no physical answers to prayer. Personal life is not the essence of the soul, but its phenomenon, and the imperfection of the individual is but a part of the perfection of the whole. In short Spinozism is softened and idealized.

Corresponding to Kant's distinction between the sense and the understanding, Schleiermacher distinguishes the organic from the intellectual function, the former as material and manifold, the latter as unifying, and each making and needing the other somewhat as Bergson distinguishes mechanism from freedom. All experience impels us to God, whom, nevertheless, we cannot know; yet he does not infer God to be unknowable, like Kant's *Ding-an-Sich,* from the limitations of our faculties, but because the nature of the ideas given in experience does not correspond to the God idea, which latter he thus illogically, Zeller thinks, presupposes. Our will, he says, fluctuates, but we vainly seek for the ground of will; while for Kant it is the will which first opens the intellectual world. The deepest problem— the relation between will and being—is found in personality, which is the appearance of the infinite spirit, and the compendium of the universe. It must be developed to the fullest individuality, between which and general laws there is no conflict. This noble romanticism, by which he strives to unite earnestness and scientific breadth and to rescue the abstract morals of Kant and Fichte from their subjectivity, makes our inmost nature the picture of the infinite, and personality the organ of knowing it. Here God and every moral principle are revealed, the knowledge of which we must work out into ever purer forms. Thus religion is feeling. Pure and perfect self-feeling, however, would be a knowledge of God without the world, which is impossible because the God idea can never be freed from antitheses. But conception also gives a notion of God, hence religion is not over philosophy, and while the former should be universal reason and criticism are also allowed free scope.

Over against an absolute power and causality no feeling but that of independence, or of being determined, is possible. This form of feeling is originally given with personality, before all self-activity. We dare not say that we know its cause, as substance or otherwise, hence there is no God idea, save the vague *whence* of the feeling of absolute dependence, and all attempts to personify God are gratuitous. Religion originates naturally in us, but we must actively develop it, and it remains ever imperfect; hence there are always parts of sin as well as of grace in us, the former preceding the latter, as the life of sense precedes the life of mind. Because, as feeling, it is the most individual, religious life most needs enlargement in companionship. It is aroused by intercourse and needs community. This is the basis of the church. Every experience or representation of the individual life by word or act, which arouses others responsively to produce the same state in themselves, is revelation. This is best seen in the expressive individuality of a relatively perfect type, and others are aroused to discipleship.

So far Zeller essentially agrees with his teacher, but when the latter proceeds to make Jesus typically perfect (*urbildlich*) as a historical person by virtue of his special religious or God consciousness, Zeller objects that Schleiermacher failed to prove the latter, and that Jesus in no authentic passage claims typical perfection. Jesus may be a perfect man, but he is not thus proven a God man, and as such neither his person nor the dogmatic deduction from it is natural. With surprising critical freedom, Schleiermacher, in the matured form of his system, urges that all

43

Christ's acts and words merely reveal his personality, and so far as this creates or wakens the religious life, or in other words makes grace outweigh sin, he may be called the redeemer. There is absolutely no substitute or proxy bearing of the penalty of sin. The church visible and invisible, or actual and ideal or typical, simply aids men to reproduce the image of Christ as a norm in their own lives. Thus, in explaining the creative beginning of moral life in Jesus and the church according to profound but more or less intelligible psychologic laws, in exploring the essence of religion, and in transforming its traditions to the spirit of our times, in giving even theology a new ground in modern consciousness, and in deriving all from self-consciousness, Schleiermacher's work is incomparable and imperishable. But when, as dogmatist, he treats the gospels, even John's, as historical and labors with such painful ingenuity to pour his new wine into the old vessels which Strauss and Baur were so soon and so easily to shatter, he was not only inconsistent with the freedom of his own earlier position, but brought long discredit upon his religious philosophy, the most profound and quickening in modern thought. Zeller's attitude to Schleiermacher is thus somewhat analogous to that of J. S. Mill to Comte. While reproducing and developing the spirit of his early and best period with ripened and condensed vigor, he rejects the tortuous scholasticism of his dogmatic and exegetical (according to Darner his best and most matured) systematizing, as worthless. Religion is well called a feeling, but to describe its content as one of absolute dependence is inadequate, or at least misleading. Rather it is equally the consciousness of absolute freedom in a pregnant Hegelian sense. No matter how philosophic the conception of fatalism may be made, it must ever be prejudicial to moral accountability.

Zeller's great life-work is, of course, his "History of Greek Philosophy." His characterization of the pre-Socratic philosophy, though as unlike the speculative histories of Hegel or Schwegler as possible, is a masterpiece of constructive criticism. The laborious minuteness with which every suggestion is followed up, the compass of his method, which requires familiarity with every phase of contemporary Greek life and history, the conscientious care to avoid all false idealizations and to hold every personal preference or prejudice in leash, and the constant verification by quotations have all combined to make his readers conceive of Greek thought as perhaps less pure and perfect and less transcendently wonderful than we were wont to suppose, but have invested the theme with a nearer and far more sympathetic human interest than ever before. It is, of course, impossible in our limits to enter into any detailed review of this work, but this rough sketch of its author's varied intellectual labors will not have been written in vain if it shall induce the reader to take this work seriously in hand for himself.

The oldest of the modern histories of philosophy is Stanley's (1655), which follows Diogenes' Laertius and abounds in pictures and myths. For him philosophy is a search for truth and Christianity possesses complete truth, so he stops with Christ. Then came Tiedemann's seven volumes (1791-7), from Thales to Berkeley, his standpoint being that of Leibniz, Wolfe and Locke and in strong opposition to Kant; and Tennemann's eleven volumes (1789-1819), ending with Leibniz, involving a careful study of Aristotle, but written from a rigidly Kantian standpoint. Next followed Ritter's four volumes of the "History of Ancient Philosophy" (1834), which marked the point where philosophy first felt the need of tradition and that it could no longer draw upon its own resources, the standpoint being that of Schleiermacher. Hegel's history, which appeared two years later, exaggerated the logical element in the development of thought and made previous systems a propaedeutic to his own, although he did hit off great systems with a certain felicity. In his spirit Schwegler and Ferrier later wrote. Hegel would hardly have agreed with Dilthy that the number of possible systems is limited. It was, however, Zeller who, far more than any one else, made the history of philosophy a cult. Boutroux, writing on Zeller (Rev. Phil., Jul.-Dec., 1877) says that the Hegelian principle that facts and ideals, chronological and logical order, are one and the same, is dangerous to all positive science. Nature must be observed and investigated and can not be derived and construed speculatively. From the enthrallment of the German mind by the heaven-scaling Titanism of the great speculative period ending with Hegel, whose philosophy of history was to most minds the crux of his scheme, Zeller succeeded in gradually emancipating himself and defying the influence of the master in his very stronghold by showing objectively how the history of ideas should be studied. David Strauss [1] calls his work "an imperishable monument embodying German science, English sagacity, and French elegance" and urges that it marks the epoch when the historical spirit achieved its supreme triumph in this field. This Zeller did by breaking away from the a priori Hegelism in which he had been trained, an achievement far greater than thinking himself free from a saturated orthodox theology after he began to teach it in the University, for he gravitated, early and naturally, without intense ferment, over to the same liberal viewpoint in religion which it took progressive Victorian England a quarter of a century after the publication of "Vorträge und Abhandlungen" to attain, viz., that the Bible is to be studied by the same methods as any other ancient book.

In 1856, with the complete second edition, he had finished his outline or *cadre,* and devoted the rest of his life to filling in and completing. Even though his promotion had been delayed like Jowett's and his chair changed, there

[1] E. Zeller. Revue Philosophique, July-Dec., 1877.

was no crisis, but his life was a remarkable continuum. So far as he had a system, it was eclectic, although he had a somewhat Kantian standpoint and was far from regarding certain problems in philosophy purely as literature. On the contrary, he tended to test by categories and his systematic mind inclined him to do more justice to Aristotle than to Plato. His method was chiefly philological, and Paul Shorey compares him and his religious views to Matthew Arnold. But he insisted most of all, that historical work must be done in a spirit of unreserved and sympathetic appreciation of each successive writer and that all thus must be presented from the point of view of the authors of them; that criticism of opinions should be a separate thing and that the work of the historian should be a storehouse of information for all schools alike. Hence, although some two score historians, great and small, have since gone over his ground, Benn and Ueberweg perhaps owing most to him, none have covered the period from Thales to Boethius' pathetic "Consolations of Philosophy" (A. D. 500), that is, to the Edict of Justinian closing the four philosophical schools of Athens and confiscating their property in 558 A. D., or are likely to do so, as impartially as he. Happily, this great work is now nearly all, save the Roman schools, accessible in English. It was natural that, when the great systems declined, philosophers should turn to history so that, since the first edition of Zeller, we have had not only monographs on special points and writers by the hundreds, but an *Archiv* of the history of philosophy. For a decade or two preceding 1900 several histories were written in which all lines converged to Kant and all who follow Hegel were lightly treated, but this period, with the remarkable and recent decline of the Kant cult in Germany, has passed, and it is probable that the old historic spirit in this department is also fading. We have had histories galore of special problems of philosophy, on which principle Windelband has written. The last fifty or seventy-five years have also been marked by many histories of culture and special branches of knowledge where they were unknown before, notably chemistry, mathematics, biology, physics, medicine, education, æsthetics, politics, church and theological history leading all others in time. Thus, in the last two generations, men have awakened to new interest in the evolution of their departments and some historic perspective is everywhere required. But the defect of the historic spirit in this field is still seen in the fact that so few workers in the special, and particularly the newer, domains of philosophical and psychological research have adequate knowledge of the pedigree of their methods and standpoints, and are perhaps prone to over-emphasize the latest at the expense of earlier stages of thought. Thus, whereas political and economic history is thought incomplete if it does not come down to the present day, many histories of philosophy still stop short with Hegel, or perhaps Schopenhauer, Hartmann and a few other briefer references. Till her new *statut* (1884) Russia forbade the teaching of philosophy after Augustine, and most Catholic histories still either stop with St. Thomas, or treat all that follows rather lightly. It may be the happily rarely developed apex of this unhistoric tendency that would make us all feel, did we completely shrive ourselves, a slight reluctance to give just credit to previous workers on our themes, although, happily, few of us capitulate to the vicious old maxim, *pereant illi qui nostra ante nos dixerunt.*

As an academic department, that is, on the side of its teaching, the history of philosophy has also had many difficulties to overcome, both in Germany and other lands. In Germany they rose chiefly from the dominance of the old theories which subordinated or thought lightly of philosophy as a whole. In England, and this country at first, it was thought dangerous to religious convictions as teaching students to hold no opinions, and when the Locke-Berkeley-Hume-Kant phase of it was stressed it was thought to upset the sense of reality in the young in a perilous way. In our country especially, it had but a limited number of academic representatives, led by the late George S. Morris, once my guide and philosophic friend, the translator of Ueberweg and the most scholarly of all Americans in this field. Although these various objections have been outlived, the teaching of the history of philosophy seems nevertheless to be declining.

May it not be one of the tasks of the coming genetic movement to rescue the history of opinion in this field from its present sad neglect? A census soon after Zeller went to Berlin showed that almost half of all the courses in the entire philosophic field in twenty-one German universities were historical. Now this discipline has unfortunately shrunk to very modest dimensions. Indeed, in no country has the history of philosophy ever, so far as I can see, been taught at all in the sense which Zeller meant, nor has his standpoint had a single representative among us. It has been taught, with various biases, to apply Hegelism, or as an introduction to epistemology (like the Locke-Berkeley-Hume-Kant cult), or to give verisimilitude to a Leibnizian monadic individualism. It has been explored to find support for many a conviction and has been taught well and carefully in spots and the rest ignored, but so far as the history of philosophy as a whole is concerned, taught comprehensively, undogmatically and without partisanship, we in this country still are living in a pre-Zeller age, and that is why American thinking in all departments of this field is so prone to lack historic perspective, significance and continuity. Rightly taught, I believe the history of philosophy has a humanistic culture value that is absolutely unequaled, and that it comes nearer to being the one topic of which more could justly be said in favor of making it obligatory to all academic students, whatever their destination, than any other subject whatever. The historian in this field must be far above and beyond being led captive by any one system, but must see the partial truth of all and be well oriented from all points of view to find or make his own scheme of things in a way that fits him, having the whole world's outfit of opinions at his disposal in doing so.

So much the more remarkable was it that Zeller could see that no one has caught the true historic spirit who is a partisan, idealist or realist, positivist, materialist or spiritualist, parallelist or interactionist. If he elects anyone, it must be only by a bare working majority of his faculties and he must ever be ready for referendum or recall. Zeller is no more Platonist than Aristotelian, despite Pascal's insistence that every one is born and must remain one or the other, and despite his own leanings to Aristotle. He followed the good old apothegm of Coleridge that we must be sure that we are not ignorant of another's understanding before we assume to understand his ignorance. Thus, theologian though he was at first, he insisted that philosophy should be literature and not dogma. I should say that no man was ever so well equipped for work in this field, certainly not Kuno Fischer, his great contemporary and rival, for the latter never entirely escaped the seductions of partisanship or the affectations of eloquence where only critical and judicious opinions are chiefly demanded.

Zeller's erudition seems exhaustless. He went back of Mullach's "Fragmenta," of Ritter's and Preller's "Textus Receptus" and corrected even Diogenes' "Laertius." He ransacked the ancient literature and history contemporary with each author, compared disputed readings, had a keen sense for spurious passages, exposed pseudonymous authorship and even challenged the great Aristotelian Trendelenburg and presented a rival theory of the categories of the great Stagirite. Thus Zeller was often engaged in polemics not only within but without his own field. Yet, for the most part, his lectures, very unlike his texts, were clear, interesting and even edifying, save in his *privatissimi* courses, which I did not attend. The "Expectorazionen" were often the most learned and interesting of all.

Perhaps the most important difference between Zeller and his critics is represented by the polemic of Teichmüller, supported to some extent by Heinze and Bergmann, concerning the question of the relation of Plato's ideas to things and persons. As Plato summed up all who went before him, save the Atomists, and determined about all that followed, except the Epicureans, a single word may be said here upon this subject. Zeller understood Plato to represent that his Ideas, as of the good, the beautiful, the true and the rest, were more or less transcendent, that they had their abode in the heavens or with the gods, that objects became real and characteristic by participating in them, and that whatever immortality the human soul attained was only by partaking of the life of the Ideas by reason or immediate intuition. This point of view, however well it may agree with the serious dialogues in which it is developed, is at variance with the so-called myths of. Plato, which represent the individual soul as preëxistent, choosing in advance its type of life and coming down to earth stripping off some and retaining other reminiscences of its former glory. These Zeller regards as poetic, or as Plato's theology, which is to be taken as quite distinct from his philosophy as those two are sometimes now kept, so that Plato for him was a double housekeeper.

All this Teichmüller and others deny,[1] holding that Plato's *parousia* meant the immanence of the Idea in nature, urging, too, that from this Idea Aristotle derived and developed his notion of entelechy and final purpose or cause, and that the result both these men came to from these assumptions, and which has had such untold influence, was the belief in the immortality of the soul. This view of the

[1] See a good résumé of these discussions in Die platonische Frage; Eine Streitschrift gegen Zeller, von Gustav Teichmüller. Gotha, F. A. Perthes, 1876, 127 pp.

immanence rather than the transcendence of the Ideas gives unity to Plato's system and frees it from the contradiction which Zeller found in it, but which his critics ascribed to his wrong conceptions of Plato. On this view there is no contradiction or even grave contrast between the myths and the serious teaching. This view Zeller has distinctly rejected. Without attempting to decide between the parties in such a controversy, it certainly does appear that the question was so grave as to merit rather more careful consideration of it than Zeller gave, for if it is true, it involves considerable readjustment of his entire standpoint and the rewriting of much of what he had to say about Plato.

Zeller was the first to realize that the Greek mind was the most acute in all history, and, what was perhaps quite as important, if not more so, that its development was the freest from all priestly or theological as well as from political influences and thus, in a sense, the most natural and spontaneous, so that in Greek philosophy the soul of man found its most complete expression, more so even than it did in the German systems, although Zeller thought there was a profound kinship between them. He also saw more clearly than any one before him had ever done how the Greek philosophy shaped Christian thought, determined theology, moulded the church and that, too, in a sense and to a degree that even Hatch has not fully grasped. He found here the natural history of the most gifted of races, with the greatest power of expression, the genetic story of the soul of a people from its adolescent dawn to its senescent involution and decay. All subsequent philosophical problems are implicit, and most of them explicit in it. Each system is a careful answer to the eternal questionnaire: what are nature, man, soul, truth, beauty, and the end, meaning and worth of life, as affected by temperament, age, environment, and personal *Einstellung?*

Of course no history can ever take the place of the original texts. To begin with Zeller's little epitome of his

Greek philosophy (in Germany much read and now translated) as a finder, and to proceed thence to a study of his
larger volumes for wider orientation and introduction to
sources, gives perspective and incentive. His work is an
album of portraits of men and systems, viewpoints and
interpretations of life, the most fresh, original and formative the world has ever seen. He offers us a bunch of keys
to the magnificent ancient intricate golden city of man's
soul wherein so much of our culture took its rise. Lotze
is reported to have said that, but for the hope that he might
converse with the great immortal Greeks sometime hereafter, his hope of immortality would lose much of its
charm. If Fechner's theory, which we shall see later, that,
when and so far as we re-think the thoughts of the great
dead, we in a sense reincarnate them and perpetuate their
souls be true, then the ancient worthies whom Zeller defines for us, as well as we, owe Zeller something for their
immortality. Perhaps the individual psychologist of the
future, when he shall have completed biography and history—which is the lengthened shadow of great men—may
go back of even Zeller's analysis by methods yet more fine
and subtle, but he will realize his indebtedness to this great
pioneer in his field. But however all this may be, Zeller
will remain a leader of those who, in the speculative field
which is so tempting to the self-indulgence of castle building, restrained the lust of adding his own name to the gallery of theorizers, but holding his own speculative propensi-
ties sternly in abeyance, strove by every attainable means
to take in all the others' standpoints in which to describe
men and opinions as objectively and faithfully as science
seeks to describe nature, demolishing in his soul even the
vestiges of all the Baconian *eidola*. He sought to be true
as a photographic plate is to the objects it reproduces.

Zeller was the first to treat ancient philosophers by
purely objective natural history methods without philosophical or other bias or prepossession. While, in treating the

early Greek thinkers, the problem was to construct a whole out of fragments, as the paleontologists must sometimes reconstruct extinct animals from a few fossil bones or teeth, or as the archeologists must restore an ancient temple from crumbling stones, the later completer systems, on the other hand, need the opposite treatment of condensation. Perhaps no literature so needs or so gains by careful epitomization as do the ponderous tomes of philosophers, for no life is long enough for even the specialist in this field to read and digest all the originals. Philosophy is less like water—incompressible, but more like air, the third of the old elements—very condensible. The classicist's plea that we must read all of Plato and of Aristotle and the rest in full, and perhaps in the original, to know their meaning truly, does not apply to philosophy. We need middlemen more and more to sugar off the philosophic sap, to separate the metal from the crude ore of the mine. Thus ideas and systems are made portable, some are saved from oblivion, and we are oriented to those systems or parts of them we want, and given perspective. But Zeller was not only a master craftsman in this kind of pedagogic work. Hegel said that a writer in this domain attained fame only if and in so far as he compelled others not merely to read, but to discuss and interpret him. This Zeller often does for the Ancients, and sometimes it seems as if he were telling the shades of the old thinkers in the light of modern times what they really meant to say and how and why they came to the views they held. Thus, it is not enough for him to observe all the canons of Droysen's diplomatology and historiology to get just what they did say and mean. By so much as he went beyond this he is a psychologist in the larger sense, and because he did this I have included him with the others as one of the founders of our science. In this field, as in others, history must ever be reread and rewritten, and the work of explanation grows ever broader and deeper as the data, when attained, are more and more gone back of and seen around. Thus, the tendency he started will not be complete until we regard the delineation of the ideas of Plato, Schopenhauer, and all between as what the Freudians call the patent content of an underlying vaster and more coherent latent content in which the higher psycho-analysis must find the original determinants of the systems which shaped and moulded and expressed opinions. Sometime the great systems and schools we now revere may be regarded as very much edited and refined types of folklore, partial satisfactions of so many kinds of instinctive wishes to believe, psychological documents of attitudes, *Anlagen und Einstellungen,* and then such work as Zeller did will be the point of departure for this further comparative psychology of philosophy— philosophy being, perhaps, the best expression of psychic temperament and constitution.

Nowhere as in philosophy does a knowledge of its history make such havoc with our originalities. It has been said that in philosophy the period of from perhaps one to three decades preceding his own work seems to fall in the blind spot of every author. This is the point where the formal histories usually end, so that one can reproduce the ideas of writers who precede oneself by about this interval with impunity, and this is often done, if not consciously at least unconsciously. Moreover, mathematics, physics, chemistry, biology, geology and the rest of the sciences have had continuous progress, taking up all that is of value and dropping the dross, so that it is less needful for an expert in these lines to study the history of his science, and interest in it is largely a matter of taste or curiosity and gives the student of it a lively sense of how far his own day is beyond that of the founders, or a feeling of altitude that may be almost dizzying. It is far different, however, in philosophy, although not a few scientists have held it a reproach that philosophy is so largely historic. Why not, we are asked, teach only what is now true and accepted

5

in your domain, and not waste time on the antiquities of the subject? How, in this day of the twilight of the speculative systems, shall we take our stand between this view and the so often expressed idea of Hegel that philosophy is mainly the history of philosophy? Why, in this field, are men always reverting to the old masters, now as exegetes and disciples, now as rehabilitating ancient standpoints in the garb of new opinions, and classifying and naming the latest systems after the great dead, Platonic, Lockian, Fichtean and the rest? The only answer I can give is to point to the fact of the perennial humanistic interest which attaches to all products of the human mind when it lets itself go with a certain abandon. It was this which made Froschammer call all philosophy a more or less free fling of the higher imagination, not only interpreting but supplementing fact and science. Most of all does it behoove those who affect to be at the same time experimental psychologists and metaphysical epistemologists to see to it that the history of philosophic opinion is given its due place. The pure laboratory psychologist who cultivates toward it the indifference of the scientist toward the historic factor in his line has been very effective in setting the present fashion of neglect of the historic spirit, so that there are many inductive psychologists to-day who feel little need of history since Weber's law, and whose horizon at the farthest only extends to the origin of associationism, possibly with a touch of Kant, like Klemm ("Geschichte der Psychologie," 1911, 388 p.) and, like him, dismiss what preceded as pre-scientific.

Here, then, are five ways: First, that advocated at the (Washington, D. C.) 1911 meeting of the Psychological Association by Münsterberg, that such philosophic themes as epistemology and the relations of the soul to the body and other speculative themes should always and everywhere be taught as a part of psychology, even to medical students. Men of this type insist that even psychological themes should never be unmindful of the light shed upon them by Descartes, Leibniz, Kant, Fichte and the rest. They are prone to test their experimental results by philosophical rubrics; for them, at least, certain philosophical views are dogma, and they feel free to modulate over at any time from one to the other. Secondly, some, like Wundt, keep up their philosophical and historic interests, which, indeed, may dominate their thinking, but also strive to maintain two separate compartments, one rigidly scientific and the other frankly speculative or deductive. This attempt, strenuous and honest as it may be, almost necessarily fails to work because of the limitations of the human mind, and in Wundt, *e. g.*, we see in his doctrine of apperception, his tri-dimensionality of feelings and his discussion of the ego how impossible it is to keep these two standpoints rigidly separated, or to evict metaphysical proclivities even from the laboratory. Third, we have a few psychologists whose thinking is entirely dominated by the laboratory and who are frankly if not ostentatiously innocent of philosophical knowledge. For them, all that preceded is as alchemy to the chemist, or as astrology to the astronomer—antiquarian and negligible material. Fourth, come those who conceive the philosophy of the past always as literature, never as dogma, and of the highest cultural value to be used as most of the three-score writers of *Logos* would have it, as a means of refining and perfecting the individual mentally, emotionally, and morally.

Eucken, Reuter and other collaborators, partly under the inspiration of Nietzsche, insist on the utmost possible development toward the Superman as the supreme human duty. They are moralists and romanticists and have cut loose from science to seek a *Wiedergeburt* by seeking to be again inspired by the spirit of Fichte, Schelling and Hegel, while ignoring and criticizing their letter. In this way they strive to give new worths, values, meanings to life. Their *Weltanschauung* they describe as *überlebende* or as

Lebendigleben. Life alone is the true reality. The Apollonian idea is higher than the Dionysic. The theologian, Trolsch, urges that true Christianity is found in the higher philosophic point of view and that the chief value of science is its moral content. There is a touch of mysticism of the Eckerhardt type. Simmell describes death as *Lebenswandelung* and Trolsch says the logos is the supreme thing in Christianity. This movement is as interesting as was the asceticism of Ruskin, William Morris, Cobden Sanderson, Oscar Wilde. As they attempted to revive the best things in the mediæval guilds, and as Wagner at one period strove to bring back Germany from Christianity to a sublimation of the ancient Teutonic myths, so this movement would conserve and spiritualize philosophy.

From this viewpoint, the systems are choice expressions of the highest aspirations of man. They are the Bible of the intellect, will and heart, but these scriptures are to be freely subjected to the highest criticism and to be studied and used as instruments for the attainment of ceaseless personal betterment, as arsenals of suggestion, aperçus, incitements to keep the soul young and growing. Systems are for the higher individual pedagogy of self-evolution, and their supreme value is found in edification. None of them are finalities and their sanction is that they work well now, giving those who know them openness, plasticity, breadth of sympathy and of mental horizon, and keeping the mental soil loose and irrigated. In these psychic altitudes the atmosphere is serene and ethereal and in it the religious zests that made the old faiths and cults and philosophy are kept fresh and vital. From this viewpoint philosophy affords the purest and highest of all forms of culture and is needful for all liberal and educated men, scientific psychologists never excepted. With this view the pedagogue must have cordial sympathy. But a fifth and yet higher standpoint is just emerging and that is that the old systems, one and all, are to us challenging data

58

for further psycho-analysis, like myths, cults, religions and dreams and illusions. We do not really know the old systems till we understand their psychological motivation in both the age and the individual. How and why did these men in this age formulate the great questions of life and mind thus and give such answers. What was the *Zeitgeist*, environment, diathesis, the folk thought, aspiration, political and economic situation? What was their deeper meaning? What did the writers intend by what they said and what was left unsaid, and why? How have others sought to express the same thing in the same or other fields? How can we find or work out a way to the comparative standpoint and determine the canons of higher criticism for them all, and, above all, how can we express all they meant in terms of our own age? Perhaps something like this is to be the culminating theme of the genetic psychology of the future. If this be so, then the relations of the history of philosophy to psychology are those of a challenging and supreme but unsolved problem. We must not forget, however, that this is only a postulate, for this tendency is yet in its infancy.

EDUARD ZELLER

Platonische Studien. Tübingen, Osiander, 1839.

Die Philosophie der Griechen in ihrer geschichtlichen Entwicklung. Tübingen, Fues, 1844-52. 3 Bde. in 5. This work has been translated as follows, all from third edition:

A history of Greek philosophy from the earliest period to the time of Socrates, tr. by S. F. Alleyne. London, Longmans, 1881, 2 vols.

Socrates and the Socratic schools, tr. by O. J. Reichel. London, Longmans, 1885. 410 p.

Plato and the old academy, tr. by S. F. Alleyne and A. Goodwin. London, Longmans, 1876. 629 p.

Aristotle and the earlier Peripatetics, tr. by B. D. F.

Costello and J. H. Muirhead. London, Longmans, 1897.
2 vols.

The Stoics, Epicureans and Sceptics, tr. by O. J.
Reichel. London, Longmans, 1885. 585 p.

History of eclecticism in Greek philosophy, tr. by S.
F. Alleyne. London, Longmans, 1883. 383 p.

Register zu dem ganzen Werke. (Die Philosophie der
Griechen) Leipzig, Fues, 1868. 79 p.

Das theologische System Zwingli's. Tübingen, Fues,
1853. 216 p.

Die Apostelgeschichte nach ihrem Inhalt und Ursprung
kritisch untersucht. Stuttgart, Mäcken, 1854. 524 p. Tr.
by J. Dare, London, Theological Translation Fund Library,
1873.

De Hermodoro Ephesio et Hermodoro Platonico. Marburg, Elwert, 1860. 26 p.

Vorträge und Abhandlungengeschichtl. Inhalts, Leipzig, Fues, 1865. 504 p.

Ueber die Anachronismen in den platonischen Ges-
prächen. Berlin, 1873. 20 p. (Aus Abhandlungen, d. k.
Akad. der Wiss. zu Berlin).

Staat und Kirche. Vorlesungen an der Universitat zu
Berlin gehalten. Leipzig, Fues, 1873. 250 p.

David Friedrich Strauss in seinem Leben und seinem
Schriften geschildert. Bonn, Strauss, 1874. 126 p. Tr.,
London, 1874.

Geschichte der deutschen Philosophie seit Leibniz.
München, Oldenburg, 1874. 744 p. (Bd. 13 von Geschichte
der Wiss. in Deutschland. 2te. Aufl.)

Vorträge und Abhandlungen. Leipzig, Fues, 1875-
1884. 2te Auf. 3 vols. One essay of these, Strauss und
Renan, has been translated, London, Trübner, 1886. 110 p.

Ueber die Benützung der aristotelischen Metaphysik in
den Schriften der alteren Peripatetiker. Berlin, 1877.
25 pp. (Aus Abhandlungen d. k. Akad. d. Wiss. zu Berlin.)

Ueber die Messung psychischer Vorgänge. 1881. 16 p.

(Berlin Akad. Wissens. Philos-Histclasse. Abhandlungen p. 1.)

Grundriss der Geschichte der griechischen Philosophie. Leipzig, Fues, 1883. 317 p., tr. by S. F. Alleyne and E. Abbott. London, Longmans, 1886. 363 p.

Friedrich der Grosse in seinem Verhältnis zu der Philosophie seiner Zeit und der Vorzeit. 1885. 26 p. (Deutsche Rundschau, v. 44, p. 336.)

Friedrich der Grosse als Philosoph. Berlin, Weidmann, 1886. 298 p.

Gymnasium und Universität. 1890. 24 p. (Deutsche Rundschau, v. 62, p. 216.)

Ueber Systeme und Systemsbildung. 1899. 14 p. (Deutsche Rundschau, v. 101, p. 78.)

Kleine Schriften. Unter Mitwirkung v. H. Diels und K. Holl, hrsg. von O. Leuze. Berlin, S. Reimer, 1910. 602 p.

Strassburger Abhandlungen zur Philosophie. E. Zeller zu seinem siebenzigsten Lebenstagen. 1884.

Philosophische Aufsatze: E. Zeller und sein 50. Jähr. Doctor-Jubiläum gewidmet. Leipzig, Fues, 1887 422 p.

RUDOLPH HERMANN LOTZE
1817–1881

RUDOLPH HERMANN LOTZE

RUDOLPH HERMANN LOTZE

1817-1881

Rudolph Hermann Lotze was the son of a military physician and was born in 1817. He studied for six years at the excellent gymnasium of Zittau, where his father's regiment was stationed and where he made his first slight acquaintance with philosophy. When he was twelve years of age his father died. He entered the University of Leipzig at the age of seventeen and remained four years, devoting himself chiefly to medicine, but dipping into poetry and art and attending one course, that of the Hegelian, Christ. Weisse, in philosophy. At the age of twenty-one he became a doctor of medicine and practiced one year at his home; then became docent in medicine for a year in Leipzig and then changed to philosophy, his first lectures being on pastoral medicine, general pathology and nervous diseases, natural philosophy and anthropology, the encyclopedia, organic physics and therapeutics to groups of from seven to forty-three students. His style in writing and lecturing was monotonous and unattractive, and his sentences often long and hard. Personally he was small, of very simple manners, with peculiarly quaint and old-fashioned taste in dress. In Leipzig he saw a great deal of Fechner and frequented his circle as a very silent listener. Here, too, he wrote and published a volume of poems of 244 pages, now out of print. They are on the moon, stars, night, wind, sea, dreams, tears and show deep feeling, but only the merits of a dilettante.

R. Falckenberg [1] and others have given us interesting sketches of Lotze's personality, career and opinions. In 1844, at the age of twenty-seven, he was called to Göttingen to succeed Herbart, who had just died, and here he remained for thirty-seven years and did most of his work. He usually lectured at 10 A. M. and 4 P. M. daily, and the number of attendants on his various courses during all these years has been computed and found to range between 6 and 99. The number of times he repeated his courses has been carefully computed. For 37 years he gave courses on psychology; for 29 on morals; for 26 on logic; for 24 on mathematics; for 11 on history of philosophy, and on other courses less. Among the most noted of his pupils at Göttingen were Teichmüller, Stumpf, and Longenbeck, also G. E. Müller, who succeeded him at Göttingen. It was his influence that obtained Brentano his chair in Vienna in 1874. It was his habit to have his younger friends and students at his house Tuesday evenings at a *Kranchen*. He had three sons, the oldest of whom became a physician and surgeon. In his early years he lectured on general pathology and therapeutics, and in Wagner's "Handwörterbuch der Physiologie" he wrote articles that caused a great deal of discussion on life, sex, and instinct. It was here that he composed his "Microcosm," relieving its strain by making a Latin version of "Antigone." In 1881, upon the death of Harms and through the influence of Zeller, who made a special visit to Göttingen to see if he was favorable, and also of Helmholtz, who was his ardent advocate, he was called to Berlin, and, after much discussion and perhaps over-persuasion, he accepted. He began two courses of lectures here on April 1, 1881, one on psychology,

---

[1] Hermann Lotze, von Richard Falckenberg. Stuttgart, Frommann, 1901, 206 p. Moderne Philosophen, von. M. Kronenberg. München, Beck, 1899. H. Lotze, pp. 2-75. Lectures and Essays on Natural Theology and Ethics, by Wm. Wallace, Oxford, Clarendon Press, 1898. Hermann Lotze, pp. 481-510.

which was far better attended than in Göttingen, and one on metaphysics, which did not prove to be attractive. He died of pneumonia three months later, July 1, 1881, at the age of 64, and was buried beside his wife in Göttingen. He was a remarkable letter writer and many of his epistles, especially to Hertzel, Fechner, and Strümpel, are preserved. His "Microcosm" has been translated and also his "Metaphysics" and "Ethics." His manner of lecturing was from summaries based upon very brief notes which he amplified in class. He rarely if ever read. The dictata of his lectures on logic, metaphysics, ethics, psychology, æsthetics, and religion were translated by Professor Ladd and printed in a series of little handbooks (Boston, 1884-86).

Philosophy in Germany seems to have reached its lowest ebb more than a half century ago, when Lotze's influence began to be felt, in the reaction against absolute idealism. The "conspiracy of silence" against Schopenhauer was not yet broken. Hartmann, as his autobiography shows us, was still in the second of Shakespeare's seven ages of man. Fechner, Trendelenburg, Zeller, Fischer, on the one hand, and on the other, Brücke, Helmholtz, Reymond, Ludwig, the now famous pupils of E. H. Weber and Johannes Müller, who with their co-laborers have founded the new psychology, had only fairly begun their career of discovery. Herbart was slowly but surely becoming a mighty influence by stimulating more than by indoctrinating his readers. Schleiermacher was read scarcely more than now; and the *"Gemüth-religion"* was, as it has been ever since, but little understood even by his countrymen, partly because it has always been so modified and even perverted by his pupils, especially by Dörner, and still more because it occupied the broad middle ground between the two all-seductive extremes of Strauss and Feuerbach on the left and Hengstenberg and the orthodox reaction on the right. The cry, "Back to Kant!" which has now made his works in some sense a philosophical Septuagint, had not resounded. The claims of many academic teachers for the supremacy of speculation were never more absolute, and never more unheeded. Most of them stood in the unphilosophical condition of more or less avowed pupilage to some one of the systems of the heroic age of idealism, the influences of which were far too pervasive and dominant to allow free individual development or independent criticism or even history. More than any other existing philosophical periodical, the *Halle Zeitschrift* now occupies the standpoint, and discusses the questions of this period.

If we extend the view to France, we find that, in spite of the Revolution of 1850 and the influence of Fourier and Simon, the dead official eclecticism of Cousin, which considered philosophy a shop, and opinions ready-made furniture among which each could pick and choose at will, was still dominant, although it had already begun to lapse from a rigid, almost priestly censorship, to the literary standpoint, from which, according to Renan, all truth is best seen in a play of light and shade, and God himself is found to be nothing more substantial than the category of the ideal. Positivism, which has since taken so deep a hold on French scientific men, was comparatively unknown. In England and the United States, Hamilton, Butler, Paley, Edwards, and, of course, Aristotle, and to a less extent Plato, were widely read and studied. Most admirers of Coleridge considered him as an isolated prodigy, and were unaware how directly he drew from German sources, particularly from Schelling. Berkeley was sometimes seriously, but more often curiously, read, and his idealism no less often misunderstood and even caricatured. Hume's philosophy was widely discredited by his religious opinions. Locke was everywhere read, but generally with a certain not purely philosophical reservation. Reid and Stewart were still classic. Abercrombie, and even "Watts on the

68

Mind,'' were at least respectable authorities in the schools. If not always physics, philosophy often did signify little more than sound common sense. Materialism and idealism were the Scylla and Charybdis of independent speculation; but immoral as the tendencies of the one system, and insane as those of the other, were deemed, German pantheism, which had begun to loom vaguely and awfully in the background, had more tragic sublimity than either; for it lay far beyond the boundary-line in passing which reason must forever lapse into irretrievable error and infatuation. Self-knowledge was highly spoken of; but there was a prejudice against every sort of self-study or introspection as unpractical and paralyzing, save in a purely religious or ethical sense, which was simply superstitious. This standpoint is still not uncommon in some of our smaller colleges.

For those who combine a love of modern science with a taste for the traditions of philosophy the writings of Lotze have a peculiar interest, while for those who knew him well his character has a still greater charm. A recognized authority in three of the medical sciences to which he made important contributions, the author of the best of all critical histories of æsthetics, and possessed of what his friends called a veritable genius for the quiet enjoyment of art and nature, one of the most revered and influential of all modern academic teachers of philosophy, of simple manners and tastes, and until the death of his wife and the marriage of his three sons, by which he was left comparatively alone, exceptionally happy in his domestic relations, he illustrated and reflected in his life and temperament all that is best in his teachings. The question whether the doctrine has had the greater or primary influence upon the man or vice versa seems quite vain. His opinions are never striking, and his career was scarcely more eventful than that of Kant. Yet very few have succeeded in giving more all-sided expression to their own natural personality—which he calls the highest fruition of philosophic endeavor—with such a rich and varied wealth of culture. He very rarely quotes or even names other writers, but muses and soliloquizes along from one subject to another with little method save an almost fantastic regularity in the number and length of his books, chapters and paragraphs, dropping suggestions which stimulate but seldom satisfy curiosity. Wide as is the range of his knowledge, his mental digestion and assimilation are so perfect that even trite facts present new and interesting facets in his pages, and the reader is brought face to face, and quite often heart to heart, with new-old subject-matter stripped bare of all the circumstances of names, dates, apparatus, etc. He rarely antagonizes the views of others, and perhaps had hardly an enemy or ill-wisher in the whole world of science or letters, but men of nearly all shades of opinion and belief speak of him with respect or at least with consideration. He very rarely dogmatizes. It was his poet-instinct, he tells us, which first drew him to philosophy. This, like theology, he considers as essentially the expression of sentiments, instincts, and needs which in a true and broad sense of the word are best termed æsthetic. So far from desiring to indoctrinate, he repeatedly insists that he writes in order to share his doubts and ignorance about ultimate questions—which form the bond of deepest sympathy between men—no less than to contribute his moiety of details to lighten, though but for a moment, the darkness of some mind or the oppression of some heart. He has no closed system, is more fond of raising than answering questions, and designedly leaves his students for the most part, whatever their training, standpoint, or mental predisposition, more rarely followers of him than confirmed and strengthened in their own natural tendencies, but more sympathetic, independent, and with an intellectual horizon broadened and variegated with a wealth of suggestive *aperçus* which make rational reflection ever after the most satisfying and strengthening, instead of—

as it is too often apt to be—the most weakening and unsettling of all occupations. He has no school in the old feudal sense of half a century ago, when many had no other intellectual ideal than to look at the universe through Hegel's eyes, or to see the world that Fichte or Schelling saw. Such discipleship is as impossible in our day as the fealty-oath of the old Scottish clansman would be. But it may be safely said that there are now few thinking men over forty-five in Germany who are not more or less indebted to Lotze for mental poise, intellectual tastes, or elements of a general culture which enable them to look beyond their own individual department of activity. Students, of course, attend philosophical collegiæ with very little of the enthusiasm or partisanship of former days, and still less with the expectation of deriving any material advantage therefrom, but with a purer and more intelligent interest in culture for its own sake, or, more specifically, in order to take a free, wide, and, above all, an independent look over and beyond the specialties among which they must choose a career. It is because professions are yearly more exacting, exclusive, and narrowing both in preparation and in pursuit, that lectures and books like Lotze's are particularly salutary and popular. A specialist, even in philosophy as generally understood, will find but little that is new in his own line, for Lotze's aim is to present an outline of the sum of human knowledge which shall be mainly correct in its proportions or in the place and importance given to its various departments. Hence the title of his most important work, ''The Microcosm,'' or, as he explains it, the ideal man as a symmetrical copy or reflection of the macrocosm or universe. To know ourselves we must know the structure of the world of which we are the summit.

Lotze attained his standpoints on most matters in his field relatively early in life, and in this respect differs radically from Schelling, who wrote himself clear in successive systems, or Kant, whose voyage of discovery took him until past middle life. But by the age of twenty-six Lotze had formulated many of his most characteristic views. The relations between physics and metaphysics, the body and the soul, nature and history, mind and matter, psychology and logic, the real and the ideal, God and the world— these are his favorite themes. It should not be forgotten, too, that his viewpoints were determined somewhat by his early poetic attitudes. Kurz's "German Literature" calls his poetry obscure but full of promise, while Gottschall thinks him mystical. The volume of poems appeared on the eve of his engagement to his future wife, which perhaps made in his soul a springtime of emotions. He had a long struggle to emancipate himself from the Hegelianism of his teacher, Weisse. When his "Metaphysics" appeared in 1814, it marked a crisis, for here he broke with Hegel and also showed that he was no follower of his own predecessor, Herbart.

Lotze is thus a humanist as opposed to a specialist, and this brief sketch of his opinions may well begin by a reference to his classicism and orientalism. Neither Herder nor Schiller, whose views he often reproduces, was more awed by the poetic arbitrariness of mythology, which, failing to besoul the immediate world of things, escapes the oppression of the blind forces of Nature and preserves freedom for the human spirit by coming to consciousness in a new-created world of its own. The Mosaic account of creation, which refers all things to one cause, and that an arbitrary omnipotent Word, is the consummation of this reaction of the higher instincts of the soul against the natural fatalism of common minds. Here humanity is erect, personality is independent and supreme in, or rather above, the world. But many minds pass to a second stage wherein an unconscious yet rational force is postulated back of and beneath things. Attraction is a longing, creation and growth a willing, harmony and adaptation a reasoning impulse, one but impersonal. This view, again, has too often given place to the scientific one that Nature is all, her fixed and invariable laws universal, and even men automata. Opposition to this view became the ground motive of all Lotze's philosophizing, and as his early partiality for this standpoint later gave his materialistic friends occasion to charge him with apostasy, so his later concessions to it may surprise and disconcert many English readers who have heard him quoted as a great champion of religion.

The first question the geneticist asks concerning a philosopher's system is, what were the underlying motivations that prompted it? It is now no longer enough to say that a philosopher sought the truth, for all do that, but we must know what led the thinker to philosophize and what he wished to accomplish by his scheme of things. It is especially pertinent from Lotze's own standpoint—from which everything is purposive and can only be explained on that basis—to ask this question concerning his scheme, and of no one is the answer clearer. He philosophized to harmonize two views of the world in his own soul and in that of others. On the one hand, science, with its severe logic of causation and mechanism, law, order, and the conservation of energy, investigates, measures, proves, seeks ever increasing exactness and uniformity, prefers physical types of thought and even material objective tropes and imagery to those that are subjective, and believes that when its work is done the cosmos will be shown in all its parts to be a mechanism of atoms and forces, perfectly ordered, certain, necessitous, under the complete reign of law. These methods and assumptions have wrought marvels and have their inspiration which all must feel.

But, on the other hand, there is the human heart, with its needs, hopes, wishes, and even dreams. There are what Lotze is fond of calling "a philosophy of feelings," "prophetic yearnings," etc. There are the imagination and its creations in art, poetry, literature, religion. There are philosophic speculations and supersensuous things that cannot be proven. There are the eternal verities of religion and also the world of ideas and ideals of which Herder had attempted to write the history. There are convictions we cling to which are beyond the reach of demonstration. Above all, there are eternal moral principles and values truer and more real than anything else. There is an ethical order pervading the entire life of man which science cannot touch.

These two views are as different, if I may attempt an illustration, as the moon of science and the moon of poetry, myth, and sentiment. To science, the moon is a corpse, a dead world, very cold, lifeless, airless, hung in the sky as a ghastly prophecy of what our earth will one day become, a perpetual *memento mori,* which is like a death's head at the feast. To the heart, on the other hand, the moon is not only our nearest celestial neighbor, but is eloquent of love, is soothing, beneficent, the measurer that metes out the year in weeks and months, the controller of tides in the sea and in our physiological organism, the lord of the weather, an object prayed to by children now and worshipped as the supreme deity in many ancient religions, and for denying the divinity of which Socrates was condemned to die.

Nearly all Lotze's philosophy, even more than Bergson's who consciously or unconsciously follows so many similar lines, is an attempt to mediate between these two points of view; to prevent the encroachment of either upon the other; to show that and how every whole soul must and can cling to both at the same time. The waste and devastation caused where either discredits the other is the supreme tragedy of our day. The fancied opposition between them cleaves the very soul of cultured man in twain. Lotze advocates no double housekeeping by which we live alternately in two compartments of the soul, ignoring the claims of now one, now the other, but he would make the human soul whole again by having the spirit of each penetrate the other. It is not only an unprecedented waste of human efficiency that science and humanism are so at variance, but it is a culture-disaster and tragedy for both sides alike, for each needs the other, even for its own good. He felt a veritable call, not so much to arbitrate, as to bring out the harmony which he felt to be preëstablished between them. The estrangement was pathetic, especially then and most of all for the young. Lotze was himself a poet and a philosopher, as well as a scientist, and in his early Leipzig period it seemed for a time uncertain which muse was to claim him. His formative period was at the nadir of philosophic interest, when the great systems were not only neglected, but despised, and yet to him philosophy was the culmination of all humanistic influences, although he knew that the systems of the near and far past must be reconstructed if philosophy was to be reinstated. He shared the current antipathy to the high a priori methods and results of Schelling and Hegel, but felt the moral inspiration of Kant and Fichte. He was irresistibly drawn toward the "Monadology" of Leibniz because it gave a basis for his individualism, but he was repelled by Herbart's attempt to, as he said, "scientize" the soul, deplete the rich, all-sided monads mirroring the universe to mere barren monotonous *reales,* and to resolve the play of concepts into mechanics and mathematics, which latter he thought should never be allowed to find any secure foothold in the domain of the soul where freedom and moral worths are supreme. Thus the light in the head must not go out when it is taken to the heart, and the warmth of the heart must suffuse the intellect.

His notion of atoms is extremely typical of his mental disposition. Atoms need not be absolutely simple or unextended. It is enough to say that they are hyper-sensuous. Whether they are material or dynamic cannot yet be determined and, in fact, makes little difference. Atoms are

simply the last element to which analytic thought is able
to refer the changes in Nature. For every application of
the doctrine it is also practically the same whether active
forces come to atoms from without for every momentary
emergency, or inhere in them and are brought out into
action by relations. One thing, however, is certain, every
outer refers to an inner change in the atom. Thus, they
seem to us to live and work as it were out from themselves.
Should their inner condition change, the laws of Nature
would be changing, as, indeed, they probably are, but too
slowly to be observed in the historic period. Indeed, the
affinities of the constituent elements of atoms may be
permanent and constant in only a relative sense. Whence
comes change? Time is only its passive medium and never
its cause. Perhaps even atoms, although the most stable
and primitive of all things, have their periods and are
circuiting back to an earlier condition. They may even
already have had thousands of changes and conditions.
Certainly we do not eternalize memory by making it inherent in them.

The grounds of all life, he says, are chemical changes.
These are not modified or controlled by any vital force, but
themselves constitute all those processes of assimilation
and secretion by which the body grows, is nourished, and
keeps itself in repair. These same forces also bring decay
and death. Although our impressions and our reactions
upon them are so different that it helps but little to refer the
one to the other, we have no right to assume even a specific
irritability, which may not be explained, like all else, by
"the gradual and gentle reciprocity by which each part and
element of the body influences the others." All animal
tissues, save in some degree the parenchyma, which may
be the active element in all, show some sort of punctiform
structure. This may be the slightest perceptible granula-
tion or may be the finished cell, and originated no doubt
from the coagulation of a fluid, but whether by mere se-

cretion or affinity is unknown. The independent movement of cells and the individuality of their life are less marked in animal than in vegetable tissues. Water, the agent of solution, which makes organization different from crystallization, and oxygen, which consumes dead matter and organizes new, are the two chief agents in that under-flow of chemism which causes not only animal heat but is perhaps the bearer of that moving impulse which life needs for beginning and completing its development. It almost seems as if the end of life were not merely to repair loss but to eradicate all previous impressions, for, while we see change begetting limits which seem gradually to exhaust the possibility of change, the body remains after all only a candle, which consumes fastest when its flame is steadiest.

On a background of inorganic, organic chemism seems able to supply all needed new or higher forces. If we try to form a general picture of life we can think of ourselves only as a *whirlpool or eddy* in the straight current of natural forces. As the waves made the reef which causes them so they will wear it away. The living body is like a rainbow, with no fixed substratum, or it gathers forces as a lens gathers rays. As in time so in space, we can hardly distinguish our body from other objects. The air penetrates our lungs and its oxygen our whole system; we cannot tell where food begins or ceases to be a part of us. So, too, we find traces of mind, down through the animal to the vegetable world. On the other hand, there are certain parts of the body—those which are least voluntarily movable, or those where the fibers of the sympatheticus are most numerous—in which the changes are more rapid the less they are sensed as factors of conscious self-feeling. All that is high has more presuppositions and less independence than that which is low in the order of development. Thus every rational attempt to feel ourselves as over against the world, is vain. We are at bottom, and shall ever be only a part of nature. Nearly all that has ever been urged of the influence of environment and heredity, of the universality and validity of laws and associations, and of the dependencies of the mind upon the body—his medical psychology first establishing the department of mental physiology—Lotze fully admits, and predicts that far more is yet to be discovered in the same direction.

The above is essentially the standpoint of modern science and he terms it the mechanical view of the universe, but insists that it is but one, and that a subordinate side of man and Nature. His formula is that mechanism is universal in extent, but everywhere secondary in importance. In the first place, he says, this view does not satisfy. A physiologist, *e. g.*, is justly glad to discover a mechanical explanation of some phenomenon which was formerly referred to vitality or to the equally hypothetical irritability, but, if he will reflect, he will find that his satisfaction is not that he knows more exactly, but that thus he comes a step nearer to certainty in intuiting some ulterior truth. The pride of a remorseless investigator, who values new views in proportion as they oppose old and especially sacred prejudices, is a false heroism and is far removed from scientific impartiality. It is true in a sense that observations are the facts and theories the fables of science, but the latter are often far more important than the former, for they are the expression of those half unconscious hopes and wishes which direct and inspire every inquiry. Besides, men fall into pessimism, as at present, according as the needs of the *Gemüth* are unanswered, or its idols broken. Although the special advocate of the old and the all, he says that the feeling that reason and religion are opposed is an unnecessary misery we bring upon ourselves by stopping short before investigations are finished, and it would be obviated by granting that science cannot explain the origin of things and that religion has nothing to do with mechanism. Lotze would by no means say with Jacobi that he was a heathen in understanding but a Christian in heart. That, as we shall see later, would be saying both too much and too little, but, like him, he feels that intellectual culture alone is a *caput mortuum* without faith, which is life.

The positive part of Lotze's doctrine is summed up in his oft repeated phrases that only that which has worth really is, or that the world of forms and means is subordinate to the world of worth and ends. There is an intellectual realm, he says, where ideals are real without their instrumentalities; where the highest happiness exists without being bound to its conditions, and in which the intuitions of truth do not depend upon either their logical connections or their causal relations. He glorifies feeling, with its inexhaustible manifoldness, as being more truly the nature of *Geist* than even knowledge. Again he declares that what ought to be is all that is really real in the world. The universe is all miracle and poetry; it is lawful and prosaic only to a one-sided apprehension. There may even be, he says, in logic final synthetic truths, not merely actual, but æsthetical and proven by the absurdity of the opposite and not by the impossibility of thinking them. In fact, logical progress is henceforth to consist not in the formulation of new laws of thought, but in increasing knowledge of what is presupposed as the highest self-unfolding principle. It is growth in *Selbstverständlichkeit*. All logical relations and all associations of ideas tell us only what is done (by external circumstances, etc.) on parts of a content which lies beyond, which we are apt to forget, and over the nature of which they have no power. This content—pure being, beauty, goodness, personality, etc.— is as diverse as the web of relations in which it is involved. Plurality, likeness, wholeness, and the rest tell us nothing of it. Our conceptions follow their own laws, which correspond very little with the laws of this real transcendent world, which they have broken up into a universe of glimpses so stale to the vulgar, so ravishing to the poetic mind even in their weirdest reconstructions. The soul must and will have or make objective expressions for its own needs and nature. It clings to outgrown superstitions, because there is a part of its essence unuttered in the modern world of understanding. In proportion as the impulse of development into conscious life is strong does it often cling to the most absurd and perhaps repulsive forms of objectivity, which are sacred to it and should always be respected as such. Here we are strongly reminded of Fichte's practical ego which ever strives beyond itself to establish an ideal world of moral goods, and even of Renouvier's theory of rationality as a sentiment. Lotze, however, would not say that a form of reason is a matter of taste, still less would he deny the reality of the objective facts of religion. His principle far more than Fichte's is one of passive contemplation, but he lays very little, if any, worth on the external evidences of religion, or even on its theogonies, miracles, Bibles, or churches. The soul must and will know its own wherever found with a quickness and certainty of intuition which leaves proof far behind. The supreme postulate of logic is some one major premise for all its conclusions, and this must express the movement of the collective cosmos. This bottom principle is nowhere defined, but is best described in his "Metaphysics," just issued, as teleological. That it is such is the final and highest fact of intuition.

In much from which the above is epitomized we are led to fear that, in his distaste for mechanism, Lotze has forgotten that clearness of thought and language is one of the many goods which should be realized. Yet true, the culture he tells us, which invests all periods of life with boundless interest, and to which we owe all its worths, which has given man many instead of few pleasures in the world, can raise us to a "unity of creator and created too deep for even mystic words." We must not grow weary of meditation or seek to attain all these things at a gush. We must not always riot in contemplation, but be faithful to the little while inspired by the great.

The absolute idealistic standpoint is scarcely less distasteful to Lotze than the mechanical. His training in the medical sciences gave him an aversion to Hegel still more pronounced than to Herbart. The former, he says, subjected both solutions of the world to a *reductio ad absurdum* by trying to force a union between them. He made a triadic machine of the absolute idea which created and constituted his intelligible universe. Even religion has become mechanical. "Philosophy," he says, "thought it was giving to Him who is more than can be called idea an honorable elucidation, when it raised Him out of the dimness of being clung to by the whole heart and soul to the dignity of a notion objectified in pure thought and proven by logic." In his lectures on the philosophy of religion he has almost nothing to say of Christianity, mainly, no doubt, as is readily inferred from his mental character and position, because he has far more interest in those questions common to all religions than in the special solution of Christianity. Granted his æsthetic-teleological principle supreme at the center of the world, which he terms the personality of God, together with the existence of noble souls after death, and his religious creed is about complete. The mechanization of the church, which should be at least the advocate of a broad humanistic culture, and which should make common cause with philosophy in all its more anti-materialistic and subjective sides, instead of suspecting and criticizing its tendencies, is to him one of the saddest aspects of modern times. Instead of resisting this current, authorized religious teachers have made themselves to some extent responsible for it.

The simple facts of experience do not satisfy the mind as a whole in the exercise of its imperative "ought to be," for fragments must be completed and contradictions harmonized in order to satisfy the innate instinct for truth which craves totality. This, at bottom, is an ethical emotion which comes with enthusiasm if not vision. It is the good, the beautiful, the really abiding. There is another world beyond the ordinary lapse of events within and without, "a sight of that immortal sea that brought us hither" which fades in the light of common day. There are obstinate questionings which impels us to true being, which is essentially ethical. To develop this is the aim of philosophy and, in doing this, it must push much farther the common distinction between reality and illusion, give us unity, and elevate the transient insights and convictions of the best men into the permanent possession of all. Thus humanity must have a humanistic interest. Lotze cared little for knowledge for its own sake or for mere intellecualism, or for the self-development of the idea, or evolution, or progress, or mere plan, or method. There must be something that has inherent intrinsic value, something ideal and beautiful. For him the idea of the good is only attained when we see that the world of values is supreme, and that is the key to the world of forms. He disagrees with the elder Fichte's subjective absolute idealism and with his apotheosis of action and prefers "the quiet bliss of beauty, the sanctity of that disposition which neither does nor desires the intrinsic self-consistency of truth with the place of its harmonies." These things are "too essential in the constitution of that postulated ideal world to let me do otherwise than look upon the restlessness of action as merely the means for reaching that higher aim." The truth of work is the Aristotelian $\sigma\chi o\lambda\acute{\eta}$ or leisurely enjoyment of it. Progress and evolution are not goods in themselves. One of his early theses was that there is no progress, "that the difference between civilization and its obstacles is a constant quantity." Men are prone to mistake the means for the end, and the self-applause of material advancement is a delusion, for every new step brings with it new dangers to be guarded against. We glorify machinery, but this never creates energy, but only transforms it so that it can be used. His criticism of Kant is directed against this formalism, for mere conformity to law for its own sake can never be a motive with a man of culture, nor does he care much for method in the sense of Spinoza or Hegel. His metaphysical system is teleological idealism and his categories are what he deems the fundamental conceptions that arise from the conviction that the cause and substance of all is its moral meaning. This conviction is impressed upon the mind not by intellect alone, but by a feeling of what ought to be. Thus Plato and Leibniz were closest to him. Duty for duty's sake is subordinated to the good and beautiful. Thus he broke with Kant's divorce between duty and pleasure by holding that there is no good that is not pleasant. He could not accept the view that virtue is merely the recognition of supreme law. Moreover, the personal must never be lost sight of. Personality is not merely a transition toward an impersonal absolute and we have no obligation to help along a process uninteresting to us. The human heart is richer than all laws; forces and ideas imply a thinker; action, a doer. Thus metaphysics must, first of all, satisfy the permanent wants of our moral nature and a true obligation must be unconditional. The world cannot be interpreted according to a plan upon which the commands that should rule our behavior can be deduced. Still less can we formulate duty from the developmental history of our species. Pleasure is really "the seal set upon a perfect life," and we crave it not because we are selfish, but because without it the world would be absurd. Pleasure is not merely a means of enjoyment, but "the light air in which every objective excellence and beauty of the actual first becomes luminous." Even science cannot compensate for the loss of the immediate vividness of æsthetic enjoyment. He recognized that the truth of science and of imagination and poetry are different and what he really sought was to bring what is true in philosophy within the reach of the average man of culture.

Phenomena always stand in a double relation. On the one hand, they require a substrate or substance of which they are phenomena, and, in the second place, there must always be something to which they are phenomena revealing that substance. Put in other terms, phenomena are a medium between two things: that *of* which they are a manifestation and that *to* which they are a manifestation. These two are their purpose, their *raison d'être*. From this it follows that phenomena are not merely subjective. They are also objective manifestations. On the one hand, their existence does not depend on their being perceived, as Berkeley said, because they have an existence all their own, owing to their substrate, but apart from it. On the other hand, they exist to be perceived, and are unfinished and purposeless until they are perceived. If substance is their efficient, a perceiving mind is their final cause. Thus, phenomena in the world of sense are the means by which the teleological process which binds things together and works with ontological forms is revealed to the human mind, so that there is a parallelism between the phenomenal and the ontological forms. This parallelism is one special case of the more general parallelism which exists between the real and the ideal, between things and thought, thought and speech, etc. Idealists often assume a difference between real existence and knowledge of it as if by being known or humanized things were changed into something different from what they are in fact. It is said that we do not know things as they actually are in themselves, so that there is one universal human error. All this Lotze denies. He says that such thought fails to recognize that the universe is made to be known, that to become known is a part of its very essence, and that this should always be taken into account. The world of objects is only one part and they are not complete until they are known, as flowering plants have no secure existence and are not truly known without the insects that fertilize them. Instead of being deprived of part of their reality in the act of knowledge, it is only by this act that they become completely what they are.

From this general characterization we pass to a brief epitome of some of his most striking chapters from his various works, where they often occur without any conceivable system under such titles as men and animals, unity of nature, language, soul, history, religious life, beauty and art, body, mind, etc. In considering, e. g., the enjoyment of life and work he says that men are not like plants, with constant needs and supplies. At first they had only to take what nature provided, to reap without sowing. Greek education was designed to fit men to use leisure time pleasantly, and labor was slavish. After the Crusades had opened the world a little, guilds and callings were established wherein work and pleasure were combined. Now since America has been discovered and the world known as a whole; since people are mingled and science has furnished means of commanding nature; and since machines, revolutionizing one industry after another—machines making machines in endless perspective—have brought men together into crowded cities, specializing labor to a lifeless routine, human life, its conditions, wants, ideals—its very nature, in short—have been radically changed. A tool requires a whole man to work it; not so the tending of a machine. Men put no heart, no soul, no conscience into their work. They pass from one industry to another. If they amass wealth they lack culture to enjoy it, and we have often the sad spectacle of a rich-poor man, retiring to enjoy living, failing to do so, and plunging into business again to save himself from ennui. Industrial expositions have become the great modern festivals. The magnitude of the labor question and of social democracy is due to the mental dissatisfaction with manufacturing life, where men marry young, foreseeing all their life—that its end will be but little better than its beginning—and where the life really lived is not the true one. They live in day dreams, nursing fancied wrongs and artificial sentiments, musing over schemes of change, while at the same time the necessities of life require increasing labor, and competition becomes daily more fatal to the weak. We boast of ruling Nature, but we have done so by an organization of her forces, which is so complex and uncontrollable that men were never so helplessly dependent upon her as at present, never so intent upon plundering her, and never so forgetful of loving her. Workmen are less and less able to foresee or resist changes in the market. Realizing their mutual dependence—that each suffers with the others—they unite in share companies, coöperative and insurance societies, till it seems as if shortly land itself would cease to be private property, but would be plowed or reaped on shares, and that perhaps even family life and nationality may be eventually fused in socialistic and international solidarities. The chief virtues of many professions and pursuits have already become those of machines—which may indeed soon come to discharge human duties. Business, in fine, that strange monstrous creation of modern life, which obeys its own half-unknown and entirely uncontrolled laws, which has destroyed our manners, created large unmarried classes, deluded some to count it progress that women are allowed to labor, study, and vote with men, which uniformalized and materialized modern aims and ideals, and at the same time stultified individualism to the point of looking upon differences of opinion, like different species of animals, as ultimate facts in nature, seems likely to drive work, in its former honest, man-making, and joyous sense, out of the world. Men now feel that the vague conception of their own incompleteness is not adequately or else not securely enough expressed in the expectation of a future life complementing the de-

ficiencies of this, as has so long been the case in great
business communities and nations, but they demand a sub-
lunary fruition of all their powers and capacities. Popular science, with its half culture, has aided not a little
in this general unsettling, encouraging the consensus of the
incompetent, as we might define social democracy, which
is now ready with its verdict upon almost every special
question in the whole range of human knowledge and experience.

We pass to another chapter in which he curiously claims
to have done for personal adornment a service comparable to what Kepler has done for astronomy. By his three
laws he thinks he has psychologically explained man's satisfaction in the various classes of clothing. If we touch
an object with a stick, he says, we intuitively analyze our
sensations into those felt by contact of the hand with the
stick, and ascribe the rest to the object at the other end
of the stick, and thus our own consciousness "runs through
all which touches us" in a peculiar manner. The first
pleasure we feel in attire comes from all that lengthens the
body in this sense, by prolongation of our personality at
the head or feet—high shoes, stilts, hats, headdresses, etc.
The worth of these for feeling varies with every change of
the height and shifting of the center of gravity. There is
special pleasure when equilibrium is the least trifle endangered. We feel the wind, our own motion, etc., by very
different sensations in hats that are high, broad, and
obliquely poised, or heavy, respectively. Secondly, all
hanging, fluttering, or swinging garments or ornaments,
by their changing tensions in different directions, cause
us to feel ourselves most agreeably in the peripheral track
or graceful curves of their free moving ends. A trail
dragging along the earth is like a new organ, endowing
us with a new sense. Ribbons, earrings, watch chain, sashes,
long, flowing hair are worn, especially by the young, not
merely for display, but to gratify the exquisite pressure-

sense so peculiar to youth. Lastly comes the impression we derive from our own clothing and its strength, thickness, texture, or stiffness, which our self-feeling imputes, as it were, to the form or poise of our own body. The pressure of a corset, he says, awakens the feeling of a stronger and more elastic existence. So girdles, bracelets, and, above all, the first trousers with braces give a pleasing sense of sturdy, inflexible uprightness or rigidity. He even declares that we admire the folds or smoothness of a graceful and well-fitting garment not for its own beauty but because we unconsciously reproduce in our own minds the agreeable sensations of the wearer's body. So, too, a false arm or leg half deceives even the wearer as to the boundaries of his own corporeal existence.

The object of art, he thinks, is to find new meanings of reality. Poetry attempts to represent the developmental history of the secret personality. Music reveals the general form and relations of the elements of reality as immediately known. In the broader sense, however, of which these are only specific expressions, art includes manners, style of life, ideals, common interests, dress, domestic habits, and surroundings, etc. The rococo style, which he considers one of the most perverse of all directions of taste— extending to common utensils, all the details of etiquette, etc.—is the object of his special aversion. It destroys the very nature of what it would beautify, and stands for the sovereignty of arbitrariness. This has given place to the still more unæsthetic heterogeneity of art-forms which not only tolerates monstrous galleries of pictures and statuary in which the impression of one masterpiece is neutralized by others, but concerts where, in a single evening, the characteristics of a dozen composers, representing as many different directions of artistic endeavor, are illustrated. These are barbarities in art and have no more root in modern life than carnivals. So, too, the noble institution of the seventh day of rest is a rhythm pervading the

forms, but no longer the heart of society. We seek mainly
pastime and change, and in this view it would seem that
art was never so far from life as now. On the other hand,
the French language has been made the cleverest, briefest,
most pleasant, and thus the best and most universal of all
prose simply because conversation has been freest and all
standpoints and all specialties have been best represented
in social life. Unlike German, it has been able and content to learn from without imitating antiquity. Inherit-
ing the results of long and consistent national culture and
reflection, it has developed a prompt and businesslike facility of fixing modern expressions upon modern notions and
interests. On the one hand, modern culture favors the
critico-literary way of looking at things. It finds its most
æsthetic pleasure in understanding the manners and means
and history of the arts, in knowing how they are done,
in making collections and perhaps in thinking how much
pleasure may sometimes come from pure and direct enjoyment of its treasures. The poetic element is shut out
from society as a fantastic irregularity. The choicest part
of our culture we do not express, feeling that its exhibi-
tion would be a sort of desecration, and thus art is deprived not only of enthusiasm and inspiration but even
of ideals. Now every age, nation, or man must first develop
an ideal instead of finding it ready made, and then must
proceed to realize it. Only after the individual artist has
found his own personal satisfaction in some definite sense
of reality or worth which in previous ages of art was in-
herited, but which is now quite as likely to be new and
unconventional as otherwise, can he apply himself to the
study of the forms and means of expression. Art has been
said to excuse all differences and diversities. When matters of taste can be questioned all beauty in the outward
forms of life in this sense is at an end and instead of the
interesting display of individualism in costumes and manners we have the laws of fashion and etiquette. Yet this

89

age is unfolding a distinct ideal type of life. It is characterized by the words accuracy, purity, compendiousness, great effects by small means, and with little display. We admire the elegance of the shortest and easiest method and dislike ceremoniousness. As architecture has been called frozen, so, but more scientifically, mathematics may be called dried music. What may be designated as the mathematical elements, as characterized above, may be called from the æsthetic standpoint the hopeful good genius of our time.

Lotze recognizes two sources of religious ideas: nature and social life. The former, or the cosmological element, is predominant in the heathen, the latter, or the ethical, in the Jewish and Christian religions. The Catholic church first gave ideal and metaphysical conceptions power over individuals by organizing and instituting them with an absoluteness which was truly Oriental. Its chief error was in imposing upon men's minds premature images and formulæ of the perfect instead of cultivating the means of practically realizing perfection. Activity is the passion of the West. Here men must work and experiment and not speculate. Here are history and progress. The world is not finished without the individual's effort. Yet recent Christian theology and philosophy have again come to interest themselves mainly in cosmological questions. God is sought in Nature, or in creative emanations more than in his unfathomable acts of love; we try to understand the metaphysical significance of Christ rather than the ethical majesty of his self-sacrifice. The doctrine of the Trinity is the most puzzling of the bequests by philosophy to theology. It is the confession of inability to identify in thought what, according to the laws of thought, must be one. In religion we need the strongest practical sense to overcome the effects of the confusing theories which mark man's struggles to see the whole. Apart from the æsthetic value of its legends, the ethical element is the essential thing in religion. The observation of Nature leads to the notion of a supernatural power, but rarely to the discovery of moral truth, as, *e. g.*, the duty of self-sacrifice. These spring from a native instinct. The chief duty of every man is to cultivate this instinct by answering for himself the question of what ought to be. Different circumstances, tastes, endowments, etc., make the end of life, and thus all its worths, different for each individual. The higher the standpoint of culture, or the more changeable the equilibrium of various moods, the more complicated and the more often erroneous does this become. Yet as man is but a part of a larger problem, as teleology in nature and native intuitions and powers in the soul of man are only different aspects of the same problem, so, too, paraphrasing a well-known saying, it is possible that, as a little philosophy leads us from, so, much leads us back again, to Orientalism. At any rate, a man of religious mind feels, without being pantheistic, that, though he and all that he possesses may be fragile, he has a world calling, and that the significance of his work in the universe is tested, not by its amount, still less by its kind, but by its fidelity. Labor of the first rank is devoted to the highest ends.

One of the chief traits of Lotze's philosophy, if not his culminating thought, is his much-discussed conception of substance, by which he seeks to unite individuation and pantheism. The Eleatics, Spinoza, and extreme absolute idealists and ontologists of a mystic Oriental type conceived substance as the supreme infinite reality, as the primordial beginning and the end of all things, and thought it the *summum genus* of induction, the major premise of deduction, mediated perhaps by the king of categories, being. Particular things, *genera,* or persons, must be derived from it or become real so far as they participate in it. On the other hand, vigorous thinkers like Leibniz, with his monads, and Herbart with his reals, if they did not pluralize substance, made it inherent in individuals, and most of them either derive both the reality and the unity of being from these parts or postulate it independently and then connect or else infer it by deduction from things. For these two affirmations or tendencies in the history of thought Lotze sought a more complete harmony. Thought, he urged, requires that we start with a substantial core of things and minds. We thus get the first apparent general reality by thinking things together causally. Substance, in the soul, is that which persists amid mental change. It is the independent bearer of psychic functions and the unifier of diverse psychic elements. Causation is a bond between the inwardness of things. It is also the power that controls them, and thus we may even call it God, although in a sense too high to involve personification—which means limitation. But this all-pervading substance does not subjugate or determine individualities. Substance is not thus for Lotze a merely imaginary addition to things, as Locke thought. Again, unity does not consist simply in pure being as such, as with Aristotle, nor is it a common energizing principle, as with Herbart and Leibniz. The latter simply postulate unity, while Lotze reaches his substance idea by knitting things together by causative thought. Hence, for him, ultimate substance is always in process of becoming. Even the unity of the soul substance is the product of causal inference. Every single thing has some substantiality about it. Thus he uses the substance idea, which has so often been the maw in which all things concrete and particular are swallowed up, to confirm the essential reality of both objects and of souls, which he thus conceives as perdurable. This problem was the leading motive of his "Metaphysics" and his "Ethics." Perhaps most criticisms of his system have been directed against this effort to harmonize personalism and pantheism. Most objections, however, he anticipated and met by urging that both the standpoints he would harmonize must be true, for they both carried within them-

selves the immediate intuition of their value and worth, so
that plenary conviction of one should never exceed that of
the other, and if his demonstration of their ultimate identity was faulty a better must be found and worked out
with no abatement of belief in the interim.

Lotze, perhaps better than any other, marks the transition from a metaphysical psychology to one based on induction from psychical and bodily states. His "Medical
Psychology" (1852) best marks this passage from the old to
the new. He sought to give both their due, to make peace
between them, and to be at once a physiologist and a metaphysician of the soul. In psychology, as in every other
philosophic discipline he touched, he strove to be a recon-
ciliator, with the result that his system has taken its place
as representing a period of transition of the greatest im
portance in its time, but now becoming an *überwundener
Standpunkt*. When others sought to differentiate, he
sought to integrate, so that, if his bridges were faultily
built or insecurely buttressed, and if some are falling or
superseded, still they made possible a great and profitable
traffic and greatly helped on evolution without revolution
in their day. Thus, historically, modern scientific psychology owes him a great debt, for he not only mitigated the
prejudices of the old philosophic camp but mobilized it
for further advance. If we would now evict some of his
metaphysics from our laboratories and clinics, let us not
forget that he made the traditions of the old speculative
systems and even of religion friendly and even gift-bearing
to our science when it was helpless and in its swaddling
clothes.

With Lotze even association is determined by a struggle
of the emotional values of concepts with each other. It
is not interpreted as a struggle of their own reproductive
tendencies among themselves, that is, they act directly on
each other and not through the mediation of ideas. Feeling indeed is not aroused, nor does it acquire its signifi-

cance through association, which is rather determined by it. Will, on the other hand, for Lotze is causeless and can only choose between reproduced concepts and cannot otherwise influence them, and thus memory is conditioned unconsciously, though not physically.

We have no space for further epitome, and shall be content if our sketch induce others to read for themselves the sanest and healthiest of perhaps all philosophers since Aristotle. Lotze has successfully solved one of the most difficult of modern pedagogical problems, viz.: how to inspire young men with a love of general culture which shall not be inconsistent with but subordinate to special training. Even Carus assured his pupils that no one can nowadays be a philosopher without being at the same time an expert in at least some one particular branch of science. Few of our American humanists have yet learned to do this. There were a few years ago in Germany probably several scores of young Americans, either inspired by the example and fame or else following the advice of more or less eminent humanistic teachers at home, who heard lectures in half a dozen specialties in as many universities during a stay of two or three years without a thought of becoming practically acquainted with any, but with an idea of a general culture which they expected to bring into use later in the pulpit or lecture room in mediating between sciences, or, more probably, between science and religion. From such students, some twenty years ago, one could obtain a quite mystic notion of a "specialist" as a man whose omniscience in his own branch is only equaled by the density of his ignorance beyond the sharp line of his own department, where in his blindness he must be carefully led and educated. Men like these held that Rev. Joseph Cook [1] had

[1] The Boston Monday Lectureship, which in the later seventies crowded Tremont Temple for twenty Monday noons per annum for five years to hear the Reverend Joseph Cook, some of whose annual volumes reached a sixteenth edition, first made Lotze, who was the

established a new profession and opened a new career for men of an eclectic turn of mind. But to-day sciences, as comparative, genetic, etc., are becoming more and more an organic whole, and even if it be too much to say that he who knows one must know much of many and something of all, it is certainly true that he who does not know one thoroughly knows nothing of the spirit, method, or end of any. We are convinced that much of the authority which theology and philosophy have assumed over the special sciences will hereafter be deemed leveling in a socialistic sense, as the tyranny of incompetence and the commonplace. The importance and scope of new ideas and *aperçus* are apt to be overestimated at first, especially by

lecturer's oft-mentioned hero, popular in this country. He was described as "on his knees before a personal God," "who rent materialism thus, thus!" as Mr. Cook tore his manuscript before a transported audience. "The microscope begins to have visions of immortality," "everything scientific is biblical and everything biblical is scientific." With a few of Lotze's prophylactic axioms graven on his memory, which were represented as causing dismay among all orders of intellectual unregeneracy, even the clergyman, we were told, could study science without impairing the temper of his faith. "An involution must precede every evolution," hence God. Mr. Cook even dramatically represented Lotze as standing upon his platform, swinging the apocalyptic millstones and mutilating the decent corpse of a dead materialism. To Mr. Cook, God, immortality, materialism and all the rest were terms of exact and settled connotation to be used without fallacy in an endless chain of syllogisms, instead of extremely complex concepts varying with every shade of culture and experience. Such stalwart pedagogic methods may have done good against the deadening tyranny of orthodox opinion in that day, which so impoverished intellectual and moral life in our country. Mr. Cook's foible of science may have given a new and appetizing flavor to the sentiment of conviction, but his representation of Lotzianism was most unfortunately misleading. His method encouraged scores of young clergymen to try their 'prentice hand upon the scientists with some new *coup* of their protagonist. How Lotze, as we have seen, would have shuddered at the thought that his name was inscribed on a church banner heading a crusade against science! It may be pertinent to add that the limits of minds which are not experienced in observing how reflection causes them to lose their absoluteness and shade off into others. We know no modern writer who makes knowledge a part of his own mental fiber more thoroughly than Lotze. In fact, the professor is so sunk in the academician that there is nowhere, save in his "Æsthetics," a trace of cram; and he has a truly philosophical distaste for exceptional, striking, and strong statements.

No system, however, is perfect, and we believe his to have one fundamental and several minor errors. In the first place his theory of the world seems to us too intensely individualistic. This principle the *Zeitgeist* is repressing in both morals and science, and yet Lotze uses

Mr. Cook's credulity became more and more shifting and that he at last came to make a confusingly qualified defense of "certain facts" of spiritualism. If a conch shell can be slipped through the wooden bottom of a chair, that to him gives us reason to believe that the risen Jesus could pass through closed doors, while the materialization of hands demonstrates the reality of the finger that wrote on Belshazzar's walls. Modern spiritism is the refined quintessence of the superstition of ages, compared with which the historic period is but a day. If there have been centuries of enlightenment and civilization, it is because this darkness has here and there cleared up for a space. It settled again in the first Christian centuries as Cabalism, Emanationism and neo-platonism, with their hierarchies of spirit hosts, romanizing the Church, strangling natural and medical science in the third and fourth centuries, and later bringing darkness, plagues, moral corruption, Paracelsianism, etc., from which we are now struggling to emerge. It has always been the common enemy of the Church and science, both of which Mr. Cook challenged to accept "its fundamental facts." Give me an eternal sleep far rather than the vulgarly gaudy spirit-life revealed in the coarser literature which has been designated here as "the most dismally superstitious of all modern prints." This, too, is the sentiment, so far as I can learn, of every authority in the German Church without exception. Mr. Cook quoted a few German savants who were at one time most impressed by it and wrongly made Lotze, Fechner and others its vouchers, although after a storm of protests he virtually retracted his endorsement, saying, "spiritualism is Potiphar's wife and my name is Joseph."

it to convince us of the immortality of the soul, the personality of God, and the absolute value of æsthetic enjoyment. Rejecting the common arguments for immortality he holds that it is chiefly proven by the power of embracing all our bodily conditions in one act and as one object of self-consciousness, and is mediated by the mysterious fiberless parenchyma. The immortal part is, of course, the subject to which this appears; and yet he concludes, in his usual collapsing fashion, that, after all, soul and body may be parts of one higher unity. So, too, the idea of a personal God as the consummation of the teleological principle is the highest of "the Goods" which are a sufficient cause for all that is. There is no apprehensible unrelated being. The latter is not a background or homogeneous substance from which things come out, but it is relation, the postulate of all reality, the ground of all difference—the *what* or the essence of things. It can never make a thing unique in the world, but can only give to it and its class a more or less different sphere of relations—as, *e. g.*, causes or effects. Correspondence, and especially reciprocity, imply a constant substantial unity. Space is a form of intuition in which things represent their supersensuous relations to each other to our consciousness. Things do not exist in space but it in them. The supersensuous order upon which the spacial order of the world depends must not be conceived as the intellectual complement of space. It is rather a web of aspacial relations woven each moment anew by things affecting each other directly without any mechanical (*i. e.*, causal) intervention. This does not destroy the reality of monadic things, whether atoms or individuals, but it shows us that all actual reality is spirituality, or being for itself (*Geistigkeit-für-sich-sein*). This is selfhood, the essence of all personality, and does not consist in positing an ego and a non-ego over against each other, for even self-consciousness, in the ordinary sense, which is a faint illustration of being-for-self, may dispense with a substantial objective world. This is to be used as a means which can be later disallowed. Souls which can come to need nothing but themselves, but sustain their development "in eternal inner movement without beginning," have attained the true immortality of being-for-self, which is the consummation of self-knowledge. This is not the immortality of impersonal matter or of the pantheistic idea, but it is pure personality, the highest form of which is God himself, who is known, if at all, immediately and directly; who can be known only by resembling him, and to know whom is a blessedness so great that it may be called the consummation of all the teleological ends of creation which we can as yet conceive. He has even been thought to believe that no one has yet attained immortality, but that the drift of things points that way, so that later, when men are fully evolved, they will probably attain it—a few of the best first, and others later, as they reach the standard.

This is the best résumé we can give of the famous ninth book of the "Microcosmus," with the help of the elucidation thrown upon it from his "Metaphysics." The *Gemüth* is thus made the organ of a transcendental world, and he even says that feeling, more than knowledge, is the true nature of *Geist*. The soul loves the fancy that atoms have internal states, hence they very likely have. But why could not Kirschmann, *e. g.*, argue that his foundation of realism or the existence of "spiritual spheres" in the vacuous interspace between ethereal undulations where, he said, perception takes place has the same supreme æsthetic current? We cannot know what is till we know what should be, says Lotze. Fidelity in working, not success in work, is our calling. To God all activity is practice, discipline, and not accomplishment. The existence of this world of transcendental meanings, personalities, and values is intuited and felt, not inferred; yet in asserting its reality even Lotze is often dogmatic. No one, we urge, can deny that so far as God or things are for self they are not for us, but must remain as inscrutable as if they were in the fourth dimension of space or Professor Crooke's fourth form of matter. Like the latter, being-for-self may perhaps exist, but so far from being yet a scientifically discussable question there is no probability that we shall ever be able to do more than to assert or deny its bare existence. Man has never been content to receive his own being at second hand as a product of nature, when he lives it himself. So, too, if the spiritual life of a Supreme Being is, as Lotze says, so intense that even when turning away from the supernatural we cannot destroy it, reason can have externally little weight in proving or disproving it, and his argumentation is superfluous. To retort in his own nomenclature, his reasons for the existence of a personal God are too mechanical.

This he seems himself sometimes to see and to concede. But granting his direct intuition as the highest self proof of God the question immediately arises, why is not this æsthetic-ethic sentiment which has the Divine for its object more fully characterized and analyzed, as we have a right to expect from one who makes psychology the foundation of his philosophizing? We should be told at least something of its origin and development, of what baser elements it is compounded, what are its more familiar illustrations and relations, etc. We especially need some explanation of why theological conceptions are more satisfying to it than are the countless new sources of poetic inspiration opened up by science, which Helmholtz, e. g., thinks far deeper and richer than those of all poetry, mythologies, and religions combined, but to which Lotze seems all the while, for a scientific man, strangely unsusceptible. There is no possible means of determining whether the pleasure of the one in considering the laws and forces of electrical phenomena, or that of the other in contemplating a supreme ethical personality, is the more intense, complex, or high, and if there were it would prove nothing. Not only do the formulæ of the theory of knowledge (*Erkentniss-theorie*) invest all the objects of feeling with the same uncertainty, dependency, and conditionality as they do the objects of perception, but the former lack the *consensus omnium gentium* which gives at least practical validity to the latter. The world of law or mechanism may be destined to be superseded by a new order of things, but there must be no break or discontinuity in the development. Science must work out its own salvation by its own methods. Wherever we touch nature there is residuary mystery—miracle, if you choose. There is room enough in the world of to-day for every conceivable theory to be true, for wide as is the intellectual horizon there is always a beyond for those who love "double-householding," and it is always possible to speak or think in any one of several psychological registers. But this, whether fortunately or unfortunately, will never satisfy those who believe that there is at bottom but one mental faculty, but one Nature, one truth in the world which is always here and now, so that we can hope to know all only by patiently learning to know one thing thoroughly and well. Æsthetic contemplation is one of the noblest satisfactions, or, according to Lotze, goods of life, and its cultivation is one of our chief duties; but science may also become the highest and the strongest motive and its practical utilization is still higher and more needed in the world in enlarging the boundaries of human knowledge and in finding new laws and controlling new forces. The history of opinion teaches nothing more impressively or more repeatedly than that truth has nothing to do with our likes or wishes. There is almost nothing in the natural world, or the world of imagination, which has not at some place and time been the object of belief, love or reverence, fear, or hate. The heart and its intuitions always seek or perhaps fancy that they have found the abiding, but are always finding their hoped-for finality premature.

RUDOLPH HERMANN LOTZE

We have space only to indicate the nature of our objections here, and, in passing, to notice the final form of Lotze's famous theory of the perception of space,[1] which has undergone many minor modifications since it was first promulgated,[2] but which we consider inadequate and essentially inconsistent. He finally comes to describe his famous "local signs," or elements of space perception, as "purely intensive," "with no geometric relations," "foreign to every notion of space," but "bound together by relations of an entirely different species," so that we know the position of even parts of our own body not by extradition but by a veritable reconstruction, and so that we cannot be truly said to distinguish even these sensations in space. The soul, it is throughout assumed, is absolutely independent of space, if not "punctual"; yet it has a "tendency," or a "faculty," to arrange this class of signs into an order which we call space. Why it tends to arrange them in this rather than any other order, "on account of the marvelous hold of geometric intuitions, we have not the least idea." Inquiry into the origin or further nature of the faculty which produces space from an aggregation of spacial zeros is condemned as hopeless. He objects to the term "tendency to movement" because it is ambiguous. His "local signs" are only psychic and the localization they provoke is an act of imagination "without any approach or resemblance to any sort of motion." He believes on the whole that no innervation which does not produce muscular tension can occasion any sensation even though we have a knowledge of our own desire to act. Yet modifications of tension even if balanced are the effects of partial movements, together with the images of motions suggested to or willed by the mind, and make up a large part of the system of local signs as intensively con-

[1] See his article, Sur la formation de la notion d'espace. Revue Scientifique, Oct., 1877.
[2] See Lotze's Medicinische Psychologie, Bd. I, Kap. 4.

structed, especially for the eye. Lotze thus utterly fails
to see that no conceivable logical or real transition from an
intensive to an extensive series is possible and that it is
quite as justifiable to argue quality an "idol" and quantity immediately perceived. Every form of the theory of
the "punctuality" of the soul, a doctrine strenuously opposed by writers of such profound psychological weight as
Aristotle, Ueberweg, Ulrici, Fechner, Lange, Weisse, etc.,
which has nothing to recommend it in its pedigree or in
the anatomy or physiology of the lower forms of animal
life, and which rests upon a perversion of thought, is sure
to assume ready made space as a matrix or bed in which
its intensive punctualities are set. Upon his premise the
very term "local signs" should be disallowed. They designate mystic incarnations of the nonspacial in space.
Either they are not local or else they are themselves position and not merely signs of position. For Lotze they became as purely *dei ex machina* as Leibniz's monads or
Herbart's reals. Instead of taking extension, real or ideal,
to pieces and reconstructing it into a series of an entirely
different order, we could far sooner believe that, as motion
is immediately felt within the body, so peripheral space
is not first apprehended as a plurality of like or unlike
impressions, but as a simple unity, never entirely ab-
stracted from some kind of content in which further thinking comes to distinguish not merely parts but limits, form,
locality, and various degrees and modes of occupancy or
extension with ever-increasing manifoldness and accuracy.
Some have thought to save the doctrine of local signs by
urging that the retinal and dermal order of space relations
is in some way represented in the central (thalamic or hip-
pocampal) regions, and that experience has only to trans-
late this brain space, immediately known, into corresponding terms of peripheral extension. If the brain cannot immediately discriminate its own dimensions, much less can
it those of the body and the external world, it is said, and

we are referred to the questionable embryological theory that the whole nervous system is developed from the epiblast and that as it unfolded it carried in its own constitution latent traditions of outness. It is still more often urged that nervous centers have direct intuition of the position and distribution of peripheral fibers, as a dim *tabula rasa*, on which sensations of touch are located where they are excited. All that can be said to all such theories is that, conjectural and improbable as they seem, it is impossible in the present state of knowledge entirely to refute them.

Indeed, the line cannot be drawn too hard and fast between speculations like Lotze's and a truly scientific philosophy. True, he contributed much to establish physiology as an independent and practical science, and in his pathology he so vigorously attacked the then dominant medical theory of crises in disease, of which he gave a new definition, that some physicians still point to his work as the beginning of the end of the general public distrust into which the medical profession had then fallen in Germany; but his mind and his best work are essentially poetic, and as such the charm with which he invests his somewhat paleontological conceptions of the world will add, it is not too much to say, essentially to the noble enjoyment which those who read him will know how to extract from life. His tastes ceased to be scientific, he never did important scientific work, and he lost caste among scientific men. So far from representing their opinions or tendencies he came to share both the neglect and the suspicion which is the traditional attitude of science toward metaphysics. He was too conservative to be an impartial observer or experimenter. He even hesitated to admit that every conclusion of philosophy is conditioned by psychology, and that there can be no finalities in the former till foundations are secure in the latter, as all interpretations of the theory of cognition seem to logically require. So, too, his knowledge of the world in

8   103

general, which makes so large a factor of his philosophizing, seems so vague and hazy, unreal and unpractical, that the reader passively acquiesces often more because he feels every kindly prepossession in favor of so well-mannered and sweet-tempered an author than because he is provoked to react by coming upon coincident reflections with his own. In making a new discovery in the study of nature some minds are most content in devising and arranging the apparatus, and when the mechanism is perfect and works well they have already reached the point of supreme scientific pleasure. With others such pleasure is experienced only in ascertaining how nature responds to the question addressed her, that is in obtaining results. This class only we consider philosophic. With others interest culminates in reflecting on the agreement or disagreement of the new observations with previously expressed theories or previously published results; it is, in short, a matter of public pride and consistency. There are yet others who are supremely interested in considering afterward how the new result affects their own hopes and wishes or their previous tastes and desires. Lotze belongs to the latter class. He is, in short, through and through a sentimentalist—taking the word, however, in its finest and noblest meaning.

It is because it is life and not formalization that feeling is free, and it is the most sacred office of philosophy to keep it so. Its freedom, however, is imperiled not by the constraints of the outward material world but by the more intimate idols of its own creation. In its ceaseless struggle for self-assertion, the soul, in Herbartian phrase, is always seeking a more stable outer and inner equilibrium. The first, over against the external world of the senses, it finds in science, with its constancy in fact and law; the second, over against the myths and theories, in which it has formerly sought glimpses of self-knowledge, it finds in philosophy, which, strictly interpreted, is the same for no two individuals, and remains no two successive days in growing minds without change. Hard as it sometimes is to give up hypotheses which have grown improbable in science, those who, with pious hands, trim and feed the lamp of philosophy are often required to make still more painful sacrifices. Lotze hears the call—no one more distinctly—but he lacks the hardy heroism of soul to obey. His demands on the world for individual æsthetic enjoyment are exorbitant and almost unparalleled. It never occurs to him that man's right to happiness at all is as yet quite unproven. He is very far from schooling himself, like Stuart Mill, to be content with a little happiness, and that at long intervals. He finds no satisfaction in the hope that the future will be better than the past or the present. His refined and subtle hedonism teaches that, respecting extra-scientific matters, we should at least try to believe what pleases us. But this we deem nothing less than immoral and even "socialistic" in its effects. Man is placed in the world to labor. Half his body is muscle. It costs harder and harder work to live, rear a family, be respectable, and provide for being decently buried. What right has this philosopher, idly sitting in his isolated study, to talk with such moving, maddening pathos about a world of worths and goods to be purely and perfectly enjoyed, while his own department was never more hopeful and in such crying need of labor and self-sacrificing devotion as now? We want to push on the psycho-physic studies which Fechner has begun and left in the most interesting and suggestive stage of incompleteness; to carry on the analysis of æsthetic sensations begun by the Helmholtz school, and to determine how far physiological psychology can justify the new as well as the old methods and critical judgments of art; to advance investigations respecting the structure and functions of nervous tracts and centers; to know more about the senses, the muscles, and will, the origin of man, and the unfoldment of his faculties; to find the true value of the new introspection—all in the hope of learning something more thereby about the validity of human experience, the scope, laws, and limits of knowledge, and, above all, the nature and forms of duty. That, with his fitting scientific training and early bias, Lotze has contributed little or nothing to the solution of any of these questions we are sometimes tempted to consider as no less than reprehensible, for, great good as he has done, he ought, with his rare gifts, to have done far more had he not been tempted by the sirens of æsthetic optimism to revery and pensive quietism.

Again, there are certain things in Lotze which we have never been able to harmonize. We have not been able to know mind aright, he argues, because we have conceived its faculties under so many physical analogies, because we picture the facts of memory as having properties like inertia, because we image mind as in space, or as having properties of light, or of electricity, like Hegel, or we speak of impressions as dim or weak, and conceptions as broad or positive and negative, etc. But such, and indeed all, naming, he reminds us, can never explain but always itself needs explanation. These descriptions may break up one great into many small mysteries, or parallel one series of secrets with another—as his cosmological are paralleled by his ontological forms. But why is not the mind also made to be known, and why is not being known a part of its existence, and essential to its completeness, as, when he is trying to explain away "the universal human error," which has separated subject and object, he tells us becoming known is to the completeness of the external world? Why should the things in themselves of sensation and self-consciousness respectively be subjected to laws so radically different? As the strongest argument for immortality, as we have seen, he urges that consciousness is really unitary because it appears to us to be so. How shall we know that this also is not a physical analogy, and that the soul does not truly exist because it is not truly known? Above all, how is this reconciled with his strange definition of phenomena as intermediates or means between personal souls, for whom all things exist, on the one hand, and the transcendent essence of things on the other, and as thus only half dependent for their existence on being perceived? If the universe is composed of personal spirits with "free inner spontaneity" consenting to be harnessed into mechanism in order to realize and unfold in corporeal form the beauty and goodness of the eternal idea, and, if "personality can never be understood by persons," then the whole psychological tendency of recent biological and even physical science is the greatest illusion of modern culture. For ourselves we are more than ever persuaded that true science and true philosophy give to more than they take from both poetry and religion.

Sometimes we are best helped to understand a thinker of this type by seeing how others of different types or schools of thought regard him. For this purpose I select the following from his chief critics in four different camps:

L. Stählin,[1] the orthodox theologian, while praising Lotze's rehabilitation of philosophy at a time when it was prostrate in the dust, and without quarrel with Bowne-Meyer in calling Lotze the greatest metaphysician of his day, or with Caspari, who thinks he marked an epoch in himself, still decides that his system is full of contradictions. Lotze is at his best in inquiries from various standpoints into various aspects of the problems he discussed, but Stählin insists that he broke with all traditions in making the soul the true *Ding-an-sich*, and destroyed the living God by defining him as the "one substance, the absolutely good and the all-personality." If substance is all that is, then finite things are mere modifications of it, and it cannot be absolute but is conditioned. If the soul is spirit,

[1] Kant, Lotze and Ritschl, Edinburgh, T. & T. Clark, 1889, pp. 161 et seq.

it can be no *Ding-an-sich*. The mere standing-in-relation of things is no proof of their substantial unity. As a critical realist, he has not confuted the critical idealism of Kant. If the soul were a thing in itself, it never could be known. Lotze can equally be proven to be a skeptic of the pre-Kantian-Hume type, or a thoroughgoing idealist. "He is really a syncretic scholastic, and his scheme cannot be accepted as a solid foundation on which to reërect the edifice of theological science."

Wrenschner,[1] the monist, argues that Lotze is no dualist, but a monist on account of his pan-psychism. Compare his doctrine that all finite things root in an infinite substance, that all that is real is *geistlich,* and also his interaction theory, which in his mind is not entirely inconsistent with the parallelistic view of the independent causation of all that is psychic, and his notion that the freedom of what he calls the *Für-sich-sein* of the soul, which makes it seem independent of the body, is acquired. On the other hand, his dualistic proclivities are no less pronounced, so that here, too, his harmonizing instincts have caused him to be claimed by both parties, as indeed he has been by both parallelists and interactionists. He never sacrificed a view that appealed to his own soul as valid and worthful because of its logical inconsistencies with other viewpoints, but assuming that sentiment of conviction is supreme, if there was discrepancy or even contradiction, he at once sought some causal or other nexus, sometimes even when the opposition seemed diametrical. Spinoza said that it is not the thinker's business to love or to hate, but only to understand things, and yet Ritschl based all his new theology upon Lotze's *Werthurteil* to affirm the supremacy of morals.

Schiller,[2] the pragmatist, denies that Lotze needs any

[1] Der Monismus; dargestellt in Beiträgen seiner Vertreter. Ed. by Arthur Drews, Jena, Diederick, 1908, 2 vols.

[2] Lotze's Monism in Humanism; Philosophical Essays, by F. C. S. Schiller, London, Macmillan & Co., 1903, 297 pp.

underlying unity, and says that his process of reasoning in obtaining it is unsound, that it explains nothing when attained, that it has nothing to do with God or even with Lotze's conception of him, so that it contributes nothing even to religion. Lotze was impelled to assume unity by the metaphysical difficulties involved in his idea of cause or the interinfluence of things. This means that things could not be really separate. This unity, granted and made real, explains all that has been thought transient as immanent interaction, and this he frankly calls the absolute and then goes on to treat it as prior to and more real than the things it connects. Things are nothing but the actions of the absolute upon spiritual beings, which, by being centers of experience, are thus made independent of the absolute. Lotze's unity is no more real than his plurality. It is not by virtue of the substance contained in things that they are what they are, but because they are able to produce the appearance of having a substance in them, he says, suggesting that a thing is what it does, and so he is at root a pragmatist, had he only known it.

Henry Jones,[1] the Hegelian, says that Lotze felt that he must first of all clear the ground of the false pretensions that philosophers, particularly Hegel, had set up for thought, viz., that they identified it with reality and converted a rich living world into a fixed system of abstract categories. Thus Lotze begins by an analytic attempt to find out what in reality is the nature of thought and also its limits. He finds (a) that it is not an ontological principle. It does not constitute but only represents reality, and that not very accurately. These ideal representations we call truth, and truth may correspond to the actual universe but is no part of it, but simply a function of human intelligence. (b) It is only one function among others, that is, besides thinking there also are feeling, will, senses, imagination. Thought merely conceives, judges, and rea-

[1] The Philosophy of Lotze, Glasgow, 1895, 393 pp.

sons. (c) Even to perform the functions left to it, thought
has to have the above other activities, such as sensation,
faith, or appreciation of worth, etc., and is dependent upon
them for its ideals, impulses, criteria. When thus provided with its material, thought arranges and substitutes
rational necessity for contingent connection between mental
phenomena, and so is wholly formal. (d) The systematic
world thus created by thought from its data is purely ideal
and not a world of things. There are no classes in the
outer world of reality, no subject, predicate, or copula, and
the reasonings that connect ideas are very different from
the causes that connect objects. Products of thought are
not even similar to anything in reality. Things do not
conceive or enter into classes. Thus the thought world
is at no point in contact with the real world. (e) The
results of thought would not be recognized as representing
reality if thought was the only intelligent power in man.
The knowledge that things are is due to other functions.
Furnished with these, then, thought may show what they
are and reveal their meanings, but meaning is never what
a thing is, but what it appears when translated from reality to ideality. Thought never shows what an object is in
and of itself, but only whether it is like or unlike, equal
or unequal to, or otherwise related to other objects. Thus
the core of reality entirely escapes thought. An intuitive
intelligence might conceivably give us this inner core and
rerepresent that imperious personality that constitutes the
inner consciousness of intelligent things, but our intelligence is only discursive or reflective, and creeps from one
feature to another, showing only relations. Thus thought
is not constitutive even of intelligence as such, but is an
indirect process that man has to undertake to make up for
the inadequacy of his perceptions. It is a symbol of man's
incompetence as well as his only means of acquiring such
knowledge as is possible.

Now from this Jones says that it follows that the idealistic reconstruction of belief that has so strongly influenced the modern world is entirely broken down. Thought is apart and insignificant, independent in man's mental equipment, and the work of metaphysics must be done over again, and some other ontological principle must be found. Again, the theologians who oppose reducing God to logical processes are encouraged, for, aside from all systematized thought, there is a field for immediate intuition. Thus thought is a composite, and reason has nothing to do with religion, but only with theology. Again, Lotze's investigations have stimulated others, and in Scotland there has been a remarkable development of logical lines on Lotze's basis, as well as by Brandeis and Bosanquet, and this development of his position seems to Jones to issue in its refutation. Lotze's main contribution, therefore, is really in defending the idealism he sought to overthrow. His is a pseudo-dialectic product. The helplessness of such thought as his shows it to be a logical fiction. So Lotze leads from a formal to a constituent, or from a subjective and epistemological to an objective and ontological view of thought.

In the carefully phrased statements of his "Dictata" (now translated in six booklets on as many of the topics he chiefly taught), which consist of condensed expressions his students were to copy, Lotze is systematic, precise, formal almost to a fault, yet each of these outlines covers but a small part of the ground usually included in the subject under treatment. Each presents an ordered collection of viewpoints that seem to the author central, and no more. In the psychology syllabus, e. g., he discusses sensations, the course of ideas, attention, space, feelings, emotions, and in the last, or theoretical, half, the reciprocity of the soul and body, with chapters each upon the seat, time, relations, essence, states, and realm of the soul—and that is all. So in the other topics his range is narrow even where his treatment of the themes chosen is full. Even in his larger ethics, logic, and metaphysics he does not hesitate upon occasion to pass from one domain to another, regarding these demarcations as mere pedagogic devices and fences to prevent the investigator from pursuing his subject wherever it leads. Hence, there is a great deal of substantial repetition. To this all lines converge and from it they diverge. He was also through and through a consciousness-philosopher, and his ultimate quest was *Für-sich-sein*. Of the immortality of the soul he spoke with great reservation, usually as something which was beyond the domain of philosophy, but in general he seems to have held that immortality was attained whenever souls had made themselves of intrinsic worth, and therefore essential parts in the relational and especially in the moral order of the world. Whether the race has this kind of immortality is left unsettled.

We may regard the chief traditions or philosophemes in the history of thought as three, now characterized somewhat as follows: The first took earliest shape as the *concept* under the obstetric art of Socrates, and was better defined by Plato's doctrine of ideas or forms. In another way it appears again in Aristotle's theory of *categories*, half deduced, half gathered from the agora, and which Kant assumed without criticism and with too little change; and later in the *universals*, innate ideas, exemplary forms and species of the schoolmen, as Hegel's diamond network, which made the universe real because it made it rational, as the pure entities in the artistic contemplation of which Schopenhauer thought the soul found its only surcease from pain, and even as the *natura ipsissima* of God himself, to know which was conscious immortality; while it is no less historically represented in the theory of fixed types in nature, which have constituted the chief obstacle which evolution has had to encounter in every field and form. This assumption of fixed substantial norms or forms—precious because brought forth by such severe tra-

112

vail of soul—now thought to be immanent, now transcendent, here in the field of nature, there of mind, partly in-
herited from the Greeks, yet instinctive in every mind,
needs to be traced through its many forms, as the key to
much of the thought and many of the great controversies
of the world. Properly treated, this point of view is of
the highest educational value. On every hand, however,
are rutty, ultracategorical minds and books whose whole
philosophizing consists in adopting or adapting some one
set of categories from the many by no means accordant
tables of them, and pigeon-holing among them all facts
of matter or mind with an often ill-concealed "air of re-
pressed omniscience," as if they were hierophants initiat-
ing into esoteric mysteries and jealously guarding all metaphysical orthodoxies. Easily made changes in the name,
number, order, or prominence of these norms meet any
exigencies of controversy or morals, and, few as they are,
and many as are the books, the combinations are by no
means exhausted, nor the vast mental spaces explored that
can be thus "triangulated" by their definition alone. Substance, cause, time, space, and all the rest are not simple,
as is assumed, in the sense of being indecomposable by
psychic analysis. They mark the points where thinking
stops as well as starts, and no definition of them can be so
exact as to sustain a long argument unswervingly. Without such norms, knowledge and experience could no more
become objects of science than could physical nature if
there were no laws, but they will submit to more adequate
formulation if we study their validity rather than their fit
or consistency. The influence of psychology upon the creations of speculative genius in this field is not unlike that
of science upon poetry. It is opening a new world, and
rendering the charm of the old still more subtle.

The second historic standpoint is the mechanical.
Though older than Democritus, it entered the modern world
as a result of the great discoveries and inventions which

heralded the Reformation. Descartes, who could not think except in visual and mathematical terms; Borelli, by his great work on the motions of animals; and the iatro-mechanical school of medicine thus founded (which treated digestion as trituration, secretion as sifting, circulation as hydrodynamics, and nerve action as vibration, and which made mathematics for a long time the preliminary study of physicians) represent its "storm and stress" period. Part of the force of this tendency expended itself in practical inventions, part was lost in the vagaries of popular materialism, and the best of its impulses were revived and are still felt in the German school of physiology since Weber, which has raised the whole art and science of medicine in that country from a very low to its present commanding estate. Not content with the attempt to reduce inanimate nature to terms of measurable force and matter, it prompted Herbart's effort to state the mutual action of concepts in exact static and dynamic terms, proposed the psycho-physic law and the hedonistic calculus, and a logic so exact as to be literally mechanical, and ever since Spinoza it has cherished the hope that philosophic problems might be reasoned out by geometrical methods, and has favored mechanism in thought and morals by emphasizing every material trope and analogy. It is the standpoint of which Lange is the best historian, and against which the main current of Lotze's philosophizing was from the first directed, and which he called universal in extent, but everywhere subordinate in function. If on the one hand it is often less respectful to the great traditions of humanity; if it breeds an indifference to many themes yet held in highest reverence, that recall the old agnostic maxim, *quæ supra nos, quid ad nos;* if taken extremely it eliminates freedom, responsibility, and immateriality from the problem of life—let us not forget that it has also brought the human mind to a sharper focus with less dispersive fringes than ever before in the history of thought, on all things within its range, even though others beyond it are blurred and distorted.

For the third historic standpoint I know no better name than that of self-consciousness, a far narrower term and thing than self-knowledge. The remote result of the Reformation was to raise the question in a few of the most vigorous and serious minds of Europe: What if even our philosophy, too, be but the most refined of superstitions, and all articulate systems idolatry? What if we must make a *tabula rasa* of all current hypotheses and presuppositions about ultimate truth, and seek some kind of *ataraxia* in knowing that we can know nothing. Self-examination reduced them to the condition of primitive thinkers with no consensus, facing a universe perhaps too vast to have any character assignable by man, because greater than all that can be called thought; standing before, as it were, an unrevealed logos, an unrelated absolute, an unheteronomized ought, an unobjectified will. Hume would not have said that we must doubt all that we cannot prove, yet it was natural in an age of such rapidly deepening self-involution of thought that he should be taken far more seriously than he meant by Kant, who, more than any other, has made men content with a rational and practical arrangement of concepts, even if they cannot express the real nature of things, but only our thought of them. From this standpoint many have seemed to seek proof of, if not, indeed, a substitute for, the objective validity of ideas in the fit and consistency with which they can be juxtaposed, assuming that from their contact in individual minds the only real continuity in thought can be inferred. Others, by an introspective involution of thought, have believed that thus thought could be made as deep as the ego and as broad as the all, and raised to a potence almost divinely creative. Taken extremely and alone, or in some of its manifold combinations with the first standpoint, this philosophic tradition tends to reduce both the world of matter

115

and all the great realities of religion to a system of long-accumulating deposits and projections of the human consciousness, or to resolve nature as well as theology into anthropology. Man's mind is the measure of all things. The secondary and even the primary qualities of matter and all spiritual goods are alike subjectively conditioned or even constituted. The degenerate forms and products of this philosophic direction are too complex to be traced here.

These three spheres of thought, to tracing the details of which through the various systems the history of philosophy is devoted, are still to a great extent unharmonized. The psychologist, at least, is not satisfied with any attempt to reduce the categories to an organic unity of consciousness. The Greek conception of idea or form and the self-affirmation of Protestantism are now seen to be segments of a larger orbit of thought than this. The second of the above standpoints is not yet satisfactorily mediated by the notion of fixed and constant types of any sort, and mechanism stops short of consciousness. To secure the unique culture-power of the first and last of the traditions of philosophy to students of science, and of the second to students of general history and the humanities, is the chief duty, and to aid in mediating the new and higher unity now impending between the three is, in my opinion, the chief task of the psychologist to-day. If there was ever a time when the student and teacher of religion needed to ponder these problems, to be fit for his work amid the light and heat of popular interest and discussion which these large adjustments are now exciting, it is to-day. It is the function, not of psychology, but of revelation only, to give absolute truth; but we must not forget in our land, where the very depth and strength of religious instincts make us too satisfied with narrow and inadequate mental expressions of them, that the first step toward securing an adequate theoretic training of those sentiments in which

116

religion and morality have their common root is to rescue the higher mythopœic faculties from the present degradation to which prejudice and crass theories have brought them. That deeper psychologic insights, in directions to which attention in this field is already turning, are to effect a complete atonement between modern culture and religious sentiments and verities is now becoming more and more apparent. The development of these insights will gravely affect the future of religion. Will not geneticism, as hinted at the close of the last chapter, furnish the fourth, higher, mediating standpoint?

Perhaps there never was a saner, safer philosopher with a more Emersonian combination of sweetness and light than Lotze. He was "more fine and suggestive than large and vigorous" (Falckenberg), with greater reserve than Fechner; cautious, always moderate, sensible, and in good taste. His metaphysics and even his logic were rather for the sake of his æsthetics and ethics. His system is more classic and less romantic than that of Hartmann. If he evolved few great or original ideas, he never said a foolish or *outré* thing or one which lent itself to caricature. He revered philosophy as the queen of the sciences, and was her faithful minister, even though she was deposed, and he lived in hope of seeing her restored to her ancient throne. He never made an enemy, and disciples of other schools were more prone to find points of agreement than of difference with him. Save Baumann, Stumpf, Busse, and Falckenberg, perhaps in that order, he had no disciples in Germany in his own department, but had much influence in the heyday of his fame with liberal theologians. The group of philosophical and æsthetic spirits that have lately founded and supported *Logos* continue his spirit, but have departed in some respects far from his letter. In England he has had no permanent followers, but in France in Bergson more perhaps than in any other living man his soul is marching on. Only Bergson holds to two

117

systems of philosophy, one superposed upon the other, and he makes no attempt to harmonize but only to contrast them. In this country Bowne and Ladd have diffused his principles and made for him a number of adherents, especially among conservative and semi-theological academic teachers.

Lotze, however, had no wish to establish a school, but rather to prescribe cures for distracted souls as a kind of pastor-physician. He used ideas to infect men with his temperament, to lure them to the sanity, unity, poise, and repose that both nature and nurture had given him. At bottom, his was a philosophy of feeling, and his ultimate appeal was to the *Gemüth* which he would make an oracle no less supreme than Schleiermacher had sought to make it for theology, Horwicz for psychology, Magnan for psychiatry, and, in a way, Freud for psychoneurosis. Much as he reconstructed and eliminated from the other systems, it was only to save all that was tenable in them that edified, and, although the residues he saved he tried to make to fit logically, if he did not succeed in convincing reason, he still appealed to the heart. Every principle and idea that affected the sentiment of belief and conviction must be a part of a harmonious intellectual whole, and contradiction and inconsistency must at least be postulated as eliminable. His trust in the instinct of belief was implicit, and he held that if intuitive creedal affirmations did not fit each other it was so much the worse for them. Of course, he thought he had welded basal verities, certified by his criteria, indiscerptibly together, so that he could never deem his own system eclectic, but coherent and rigorously sequential, although few men with a well-developed critical diathesis now accept his syntheses as they stand.

Thinking in such syntheses as he strove to make is premature, and perhaps can never be final, but a better harmony than that he sought is slowly coming, though in a very different way, viz., by the slow natural progress of science into the domain of humanistic interests. The psychology of the feelings is at the door and will justify their viewpoints. The higher criticism is fulfilling, not destroying, religious values. Æsthetics is beginning to be more scientific than his. The higher anthropology of myth, custom, and belief has made rapid strides since his day and is showing the truth of even superstitious, and what erstwhile seemed senseless, cults. His very narrow views of instinct are already superseded. Vitalism is coming to the fore in biology. The value of mental states is being understood in therapy and even hygiene. We are even interpreting the old orthodoxies out of what they say into the larger, deeper terms of what they mean. The criminology that regards crime as a disease seems to have already done its best work and to be just now beginning to recognize again the element of personal guilt with a sphere of freedom and consequent responsibility, and we are even striving to penetrate the mysteries of the original creations and spontaneities of genius. Thus the iron laws of mechanism as he understood them are no longer so universal or oppressive. His conceptions of modern psychology and especially of genetic aspects are now antiquated. His ideas of psychic evolution were so crude as to be almost valueless, and yet the modern psychologist who has not read Lotze and come to terms with him not only lacks perspective but has undeveloped possibilities slumbering in him of which he does not dream.

BIBLIOGRAPHY

Hermann Lotze: sa vie et ses écrits, par E. Rehnish. In Revue Philosophique, Vol. XII, 1881; pp. 321-336.

Hartmann und Lotze, von G. Hartung. Phil. Monatshefte, XXI, 1885; pp. 1-20.

Darstellung und Kritik der Lotz'schen Lehre von den Localzeichen, von Reinhold Geyer. *Ibid.*, pp. 513-560.

Lotze's praktische Philosophie in ihren Grundzügen, von Thr. Achelis. Phil. Monatshefte, XXII, 1886; pp. 577-609.

Lotze's Lehren über Raum und Zeit und R. Geijer's Beurtheilung derselben, von H. Höffding. Phil. Monatshefte, XXIV, 1888; pp. 422-440.

Lotze's Metaphysik, von Johann Wolff. Phil. Jahrbuch, 4, 1891; pp. 138-160. 5, 1892; pp. 26-41. *Ibid.*, 133-151. *Ibid.*, 285-315.

Lotze's moral idealism, by G. Santayana. Mind, 15, 1890; pp. 191-212.

Lotze's antithesis between thought and things, by A. Eastwod. Mind, N. S. 3, 1892; pp. 305-324. *Ibid.*, 470-488.

Lotze's Ansicht über die Reproduction der Vorstellungen, von Friedrich Pol. Norden, Diedr. Soltau, 1903; 54p.

Lotze's Substanzbegriff, von Sali Levi. Heidelberg, D. Straus, 1906; 45p.

Lotze's Lehre vom Ding-an-sich und Ich-an-sich, von Arthur Löwenstamm. Breslau, H. Fleischmann, 1906; 56p.

RUDOLF HERMANN LOTZE

Geschichte der Æsthetik in Deutschland. München, J. G. Cotta, 1868.

Metaphysics in three books; ontology, cosmology, and psychology; Eng. trans., ed. by B. Bosanquet; 2d ed. Ox., Clarendon press, 1887; 2 v. (Clarendon press ser.)

Logic in three books; of thought, of investigation, and of knowledge; Eng. trans., ed. by B. Bosanquet; 2d ed. Ox., Clarendon press, 1888; 2 v. (Clarendon press ser.)

Pädagogische Psychologie in ihrer Anwendung auf die Schulpraxis und auf die Erziehung, von F. Bartels. Jena, Mauke, 1891. 2 pts. in 1 v.

Medizinische Psychologie; oder Physiologie der Seele. Weidmann, Lpz., 1852. 632p.

Microcosmus; an essay concerning man and his relation to the world; tr. fr. the Ger. by E. Hamilton and E. E. C. Jones; 2d ed. N. Y., Scribner, 1887. 2 v. in 1.

Outlines of philosophy; tr. and ed. by G. T. Ladd. Bost., Ginn, 1885-1901. 6 v.

Outlines of psychology; dictated portions of the lectures; tr. and ed. by G. T. Ladd. Bost., Ginn, 1886. 157p. (Lotze's Outlines of philosophy, v. 4.)

Outlines of psychology; dictations from lectures by Lotze; tr., with a chapter on the anatomy of the brain, by C. L. Herrick; illus. Williams, Minneapolis, 18—. 150p.

Outlines of logic. Boston, Ginn & Co.

Outlines of æsthetics. Boston, Ginn & Co.

Allgemeine Pathologie und Therapie als mechanische Naturwissenschaften. Leipzig, 1842-48.

Allgemeine Physiologie des menschlichen Körpers. Göttingen, 1851; pp. 632.

Geschichte der deutschen Philosophie seit Kant. Dictata aus den Vorlesungen. Leipzig, 1882.

Grundzüge der Naturphilosophie. Dictata aus den Vorlesungen von H. Ladd. Leipzig, 1884; pp. 84.

Kleine Schriften; ed. D. Peipers. Leipzig, 1885-91. 3 Bde.

Ueber die Bedingungen der Kunstschönheit. Göttingen Studien, 1847.

Ueber den Begriff der Schönheit. Göttingen Studien, 1845.

Ein Wallfahrt von Antwerpen nach Jerusalem aus dem Jahre 1517. Leipzig, 1866.

System der Philosophie. Bd. 1: Logik, Leipzig, 1874; 2 Aufl., 1880; Bd. 2: Metaphysik, 1879; 2 Aufl., 1884.

Outlines of metaphysics. Boston, Ginn & Co.

Outlines of philosophy of religion. Boston, Ginn & Co.

GUSTAV THEODOR FECHNER
1801–1887

GUSTAV THEODOR FECHNER

1801-1887

Fechner sprang, on both his father's and mother's sides, from a line of rather liberal and cheerful Lutheran pastors, and this heritage made itself very strongly felt in his later and even middle life. His father, although a country pastor, was one of the first of his kind to feel the spirit of the *Aufklärung*, first to have a lightning rod on his church, and not to wear a peruke in the pulpit, despite the excitement these innovations caused among his flock, whom he told that Jesus preached without a peruke. The father died when Fechner was in his fifth year. Theodor was sent to the Gymnasium at fourteen, and at sixteen began to study surgery and medicine at the University of Leipzig, and in this city he remained the rest of his life, rarely leaving it. It grew from 40,000 citizens within the promenade to a world city or *"kleine Paris,"* and was called the heart of Germany. Fechner eked out the very slender means his mother could give him by giving lessons, making translations, and doing other kinds of literary work. In his early youth he planned to make literature his calling, and his temperament was always poetic and æsthetic. In the university, however, he became an avowed atheist until he read Oken's natural history, which brought him sudden and new light, and he became an enthusiastic disciple of Schelling, saying later that he was an apple that grew on Schelling's tree, although he fell some distance from it.

Medicine then had no scientific method, and was even

more entirely empirical than when Helmholtz wrote on "Thinking in Medicine," almost implying that there was none. Its practice consisted mainly in following certain prescribed and unexplained precepts. For one interested in the intellectual side of it, it was unsatisfying, and so Fechner turned to the physiology of von Weber and dropped pathology and therapy. He passed his doctor's examination in 1822, but nevertheless refused to go through the formalities of becoming a physician, but turned to experimental physics, which he thought the best domain of experimental science. Kant had shown that the laws of nature are also the laws of mind and had held that the former must be studied in detail, but his successors shortened the way and became more theoretical, and even physics became speculative. Oken knew his subject but followed Schelling's construction of all organisms from *Urschleim,* assuming that the problem here could be solved at a stroke. This was a captivating view. God is the universe, and comes to self-knowledge in man who unites all the organisms, which in the animal world are scattered into one organism. For instance, man's five senses combine five types of animals. Skin, tongue, nose, ear, and eye animals are Oken's names for vertebrates, fish, frogs, birds, and creatures with two lids to their eyes. Fechner did not understand such sentences as "the optic nerve is an organized beam of light—the brain an organized sun—the eye an organized color, sun, or rainbow"; but what drew him to this philosophy was its view that the world is not a dead mechanism. Although he did lecture in the Schelling-Oken spirit after his habilitation in 1833, when he translated Biot's "Physics," he later left this point of view behind. He began lecturing on physics in 1824 and his speculative inclinations were sidetracked for a time as harmless humor. The central interest in physics then was electricity—Volta, Oersted, magnetism, and a little later Faraday and Ohm. Electricity was "imponderable," and we find many minor contributions of Fechner in Poggendorff's *Annalen,* in which there appeared several minor articles of his.

In 1838 he began his more or less psychological studies of subjective color experiences, which constituted his transition from physical to physiological and psychological interests. He published investigations on subjective complementary colors and how to excite them with a color top, also after and accessory images, and the phenomena of *Abklingen.* These began to appear before the end of the thirties of the last century. (Poggendorff, Bde. 44-50.) He was constantly experimenting upon himself for subjective optical effects, even glancing at the sun, working with sudden lights, and straining his eyes to observe the electromagnetic scale, and this gradually led to his later calamity. He now translated Thenard's "Chemistry," and was an editor and frequent contributor to the *Pharmaceutic Centralblatt.* When he was made *ordinarius* without salary in 1833, he married Clara Polkmann, to whom he had been engaged for three years, and the need of being economical prompted him to edit Breitkopf and Hartel's "House and Conversation Lexicon," in eight volumes (1838), for which he himself wrote many articles (Lasswitz thinks one-third of the whole), discussing such matters as marketing, shopping, various domestic industries, etc. His health grew worse from 1835 on, and he traveled. He hesitated about retaining his professorship, and gave popular lectures. We can learn little of the nature of his illness, except that he could not control his .attention, and his thoughts were very active against his will. He could not sleep, and became depressed and tense by turns. Some optical disease set in, and he was obliged to give up all reading and writing, and spend much time in a darkened room. Even dark glasses were intolerable, and he found his way about the streets almost like a blind man. The worst began in 1840, and this was the turning point to a different direction of thought and work.

This we can best introduce by glancing at some of his humorous articles, written under the name of Dr. Mises, in which he satirized medicine and the old natural philosophy. In the pamphlet entitled "Proof That the Moon Is Made of Iodine," he derided the tendency to regard iodine as a panacea, and also made sport of Oken.[1] The latter appears in such sentences as "warmth and light are nothing but the two poles of fire, or its plus and minus," or we might name them the "debts and the assets of fire," or we might define heat as "sin or egoism, the left side or tail end, the ganglion system, or the plant organ of fire, while light is virtue, truth, the right side, the head end, the brain," for all these relations are, in fact, not entirely adequate to the idea, but approximate it in various stages by their potencies. Thus it follows that the moon, since it, like iodine, heals *Kropf*, consists of iodine and light, since it is not true light, but the efflux of the iodine. It looks yellow because of the different potentializations that iodine has undergone.

In his "Panegyric on Current Medicine and Natural Philosophy" he discusses the number of applications of drugs and medicines. Mises says we have not only many drugs for every disease, but every drug heals several diseases, so there will have to come a time when in the Materia Medica there will be enumerated under every drug not only the medicines that it can, but that it cannot, help. A book emphasizing this negative side would probably be smaller and smaller with every edition, and would in the end reduce itself to a single sentence, viz., "Every drug heals all diseases"; and therapy would also be a sentence, "Every disease is healed through every medicament."

These things, of course, have mainly historical interest, but in another pamphlet entitled "Means of Protection against Cholera" he says that it is regarded as a terrible

[1] Who was popularly introduced into this country by I. B. Stallo, Philosophy of Nature, Boston, 1848, p. 520.

guest, but even for those who fear and hate it it is a benefit. It protects mankind, depopulates and makes more room, food, and business. As there had been so recent an outbreak of cholera and another was feared, this satire was thought to go too far. He starts from the general discontent of mankind that is directed even against the cholera, which does nothing but look after human affairs with great earnestness, viz., determining population and boundaries, enforcing temperance, showing the vanity of wealth, helping out druggists, doctors, booksellers. It possibly may sometime help medicine a little.

Stapelia Mixta is a flower of neat color with sharply contrasting spots, which emits such perfume that the carrion flies lay their eggs in it by mistake. The little book by this name contains various chapters of different worth, and many which, in a second edition, were dropped. It treats of literary and æsthetic subjects, especially the symbolism of conic sections and an inverted world.

Rather charming is his "Comparative Anatomy of the Angels." These are not symbolic, but real, living angels, which stand in the organic world a little higher than man, who is not the highest nor the most beautiful. Even the ass thinks his own type ideal. The human form is a strange aggregate of surfaces and curves, hollows and elevations. There are no flat surfaces and therefore curves and specifically the sphere are the ideal forms and these change (as, indeed, Plato had said). The parts of man's body are beautiful as they approach it, but the eyeball is most complete. It is the organ of light and in light angels live. Earth is not their fitting residence. They belong to higher bodies like the sun, the stars, or light. Just as the air is the element in which man lives, so light is the element of the angels, who are simply free and independent eyes, all eye, or the eye-type in its highest and most beautiful development. Thus, what in man is a subordinate organ, in the angels is of independent worth. In animals the eyes are backward or sideward, whereas in man they look forward. But angels are single eyes. Their language is light and their tones are colors. The eye-language of love hints at the speech of angels, these creatures of the sun with their ethereal bodies. Their skin is merely connected vapors, like soap bubbles. Their transparent nature can take on colors. They change their form and expand and contract according to their feelings. They are attraction or repulsion, and with this goes the wonderful color play. They are organisms. They move by hovering and sweeping along. General gravitation, which relates all bodies, is their sense. They feel the farthest thing in the universe and the slightest change in it. They are, in short, living planets and, in fine, the planets are angels. They are less refined than the sun dwellers because farther away from the sun. This last conclusion Mises did not draw at first, but he did so later, not in jest, but in Fechner's serious theory that the earth is an organism, and men are organs of a higher being, that is, the earth.

In his "Four Paradoxes" the satire is against the fruitless endeavor to know the unknowable and the vanity of purely speculative methods. A good illustration of Dr. Mises' mode of thought may be seen in the first of the four paradoxes, entitled "The Shadow is alive," inspired, no doubt, by the story of Peter Schlemiel, the man without a shadow, and so without a soul. He asks why should it not be? We live in three and a shadow in two dimensions of space, but the third dimension is stiff and thick and very obstructive. When we turn around, the nose and all our features remain unchanged, but the shadow, if he dislikes the nose or any other feature, simply turns away and it goes. The arms are long or short and can be also taken off by turning. The shadow can walk upright on the wall or slip along the ground, flat; can break himself on an angle and yet be whole; can go through thick and thin; whereas, we have to choose our way with care. He can fall on a dung-hill without soiling even his shoes, and never suffers from a stone bruise; he is not afraid of water or fire, and can actually run through others of his own species. Now, if it is objected that shadows are not only nothing, but less than nothing, the answer is that on their side shadows do not need to believe in the life of man. A shadow may regard himself as spirit and man merely as body, the use of which is to show forth the purely immaterial existence of the shadow, to connect him with something material. Why is it not just as well to conceive the soul beside as inside the body, and that the body serves the shadow? The shadow will say, "Without body I cannot exist and, therefore, body is for my sake, to tie me down to this vale of tears, but I hope that I may not always carry about this heavy mass which is ever clinging to my heels, where there is always linked so much more evil than goodness. Striving here only to be as dark as possible, I shall eventually come into the highest realm of shadow, or pure night, where I can exist with other good shadows, blessed forever without body or light. Obviously, it is only my body that now hinders me from seeing the great Primeval Shadow in the heavens, who created me and all other shadows. The great partition between the Father of all shadows and me will soon fall." Indeed, the shadow might simply invert things and call men his shadow and servant. If the shadow vanishes the man dies, for never can any man live without him. If, again, one answers that the shadow is nothing, the reply is "which is stronger, hunger or satiety? Nature is more hungry for light where darkness is than vice versa." If one refuses to believe that the hole that a shadow makes in the light has no feeling, he must grant feeling, at least, to the surface in which this hole is found, for that would feel what was lacking in it. The surface changes constantly, and the shadow must be an individual, as the material of which a body is made is changing. The second paradox was that space has four dimensions; the third,

131

that witchcraft exists; the fourth, that the world is the product not of a creative, but of a destructive principle. He loved to use his ingenuity in dignifying trifles and in defending the improbable, and was very clever with analogies. He seemed to show a superfluity of mental activity. The reader is often puzzled just how far to take Fechner in earnest, or to know whether he was reading him or Dr. Mises.

He also wrote interesting essays on Ruckert and Heine, being especially attracted by the former, and in 1841 he published a volume of his later poems. It was very congenial for him to solve puzzles and riddles and of the latter he collected a large number, which, as Dr. Mises, he published. His literary ability, however, lay not in poetry, but in art criticism, at least next to satire. In criticising works of art he ridiculed the attitudes of conventionalized figures, and seemed to hold a brief for a new naturalism. In his humor he certainly showed great originality, perhaps unequaled by anyone in this field. He notes the incongruity between his piquant and witty writings and his harmless, very monotonous life. Some think he was influenced by Jean Paul.

It was hard for Fechner to accept Darwinism, because he believed that it assumed an initial indeterminateness and a slow evolution of purposefulness. A builder would hardly give his unskilled workmen *carte blanche* to put together mixed piles of wood, stone, brick, and mortar as they were, and even with endless time at his disposal there would be very many new starts and destructions, although they might eventually learn how to construct the building. This represented Fechner's idea of Darwinism. He himself thought there must be stability with variation but diminishing change. Nature first shows constancy and repetition. The struggle for existence could help only after differentiation had set in. Correlation is more than chance. Differentiation was once far more rapid.

132

GUSTAV THEODOR FECHNER

"The highest good," or the supreme end of all thought and action, is the maximum of pleasure, not of the individual, but of all, and on this he based all his rules for morals. God, too, loved and sought happiness, so his moral principle had a religious basis. Thus only we can educate the conscience, which consists in the feeling that our will and conduct are harmonized with God's will. He says, referring to his own experience, that the diseases that God sends men are best cured by conforming to the laws of nature.

Here, roughly stated, is his thought in the "Book of Life after Death," the best of his mystical writings before his crisis, though greatly amplified after. A human fœtus before birth might reason thus: "Here I am comfortable, warm, fed, sleeping in darkness and growing without effort. When I must leave this place all I observe convinces me that it must be as putrid excrement, for what is called birth will be my death. Therefore, let me get the very most and best out of my present period of existence, for it is all I shall experience of life." How different the sequel after birth—life in the blessed light of day, the use of the senses, all Nature, social life, activities, joy, sorrows! Here we sleep only one-third of the time. But, surely, when this second life ends there will come the end of the moldering, excremental corpse. But no, there is a third life, all waking. Leaving the body at death is only escaping a second womb and placenta to a life as much better than the second as the second is than the first. What we now call death is only a new birth into a higher life, which is perdurable and is to the other as the life of a bird to that of an earthworm.

How now do the dead live on? First and chiefly in us. Fechner takes his leading concept from the mystic way in which Christ lives in his followers, who are members of his body and branches of his vine. To this larger life of his in the church, his earthly career is only a grain of mustard seed. Gloriously his soul has gone marching on.

Just so the dead press in upon us, yearning to add their strength to ours, for thus they not merely live, but grow. New impulsions and sudden insights in us are inspirations from them. Not only do the great and good dead influence and pervade us all the time, but we are exposed also to the bad. Many of them are always bad, and so if our will is weak and our personality unorganized, they may dominate us. Their visitation is insistent. They do not crave incarnation in the flesh like Plato's spirits, but in our moral life, that therein they may be made perfect. We all have in us sparks from the lives of Luther, Goethe, Napoleon, etc., who think and act in us "no longer restrained by the limitations of the body, but poured forth upon the world which in their lifetime they molded, gladdened, swayed, and by their personality they now supply us with influences which we never discern as coming from them." Each great dead soul extends itself into many and unites them in a spiritual organism. Thus, the dead converse with each other in us. They also fight the good and the bad in each other in us, causing strife in our souls. From them come rivalry, sects, wars. Men are driven blindly by alien spirits, though they know it not. When we remember and attend to them, they do the same to us. It is, however, idle to seek for our departed friends in any other objective way, but when we think of them then they are truly present. They are particularly near every monument or memorial or biographer, and listen with satisfaction and expansion to our every thought of them. This is a cult, not mainly of ancestors, but a kind of communion of saints dead, both with us and with each other. Close as this union is, it never endangers the principle of individuation in them, but rather enhances it. If, while living, we live in harmony with spirits, we shall have already a place prepared with them when the body is sloughed off. The spirit world is "a tree of souls the roots of which strike into the earth but whose summit reaches the heavens." Dead geniuses and saints mediate between God and common men. Every town should have beside its church a shrine for its own great dead. The dead play upon our present life as upon a lute, even when we think we play upon ourselves. Only at death do we attain full consciousness of what we have produced in others and made out of ourselves. A man who had passed all his life in solitude, or an infant who lived but a day—both would alike be permeated and perpetuated, that is, made immortal by the influence of the spirits. Our own association of ideas typifies their union. Freed from matter, the disembodied soul will be able to pervade the animal and vegetable world as a diffusive power and may even reach the planets. Possibly the earth itself will one day return its soul to the sun, and a sun life of all earthly creatures will begin. Each soul will have its share in a transcendent body, for we are now in the ground like seeds of a giant tree which intersects with all the other trees of the forest and yet maintains its own identity. The divine comes to consciousness in us and thus we never die. Phantasms of the dead may be both subjective concepts and objective realities. We cannot know, yet wraiths and actual phantasms of the dead are highly improbable. If they exist, they are only degenerate, abortive or decaying, decomposing spirits that come into the range of our senses, so low have they fallen. The dead and living could not communicate in this way. To do so would be partial death for the living, for revenants, if such there be, are the scum and off-scouring of the spirit world. There is, however, a higher soul in which we and all things live, move, and have our being, and in which and only in which spirits are real. We are, in fact, what we have become. The brain is a kind of seed which decays that the soul may live. The individual soul may mount on the collective souls of the dead as a sparrow is carried up on an eagle's back to heights it never could attain, but, when there, can fly off and even a little higher. At death the soul seems to drop

10   135

below a threshold and the spark of consciousness might be conceived to go out but for the fact that the soul is not projected into an empty world but into one where it incessantly meets varying resistances that keep personality above the point of submergence or any other extinction without appeal to the conservation of energy. Just as attention moves about from point to point within the body, so after death the soul moves around the world.

Perhaps failing eyesight, due to his too arduous studies of binocular vision, predisposed Fechner to mental vision, as blindness did Milton, and as temporary loss of sense perception favors such states as Swedenborg's of rapt insight into things celestial and infernal. Perhaps biology (which he knew so little, save the physiology of Johannes Müller and Ludwig, till later he damaged his eyes still further in trying to absorb Darwin) would have satisfied some of his cravings and helped bridge his two worlds of physical science and seerdom. Perhaps had he had children he would have thought more of the future of man on earth and less of his post-mortem life. In fine, had his own life been more completely rounded out and his invalidism less chronic, he would have been less curious and lustful concerning another life. Yet it is doubtful whether, had all these conditions been otherwise, it would have much changed his strong and persistent *Einstellung* for the *Jenseits,* his curiosity to examine the veil for every pinhole through which light from the beyond could come. The imagination is a totalizing faculty and in him it complemented all personal and racial impressions and strove to build a mansion for man's soul wherein all wishes were to be satisfied.

The Crisis.—For three years he was ill, and he has written the history of these years. In 1840 his eyesight began to fail him. He could neither write, read, nor endure society, and suffered all the deadly qualms of tedium. Nor did he care very much to be read to. His method of work was to jot down everything and then rewrite and combine endlessly, and this method could not be carried out with the aid of another person, and he was too old to change. He tried to dictate to his wife, but this was a failure. He finally came to the very verge of the grave and, as he said, looked death straight in the face for a long time. The medicine he had derided had its revenge in the moxa, thrice administered to bring a counter-irritant to the spine. Sometimes for weeks he would neither eat nor drink. Later he found himself able to eat fruit and, finally, strongly spiced raw ham and red wine, and on this diet he began to recover. But his eyes remained so bad that, in November, 1842, he had to stop writing even in his private notebook, could not converse even with his wife, and suffered intense pain in his eyes and teeth. He wanted to die, but, he says, "I was convinced I should win nothing by suicide, but rather in a future life my pains which I here want to escape would be continued." Sometimes his state seemed to him a kind of puppet condition. He could not control his thoughts or attention by his will. His dreams were torture. Still he always felt that his life would last. In this condition he had to spend months in a dark room and when he came to the table had to wear a mask and sometimes hardly spoke a word for days, abandoning all former pleasures. August of 1843 was the worst month, but soon came slight improvement and he could venture into the light, though even at the end of 1843 he was still thought to be incurably blind and hopelessly out of his mind. The sudden betterment came in a peculiar tense psychic state and he then felt that he was called by God to do extraordinary things, and prepared therefor by his sufferings; that he had extraordinary psychical and physical powers. The whole world began to appear to him in a new light. Its riddle was revealed. The old being was gone and "this crisis seemed a new birth." His former inclination to philosophical speculation had come to the foreground. It was a case of prophesying by convalescence. He turned away from physical investigation to that of general problems of the world.

While he was ill, Wilhelm Weber had taken his place and Fechner had a pension of 850 thalers, which was later increased by 400, making 1,250 in all. Although an opportunity soon came to return to physics, he declined, but still, to partly compensate for his pension, he did give lectures twice a week in the summer of 1846 on the highest good, last things, anthropology, the seat of the soul, its relations to the body, psychophysics, and æsthetics. The physicist, however, had become the philosopher, and for forty years he was able to continue on this new line. He now realized that, although science must be carried to its uttermost, only the inner sense of nature as a living unity can truly satisfy. His subsequent life may be characterized as pervaded by the tendency to press through the physical to the metaphysical, through the natural to the ideal, through the objective to the subjective side of things.

Although born under the reign of the great speculative systems, interest in them was steadily declining, so that during his mature years the philosophic point of view reached, perhaps, its very lowest ebb in the German reaction to science and mechanism. This was one reason why the works that Fechner put his heart most into fell dead from the press. The philosophic spirit that always and everywhere presses on from every sense and phenomenon to the transcendentally true, good, and beautiful was perhaps never, in the modern world, so near extinction as in the three middle decades of the last century in the Fatherland, just when Fechner was most active. But he felt that the higher life of thought could be vindicated, not by any critique of the faculty of knowledge like Kant's, and still less by any a priori regimentation of the sciences like that of Hegel, Fechner's pet aversion, who, he said, "unlearned men to think," nor yet by turning away from the study of nature, but only by accepting everything the sciences could tell us and pressing through them to the soul that inheres in all things. Vogt, Büchner, Moleschott and even Hegel to Fechner stood for the night side over against what he called the day side of things. They courted darkness to develop their eyes, like owls. His pet word was not reason or idea, but insight, and it was this that led him to hold that all things, even atoms, crystals, heavenly bodies, the earth, plants, all are besouled if we see them truly from within. His animism thus makes all akin. All things express in different ways the same *anima mundi* or cosmic soul which is God, who came into existence with the world, is its conscience and will, and will die when and if the world dies, but which every process, object, species, or new scientific thought and good deed helps to fuller and larger existence.

Since his death there has been a remarkable revival of interest in Fechner in Germany among philosophic thinkers, and his works are edited and reëdited, read and discussed as never before, and his kinships with other writers, particularly Leibniz, Schelling, and, most of all, Lotze, have been pointed out. Not a few have defined their positions with regard to Fechner, and Paulsen, in his Introduction to Fechner's ''Seelenfrage,'' which he deems the central part of his scheme of things, acknowledges a very close similarity of *Weltanschauung* with his own, although he read him late.

Fechner had been a very diligent reader in his early years, when his interests were chiefly in physics, but his crisis left his eyes too weak to read much, although many friends helped him out, so that his new philosophic insights developed with only a general knowledge of Kant, Schelling, Fichte, and Hegel. Kant was one pet abomination, whose invention of the *Ding-an-sich* he termed a fell plot to banish joy from the world. For Fechner epistemology did not exist. Things were just as they seemed to sense

139

and the inductions based upon it, and there was nothing noumenal or transcendent within or behind them. To teach distrust of the senses or to call our experience with nature merely phenomenal is to make true knowledge impossible, to cheapen life, and to bring discontent, unhappiness, and disenchantment into the world. We meet and know the ipsissimal God himself in the universe, not merely the effects of which he is the cause. In our daily experience with the world we are up against substance itself, not merely its attributes or modes. Matter and mind are two objectively different modes of immediate contact with reality. The psychic element, when it appears above the threshold in its own time and way as its stimulus increases logarithmically, is a real phenomenon. It is all there with nothing behind it. It is all its *Wirklichkeit*. The night view of life is that which designates all this beautiful world as only phenomenal, or as a passing subjective illusion, and puts reality more or less out of reach behind in some noumenal *Ding-an-sich* or transcendentality, both for cells and atoms. It sacrifices the *Dieseits* to a hellish *Jenseits*, which is a fetish, though made warp and woof of imagination. In fact, it means that science, though its growth is phenomenal, can never truly understand life or consciousness.

His book on "Life after Death," already discussed, after his illness was taken up more seriously. Immortality is proven by the fact that consciousness is not a property that inheres in individuals, but a general one inherent in all Nature. It was this line of thought that led to the publication of "Nanna." This was practically the first fruit of his new life. In his introduction Fechner confesses the dreamy character of his work. He had first called it "Flora" until he read Uhland's "Myth of Thor," where he found that Nanna was the wife of Balder, the light god. The name of her father, Nep, suggests *Knospe* (bud). Saxo describes how Balder's love to Nanna was inflamed as he

saw her beauty in a bath, and this Fechner thinks symbol-
izes the dew of flowers in the morning light. At Balder's
funeral Nanna's heart bursts with pain, and this suggests
the depetalization of flowers. From the under world Balder and Nanna send presents to Frigg, who presides over
married love, and these—a veil and a gold ring—suggest
the flowers of late summer. Fechner would describe the
communion of besouled plants with the light-god Balder,
and finds Nanna a more German goddess, better laden with
mystic suggestions than the Latin Flora, whom he condemns
to herbaria.

"Besouled plants" certainly does sound like a fairy
tale, as Kurd Lasswitz says in the preface of his edition
of "Nanna, or the Soul Life of Plants," the first edition
of which had been published fifty years before. If, indeed,
we could invert things and set plants upon the throne of
the earth and we become plants, we should be inclined to
ask what these restless human bipeds are running about for
and whether they have any use save to serve vegetable life.
We, the plant people would continue, remain in dignified
rest in our own place, and need to do nothing save to spread
out our roots and leaves in order to receive all divine gifts
as our due tribute. Men live to prepare carbonic acid for
our breath and die only that their decaying bodies may
furnish us nitrogen. Men have to cultivate us in flower-
pots and gardens, field and forest, and yet we consume
them in the end. If we wish to send our bacterial army
into their blood, we exterminate them, and, although they
take a small part of our fruit and leaves, it is only to
spread and fertilize our seeds. Insects as far outnumber
men as our leaves do insects, and yet even insects serve us
as love messengers to bring the pollen of our blossoms to
fertile corollas.

Plants participate in the cosmic soul life, and, indeed,
have their own souls. They live, breathe, emit perfumes,
bloom, propagate, and are beautiful, partly, surely, for

their own sake. They must have a dim kind of feeling. Animals do not speak and yet we know that their feelings are much like ours. But plants respond with exquisite sensitiveness to their environment by changes in their organization and functions. Their psyche is not concentrated in a nervous system or brain, but diffused through all their parts. They do move their parts toward food, light, air, moisture, and who can say that consciousness can not exist without a nervous system? Tones can be produced by either strings or reeds or vibrating columns of air, and psychic life may be as varied. Plants do not attend as we do and the consciousness attending the vegetative processes may be blunt, but perhaps consciousness is more vital the wider its diffusion. They must feel discomfort when deprived of food, light, and air. They must have a sense of need and an inner compulsion toward satisfaction. Plants' souls are not miniature copies of human. It is an advantage that the soul is otherwise diffused among plants than in man, and perhaps that their responses are very slow. Who can say that the water-lily has no sensation of its own beauty? These outer and inner movements of plants can hardly be purely mechanical. A flower, too, surely must feel a little pride to be worn by a beautiful lady. Plants have the great advantage of not foreseeing, e. g., that the scythe will mow them down, as even cultivated plants or animals do not. Surely, plants cannot be like blind eyes and deaf ears, but plant life is preparatory to a higher psychic life throughout Nature.

The besouling of plants really rests upon the basal idea of psychic processes corresponding to physical processes; that the psychic is only the self appearance of the material and the latter a form in which inner psychic processes can appear to others. That material processes in a physical system arise as conscious of themselves requires, however, that they reach a certain degree of intensity, which he called the threshold, a most fruitful idea not yet developed in "Nanna," but very clear in the "Zend-Avesta." Here he shows that plants have an individual consciousness to a certain degree, but that this rests on that of a general higher one without its individual character.

It was natural that this book should seem fantastic to students of nature, and it was especially attacked by the botanist Schleiden, to whom Fechner replied in 1856 in an article entitled "Professor Schleiden and the Moon," in which he defends the views in "Nanna" against this botanist and, incidentally, shows the meteorological influence of the moon and criticizes Reichenbach's *Od*, which had a certain charm for a time. Fechner thinks it is pathological. More recently the accurate knowledge of cell division, transformation of energy, the coöperation of the plant and the animal world, and especially evolution, have been helping to a view of the world favorable to psychophysical parallelism. The clearer it becomes that all the manifoldness of the living world represents only stages of development and that there are no leaps, the plainer it is that there must be a psychic continuity corresponding to that in the physical world. Perhaps if Fechner had known Kant's theory of knowledge, especially his conception of the objects of sense, he would have been confirmed in this view.

This inverted world is, of course, a fairy tale in that plants do not think and speak, but Fechner has shown how much truth there is in this "Märchen." When it was published, wise men shook their heads, but they do so a little less now, for times have changed. Its fundamental thought is that consciousness in some form pervades all Nature, and this idea is not so strange to philosophy, but is almost a consequence of the conception of the parallelism of physical and psychical, as Wundt says in substance.

Fischer [1] long ago suggested that the Greek word, $\varepsilon\iota\delta o\varsigma$

[1] Über das Princip der Organisation und die Pflanzenseele, Mainz, 1883. See also Bosé, Jagadis Chunder, Plant response as

or idea means form, and that there has been something psychic in every principle of organization of a type or species, which is comparable to a school of art or philosophy. But there can be no form without content, and, while each variety breeds true, the biological unit or phylum does not necessarily involve any psychic principle. While there is a sense in which, as Aristotle said, the whole precedes the parts, the *nisus formativus* which equips creatures with organs and functions does not imply ideation. The doctrine of a life force as something apart from physical or chemical energy has also been interpreted as implying a psychic factor. The hypothesis of a principle which presides over generation and nutrition has been substantialized as a background conception, favorable to a spiritual interpretation of physical processes, and many have postulated distinct psychic agencies and have assumed that life processes are directed by a conscious or at least unconscious purpose.

Fischer thinks life neither self-generated nor eternal, but derived from the absolute basis of all being, where it existed *in potentia*, and holds that there was never a time when all the world was dead, but that life has always existed immanent in systems of organic molecules and that the plant soul arises from a summation of molecular souls. These latter have no *Für-sich-sein* and each remains a strictly unitary being, a "moment" of the whole. He does not assume a "heaven for plant souls," but believes that they are simply resolved back again, each into its original elements, each of which persists for itself. Thus, he holds that there is no general but only an individual psychic life, although he is a monist because he holds all matter alike, and these minimal stages of psychic development to be based upon an immaterial supersensuous absolute.

a means of physiological investigation. New York, Longmans, Green & Co., 1906, 781 pp. Pringsheim, E. G., Die Reizbewegungen der Pflanzen. Berlin, Julius Springer, 1912, 326 pp.

Hence he reasons that by the principles of analogy, completion, gradation, connection, causality, and teleology plants have a psychic principle.

The botanist Němec [1] has told us that no one now denies that plants can transmit stimuli and that the only question is, whether they do it in a way comparable to animals with a nervous system. Some do it only by the propagation of hydrostatic pressure under conditions which can take place even in dead plants; others by diosmotic processes which need no special protoplasmic structure. Against the common opinion Němec thinks to demonstrate structures and functions not unlike those of the elementary nerve fibers which Apathy found in the higher Metazoans. After three years' study, Němec concludes that many vascular plants possess special structures for conducting stimuli in the cytoplasm of their cells, so that the similarity to analogous processes in animals is far closer than has hitherto been supposed. After demonstrating structures that seemed homodynamic, his conclusions were confirmed by studying experimentally the propagation of straomatic stimuli, and this indicated fibers set apart for this purpose, for their bundles could be followed directly to the seat of the bending movements, and both fibers and the function of quickly responding thus vanished again. He does not deny that these bundles may have other functions. He finds just under the dermal surface of the root cells sensitive to geotropism, and these cells are characterized by the presence of grains of starch which serve to orient the root to gravity. Their specific weight is greater than that of the protoplasm of the cell, so that they press against different parts of the surface in different positions of the root. The stimulus is transmitted with undiminished intensity, and in some plants these movable starch grains are developed to a special organ comparable with the static organs, which, in

[1] Die reizleitenden Strukturen bei den Pflanzen. Biol. Centralblatt, June 1, 1900.

Metazoa, are provided with statoliths. This author agrees with Czapek, that there is no difference in principle between many reflexes of plants and those of animals, and that not all movements of plants can be regarded as antitypes of Metazoan reflexes.

Baker (1754) and later Buffon (1748), Fontana (1787), F. Bauer (1823), Spallanzani (1777), and others dessicated simple animal forms and revived them years after by moisture, in one case eleven times over, while Doyère (1842) subjected dessicated radiolates to 150 degrees centigrade, and Schultze (1861), who experimented with macrobiotic forms, preserved them for many years. Preyer has repeated these experiments, while others have frozen frogs, fishes, leeches, bacteria, etc., and revived them again. But no man ever yet saw life originate under controlled conditions, though we do see its opposite, death, everywhere. Hence, it is more natural to suppose that life was first and that in organic matter death was a product of its decay or fall. Thus the earth is not so much our home as our mother. Plants, and even animals and man, are deposits on a rocky basis of cosmic life. A man once dreamed (is Fechner's allegory) that he saw a sphere floating in the water. He examined it under a microscope and found it curiously colored. But a higher power revealed parasites in the form of plants, animals, and men; he finally detected himself and saw that this sphere must be alive. This was the fable of his philosophy. The earth does not need cells, organs, and limbs to be organic, but it must have *causality*, which is universal, and also *finality* or purpose, to give direction to all its movements, molar and molecular. These two give stability. In every closed system all must return sometime as it began. This periodicity and recurrence are only approximative in every complex system. The cosmogenic principle is more comprehensive than either the molecular or organic, and dominates both. How Fechner would have rejoiced to see experiments like those of Bose,[1] indicating that leaves and twigs show about every form of response to stimuli, electric, chemical, and thermal—experience fatigue and even death, very much as do the lower animals. The sagacity of plants is more and more seen to approximate that of the lower animal forms.

In 1855 first appeared his "Atomenlehre," reëdited in 1864. Here Fechner comes to terms with the speculative philosophy of nature. His reaffiliation with Schelling and his desire to snatch a coal from the ashes of Herbart and Hegel do not prevent him from showing that empirical science can never rest on a speculative foundation. He did seek to show that the results of science could satisfy idealistic cravings, but to do so he had to disprove a philosophy that could dispense with investigations into Nature. The atomic theory was directly in point and he here shows the impotence and perversion of speculation. The philosophy of Kant, Fichte, Schelling, Hegel, opposed the discontinuity of matter and empty space, which for them did not exist. If their philosophy is right, there can be no true atoms and vice versa to prove the existence of atoms demolishes this type of philosophy. So his book is entitled "Physikalische Atomistik" and he assumes all the grounds for belief in atoms, of the doctrine of which he gives a pretty complete history, so that this work is of value even though the philosophy it upholds is ceasing to exist. Whether matter is continuous or discontinuous is the vital point which he discusses from the standpoint of metaphysics and of the theory of knowledge, and in such a way as to deal with the opposition between *Kraft* and *Stoff*, which was sublated in the doctrine of energy and the diffusion of matter in space. The doctrine of modern energetics is anticipated here. The question is not so much whether there are atoms or not, as it is a question

[1] Previous reference.

147

between the empirical and the speculative foundation of matter and philosophy. So the discussion is largely methodic. Atoms are not transcendental but ideal structures by which a metaphysical image of the world is freed from ethical, æsthetic, and religious questions. Atoms have nothing to do, he says, with the materialistic point of view, but are dynamic or "plerotic," and there is nothing in the theory to affect what the *Gemüth* needs. The historical fact that atomism was associated with Democritus and Epicurus and is favored by the mechanical theorists gave it the reputation of being atheistic. This he denies. In the chapters on the idea of matter, substance, and force his view culminates. Atoms, then, are not matter but laws of force, and gravity and molecularity have an organic principle at their root. Toward this the newer vitalism now tends. Fechner thought that wherever particles swerved in their movement from the directions which gravity would impose upon them, their motions might be psychically interpreted, and he invoked this principle even to account for the ellipticity of planetary orbits. Motion for him has no beginning and is the life of the world. Metals, rock, and earth have a cadaveric rigidity, and protoplasm is what is left over after these have been secreted out. Heat, if it were caused by condensation, did not exist in the primary diffusion of matter, and need not necessarily be thought to destroy preëxisting germs, especially near the periphery of cooling planets.

As to the origin of consciousness, we have a series of thresholds, upper and lower waves. The highest consciousness is God, who planned vaguely at first and is realizing his purpose in all the world processes, so that his plan progresses and becomes more definite and conscious. Thus, as Paracelsus and Jacob Böhme thought, God is growing in our experience, which, as it gives him character, also contributes to his consciousness and adds to his achievements. God comes to consciousness in us—an Hegelian sentence which its author, however, interpreted in a different sense. When the world is complete, evil and sin will cease, but neither the world nor God is yet finished. Here, again, if we analyze Fechner's consciousness, we find many ingredients of the idealistic philosophy. Probably the strongest thing in his soul was his religious instinct. He trusted his own idea. Leibniz said that he always felt some inclination to accept every new thought. Fechner, on the contrary, instinctively opposed all new ideas, especially if they were strongly vamped up by authorities.

Life and consciousness never arose, he said, but are original activities of the universe; they are two expressions of the same thing and differ only as a circle seen from within differs from one seen from without. From without all is manifold, from within all is unity, and both together constitute all there is. The soul is not punctual, but is through all the body. Those processes immediately bound up with consciousness are *psycho-physic movements* and they are primordial and cosmogenic. A memory not present to consciousness persists under its limen; it has psychophysic movement, and cannot be lost because of the conservation of energy; though the body changes, memory may last on for a lifetime and so, perhaps, though it cannot be proved, psychic elements may survive death, the psychophysical movement persisting by taking new physical elements. To be sure, there is no psycho-physic movement in a corpse, yet it may last on in the world about it. Individual consciousness is an upper wave above a lower subthalamic one representing a more generalized consciousness in which the events of personal life could not be lost when its bodily limitations fall off, as those of the fœtus do at birth. The dead share our thoughts and impart others. Thus we make our fate and there is no future penalty or reward of heaven or hell, but only further development along lines begun here. The bad will eventually pass out of existence. Thus this life is the seed in the ground. So the night-side, that sees in nature only a passing illusion, fades into the day. This view gave him courage to endure his long and disheartening illness and inspired him during it and was embodied in his poems, which are quite Wordsworthian.

Each sense is independent of the other, has its own specific energy and may be imagined as acting in isolation from all others, but consciousness and the brain associate and compound their data. So each man, animal, and plant lives out its own life but is integrated in the same way in the larger world-soul. Fechner took great pleasure in elaborating this analogy. If an adult loses his eyes his visual imagination still works, even though in a more generic form. So when we die we live on more generically in the world-soul. A leaf falls but its activity has modified twig, branch, and even trunk and root. So our personal lives when they go out survive as earth-memories. Like all that lives, we are sense-organs, not so much of one absolute as of the concrete world-soul. We are each leaves of the great Yggdrasil or universe-tree. The earth-soul is infinitely perfect. It has no need of outer things and need not run after food, light, or air, but has them all. It develops from within and has all it needs without effort. It requires no limbs or special senses, for all things are its organs. It has no heart for the circulation of its fluids and no brain for integration, but like some of the Protozoa, though infinitely larger, it is *en rapport* with everything. It is infinitely superior to all these things, but uses them in us and in every form of organic life. It is spiritual first and chiefest, and mechanical only later. So, too, all the other planets and stars are besouled. They are the real and only angels, superior like the world-soul to all their denizens. Again, just as our senses are integrated in and by the brain and the self, so all the world-angels of the solar system are organs of its still greater soul and all other star systems unite into another still higher, and so on, from synthesis to synthesis, in infinite perspective. Thus for Fechner the spiritual and animistic view must explain the mechanical, and not vice versa. This view might be compared with Preyer, who rather crassifies if not vulgarizes it by urging that the inanimate world is the corpse of defunct protoplasm.

From 1860 until his death in 1887 Fechner was chiefly interested in his "Psycho-physics," but this change of interest was more apparent than real, as Wundt says. The goal remained the same as in the "Zend-Avesta," for the poles of his sphere of thought are the same, though the latter turned on a heavenly and the former on the earthly axis of empirical science. The motif in both cases is to connect soul and body, spirit and matter, God and the world. In one he works from the *Jenseits* to the *Dieseits,* and in the other he reverses his course, but the two termini and the path between are the same.

The physical world is one of law and we must assume that the spiritual world is no less so. There must then, a priori, be some exact mathematical relation between the physical and psychical, some law of concomitant variations, for all that is psychic is but the self-appearance of the physical and a material process runs parallel to every conscious process. But how can we measure the psychical by the physical? This was a new ambition and a new problem over which Fechner brooded long, as Descartes did over his. And as Descartes hit suddenly upon his idea of the analytic method, so Fechner, on the morning of October 22, 1850, while still in bed, first hit upon the thought that the increase of the subjective intensity of a sensation is proportional to the increase in the strength of the stimulus; that there might be two series, the psychic increasing arithmetically or by a constant difference, and the physical increasing geometrically or by a constant multiple. This thought made his book of logarithms almost sacred, for in it he found the norms he sought. From that

11   151

time he began to weigh and measure. We can say that one line or weight is twice as long or as heavy as another, but with less accuracy of a noise or a ray of light that it is twice as loud or bright as another. We cannot say that one sound is ten times as strong nor one light ten times as bright as another, nor if ten guns were fired at once would we recognize it if an eleventh gun were added. Here Fechner develops his doctrine of the threshold and the measure of sensibility, and the theory by which from the latter he can reach the measure of the stimulus. But there are many stimuli that are too slight to cause sensations and so he passes to the idea of a differential threshold. The stars do not come out in the sunshine because the difference between them and the bright sky is too small to be perceived. We hear a distant waterfall when the noise of the day has subsided. E. H. Weber had found that two lines were not recognized as different in length until one was at least one-fiftieth smaller than the other. This showed that the sensibility for the difference between the stimuli is dependent upon the magnitude of the stimuli, and in such a way that the greater the initial stimulus is, the greater must be the difference in order for it to be perceived. If one cannot recognize the difference between 40 and 41 grams, one cannot recognize it between 80 and 82, or 400 and 410. Fechner also studied faint shades on white backgrounds in different intensities of light. Sensation, therefore, does not depend on the absolute amount of the stimulus, but on its relative gradations, and thus he developed his three methods: (a) just observable differences; (b) right and wrong cases; (c) average error, the first being easiest, simplest, and quickest. Fechner's formula was that the sensation is proportionate to the logarithm of the stimulus. A beautiful instance is the gradation of the magnitude of stars by astronomers by their objective brightness, which, it was found, varies by a constant multiple of about two and one-half. This measurement of sensations by stimuli he calls outer psycho-physics. For inner psycho-physics he draws further consequences, and here we find his doctrine of consciousness. In his "Elements of Psycho-physics" he has two excursions. In the first he treats the law of conservation of living force, which we call energy, which was remarkable because developed in 1860 and which shows how Fechner was evolving his notion of the unity of natural forces. Every psychic process presumes an exchange of energy which is only parallel to the physical process, and never involves any transition between the psychical and physical. There is only one psycho-physic energy, and psychic life is not a translation of one into the other, but is only the inner side of the same thing, so the psychic never loses any of its value. The second excursion treats of the seat of the soul, where he crosses swords with Herbart's and Lotze's punctual theory—that consciousness can inhere in a monad or atom. Against this Fechner holds that consciousness is the inner unity of a corporeal system and that the conservation of the soul rests upon a solidary coöperation of all parts and activities of the body and their reciprocal activities. In these tedious investigations, now passed with slight mention in some of our text-books on psychology and in some, I observe, entirely omitted, experimental psychology began. On the basis of Weber's law (for touch), the difference between the threshold for stimulation and for consciousness was established. Fechner held that this law applied to the relations between the external stimulus (not the psycho-physic movement within the nervous system) and the sensation, because, he said, the differential threshold must have a neuro-psychic basis and because "the constancy of the relative magnitude of the differential threshold shows an immediate connection with Weber's law, which is thus valid between psychical and physical and not between the nervous factors and the course of the physical excitation." Hence we have his "parallel law," by which the difference between two stimuli is sensed as equally great if the excitability of both increases alike up and down the scale.

Thus he took Weber's law inward in his "inner psycho-physics" and concerned himself with all of those changes of sensation and psycho-physic motion not caused directly by the outer stimulus, such as changes from sleep to wak-ing, movements of the attention, memory, images, etc. So in waking and sleeping the total, while in attention the partial threshold for special objects of consciousness holds. Thus, consciousness is a wave or a system of them (wave phenomena were then commanding great scientific atten-tion). Thus, as attention is in the soul related to processes not in its own field, so the individual consciousness bottoms on the universal consciousness and modifies it just as the tiniest ripple raised by a breeze modifies the smaller and that the larger and, finally, that the tidal wave that sweeps round the earth and is modified by it. Thus, again, we are in the "Zarethustra." Weber, too, worked several decades on his classic study of touch, which, no doubt, inspired Fechner's minute painstaking and objective method and spirit. Perhaps Fechner gave Weber too much credit. He surely did not do so to make him a voucher for his addi-tions to and variations from his law, which Weber would not have accepted. Natural gratitude and magnanimity, and perhaps emulation of his master's thoroughness, are sufficient explanation.

The objections to Fechner's psycho-physic law were of two kinds: (1) Against the reliability of the inner struc-ture of psycho-physics and the certainty of its results, i. e., against the validity of Weber's law and the method of con-ducting experiments, or against this application of mathe-matics and the derivation of the formula of measurements; (2) the more central objection was against the possibility of psycho-physics in general, that is, another evaluation of the results was deduced than the conclusions that Fechner had drawn. This gave him great opportunity to unite his speculative gifts and his scientific empiricism, and he thought, also, that the very name—psycho-physics—suggested a new union between the sciences that dealt with the soul and those that dealt with matter. He justified this all his life and as late as 1877 in his "In Sachen der Psycho-physik" defends himself against Helmholtz, Aubert Mach, Bernstein, Plateau, Delbœuf, Brentano, Hering and other objectors. He made much of the differences between his critics and said, "the Babylonic tower was not finished because the workmen could not agree how to build it. My psychological structure will remain because the workmen who want to tear it down do not agree." Almost all those interested in these subjects, even physiologists and philosophers, defined their position with regard to psycho-physics, the most exhaustive critic being G. E. Müller in his "Zur Grundlegung der Psycho-physik." This called forth Fechner's "Revision" (1882), which Fechner wanted to take the place of his "Psycho-physik" and which Wundt edited in 1889 after Fechner's death. At the age of eighty Fechner wrote a seventy-page article in Wundt's *Studien* on the relations between the psychic principle of measurement and Weber's law which Wundt called "the clearest and most complete statement of the problem that, during all his forty years of devotion to it, had ever been made."

Weber's law probably does not have so wide an application as Fechner ascribed to it. Again Fechner assumed that we have in the logarithm of the external stimulus a measure of the sensation in exact terms, that is, a definite ratio between the outer stimulus and the appearance of its results in consciousness or an evaluation of the stimulus in terms of sensation. There comes in, however, the very complex process of neural action which has been little understood. Hence the psycho-physic interpretation of the formula has a rival in the physiological interpretation, which assumes that the estimation of the stimulus gives a different result from immediate measurement because the nervous processes in passing from the sense organ to the brain undergo change of magnitude.

Wundt's psychic interpretation of the formula is a third. For him it is an expression of a still more general psychological law, viz., that we always measure our conscious states by one another, or compare them. Hence, we know only the relative and not the absolute value of states of consciousness. We must distinguish between what we measure as sensation in Fechner's formula and that which gives the sensation the character of consciousness, which we cannot measure, the first being the physiological, the latter the psychological sensation. In this way all the progress made by Fechner's psycho-physics can be recognized without, nevertheless, ascribing to consciousness mathematical magnitude.

Fechner believed that, in doubting his conception of psychic measurement, the whole theory of consciousness as the self-appearance of matter was jeopardized. This does not follow. It is only necessary to see in that which Fechner measured as subjective appearance an individual content—not the essential psychic phenomenon or property of consciousness, which does not change with its content, but only expresses its relation to the unity of the ego. The objective things which, as so-called outer stimuli, can be measured by science, and the subjective phenomena which the individual perceives, are both, in relation to their content (*i. e.*, sound, light, pressure, etc.), quantities and qualities. They differ from one another, however, in that in the stimuli the entire connection of the world or the coöperation of all human experience is measurable, while in the subjective estimation of the stimuli only a single individual or a single organ determines the measurement. If this subjective measurement gives another result from the objective, this only means that the object of the measurement has altered, since in the subjective judgment of a given process in the world of phenomena only an individual section of it is involved, *i. e.*, the nervous system of one person. The second difference between the objective and the subjective, or psychic, property is not involved in this, for the psychic property consists in the fact that in the subjective processes we make the unity ourselves. The psychic phenomena, as such, need special measurement, since all that can be measured in consciousness is the content of the parallel physical processes. The content that appears in the subject is a section of the objective world and this functional connection between the subjective and the objective measurements of the conscious content is what Fechner really deserves credit for establishing, says Wundt.

We may, therefore, reject Fechner's interpretation of his formula as far as we please, but still he will always deserve the honor of having called into life a new science, viz., experimental psychology. The psychic experience itself is so purely the property of the individual, so fugitive and complex, that it can not be measured, or described, or observed, or imparted. On Fechner's ground, Wundt was able to mark a new step by the foundation of the first institute for experimental psychology in 1879. Of this Fechner wrote jestingly, "You are doing this thing on such a large scale that in a few years you will have cleaned up the whole field of psycho-physics." But despite the many laboratories and investigators, this final clean-up is not yet in sight and far more questions have been asked than answered. It is marvelous, however, that Fechner, without any assistance, made the first attempts to find the long wished for formula by which the relation between mind and matter might be scientifically wrought out with the above ratio between psychical and physical intensities. A relatively like increase of physical energy meant an absolute increment of psychic intensity. "The chief value of this function to him was that (since the logarithm of a certain size of increment would be zero and then negative) it might tell us something of the threshold of consciousness and would justify the inference that the concepts sunk under the threshold were present in a more general consciousness.'' With this idea, he began his experiments on tone and sight and became the world's expert on the *threshold*, beneath which lay his philosophy and his heart.

In its subsequent development, then, the physiologists have regarded the logarithmic proportionality as between the outer stimulus and the central process; and the psychologists have deemed it only a general expression of the relativity between psychic states and processes, while Fechner's own idea that it expressed the relation of the individual's consciousness to a general subliminal one, and was thus an expression or simple stage of a psycho-physical hierarchy of the world, has been ignored. Indeed, many experimenters in this field have never read his inner psycho-physics. He failed to convince his contemporaries that a psycho-physic movement could last on under the threshold indefinitely and then reappear, so that he had to accept their silent verdict of neglect with what resignation he could. Wundt compares him with Kepler, who in working out his third law, stating the relations of the rotation of the planets to their average distances from the sun, thought he had also found the harmonic tone interval for the cosmos, for the future development of which he believed his law gave the norm. Kepler's law, however, stands, although the false speculation that accompanied it has passed, and so it will be with Fechner and his inner psycho-physics. He certainly first introduced experimental methods, which Herbart perhaps suggested and which Johannes Müller, in his iatric speculations, had only dreamed of. To his ''right and wrong cases,'' ''average error,'' and ''just observable differences'' we psychologists shall always owe a great debt. All workers in this field ought to look to Fechner as a founder of their science.

The ''Zend-Avesta'' gives a theory according to which the earth is an exalted spiritual being, the bearer of human consciousness and midway between God and man. It represents an old natural religion which needs only to be reformed and modernized. Fechner here treats of the things of heaven and earth. He sums up his animism and transcendentalism, and all that he wrote in his later period is rooted in this book. In its 800 pages he sets forth the articles of his creed or his faith, in what both the theoretical and practical interests of man need to satisfy his soul, and supplement his intellectual desires, as Plato's myths, which are his theology, did his. He admits that every conclusion he here reaches is unprovable. The substance of the volumes may be roughly epitomized essentially in his own terms, as follows: There is one God, eternal, infinite, omnipresent, omnipotent, omniscient, good, just, pitiful, through whom all that is arises and ceases, who lives and works in all energy, Nature, and knowledge, who loves all things as a part of his self-love, who would bring everything to perfect goodness, and punishes the bad only to reform it. Men, animals, and plants are all alike God's children. They participate in his spirit, which he imparts to them all. Through this they are united to him in complete organic and genetic unity, although only man can attain knowledge of this. Christ was God's child only in a higher degree than are plants, animals, and other men, and, he knew this, his inner divinity, better than they. So he is the prime mediator, but neither he nor any of his deeds or thoughts are extra-, anti- or super-natural. Indeed, nothing can be so as he is only the culmination and exemplar of the highest point yet reached by man. His life is only a series of natural psychic phenomena of a higher order. Thus it is wrong to conceive him as having been born or died, for he is only the eternal representative of the divine soul of the cosmos, which has here found its highest organ of expression in human consciousness. The eternal way of salvation is to penetrate to and love the inmost divine soul of things, to work with it, to help on the creative impulse, which we can now best do by helping our fellowmen and coming habitually to feel a supernal impulsion behind us in all we do, think, or feel. Those who best do this advance the kingdom of God, which is the good, the true, and the beautiful in both themselves and others. They constitute the church, now militant, but sure to be ultimately triumphant. The body of Christ consists of the souls of these saints in communion. Our membership in the church, baptism, and the sacrament of communion, rightly reinterpreted, may well remain the best symbols. Resurrection and eternal life are true in the sense that this life is only the seed in the dark, cold ground that must die to grow, blossom, and bear fruit, for thus we make the larger, truer life beyond out of the material of experience in this—a life which depends on how we order our mundane existence. When we attain it, we shall see face to face, know and be known with clairvoyant minds, and that state is heaven. God's ordinances and commands are designed to promote the greatest possible happiness of the individual and his fellow beings and to impel him to subordinate himself to the common weal. Evil always punishes and virtue always rewards itself (here he skirts on familiar Kantian ground). These rewards are not and punishments are not commonly attained in this world and so virtue and happiness must unite in *Jenseits*. Ultimately, however, the bad will perish and the good survive eternally. The good and the true are ultimately one and inseparable, and no knowledge can stand that is not helpful to good (which suggests a pragmatic sanction for these beliefs). All that seems new is only the transformed revelation of the world (Nietzsche's eternal recurrence).

Somewhat thus does Fechner sum up in theological terms the results of this most mystical of all his works, putting new wine of meaning into these old bottles of phraseology, seeking to state a faith which he thinks a cultivated man may hold and be not less but more scientific, defying throughout Kant's warning against transcendentalizing the use of reason. He chose the name "Zend-Avesta," which signifies "living word," not so much to suggest a western type or analogy of Parseeism, as a symbol of the light from the Orient in general which great scholars had begun to show forth to the world in ways so impressive, and 'for which Schopenhauer and many others were showing a very strong psychic tropism. To this Fechner reacted with intense vigor, but upon an inadequate knowledge that suggests the influence of the then new type of Biblical exegesis upon the mind of Jacob Böhme. Many of the mystic intimations herein concealed are revealed more clearly in his later gnostic wrestlings and yearnings with the unknowable. Perhaps science must have its own theology or, like the undevout astronomer, be mad, and, assuming this to be the case, we have here his version of what it should be.

Even in the "Avesta" angels appear as middlemen between man and God and the stars and especially the earth as angels who execute God's laws. The earth is far better organized than are its inhabitants, and all dwellers on earth are its organs and have intercourse through its consciousness. Just as impressions of light, sound, etc., are isolated save for the unity of the mind, so all individuals combined make a living unity; just as the qualities of objects that come from the different senses unite in the object, and by this union their existence is enhanced, although their individuality is not impaired, so the relation of soul and body is an identity and the spiritual is the self-appearance of the material. The material is only the form in which a spiritual substance appears to another spirit. If it be urged that plants are conscious but do not have souls, it may be said that the soul is an individual consciousness that does not vanish with the body. The unity of a body is in its processes and operations. Their true material and their true spiritual content all inhabitants of the earth have in the bodies which live on in the earth-spirit. If before they were intuitions, now they are the memories of the earth, and when the earth dies, as the stars do, they will still live on in the higher unity to which they belong in the universe, namely, in God's spirit. Death is not a separation of body and soul, for there is no such thing as separation possible. It is the reception of the body into a larger body and of the soul into a larger soul, so that both are immortal. Religious feeling he deems the highest possession of mankind and out of this conviction sprang the "Avesta." This feeling was associated by him with historical Christianity. His wife was a very strict orthodox Lutheran Christian and he exclaims, "After all, I insist that I am and remain a Christian, and my purpose throughout this work is not to sever, but to make closer this bond." He wanted to shell the kernel out of Christianity and thought that his apprehension was an adequate development of it, and he quotes Bible texts, hymns, and theologians. He was very intimately associated with the theologian Ch. Weisse, with whom he discussed all these questions, although they did not always agree, for Weisse was a Hegelian and Fechner inductive. But the time was unpropitious. The German people, to be sure, had just begun to realize that they had a soul, but felt little inclined to ascribe one to plants.

Fechner always had an intense interest in art. His older brother, Edward, was a painter and he himself was a friend of Dr. Härtel, chief of the Breitkopf-Härtel firm, where artists congregated. Since Fechner held that all knowledge must be empirical and inductive, and that everything had its inner meaning in the striving toward the maximum of general pleasure, he greatly limited the method and the problem of æsthetics. The old he called æsthetics *von oben;* his new, *von unten.* It was a part of general hedonics. Only from observation and experience and an analysis of works of art could rules be derived according to which an object might be judged æsthetically, and could there be a science. Hence it must be experimental. The golden section is such a division of a line as corresponds to the ratio of 8:5, or 13:8, or 21:13, etc.; that is, it is an irrational relation. Zeissing (from 1854-1856) had made many measurements of natural objects and human forms which seemed pleasing and even thought that he found the golden section in the dimensions of the Madonnas of Raphael and in Holbein's and other works of art, but not in either the very early or very modern painters. But Fechner said that we must not go to complex works of art but to simpler figures to determine the question, and developed three methods. The first was that of choice from among a number of angles, ellipses, crosses, etc., from which the observer was to select the most beautiful. The second, or reproduction method, was to have the pleasing forms constructed according to the taste of the subject. And the third method was to measure common forms in general use. Thus he measured all kinds of ornaments, crosses, bookbindings, dimensions of pages, writing paper and envelopes, cards of all kinds, slates, and even confectionery, snuff-boxes, bricks, windows, doors, pictures, etc. The first method, that of choice, he applied chiefly to crosses and rectangles. He concluded that, of all rectangular forms, the square and rectangles similar to it, on the one hand, and long rectangles on the other, were the most displeasing. The simple ratios 2:1, 4:3, 5:4, 6:5, which, as every one knows, are the vibration numbers needed for harmony notes, have no advantage as representing the relations in the sides of a rectangle. The relation 3:2 is better because nearer the golden section, and other figures were favored somewhat in proportion as they approximated the golden section. He made ten rectangles and found that 35 per cent. of the preferences were for the one which was built on the principle of the golden section. But in the division of horizontal lines equality is far more preferred. In vertical crosses the relation of any upright part to the cross and of that part to the portion projecting above did not favor this relation, but that of 2:1. He was so absorbed in this that he made a trip to Basle in 1867, his only long trip without his wife. He also asked all visitors in the Dresden Gallery to write answers to his questionnaire, and out of 11,000 visitors 113 did so. But he found that of these only 34 gave answers that favored his theory, and in a later work he expressed his resignation to the unfortunate fate of his experimental æsthetics in this respect.

His comprehensive "Vorschule der Ästhetik" (1886) was not a system but a rather rhapsodic treatment of various questions in this field *von unten*. He does, however, formulate a number of rules or principles of æsthetic pleasure which he discovered from his powers of fine psychological analysis of the æsthetic effects on himself, *e. g.*, the first condition is that the impression must rise above the threshold of pleasure. The quality of pleasing is not enough but there must be a quantity of a definite degree. Objects which are below the æsthetic threshold, like a poem in a foreign tongue, or the contents of a poem stated in bald prose, may predispose to æsthetic pleasure, but act below the threshold. The threshold is usually passed by summation of different impressions, each factor of which is alone too weak, and so æsthetic results are composite and manifold. Hence, he derives the principle of the union of diverse elements, all of which must tend toward the same end. That is, there must be nothing that contradicts. The like and the unlike, the harmonious and contradictory need not entirely vanish for consciousness, but with the contrast there must be, at the same time, a summation and atonement above the threshold. This makes the whole stand out under the law of clearness. Besides the difference there must be an associative factor. An orange makes a very different impression from a polished yellow ball resembling it. Red is pleasing on the cheek of a youth but not on the nose or hand, nor when it is due to cosmetics, because only when rightly placed does it suggest health and youth. Various other principles that he discusses are those of contrast, sequence, atonement, practice, wont, tedium, persistence, and change in the way of regarding the picture, economic relations, etc. His treatment of association is perhaps the chief merit of his æsthetics *von unten*. He insisted with the very greatest energy on distinguishing the direct from the associative factors, a point which, to be sure, was not entirely new with him. Lotze also had emphasized the association principle, which was described as introducing a new deity into æsthetics. The chief merit of Fechner's analytic and experimental æsthetics is that it proved that there are conditions of æsthetic pleasure which lie in the nature of sense impressions and combinations and excite pleasure or displeasure as they change, with the same necessity as do natural laws. They do not teach how to create a great work of art, but they do give relations that no artist can violate with impunity. Of course, statistical æsthetics must limit itself to a certain number of people. It presupposes that the beautiful is different from the pleasant, useful, or good; it determines the marks or tokens of beauty; and leads up to the critique of the idea of beauty, in which again he defies Kant.

Ending his æsthetics at the age of seventy-eight, Fechner felt the need of summarizing his *Lebensanschauungen,* which was composed of so many diverse elements, and this he did in the final form in "Tagesansicht gegenüber den Nachtsansicht" (1879). Here he attempts to give his general faith in a living world, through which God shines, so that his theocratic scheme of things is here most coherently stated. God is the psycho-physic All-being, law, consciousness, and the world is besouled. Over against this day-view is the night-view, which holds that consciousness is connected only with the single subjective centers which exist as men and animals over against each other, with their limited number and duration, while to it the whole fragrant, resonant, glowing world, with all its colors, remains night. The stars that keep their appointed courses, the ether waves, all the mechanical operations of the universe—it is absurd to think of these as without sensation. There is no hope, comfort, or satisfaction save in the faith that the world tingles with life and feeling.

From these views Fechner glances at the results of his own scientific activity. Occasionally he gives vent to a feeling of bitterness that his views had been so unsuccessful, misunderstood, and unappreciated. But his confidence that the day-view will conquer the night-view in the end is unshaken, and this seems likely now to come true, although he was wrong in stigmatizing all who did not share his view of pan-consciousness so pitilessly as faithless and of the night. Here, too, he expresses his view of spiritism. Reason, he thinks, must direct the strong mystic instinct of men or they become fanatics. He was particularly attracted to the unexplored regions of the soul and so he became interested in somnambulism, attended séances when table-tapping came into vogue, wrote on Reichenbach's *Od,* took part in the sittings of Slade, along with the astronomer Zöllner, the physicist W. Weber, and the mathematician Scheibner. He participated with zeal in these sittings, and neither he nor his companions were able to detect the trickery, but he withdrew and never could have been called an adherent of spiritism, though he believed that, after his own observations and that of many other reliable witnesses, we had no right to reject all spiritistic phenomena summarily as imposture. Of course, they must be rejected or recognized, and he thought the facts sufficiently proven, but still he remained skeptical to the spiritistic explanation. He was said to be a secret convert, but this, says Lasswitz, is false. He held it for *Unfug* and the facts he deemed pathological. He realized the trivial character of the ghosts and their communications. Indeed, he did not care very much whether there are spirits or not, because the day-view did not need spiritism, although he could accept it without disturbing his system. In normal life there are plenty of invasions of the *Diesseits* from the *Jenseits*. The spirits of the dead live not only historically in their operations, but as parts of the earth-spirit and individually in the general life of planets and of man. This is their normal mode of operation. From his point of view it is conceivable that more or less pathological states may occur in the general life of planets which may be perceived through the abnormal processes of spiritism. It is not well, however, to evoke these arbitrarily, for they are injurious. ''The day-view can subsist without or with spiritism, but it is better that it continue without than with it.'' It would be bad for the day-view and religion if it had to base its faith on spiritism. If one needs outer authority, it is better to turn to Scripture than to slate-writing. Thus though spiritism was repellent to him, he did like to see its phenomena.

It was at this stage that I lived near him for an academic year, and called occasionally (introduced by a card from Wundt), as a student who was trying to understand psycho-physics. Once our conversation drifted to Slade and he told me of a solid wooden ring put over a solid spool-head much too big for it and of another wooden ring on the one upright leg of a tripod table, and also of a message written between two sealed slates, at which both he and his wife, who was always present at our interviews, shook their heads and expressed doubt. He sent me to Zöllner, who showed me these things, and asked impressively how they could be done save in a space of more than three dimensions. He said he had shown them to his class, which I also visited, but which had dwindled to six, evidently students inspired by curiosity to hear this once great astronomer, now sick and senile, lecturing on the psychology of astronomy, to which latter science he had in his day made valuable contributions, especially concerning comets.

Fechner's domestic life was happy and his wife outlived him. He was very fond of correspondence. From 1860 on he almost always took some vacation trip. His eyes grew bad again and he was several times operated on for cataract. His friend Weisse died in 1876, Härtel in 1875, Weber in 1878, Zöllner in 1882, and these men were very near him. He was greatly pleased at the very general and unexpected celebrations of his eightieth birthday in 1881, his golden wedding in 1883, and the fiftieth jubilee of his *ordinarius* professorship in 1884, in which the church and university authorities united, the bells being rung in his honor. He kept at work until November 6, 1887, and died on the eighteenth.

At Fechner's grave Wundt well summed up his activity as follows: "Perhaps in none of his other scientific achievements did his rare unity of gifts shine forth more brilliantly than in his psycho-physic work. It required a knowledge of the principles of exact physico-mathematical method and also a strong yearning to penetrate the deepest problems of human existence such as perhaps up to date he alone has possessed. To this work, too, he brought an originality of thought which enabled him to transform the traditional material and methods freely, according to his own needs, and he had no hesitation in striking out new and unexplored paths. The limited observations of E. H. Weber, which were remarkable on account of their genial simplicity, and the isolated, often more accidental than planned, methods and results of other physiologists—these were the limited material out of which Fechner built up this new science. What he himself contributed in exact observations by their thoroughness and mathematical completeness had great value. Although with his limitation of means and assistance he could not finally solve very many questions, the clearness with which he formulated the somewhat scrappy and gappy material and created and carried through his exact methods is one of the very great achievements that the science of our day has to show. His original application of the principle of probabilities, which had hitherto been applied only to objective measurements, to the domain of subjective perception, is, of itself and quite apart from the end it had in view, of the very highest theoretical interest."

Wundt,[1] to whom Fechner's papers were given after his death, describes his isolated life in the tiniest quarters in a flat, with a well-worn deal table and a plain little bookcase which contained more of his manuscripts than books, and with his thumbed and dog-eared logarithmic tables always at hand. He was busy chiefly with his own thoughts, living in the simplest, plainest way, taking his daily walks with his wife with great regularity, going home to jot down in a very large hand, quite illegible to others, his first thoughts, and then elaborating and rewriting them over and over again. He recomputed all his figures and tables many times to eliminate every possible error, so that they are mathematically perfect. He was always eager to converse and often followed up a discussion with letters to his visitors full of after-thoughts, but he was averse to conversation on all his mystic, theosophic views, which became more and more his own private and absorbing theme of contemplation. Indeed, so reticent was he that even his wife knew nothing of the manuscript of his very important "Collective Masslehre," on which he had worked hard and in silence for ten years, which was found after his death and edited *in extenso* in the Proceedings of the Saxon Academy of Sciences by Lipps. Nature and religion were the poles of his self-evolved scheme of things, says Wundt, and his methods were induction, strict and severe, and analogy, wide and free.

[1] Gustav Theodor Fechner. Rede zur Feier seines Hundertjährigen Geburtstages, Leipzig, 1901, pp. 92.

Fechner made his début into the realm of philosophy at a most unfavorable time. All the subjective systems were discredited, the special sciences had contracted their boundaries, and religion, too, had retired into its stronghold of orthodoxy, intimidated by Baur, Feuerbach, and Strauss. Both science and religion had been disappointed in their hope of aid from philosophy, which they now felt had betrayed them. Fechner's oft repeated call to both was to awake. His creed, if mystic, contained nothing that science could possibly object to any more than it could to poetry. He held that the laws of science rested upon faith, but his offer of mediation between them, when each so sorely needed the other, fell on deaf ears. Philosophy, the old mediator, was dead and no other was wanted. The life-long neglect, not to say contempt, which was felt for him as a dreamer, he suffered from, but it did not disharmonize nor divert him. Indeed, he charged no conspiracy of silence as did Schopenhauer, nor did he swerve to adjacent fields where the recognition would have been prompt, but he wrought on as if by an irresistible prophetic imperative impulsion, vocation, or call to force his insights upon an unwilling world, with the thought that it sorely needed them; and as he realized that he would never reach recognition during his lifetime and saw that even science, to which his early life was so devoted, had rejected him, he comforted himself with the belief that posterity would see.

How shall we judge Fechner's philosophy, which developed in his early life as a conscious though fond play of fancy and later became the very core of his being? It does not seem sufficient to call him, as Wundt does, the renewer and completer of the romantic Nature-philosophy of the Schelling type. His scheme was too essentially his own creation, and yet, too, it was at the same time one of the best expressions of the animistic instinct of the human soul directed toward the great all-mother Nature, which culminated in the Romantic school, but which he carried still further. Although he marshaled such an array of tropes and analogies and strove so valiantly to prove it, he was by no means its finisher, for the world now seems likely to hear much more of it. James, who, in his "Psychology" (I, p. 549), says "his *massformel* and the conception of it as an ultimate psycho-physic law will remain an idol of the den if ever there was one," and adds, "it would be terrible if such a dear old man as this could saddle a science forever with his patent whimsies," lived to do ample penance to Fechner in his pluralistic universe, though he does violence to him by claiming him as a pragmatist, and Macdougall in his latest work avows himself an animist in a sense not unlike Fechner's.

To Fechner the soul was not unlike an iceberg which is eight-ninths under the water's surface or threshold out in a denser and darker medium, but the tides of which, and not the wind above, determine its course, often in the teeth of a gale. He measured what was above this threshold only in order to draw inferences concerning what was below it, but here this figure limps, for when the top of the iceberg melts off the bottom of it does not go on and down into the pelagic depths, nor does it become a diffusive power. Jacobi said that the light kindled in his heart went out when he took it to his head. Not so with Fechner. He was a prose poet who supplemented science by myth as Plato did, though not in his manner. He strove to give the mansion which he built for the soul a basis upon the solid ground of scientific fact. He was far more interested in the post- than in the pre-existence of the soul, and hence cared little for the developmental history of the psyche, and never dreamed that psychogenesis might become a new and higher dispensation of Darwinism. Few men have ever been more independent or original or trusted their own intuitions more implicitly than he, or held their course more truly in the face of all contemporary tendencies and opinions. He revered facts

171

like a true scientist, but revered the visions of his imagination like a true soldier of the Holy Ghost. He borrowed from all the great systems of his day and was held captive by none, and certainly he found a new answer to the old riddle of the Sphinx—if a man die, shall he live again? Only a threshold separates this life from the next, and the threshold that separates imperceptibility from perception and ideas not in consciousness from those in the fovea of attention is the same in kind as that which separates existence here from that beyond the grave. Indeed, there is no separation in either case, but only an unbroken continuum. There is no real death but something psychic wherever there is matter or energy. Matter is not extinct but only sleeping, dreaming mind. He would not lose sight of the whole in studying the parts, for each without the other becomes unknown.

Regarded from the standpoint of the psychology of senescence, Fechner looked to be older than his years. He at 86, and Zeller at 94, when death came to them, both had the supreme felicity of having rounded out and finished their lifework. Both left little they had ever begun uncompleted, but how very different the two pictures of old age! Zeller was ceaselessly revising revisions of his earlier works, qualifying the degree of probability of this and that, adding new footnotes and intent only upon more accurate presentation of the views of others in the past. Fechner was even more intent, until the very end, upon the problems of the future. He was peering over the great threshold he was about to cross and grasping eagerly at every new trope, metaphor, simile, and symbol that made the *Jenseit* seem more real and near and definite, somewhat as Maeterlinck now does,[1] or in the spirit of Plotinus, different as was his interpretation of the old Indic metempsychosis. The plans of both these lives had been accomplished and they were not, like those of Hartmann and

[1] See especially his "Death," London, 1911.

Lotze, broken off with numbers on the program yet to be performed. If the historian Zeller must de-individualize himself to show forth others' opinions with no subjective distortion, the childless, solitary Fechner was over-individualized, embodying an almost unique type of the species in himself, and thus the strange deep dynamism of the instinct to survival, even if it be unconscious, was absorbing. In the present revival of interest in him, his soul has come back and is marching on in just the way that he would have desired to achieve immortality.

Perhaps self-consciousness is not even the manifest content of the soul, but a veil which conceals both patent and latent content. Perhaps it is a mishap, the distemper of the mind caused by impingement or friction with the environment like foam, where the propulsive current of the will to live impinges on obstacles, or like the spindrift from the cyme of waves where they meet a counterwind and become spray. Perhaps below its sea level or threshold there is a great deep of infra-consciousness that animates all nature and perhaps our loud and strident sense of self is like the aërial humidity making clouds and rain, ever rising and falling but all coming out of the boundless deep to which they all turn again home. Perhaps unfallen man was never meant to be introspective but only extrospective, for thus most of the work of science has been done. Self-study may be chiefly corrective or therapeutic, and when we die we perhaps do not enter Nirvana but become a part of all of our common Mother Nature by way of apocatastasis so that as our "bark sinks it is to a higher sea" and every self becomes a diffusive power mingling with the universe and its elements. Death may simply sweep away the limitations between us and the great autos or cosmos, and we may be conserved chiefly as energy is so that as we go down the threshold below threshold we close in with all we flowed from. There may be only a sense of alleviation of our deep and unconscious nostalgia

173

in the great harvest home of souls, a sense of rest and of return that is too deep to be conscious. Some such sentiment as this, mystic but ineffably charming, seems to me to be the root of about all that this mystic prose-poet, seer, and scientist, the most Oriental perhaps of all Occidental minds, ever did and said. If so, to understand him we must ponder and find his relations with such men as Proclus, Plotinus, Böhme, and Eckhardt, but above all with the pundits and sages of Buddhistic India.

GUSTAV THEODOR FECHNER

Gustav Theodor Fechner (Dr. Mises); ein deutsches Gelehrtenleben, von Johannes Emil Kunke. Leipzig, Breitkopf & Härtel, 1892; 372 p, 4th ed. Revised just after the author's death.

Panegyrikus des jetzigen Medicin und Naturgeschichte, Dr. Mises. Leipzig, Lehnhold, 1822.

Katechismus der Logik oder Denklehre. Leipzig, 1823.

Katechismus oder Examinatorium über die Physiologie des Menschen. Leipzig, 1823.

Stapelia mixta (Dr. Mises). Leipzig, 1824.

Vergleichende Anatomie der Engel (Dr. Mises). Leipzig, 1825.

Resultate der bisherigen Pflanzenanalysen. 1829.

Elementar-Lehrbuch der Elektromagnetismus. Leipzig, 1830.

Repertorium der neuen Entdeckungen in der unorganischen Chemie. 3 Bd. Leipzig, 1830-32.

Repertorium der neuren Entdeckungen in der organischen Chemie. 2 Bd. Leipzig, Voss, 1830-32.

Massbestimmungen über die galvanische Kette. Leipzig, 1831.

Repertorium des Experimentalphysik, enthaltend eine vollständige Zusammenstellung der neuern Fortschritte dieser Wissenschaft. Leipzig, Voss, 1832.

Beweis das der Mond aus Iodine bestehe (Dr. Mises). Leipzig, Voss, 1832.

Schutzmittel für den Cholera (Dr. Mises). Leipzig, Voss, 1832.

Ueber die subjectiven Complementärfarben. Poggendorff's Annalen der Physik und Chemie. Bd. 44, 1838.

Ueber die subjectiven Nachbilder und Uebenbilder. Poggendorff's, Bd. 50, 1840.

Gedichte. Leipzig, Breitkopf und Härtel, 1841.

Das Hauslexikon, vollständiges Handbuch praktischer Lebenskentnisse für alle Stände. Leipzig, 1841, 8 Bd.

Ueber das höchste Gut. Leipzig, Breitkopf und Härtel, 1846.

Vier Paradoxa (Dr. Mises). Leipzig, Voss, 1846.

Nanna: oder, über das Seelenleben der Pflanzen, Leipzig, Voss, 1848, 399 p. 3d ed. 1903.

Ueber die mathematische Behandlung organischer Gestalten. Ber. der kgl. Sächs. Ges. der Wiss. Math-phys. Cl. 1849.

Ueber das Causalgesetz. Ber. der kgl. Sächs. Ges. der Wiss. Math-phys. Cl. 1849.

Räthselbüchlein. Leipzig, G. Wigand, 1850. 96 p. (4th ed. 1875, 128 p.)

Zend-Avesta; oder, über die Dinge des Himmels und des Jenseits, vom Standpunkt der Naturbetrachtung. Hamburg, Voss, 1851. 3 Thle. (2d ed., 1906, 2 v.)

Ueber die physikalische und philosophische Atomenlehre. Leipzig, Mendelssohn, 1855. 210 p. (2d enl. ed., 1864.)

Professor Schleiden und der Mond. Leipzig, Gumprecht, 1856. 427 p.

Ueber ein wichtiges psychophysisches Gesetz und dessen Beziehung zur Schätzung der Sterngrossen. Leipzig, Hirzel, 1858. 77 p.

Ueber einige Verhältnisse des binocularen Sehens. Leipzig, 1860. 228 p.

Ueber die Seelenfrage; ein Gang durch die sichtbare Welt, um die unsichtbare zu finden. Leipzig, Amelang, 1861. 229 p. (2d ed. rev. by Eduard Spranger. Hamburg, Voss, 1907.)

Elemente der Psychophysik. Leipzig, Breitkopf, 1861. 2 v.

Die drei Motive und Gründe des Glaubens. Leipzig, Breitkopf und Härtel, 1863. 256 p. (2d ed., 1910. 169 p.)

Das Büchlein vom Leben nach dem Tode. Hamburg, Voss, 1866, 85 p. (5th ed. 1903). (Tr. from the German by Mary C. Wadsworth, Boston, Little, Brown, 1904.)

Zur Deutungsfrage und Geschichte der Holbein'schen Madonna. Leipzig, R. Weigel, 1866. 45 p.

Die historischen Quellen und Verhandlungen über die Holbein'schen Madonna. Leipzig, R. Weigel, 1866. 74 p.

Ueber die Aechtheitfrage der Holbein'schen Madonna Leipzig, Breitkopf und Härtel, 1871. 167 p.

Zur experimentalen Æsthetik. Leipzig, Hirzel, 1871. 81 p. (Auf. Abhandlungen der Math-phys. Classe der Königl. Ges. d. Wiss.)

Bericht über das auf der Dresdner Holbein-Ausstellung ausgelegte Album. Leipzig, Breitkopf und Härtel, 1872. 45 p.

Einige Ideen zur Schöffungs- und Entwickelungsgeschichte der Organismen. Leipzig, Breitkopf, 1873. 108 p.

Ueber den Ausgangswerth der kleinsten Abweichungssumme, dessen Bestimmung., Verwendg. und Verallgemeinerg. Leipzig, Hirzel, 1874. 76 p. (Aus Abhandlgn. der könig. sachs. Gesselschaft der Wiss.)

Kleine Schriften (Dr. Mises). Leipzig, Breitkopf und Härtel, 1875. 560 p.

Erinnerungen an die letzten Tage des Odlehre und ihres Urhebers (C. von Reichenbach). Leipzig, Breitkopf und Härtel, 1876. 55 p.

Vorschule der Æsthetik; two volumes in one. Leipzig, Breitkopf und Härtel, 1876.

GUSTAV THEODOR FECHNER

In Sachen der Psycho-physik. Leipzig, Breitkopf und Härtel, 1877. 220 p.

Die Tagesansicht gegenüber der Nachtansicht. Leipzig, Breitkopf und Härtel, 1879. 274 p.

Revision der Hauptpunkte der Psychophysik. Leipzig, Breitkopf, 1882. 427 p.

Ueber die Frage des Weberschen Gesetzes und Periodizitätsgesetzes im Gebiete des Zeitsinnes. Leipzig, Hirzel, 1884. 108 p.

Ueber die Methode der richtigen und falschen Fälle in Anwendung auf die Massbestimmungen der Feinheit oder extensiven Empfindlichkeit des Raumsinnes. Leipzig, Hirzel, 1884. 204 p.

In Sachen des Zeitsinnes und der Methode der richtigen und falschen Fälle, gegen Estel und Lorenz. 38 p. In Wundt's Philosopischen Studien. Bd. 3, 1886, p. 1.

Ueber die psychischen Massprinzipien und das Webersche Gesetz. In Wundt's Philosopischen Studien. Bd. 4, 1887. p. 161.

Wissenschaftliche Briefe; nebst einem Briefwechsel zwischen K. von Vierordt und Fechner sowie neuen Beilagen, von Gustav Theodor Fechner und W. Preyer. Leipzig, Voss, 1890.

EDUARD VON HARTMANN
1842–1906

EDUARD VON HARTMANN

EDUARD VON HARTMANN

1842-1906

The most conspicuous figure in the philosophical world for years was unquestionably Hartmann. His opinions, however, were so largely the expression of his remarkable personality, to which attention is irresistibly drawn at so many points in reading his works, that the only logical introduction to an epitome of his philosophy is a brief characterization of the man himself. He was born on February 13, 1842, in Berlin, where nearly all of his life was passed, the only child of a captain and examiner in the artillery school, and was trained at home with the greatest tenderness and devotion by his mother and her maiden sister, although a spirit of military discipline pervaded his father's house. He entered the public school at six, three years in advance of boys of his age. Associating even at school with those older than himself, we can easily believe him when he intimates that he was precocious and somewhat spoiled. His dislike of the routine of school life, his early aversion to Cicero, Demosthenes, history, and mathematics, and his fondness for the English novelists, religious instruction, natural science, and later for Thucydides, Sophocles, mathematics, etc., are detailed with great fullness in an autobiographic sketch.[1] The most joyous day of his life was when he took leave of the Friedrichwerdische Gymnasium at the age of sixteen. His tastes were solitary and he had few bosom friends. He had already

[1] Mein Entwickelungsgang, 1874, in ''Gesammelte Studien und Aufsätze.'' Also Eduard von Hartmann, von Otto Braun, Stuttgart, 1909, 261 p.

181

taken instruction in Herbartian philosophy and had shown gifts for drawing, Latin, piano, and singing, which tastes he maintained through life.

His aversion to all the ordinary university curricula, his dislike of the barbarities of German student life on the one hand and his admiration of the *ton* in circles of young officers induced him to follow the wishes of his father and enter the artillery school in the belief that only as a soldier was it possible to be a *whole* man. Here, however, he found no genial companionship, especially in the idealistic enthusiasms which he had already begun to cherish, but this loss was more than compensated by several intimate literary and artistic friendships with daughters of family friends and with former schoolmates, to whom he expressed himself greatly indebted. He had hardly determined on the military profession when he was prostrated by an acute attack of rheumatism in both knees, which was aggravated later by a severe contusion and which at the age of twenty obliged him to contemplate another career. For one year he devoted himself to painting and then decided that he had no talent for it and turned to musical composition, only after another year to see that mediocrity awaited him also here. Now it was, he tells us, that he found that only philosophy had guided him hitherto, enabling him *con æquo animo* to regard all things *sub specie æternitatis*, and had already taught him to overcome more illusions, errors, and prejudices than it is permitted many to outgrow in the course of a lifetime. Accordingly he at once began at the age of twenty-two the "Philosophy of the Unconscious," despite the exhortation of his father to devote himself to more practical pursuits, and three years later, after the finished manuscript had lain twelve months in his desk, he was induced by an accidental acquaintance with a publisher to allow it to appear in print. He assures us that he was quite indifferent to the sudden and world-wide fame which thus early in life overtook him. His only object henceforth was the dissemination of his opinions, and critical praise and blame he now began to estimate, he says, only according to their value as advertisements.

Of the genesis of his opinions he has little to say. He had from a boy been in the habit of noting down his deepest reflections and at the age of sixteen had elaborated an argument that the soul after death lost its individuality and was absorbed in the Absolute, and had composed unnumbered aphorismic essays on Coquetry, Friendship, Honor, Conscience, Neatness, Phrenology, Kant's "Kritik," etc., etc. It was with supreme satisfaction that he was able to state that all his productions from first to last are naïve monologues written only to satisfy his own metaphysical cravings and with no very definite thought of publishing, and with little care for the public. The system he has thus developed we are told was absolutely free from every extraneous personal or material end or motive and was not, like the productions of the "professorlings," written as a basis for future habilitation, or to enforce an application for a professorship, or to win personal esteem in any society, or to make money in the book market. It was a most happy instinct that kept him from the "clique philosophy" of the professors who since the end of the heroic age of German philosophy half a century ago have been philologists whose extreme originality was a sort of scholastic eclecticism which tested and proved the criticism and observations of previous criticizers and observers in indefinite perspective, by all conceivable permutations and combinations, until now, leaving the trail of theology, they are obliged to save themselves from oblivion by retailing the discoveries of natural science. He even regretted the hours spent on the current literature of the university philosophers and longed again for idyllic ignorance of the writings of most of his philosophical contemporaries.

In the seventies, as a student, I used to visit him on Sunday afternoons in his suburban cottage. He led a purely intellectual life, was an indefatigable worker, and besides his larger treatises published many hundred pages of magazine articles and minor essays. His hours of relaxation were spent in the practice or composition of music. After the publication of the ''Philosophy of the Unconscious'' he wrote one tolerable drama entitled ''Tristan und Isolde,'' but he eschewed current literature.

His manner and personal appearance were striking. He was short and rather thick, with a head too big for his body. He walked with great difficulty, only on level ground, and preferred to wheel himself in an invalid chair. His long, abundant sandy hair and beard, and his fine poetic eye, his very rapid utterance and quick movements, his brief and ready characterization, contemptuous denunciation of those who most severely criticized his opinions, his express confidence that he was only in the beginning of his philosophical activity, all combined to give the impression of a most strongly marked and original personality, in which the keen sensitiveness of a poet and an invalid was combined with great force of purpose and power of sustained mental effort. His pessimism was almost a religion with him, and he accepted and defended with ardor in private conversation all its consequences and implications and was fond of repeating, in spite of most serious pecuniary disasters, that if one would see contented and happy faces he must go among the pessimists. His books were worn and ragged in every public library, his correspondence was extensive, and even cultivated German ladies fell to reading his philosophy and never ceased to interest themselves in the remarkable personality and the no less remarkable career of the author.

Agnes Taubert, the daughter of an artillery colonel, had long been his friend and helper, and when he was twenty-nine they were married. She remained his enthusiastic coadjutor and in 1875 published her well-known book "Der Pessimismus und seine Gegner," but six years later she died, leaving a son hardly old enough, as Hartmann said, to pronounce the Fichtean *Ich*, and after a year and a half, during which he composed his "Phänomenologie des sittlichen Bewusstseins," he married Alma Lorenz, a young teacher who had long been his sympathetic admirer and who lived to celebrate her silver wedding with him. He next composed "Die Selbstersetzung des Christentums und die Religion der Zukunft." At the age of thirty-seven his knee became worse and he henceforth went about with two crutches and a wheel chair, and he entered the longest illness of his life, during which he wrote "Die Bedeutung des Leides." At the age of thirty-nine he again had to submit to three severe operations. Meanwhile he had friends, Duprel, Venetianer, Olga Plumacher, and many others who were often with him. This was perhaps the most fertile period of his life when he wrote his "History of Metaphysics," "Psychology," his "Problem of Life," and his "System of Philosophy," all of which attracted little attention. His family consisted of a son and three daughters and he lived just outside Berlin near the Botanical Gardens till his death. He declared "Der Mensch verschalt in der Familie und mundet in die See." He took great pleasure in teaching his children, particularly music, and both afternoons and evenings he devoted to them and his friends. He was of kindly and mild manner, attentive to trifles, very fond of conversing upon the wide piazza of his little house, although quite commonly he talked with his friends propped up in his bed. Although isolated from the world he took great interest in it, but wrote out of his own life, and yet the tragedy of it is not expressed in his writings, so that we do not know how far he felt it to be tragic. After his death from obscure but acute stomach trouble, Otto Pfleiderer pronounced the eulogy at his funeral, without church service, and his wife and daughters, who had seen his soul sink into the Unconscious, were left pathetically alone. Although he once, perhaps half-humorously, advocated a club of savants whose function it should be to make post-mortem examination of each other's brains instead of to write each other's obituary notices (which he satirically characterized as the real object and the best work of certain learned societies and academies), his brain was not examined, nor were those of Zeller, Lotze, or Fechner, as all should have been, in the interests of science.

Of ''The Philosophy of the Unconscious'' (1867) a brief epitome of the leading points will suffice here. The Unconscious is the absolute subject, substance, ego, idea, or force of the universe. It contains will and intellect, which are inseparable save in the mind of man. Efficient causes are unintelligible and impossible without final. Analyze any object of nature, *e. g.*, the eye, and we shall find that there are so many elements combined in its structure, composition, and use that on a mathematical calculation of the doctrine of chances they are found almost infinitely against such a combination as really exists. Hence at the outset he rejected Darwinism. First the Unconscious is considered in natural organisms. We will, *e. g.*, to move the foot and it is as correct to say it is moved *for* us as that it is moved *by* us. It is done, we know not how, or by what agency. So animal instinct is action always according to a purpose, although without a knowledge of the purpose. Likewise in the operation of natural laws we are compelled to recognize a power which never hesitates or tires or makes mistakes. It creates the brain and then thinks and acts through it. It is as manifest in the *vis reparatrix* which replaces the broken feather of a bird's wing as in the intelligence which builds the nest. Schopenhauer considered will as primeval and held that intellect is unfolded late from its processes; Hartmann believes that will is guided from the first by knowledge. Yet the final end of all animal life is the development of consciousness, while the most intelligent and purposive action is often dominated by an unconscious bottom motive. Volition always implies dissatisfaction with the present or existing state of things and a desire to change, but always depends on intelligence for guidance.

The second book treats of the Unconscious in the organization of language, which is a creation of the instinct and mind of the race. All the fundamental principles of logic are innate and embedded as it were in language and it is one great function of reason to analyze what is here found preëxistent. Thus indeed the syllogism was developed. Speech of course does not represent the primitive elemental processes and modes of thinking. These created it as a convenient shorthand or algebra of thought. How thoughts are written out in the brain or, in other words, the retentive power of memory, is no such mystery as is the reproductive power of the mind. The former is our own work, the latter is given as by the Unconscious. All pleasure and pain, whether conscious or unconscious, which make up indeed the bulk of human experience, depend for their intensity on the strength of the volition which is favored or crossed, and thus the prick of a pin, the loss of wealth, or the reproofs of conscience are qualitatively alike and differ only in quantity. The Unconscious inductively generalizes what is of use in human experience and these results afterward appear in consciousness as a priori and we come to know our own character just as we learn that of others. The Unconscious, *e. g.*, creates the rudiments of space perception in us from local signs and then the notion of space comes into consciousness as one of its aboriginal possessions. In point of absolute fact, however, intellect creates space in us and will creates it in reality, while both are themselves essentially unspatial.

The third book is occupied with the metaphysics of the Unconscious. If we ask why the universe exists, the only answer is that it is a form which the Unconscious has assumed to rid itself of its own miseries. It is even deluded into the building of the brain wherein intellect is freed from bondage to the will in consciousness. All that the Unconscious wills is attained when it knows what it wills and yet consciousness is not directly willed, but is rather the forcing on the mind of a generically new perception, not by or according to its volitions. The world must press on and not, as Schopenhauer said, cease to will, not in order to obtain happiness or freedom, but only to develop consciousness till action becomes absolutely rational and will is eliminated by intellect.

The history of human ideals is briefly told in his characterization of the three stages of illusion: (1) In primitive ages, as now in childhood, men expected to be happy in the present earthly life with no thought of a future one. They were content to labor, suffer, and practice self-denial in the hope of spending maturer years in the unalloyed enjoyment of attainment or possession. This, however, was soon found to be deceptive. Age brought its own cares and pain, and later by a long intricate play of circumstances (2) the belief in a future life was developed. The fancied happiness beyond this life at last became so near and tangible that no risk and no sacrifice was so great during this despised and brief existence that it was not to be compensated a thousandfold hereafter. This, too, has proven an illusion. Neither the philosopher, the scientist, nor the astronomer can find any place for heaven in his ken, where the individual life can be prolonged, and (3) evolutionary theories brought the belief that happiness awaits only future generations on this earth who shall arrive farther along in the growth of the race than we. But even this is an illusion. The philosopher now sees that the future will be as the past. This life is be-all and death its end-all. The sturdiest swimmers of us all were brought into existence only to sink with bub-

bling groans into the unknown depths at last. If the life
we see and live to-day is all, how poor and sad! Here
pleasure is misery's decoy duck. Man never is and never
is to be blessed—the more consciousness, the more wretched-
ness. A satisfied wish brings a hundred louder unsatis-
fied ones. Pleasant impressions soon fade, sad ones are
indelible. Indeed it is a law of the nervous system not only
that pains increase with their duration but that pleasures
diminish and even become painful if long continued. Man's
life is a false nature. Only ignorance and superstition
find a preponderance of joy in this bankrupt world. Such
are the appalling insights which according to Hartmann
no thoughtful mind can long escape, and it is only a sublime because truly philosophical heroism which can enable
us to take the one course which duty demands in this supreme emergency, viz., to keep quietly at work as before
and make ourselves as comfortable and oblivious as possible with the consolations of art, science, family life, and
fame, and especially with the great and conscious satisfaction of superior confidential insight into the malignant
purpose of the absolute.

There seems to be no doubt that Hartmann's mind was
as exquisitely if not even morbidly susceptible as Shelley's
sensitive plant, and that he felt keenly every breath of
critical praise or blame, in spite of the generally calm and
dignified tone of his more polemic writings. He published,
bound together with his later works, a prospectus wherein
are collected, extending over many pages, scores of excerpts
from the daily and periodical press from Russia to Cali-
fornia commenting upon his system, from which a choice
anthology of polemic phrases might be culled. The bitter
discussion went on while the work passed through many
editions. Professor Michelet, the remarkable and long
sole surviving representative of pure and unadulterated
Hegelianism, expressed "honest pity" for an author who
brings such "miserable nonsense" into the philosophical

mart. J. C. Fischer pronounced it a "pyramid of absurdity," fit to excite "universal laughter." One writer averred that Hartmann had "shamefully duped the world"; another called his book a "snarl of idiotic stupidity"; "reason run mad"; "the odor of death pervading the whole volume"; "purely pathological"; "frivolity and pretense"; "the jugglery of logic"; "a plea for moral bankruptcy"; "a philosophic Dunciad"; "an apotheosis of ignorance and old Mother Night"; and similar verdicts almost by the score have been pronounced by adversaries. Dr. Hausermann feared that the doctrine of the infallibility of the Unconscious would tend to the notion of a potential infallibility of the pope.

On the other hand, Dr. Lasson considered it one of the best expressions of the tendency of modern times, admirably calculated to reconcile not only Hegel and Schopenhauer, but the classic works of German philosophy with the methods and results of modern science. Prof. Kapp called it the inauguration of a "new way of regarding the universe." Other writers too numerous to mention have acknowledged his system to be "brilliant," "genial," of a "thoroughly pure and noble moral tone," "a remarkable bit of culture history which will survive the next century," "suggestive to an unparalleled degree," etc., etc., and a writer in the *Journal of Speculative Philosophy* even called it "encouraging," elevating and ennobling. It is probably not too much to say with Dr. Kirchmann that its reception not only among scholars but throughout the reading world was unprecedented in the previous history of philosophy, and that on the whole Hartmann is treated with increasing respect even by his enemies.

It was essentially a *new* book. The author has taken an independent look at the universe for himself. He has in fact been called almost the only *modern* who has made himself distinctly heard in philosophy, while he has articulated with great definiteness and moral earnestness the

questions which the *Zeitgeist* whispers in many thoughtful
souls. His book was long in the focus of philosophical interest in Germany. In place of the absolute idea, the ego,
the *Begriff-force*—matter, motion, etc., Hartmann has
erected a new altar to the unknown God, and while he
worships at the same shrine of nescience as Herbert Spencer it is with a far more reverent and even more hopeful
mind. With him more than with his dispraisers are the
noble and inspiring traditions of the classical period of
German philosophy and for all who succeed to his influence or who would gainsay his principles he has made a
knowledge of at least the results of natural science indispensable. He vindicated the ideal against materialism,
and by at least partially satisfying the metaphysical needs
of his contemporaries made philosophy again an enthusiasm and emancipated it from extraneous literary, scientific, and even university influences. His appeal was to the
average popular consciousness with a single comprehensive
and easily comprehensible principle, and he called again
the attention of the world from petty and distracting irrel-
evancies and temporalities to the vital center of the great
questions of human destiny, nature, and duty. All who
would better understand the human soul and the intellectual influences which are at work in the world to-day
would do well to read this work thoughtfully. His argument throughout is for an intelligent purposive power gov-
erning nature, and, despite the negative predicates with
which he invests it, it goes very far toward answering the
current materialistic scribblers. It is moreover idle to try
longer to discredit even his pessimism by urging that he
is enraged at the universe because his knee was sometimes
painful or his bankers proved dishonest. It is, of course,
greatly exaggerated, but it can hardly be regarded like
that of Schopenhauer as largely curious and amusing. Excessive optimism does not incline men to indifference to
moral inaction, and so likewise that by such a scheme as his

some men should be led to suicide or a life of vice, as has been urged, seems as improbable as that Goethe's "Werther" should have produced similar results among its readers. If individual and actually attained pleasure be assumed as the measure instead of as the motive or final cause of human actions, as he both asserts and implies throughout, much that he urges of the sadness and disappointment of life will be readily admitted as true.

On the other hand, that both in personal intercourse and in the tone of most and especially the later of his writings he was often arrogant, arbitrary, and dogmatic cannot be denied. His constructions were often painfully forced, his analyses fanciful, and he was probably more than suspected of the vanity of the neologist which inclined him to express views and to form paradoxes whose strongest commendation to his own mind was that no one before him had uttered or even seen them. He was not seldom more ingenious in supporting or defending his positions than philosophical in choosing them, but the event showed no reason to believe the predictions of some of his opponents that he had no career before him save in reiterating his already expressed views, or that he would end either as a devotee or as an unmitigated quack and fanatic.

The criticisms of a modern orthodox and academic philosopher of consciousness would run, I fancy, somewhat along the following lines: The pessimism which forms the sequel of his system is inadequately motivated, and has scarcely more logical connection with the theory of the Unconscious than have the later speculations of Auguste Comte with the "Philosophie Positive." As a whole, the system has a decidedly *baroque* look, and its chapters are about as much separate essays as organic parts of a symmetrical and logically compacted and elaborated view. In choosing the Unconscious as his principle he has succeeded in what was never achieved before, viz., in committing every fallacy of formal logic at once, for he makes it not only a perpetual *deus ex machina*, who is made to play into the author's hands at every point and to whom recourse is often prematurely had to supplement his ignorance of details or of ulterior but well-established explanations, but at the same time it plays the part of a handy receptacle for every sort of residuary obscurity and inconsistency. If philosophy be, as Avenarius defined it, that mode of thinking the universe which requires the least possible expenditure of cerebral force, we must indeed allow much right to Hartmann, for the world can never be apprehended in a more simple way. But the Unconscious, as he voiced it in his first edition, is no philosophical principle, for it explains nothing nor is it explained by anything. It is the dark alternative, the dialectic opposite of all knowledge.

Hartmann's "Miscellaneous Essays," published between 1867 and 1874, and making a large volume of 729 pages, cover a wide range of topics and are mostly illustrations of his philosophical principles. We will very briefly epitomize for the reader a few of the best of these.

In the much-debated essay on Shakespeare's "Romeo and Juliet" it is urged in the teeth of a score of German critics that Romeo, though chivalric, wearing a good sword, possessing ready wit and an abundant *esprit*, is by no means manly. His love, like that of Juliet, is roused to a paroxysm at first sight, before either can know or trust the other. Juliet was wantonly careless of her parents' feelings, Romeo eventually slays himself in the instant and before even knowing how his lady died. The love here depicted was hot but not deep enough to last a lifetime, and love, at least as known in German life and letters, is deeper and richer than Shakespeare here knew how to represent it. Tragedy must show one passion destroying a *man*, and Romeo is *not* a man.

Goethe's "Faust" teaches that there is no satisfaction in knowledge, none in pleasure, but that in action is salvation. Yet after seeing the inadequacy of knowledge it is only a blind instinct which guides Faust to enlarge his sympathies and devote himself to philanthropic labor as he does in the last act of the second part. Goethe went no further, and his masterpiece remained unfinished, a blind prophecy of the Philosophy of the Unconscious, which latter explains why it is that only after a profound experience of pessimism one can truly learn how to make himself comfortable and useful in the world.

In another long essay he answers the question: "Is pessimism inconsolable?" in the negative. Sweetmeats taste as good to the pessimist as to the optimist. The great ethical problem and duty is to make selfishness powerless and hence pessimism is the strongest motive for a solidarity of races, and monism once admitted all egoism is forever impossible. Love, which is the joy of self-surrender, is a lightning flash of truth into the delusion of the individual consciousness. All great passions, arduous endeavors, or high motives make men forget and even immolate self, for death is simply rest. It is only puny Philistine souls, whose history is written only on their gravestones, who cry out loudest for the preservation of their identity in another world. The great and essential joys and sorrows of life are open to all, and it is because artificial social distinctions, richness and poverty, fame and obscurity, etc., come to be unduly magnified that the need of compensation in a future life is felt. No man is given wormwood here that he may enjoy honey hereafter. In a sense, in short, there is nothing transcendent, all is immanent. A virtue which does not carry its own reward in itself is no virtue. The only evil in the universe is to be guilty, and to feel guilty is the only punishment. Pessimism does not tend to quietism, but is the strongest of all possible motives to activity. Pain is a stronger stimulus than pleasure, and the fact that this is the best of all possible worlds, but at the same time worse than none at all, will not discourage but only give greater poise and seriousness to all healthy souls.

The nature of tragedy is a favorite theme with our author. True tragedy, which no optimist can consistently tolerate, which is quite superseded on the modern stage and in literature by the sad and the ugly, unlike these gives the highest possible elevation of soul. It is not essential that in its issue it reward virtue or punish guilt. To the spectator if not to the hero himself at last comes the insight that there is something better than life and reality, and that these may be relinquished. A more abiding sadness, which has been falsely called the highest of all tragic effects, is produced when the hero cannot die, but is forced to live on, a weary, desolate life, like Dante's souls in the Inferno, or like the Wandering Jew. Yet death produces not only the greatest present effect, but, according to pantheism, it is a type of the dissolution and resumption of all things. The pivotal acts must be voluntary acts of an unconciliatory inappeasable character and the conflict and catastrophe must be necessary.

Again he attempts to tell us how great artists bring forth their works. All works of art live in the depths of character, and must be produced often by the aid of deep meditation, but are always fundamentally spontaneous. The understanding may oversee and even criticize now and then but should never be allowed to control. The poet, he believes with Ludwig, should vanish behind his work as Nature does.

He deplores what he calls symptoms of decay in art and science. The rise of popular science, though so far less disastrous than in England and especially in France, has seduced hundreds of the best minds from original work to the public platform or press and has called into unmerited repute scores of half-trained dilettanti. In the large cities, especially Berlin, the professors, called thither for the most part in middle life from smaller places, are too apt to become salonists. They associate largely with men of their own department and an *esprit de corps* arises, often unfolding into a strict caste feeling where the local and other prejudices of members are mutually countenanced and strengthened, outgrown traditions of the schools are cemented, and in the absence of efficient and authoritative valuation of work great individual injustice is done, valuable workers silenced, and their work ignored.

In one long essay he characterizes Haeckel, whom he considers to be intellectually descended from Schelling through Johannes Müller. Jena he designates as the freest of all universities for an independent thinker. He urges that Haeckel's form of the evolutionary theory is far less mechanical than that of Darwin, in that it recognizes immanent forces, and ascribes to the former the merit of having made empirical science and philosophy henceforth not only reciprocal but necessary to each other. He regrets that Haeckel should have opposed the teleological view of the universe, and predicts that his philosophical self-training will eventually bring him to recognize the planful order and organization of nature.

Under the leadership of Professors Lazarus and Steinthal the rites, customs, superstitions, mythology, and language of primitive and uncultivated peoples, called folk-psychology (Völker-Psychologie), were made one department of philosophy. Of this Hartmann argues that its fundamental conception should be that the action of individual minds is not so much the cause as the result of the action of a collective subject of which they are less attributes or predicates, as argued by Lazarus, than embodiments. In all acts, even the freest, we will consciously to do this by these means but from a higher standpoint it is ever seen that we have at the same time been unconsciously doing other things by other means. The history of development is thus very different from the history of the conscious purposes of individuals. The latter are contradictory and often mutually canceled; the former never errs and is never out of harmony with itself or inconsistent with personal freedom. This is due to the bottom ideality of existence, not in the sense that the severed parts of a polyp each developing an independent life are identical but requiring the assumption of an absolute *prius* working consistently in and through all.

Again and similarly he argues the cause of dynamism against atomism. He well objects to Fechner's argument that atoms are at the same time material but unextended. Instead of Ulrici's view of atoms as centers of different forces working at a distance in one point of space, which yet have found size as space elements in the working sphere of their repulsion, Hartmann argues that atomic forces are the individualized expression of one pure, absolute, non-spatial, transcendent essence and that the form of this force as such is changeable only *a potentia ad actum.*

Again it is well known that Lotze when a young man published an article entitled "Life Force," in which it was argued that in animal organisms all the phenomena of life are conceivably due to different combinations and relations of elements, arrangements of conditions, etc., an essay which has been often quoted in support of a mechanical evolutionism, to the author's exceeding annoyance, and which is said to have made his later reaction to an inner teleology more pronounced. Against this and all materialistic and vitalistic theories alike Hartmann pleads for his familiar "transcendent mediatory real principle."

In one essay he praises the consistency of Leibniz as a practical optimist, who tried to mediate all antitheses in his thought and all conflict in his active philanthropic life. In another he suggests that the funds so often subscribed in Germany for the erection of monuments to distinguished writers would be better expended in permanently reducing the price of the works. In another he argues not only against capital punishment, but less restraint in prisons, which he predicts in the future will be made little model artificial states where experiments in self-government may be made for and by students of the art of statesmanship.

In a brochure of 122 pages published in 1874 entitled "The Dissolution of Christianity and the Religion of the Future," and expressly addressed only to those whose minds have been emancipated by the critical study of positive Christian dogma, Hartmann expresses his religious opinions without reserve. Christianity should no longer delay to confess itself bankrupt in the means of satisfying the religious needs of the present, which is the most irreligious period of history. The bestiality of the social democracy shows how degraded man becomes when deprived of religion, which has always been not only the chief means of popular education but the only form in which idealism has been made accessible to the masses. Yet the power of even the mummified Christianity of Catholicism to rouse its followers to fanatical enthusiasm shows that a degree of vitalizing power still remains in it which may become one element in the world religion of the future. Protestantism he designates as a mere transition-stadium from the true Christianity of the past to the ideas of modern culture and civilization. These being essentially irreconcilable, Protestantism soon became a maze of logical contradictions, yet practically it has also been a school of self-control wherein the world has been taught the valuable lesson that radicalism, while it brings men to a clearer consciousness of their rights, does not emancipate them from duties. The essence of Christianity was exhausted in the Middle Ages. Protestantism was not so much its slayer as its burier. But for its historical relations and its geographical position, which make it still a source of countless dangers to modern civilization, Catholicism has long been no less a *caput mortuum* in history than the wor-

ship of the Dalai Lama in Thibet. All religion, being necessarily an affair of feeling, must subordinate intellectual
culture as a means. Christianity entered the world, grew
strong in a period of general decadence, and preserved
the remnants of a moribund civilization, a dead language,
a mass of traditions, etc., at first as objects of superstitious wonder to the rune-revering German races, which in
the Renaissance began to prove themselves its destruction,
until now it is not only impossible for a sane man to be a
Christian in the true, unadulterated sense of the word,
but the very conception of the meaning of the word ''religion'' is almost lost to the modern world.

The *Cultur-Kampf,* he continues, in which the interests
of Catholicism and Protestantism are one as against the
true spirit of modern science, art, etc., was long doubtful
and desperate, and not till the days of Königsgratz and
Sedan, when Prussia—the center of crystallization for the
modern secular spirit—was able to bring Germany with a
united front to a renewal of the thousand years' war with
the church, was a belief in the future autonomous moral
and intellectual development of the world assured for those
who had faith in the consequent logical development of
ideas in history. All but Catholics now admit that the
Christianity even of the New Testament is a development
and Protestantism must not be content with eliminating
merely the additions and forced interpretation of the mediæval church. Radical German Protestants we are assured no longer believe with Luther that the Pauline doctrine contains the essence of Christianity; in fact Christianity has ceased to be Lutheran, Augustinian, or even
Pàuline. Later, under the influence of Schleiermacher, the
Johannean period of German dogmatics began. Now, however, since John's Gospel has been proven the latest instead of the most primitive and more especially on account
of its supposed pantheistic tendencies (as shown, *e. g.,* in
Biederman's ''Christliche Dogmatik,'' where the incompat-

ibility of the absoluteness of personality is argued from the Logos doctrine) this position has also been tacitly abandoned. It only remains, therefore, to consider the Christianity of Christ as distinct from that of the writers of the Gospels and Epistles. This the reader is assured has been done once for all by the Tübingen school. Jesus was a Jew and nothing but a Jew from first to last. He popularized upon the street the esoteric traditions of the Talmud in an ingenious and discriminating way. He was liberal, but by no means radical. The primitive and essential kernel of his doctrine is the Mosaic command to love God and our neighbor, coupled with Hillel's doctrine of moral reciprocity. Radical Protestantism is really eclectic, culling doctrines indiscriminately from Jesus, Paul, Peter, the church councils, or modern reason, and is, therefore, essentially unchristian. It is more, it is irreligious. Every religion rests upon a pessimistic contempt of the world as vain and fleeting, but the Renaissance and Reformation introduced the "optimistic intermezzo" and disposed men to make the most and best out of this earthly life. Protestantism began as a compromise and ended by calling this the best of possible worlds. Secular culture now approaches a time when it must become manifest that in attainment and possession mankind has reached all that is obtainable in this world. Then the *Gemüth*, which is the soul of religion, will be freed from the growing tyranny of the understanding, and religious questions will become once more central and supreme in human consciousness.

But the inquiry is already pertinent what ideas must enter as elements in the future religion which, as universal, must synthesize all Oriental and Occidental, all pantheistic and monotheistic tendencies. It must have "no heteronomous morality, no transcendent manipulation of redemption by extraneous merits," although it will doubtless cull some of its elements from Christianity. But man must

redeem himself. Pantheism, which fills and illumines the
dreams of mystics with reason, and which has always been,
in the words of Heine, the real, though half-concealed
religion, of Germany, which teaches that no man is out of
God or undivine, and which honors God by regarding his
being as something far nobler and higher than a personality
like ourselves, is expressed in the native impulses of pity
and love, and reconciles forever philosophy and science
with religion. Such are the vague and indeterminate and,
in Germany at least, somewhat commonplace conceptions
from which our author predicts that in a few generations
a new and world-embracing religious synthesis will be
developed.

In 1868-9, partly under the influence of the Tübingen
school, he had written a severe criticism of the New Testament, which was published in 1905 after being greatly revised and toned down ("The Christianity of the New
Testament"). In 1880 appeared his book, "The Crisis
of Christianity," criticizing speculative Protestantism. In
these works he not only criticized but condemned the belief in the existence of a personal God, since he thought
there could be nothing divine that was not impersonal and
unconscious; denied the need of any mediator or mediation, every man being his own savior if he was saved;
flouted the assumption that the end of religion is to bring
happiness now or hereafter as akin to a sensuous heaven
or work for a pay day; denounced the conception of personal immortality, holding that at death the tides that
brought us hither only "turn again home." He pilloried
what he thought the bigoted idea of a God-man, holding
that humanity itself was divine; repudiated all the historical elements of Christianity or any need of them. Christian morality is puerile because based on rewards, happiness, and heteronomous virtues. These positions he urged
with such vehemence, his criticisms were marshaled in such
array, and his negations were so all-pervading and relent-

less that he has been called "the ablest and most dangerous enemy the Christian church has ever had."

This view has been widely accepted by orthodoxy, but it is false and shallow. If he seemed to hate theology and the church, it was because of his great love for what he deemed the religion of the future, which is set forth in his "Religion of the Spirit" (1881) and his "Religious Consciousness" (1882). Here he urges that the world cannot possibly do without religion and that the church is only half-hearted and shallow-thoughted in its faith. His positive "religious religion" was not unlike that of Nietzsche, which it antedated by years, and both found their *point d'appui* in the Persian Zarethustra's conception of a necessary war between light and dark or the rational idea and blind instinct and irrational will. For their conflict the whole world-process is the drama, and from this standpoint we can first glimpse the true religion, which is to be the new dispensation of all Oriental as well as Christian faiths. Hartmann's God is the blind but all-pervading and impelling Power that utters itself in and through the entire process of cosmic evolution, which makes for righteousness in the ethical domain, which animates all his work and that of all other soldiers of the spirit, and is revealed in the lives of all the great and good light-bringers in history. Arthur Drews [1] thinks Hartmann is the most religious of all men, one called and ordained by a world-soul to be its saint, prophet, and apostle. Although Hartmann called the modern Jesus-worship a form of heathenism and the Jesus of evangelical orthodoxy a fetich, his faith was in one only unconscious principle with the two attributes, will and concept, that is, one that is omnipotent and omniscient. From this point of view he is able to make a genial synthesis be-

[1] Das Lebenswerk Eduard von Hartmann, Leipzig, Thomas, 1907, 67 pp. See also and especially his Hartmann's Philosophisches System, 2nd ed., 1906, pp. 937.

tween the pessimistic negative religion of India and the optimistic affirmative religion of Persia. Not eudæmonological pessimism or passive reflection on the excess of pain over pleasure in the world, but evolutionistic optimism, active practice, and aggressive participation in the processes of culture was his creed. He demanded not flight from reality or renunciation, but self-immolating sacrifice and work "all for God's sake." He turned from Schopenhauer's *Weltschmerz* and passive quietism to the eternal yea of Zarethustra, and did so just because he saw that pain is inevitable. Indeed, it was this that gave his piety a heroic mold. He also sought to revive the old German spirit, which he did by appealing to the heroic age of Teutonic myth as Wagner did, and also with the slogan *Das Deutschentum musst das Christentum zeigen.* Thus one eulogist calls Hartmann's creed "the deepest, most worthy religious expression of the Aryan mind, pointing out the only way in which the world can pass beyond Christianity as it must do or suffer arrest."

"The Truth and Error of Darwinism" (177 p.), published in 1875, contains by the author's admission nothing essentially new, but is an important amplification of opinions already expressed in the "Philosophy of the Unconscious." Darwinism has become popular, it is said, not from its intrinsic truthfulness but because for those who lacked the mental discipline to hold the question open there was no choice between it and more mechanical theories. Here Hartmann's friends think he incidentally anticipated Weismann. Darwinists are wrong in insisting that the transmutation of species always takes place by the summation of minimal variations in the individual, and in neglecting the embryological processes through which types are changed by germ metamorphoses. The result of this long and bitter controversy has convinced philosophical minds that Darwin's too mechanical instinct has failed to draw sufficient attention to the immanent formative force present and active at every point in Nature, which compels a teleological conception of the universe. The organic development theory, which designation Hartmann proposes as more German and more correct than Darwinism, which is derived directly from Kant and which as Haeckel well says should be called natural philosophy and not natural science, which is the most "eminent fact in the modern intellectual world and opens a prospect of limitless change for philosophical thought," has demonstrated the absolute logical inseparability of teleology and causality. They are related as means and end, and each is both impossible and unintelligible without the other. The complex bundle of hypotheses called the theory of natural selection, which Darwin himself originated by applying observations made on plants and animals artificially cultivated to organic nature at large, is analyzed into subordinate principles, themselves complex. The first, the struggle for existence, seeks to explain how types are purified and perfected. All alterations, however chemical, the anatomical enlargement of the whole or parts, the changes of periodic processes which must take account of useless qualities, as well as of those absolutely necessary for existence, can affect only external properties; no adaptation to changed environment can effect any change of morphologic type. Variability and heredity both especially postulate the recognition of an immanent teleological principle which Darwin is not disposed to admit. The direct influence of environment, which he borrowed from Geoffrey St. Hilaire, Hartmann urges is slight and superficial. The principle of use and disuse derived from Lamarck can only affect structure and weight, not form, and can account only for change of size in an organ and never for its appearance or disappearance. Change of use is, moreover, preceded by change of instinct. New conditions always cause an inner development of more or less conscious and purposive and hence unmechanical action. Sexual selection also can explain only outward decorative variations and cannot reach fundamental organs, while correlation of growth with associated variations is only the last refuge of Darwinians when they are obliged to admit that mechanical hypotheses fail and to recognize an inherent and unfathomable power working within or through atomic and vital forces.

In 1872 appeared an anonymous and lengthy criticism of Hartmann's system entitled ''The Unconscious from the Standpoint of Philosophy and the Development Theory'' in which many important concessions were made, and it was urged that even if consciousness be only a summation of the forces inherent in the lowest forms of existence these must be conceived as merely nonpurposive and morphological predispositions to intelligence and by no means as a clairvoyant unconscious intention in matter itself. The writer was minutely versed in all Hartmann's views and treated him with great deference, expressing regret that hitherto no competent antagonist had been found. Haeckel, whose pan-psychic speculations of soul cells and of memory as inherent in atoms had been thought to have some near analogies to Hartmannism, declared that this pamphlet expressed exactly his views and even Professor Schmidt,[1] who is the only eminent scientific specialist who has taken pains to examine and refute the ''Philosophy of the Unconscious'' in detail, warmly praised the anonymous pamphlet. Several years later, in an enlarged edition, Hartmann avowed himself the author of it, and refuted, although many thought quite unsatisfactorily, his own self-refutation. This performance he defended as one step in the true Socratic dialectic method of unfolding and establishing opinions, and his more implicit followers regard it as a triumphant stratagem. It has, however,

[1] Die Naturwissenschaftliche Grundlage der Philosophie des Unbewussten von Oscar Schmidt, Prof. der Zoologie u. vergl. Anat., Strassburg, 1877, 86 pp.

strengthened with many the conviction that a mind which can "confute, change hands, and still confute" in such dapper Hudibrastic style must be more ingenious than sincere, and raised the question whether a thinker who had become so much more philosophical in criticizing than in defending his own opinions might not eventually abandon the standpoint of his precocious youth and turn against his own disciples with a new principle.

In several hundred pages the author has at various times unfolded his views of the Kantian theory of cognition.[1] This he calls the essential question of philosophy and therefore of all science. He asserts the existence of something transcendentally real beyond and independent of consciousness, the knowledge of which is attained not by mere sensuous perception nor by direct inner intuition but as mediately and inductively impressed as a necessary cause of our immediate immanent experience or its effects in consciousness. The certainty thus obtained that the cosmos is a teleological process of self-determining intelligence is not absolute but practical.

In following thus far in a general way the historical order in our all too brief epitome of his opinions—for there is absolutely no other order—we come now to speak of his earlier disciples. As the word was used during the heroic age of German philosophy there are now no schools; least of all has Hartmann one. He feels himself so unique and even solitary in the intellectual world that he recognizes no master and tolerates no pupil in the full and former sense of the word. His conception of the *Ding-an-sich* he admits is a development of Kant's Æsthetics, and he allows us to call him a reconciler and modernizer of Schelling, Hegel, and Schopenhauer, each of whom is true because the other is. He even takes Darwin and the phys-

[1] See especially Das Ding an Sich und seine Beschaftenheit, 1872, and also Kritische Grundlegung des transcendentalen Realismus, 1875.

iologists under his protection, but is at vastly more pains to detail points of difference, often quite fictitious, than of essential agreement with them. On the other hand he made almost every conceivable application and development of his principles himself and left very little for his disciples to do. Moreover he no doubt unconsciously experienced the consummate luxury of the egotistic principle, which is to have a system of the universe all to one's self wherein one may live in undisputed squatter sovereignty not *by* philosophy, like the professors he derides, and certainly not *according to* philosophy, which requires, he tells us, the suppression of all egoism, but *for* philosophy.

Beginning with those who most closely represent Hartmann's own standpoint we name first Agnes Taubert,[1] the lady who became his first wife. This little volume of reflections has only a literary significance, but has been quite widely read. A larger volume by Moritz Venetianer [2] is a mystic and extreme accentuation of the besouled principle of the universe. It goes far beyond Hartmann in emphasizing the unity at the expense of the manifoldness of the universe and ends by a defense of the principle of reformed Judaism. We have plodded through many hundred dreary pages in tracing the ramifications of Hartmannism, but with no such mental nausea as in struggling with this book, over which the very spirit invoked in the Dunciad seems to have woven a resistless spell. We have tried to read it when the blessed sun of a bright spring morning shone full upon its pages and late at evening when the mind was jaded, but no mood or motive would avail. It simply will not read. The author fairly gloats over the widely gleaned recognition of the mystery of life and the limits of human knowledge by learned men of all

---

[1] Pessimismus und seine Gegner. A. Taubert, 1872.

[2] Der Allgeist. Grundzüge des Panpsychismus in Anschluss an die Philos. des. Unbew., 1874.

ages, whom he gathers into the *asylum ignorantiæ* of his system.

Volkelt's book[1] is far better. From the standpoint of new Hegelianism the author attempts to show that the unconscious logical principle is the silent and necessary presupposition of all philosophy from Kant onward. This is perhaps the best of many attempts to show that Hartmann is essentially an Hegelian in spite of himself, and it also attempts to modify his pessimistic theories.

Du Prel, a well-known popular scientist and traveler, has written a keen and well-tempered rejoinder to Prof. J. C. Fischer's coarse criticisms of Hartmann,[2] and in a later and widely read work[3] argues that Venus, the earth, Mars, the moon, the asteroids, meteors, and comets, all to be burned up at last into the cosmic mist from which they all sprang by the various atmospheres they encounter in their course, represent decaying phases of the solar and all other systems; that all sidereal bodies and orbits are selected survivals of innumerable others destroyed or thrown out of harmony by collisions; "that the truth which is a special case among all errors survives them all," and that as sensation is a fundamental property of all matter and as being is transformed material energy, so pain is lessened during the organization of a system, a world, or an animal, etc., and increased by its dissolution; and that thus, assuming from similar physical and chemical laws that forms of life analogous to those in the earth are developed at some stage of all planetary existence, so as they decay suffering gradually "deepens into the absolute and universal pain of atomic disintegration," unfolding in infinite perspective far below the horizon of animal life or individual consciousness. It would of course be unfair to call all this Hartmannism, but it is at least one of the allied vagaries

[1] Das Unbewusste und der Pessimismus, 1873.
[2] Der Gesunde Menschenverstand, 1872, 134 pp.
[3] Der Kampf um's Dasein am Himmel.

of pessimism, and all these authors were Hartmann's friends.

Another choice and elaborate pessimistic theology, written by an unknown author [1] under an assumed name, asserts that God was the primeval and absolute unity, broken up into individual existences when the universe came into being. He willed nothingness and all the processes of animate and inanimate existence are advancing stages toward the fulfillment of that will. In place of Schopenhauer's *will to live* he postulates an equally universal *will to die* and annihilation as immanent in all things and as the bottom and unconscious impulse of human life. Noble characters which compel us to admire unselfishness; works of art, in the contemplation of which we forget self and become all eye and ear to the generic ideal which is intuited in itself freed from its causal and all other relations to things; the State, wherein individuality reaches its full development by abolition of slavery, under the rule of freedom and equality for all, only that by the mutual friction of these individualities, by legality, social restraint, and competition, egoism may be again reduced and all particularism subordinated in enlarging political and other solidarities—all these are means of redemption from the only sins which are recognized, viz., pain and imperfection, not sent by a heavenly Father but freely chosen by us before the world was, *i. e.*, resulting by the free determination of the physical elements of our brains and bodies ever since the time they were all undifferentiated in the primeval cosmic gas. The highest duty for all is abstinence from that act which is the "quintessence, compendium, and focus of all the world." The author thanks the "Providence which is over all," and by whom "men are to be redeemed from sin," that he has no children and that, knowing mankind are consecrated to Nirvana, he can look

---

[1] Philosophie der Erlösung, von Phillip Mailander.

future nothingness, obscured by no mythic shadows, fully and joyously in the face.

Bahnsen [1] is a miserabilist, as original as Jean Paul and as morbid as Heine, very inchoate but with a talent for *aperçus,* whom Hartmann calls "full of the noblest blood of idealism." His own mind he considers as the elect stage where the unconscious will is peculiarly distracted and tortured. Self-torment is the end of all. He hates the very sound of the word "healthy," but for those who can construct his hysterical thought between the lines, shattered by dashes and parentheses, there is a brilliancy which makes even the most pathological of them rather amusing than otherwise. The work here quoted is extremely suggestive, novel, but of little philosophical significance.

The same may be said of the brilliant philologist,[2] Nietzsche, whose widely read essays, written in an intuitive Emersonian way, deal with the net of misunderstandings and misrepresentations sure to grow up around any one in the climate of German culture who wills to think only the truth and who has the awful power of self-expression. He believes that the noble pessimism of the opera-motives of Wagner has for its leading purposes to explain the past and not to preform the future, to show that true greatness increases the more it retires, that man will never find final ideal order in the world, and above all to reveal the omnipotence and omnipresence of unconscious motives and impulses. His "Tristan und Isolde" he calls the most metaphysical of all works of art. He joins Schopenhauer in condemning the university philosophy, which he says makes students indifferent to natural science and to history, while the study of the history of philosophy teaches them to hold no opinion whatever. The professors he

[1] Beiträge zur Charakterologie, von Julius Bahnsen, 2 vols., 1867.
[2] Unzeitmässige Betrachtungen von Friedrich Nietzsche, then a professor at Basle.

says never touch the question of central interest and the one on which they are most competent to give valuable counsel, viz., by what sort of a system of philosophy can one make the best living and win the greatest applause, and how their department can keep ahead of science (as a fox ahead of dogs). The true philosopher, he urges, must always be, as Niebuhr termed Socrates, a bad citizen. He must trouble people, lead away the youth, be more feared than favored in high places, brave the tyranny of public opinion by introducing a new degree of culture which always reverses every settled consensus—in short, he must revolutionize, as a thinker always does when he breaks out. Such a man he calls Schopenhauer, who espoused the cause of philosophy against the philosophers, and who was free because he had absolutely no pay and knew no debts of gratitude.

We have no space left to speak of the more or less definite relations in which Hartmann stands to the thought of Dühring, A. Lange, and his pupil Veihinger; to Frauenstadt who after a life spent in patching and propagating Schopenhauer later and reluctantly found himself forced to confess that his conception of the world contains irreconcilable contradictions and must be entirely reconstructed; to Biedermann, the Hegelian theologian of Zurich, who in his Christian dogmatics argues that the absoluteness of God's being is irreconcilable with his personality, or to Rehmke, his disciple, who makes large concessions to pessimism; and to scientific men who had no respect for his vagaries but let him alone, knowing that more than almost any one else he helped to popularize science and make it henceforth indispensable to philosophy and to evangelical German theology, which welcomes his vigorous championship of teleology and of an idealistic view of the world against current materialism, while it vigorously protests against his superficial and irreverent discussions of the profound problems of the Christian faith—

211

but we pass at once to one of the leading objects of this chapter, which is to briefly characterize Hartmann's contribution to ethics,[1] which in size and importance takes at least equal rank with his "Philosophy of the Unconscious."

The first and lowest form of moral consciousness, says Hartmann, was characterized by the Cyrenaics. Their naïve hedonism taught that pleasure was the end of life. The discussion of the different sorts, degrees, and consequences of enjoyment led to the true eudæmonism of the Epicureans, who taught that mental pleasure was preferable to that of the senses, and that friendship and freedom from passion and desire were the supreme forms of happiness. Aristotle, Hobbes, and especially Spinoza represent this system in greater detail. Its practical half truth is a wise and moderate *savoir vivre*, which is the highest result of what is termed the mundane positive eudæmonistic morality. As soon, however, as men begin to reflect on the disproportion between happiness and merit, the postulate of an all-wise and transcendental judge is erected, and by degrees develops into a system of rewards and punishments in a future state. To this vulgar form of egoism, best represented according to the author by the Jesus of the synoptic Gospels, earthly motives and pleasures soon come to appear low and unworthy when compared with those which are heavenly. This antithesis he regards as both false and impossible. Sensuous elements are inexpugnable from every conception of any future, especially a retributive state, and a noble Epicureanism is far better. The inevitable self-criticism of this moral scheme leads to the negative phase of Cynicism. Pleasure is seen to be impossible and the individual in this stage withdraws from the world and is indifferent to its opinions. He seeks only to lead a harmless life and avoid evil, and feels that the world can neither give him anything he desires nor take

[1] Phänomonologie des Sittlichen Bewusstseins.

from him anything he loves. This again is a partial, because a merely individual, standpoint, and the "negative transcendent moral" is sure to be inferred. Suicide, the refusal to live of asceticism, and the insight that the end and object of living is not to be happy, but to be independent of happiness, and that only those who know little and whose experience has been shallow find enjoyment in life result from various degrees of development of this stage of moral consciousness. All morality, at best, is only a palliative between full enjoyment of the world on the one hand and refusal to live on the other. In this extreme of self-negation the ultimate and inevitable bankruptcy of every egotistic moral system is manifest. The first cycle of moral consciousness ends thus in utter self-renunciation and despair.

The more complete this shipwreck of the selfish principles, the more eagerly do men grasp after heteronomous authoritative principles, and the more uncritically do they apply them to the guidance of conduct. According to the well known views of J. H. Kirchmann, this is the highest morality. Humanity, the state, etc., are infinitely higher and wiser than the individual. To obey because we are commanded now seems the highest and final moral motive. Precedent in law, good government, business, social intercourse, all depend on this instant and complete surrender of the individual will to a higher authority. The moral act brings rest but never pleasure, etc. True, replies Hartmann, the sentiments of reverence and veneration are independent of the feelings of pleasure and pain, but even these must not be unduly exalted above self-respect and independence in thought and action. The origin of paternal authority is sought in the animal instinct of defending the young. This is the first and fundamental form of all authority. Legislation stands for the control of the worst elements and individuals by the moral consciousness of the best. Custom is an unconscious which should be replaced by a conscious morality. Church authority is the most insidious and dangerous of all for both mental and moral culture. The autonomous movement by Protestantism is of great theoretical, but has proved to be of little practical worth.

With the discussion of such points the introductory, or "pseudo moral" portion of the work ends. It has shown that conscience is no simple, but a very complex, product of all varieties of instincts—feelings, opinions, tastes, etc.—and that freedom of conscience postulates merely the negation of every heteronomous element. Everything is thus far strictly in the spirit and method of Hegel's "Phenomenology." Hartmann expressly assumes the same objective standpoint and, though renouncing the dialectic method, has not, save in a few inconspicuous details, succeeded in working his way to independence of his most ingenious model, which is now coming to be considered in Germany as one of the most suggestive of all products of philosophical thought.[1]

Is there in consciousness a spontaneous ethical estimate of human actions, apart from all conformity to outer authority or influence? With the discussion of this great question the second part, which is entitled the "True Ethical Consciousness," begins and considers: (a) Ethical motives, or subjective moral principles; (b) ethical ends, or objective moral principles; (c) the ultimate and absolute moral principle. Under (a) are considered: (1) The æsthetic moral principles of taste, the existence of which enables us to answer the above question, which is purely empirical, affirmatively by asserting only the existence of such a principle without telling or knowing what it requires. Its psychological origin is here of no importance. It is considered before feeling, not because it is simpler but because its judgments are more objective and independent of per-

[1] See J. B. Baillier, Hegel's Phenomenology of Mind, London, 1910, 2 vols., pp. 823, especially in introductory chapter.

sonal well being. This is not to be confounded with Herbart's ethical sensation, which considers only the form of the act itself. Good moral taste inclines to moderation, to the avoiding of extremes and eccentricities. Yet the doctrine of the golden mean, as inferred from Aristotle, can lead only to the apotheosis of mediocrity. Harmony among the elements of the individual soul is also necessary. Evil is the undue accentuation of some one impulse, which is impossible for souls which are beautiful in the platonic sense, and which, no less than a talent for music, are born, not made. If we widen the principle to universal harmony, as Samuel Clarke strove to do by his theory of the fitness of things grounded in the will of God, or according to the Stoic principle of conformity with nature, we still find the idea of harmony indefinable, and, even if once agreed upon, disturbed by every change; hence morality is made a postulate in the Wolffian precept, *perfice te ipsem*. This is also indefinite, although it has the advantage of substituting a practical for a theoretical scheme. It leads, however, to the conception of countless ethical ideals from which, by the survival and development of the fittest, have developed the conceptions of God and Christ as good, which are the noblest of moral ideals. But there can be no absolute goodness, for ethical qualification of function requires finiteness and relativity. Hence, from the necessity of having concrete and realized ideals, springs the artistic conception of life with its heroes, madonnas, saints, etc. This is the consummation of the æsthetic principle. Life is a work of art, as in "Wilhelm Meister," the poetic embodiment of an ethico-æsthetic sentiment. But thus the world comes to seem coarse and rough, and life stagey. When taste is cultivated before reason and understanding there is an inevitable loss of energy. Form is sacrificed to substance. Man becomes most manly when he *plays* the man. Hence the principle issues in idle dilettantism. "Each to his taste," "because it pleases one," are purely subjective maxims, and bring us to a new principle—(2), moral *feeling,* which is the ultimate thing in consciousness, mediating between it and the unconscious will. This is the standpoint of the Scotch moralists since Hutcheson. But neither benevolence nor Shaftesbury's moral sense, which is characterized as the embryonic unity of moral taste and feeling before reflection, is specific enough. True, the moral culture of woman must be based directly upon this factor, but the depth of her ethical character has been overrated. The deepest motives rarely come to the surface even in man. The moral element is a complex of many elements, which Hartmann proceeds to characterize. Moral self-feeling is a commendable pride and dignity. Ethical man cannot think too highly of himself. But, so far from despising or loving to humiliate others, he respects them, according to the Kantian precept, as *self-ends.* He is never proud of works, or achievements, virtue or wealth, or even divine grace in the heart, or anything from which any members of humanity are excluded. This noble pride is always grounded on an "inner possibility of moral personality" which is open to all. It is not inconsistent with self-reproach, but is justly shy of exposing imperfections to others. It is independent, autonomous and inconsistent with the "humility of heteronomy" taught by Christian ethics. The Stoics, and especially Fichte, are its best illustrations. This, however, is an imperfect principle. Its warmth and mildness are inward, and the character grows externally cold and perhaps rough and severe. A broader standpoint is reached when we contemplate the natural depression which follows a wrong or the exaltation after a right action. This after-feeling may be merely intellectual, resulting from a right or wrong judgment, as a good or bad investment, a proven or disproven theory, etc.; or it may be "characterological," resulting from the conflict of two instincts, as in a maiden's choice between the will of her parents and of her wooer, or in the case of swallows, who must refuse to migrate with their fellows or leave their belated and callow young to perish. These are selfish impulses not necessarily moral, although they may become so by a special accident. The church has greatly emphasized the importance of regret for the irrevocable past, and even made the depth of this feeling a measure of the strength of the moral principle. It is, however, wholly bad, save in penitentiaries and among people who have developed no moral autonomy. It depresses the individual's ethical self-trust, and, in a word, demoralizes and throws him into the hands of the priests (in the confessional), and indirectly encourages him to commit secret sins, because God comes to seem more appeasable than men. Yet it cannot be said, with Spinoza, that purely rational reflection is enough. Reactive feelings, e. g., are practically inexpugnable from the moral budget. The instinct of retaliation which was once expressed in the law of equivalence—eye for eye, blood for blood, etc.—still inclines the masses to conceive state punishment as revenge, instead of a mere "prophylactic" against future wrong doing. No penalty should ever be inflicted because a law has been broken, but that laws may not be broken again. Protection of the community, not reformation of the criminal, is its object. So, too, the opposite feeling of gratitude should be restricted to a narrow sphere. The motive of every reward is that good may again be done. Anything more leads to unjust preferences, nepotism, and every species of corruption. To forgive a wrong, harmless save to the doer, and to be indifferent to a favor helpful only to one, is, however, impossible. The social instinct is almost as ineradicable as the opposite instinct of self-preservation. Instead of being, according to Grotius, the ground of legality, it is better regarded as the mediator between egoism and the true moral instincts. Isolation produces pathological conditions sometimes even in animals, but the elimination of all social inequalities would degrade and destroy even animal society. The social

instinct is specialized in sympathy, historically one of the
first feelings of social life, which is defined as a passive
reaction on the passive feelings of others. Susceptibility
to this sentiment is very fluctuating. It never impels to
acts of great magnanimity, it is suppressed by every great
idea or strong passion, as in war, and at best it has to do
only with the sufferings and never with the rights of individuals. Schopenhauer erred in asserting that love for
one's fellow men was pity, which he made the only motive
to acts of moral worth. True, every motive from its very
concept and name must appeal to our own weal or woe,
but the high moral value of sympathy springs from its
exorcism of the egoistic elements, though it must ever remain in a sense subsidiary and imperfect. Piety is "the
feeling we experience toward persons whose ethical character we respect." It is the "noblest bond between men"
and strongest defense of a strong character. The desire
to attain it is one of the deepest and best moral motives.
Toward parents, pastors, and the dead, *e. g.*, it is a free
and spontaneous rendering of homage which casts out jeal-
ousy, makes us forget small failings, and worship the autonomous character and actions of a hero from no extraneous motive. It is an invaluable propadeutic principle
and he who is too vulgarly democratic to feel it is lost
morally. The instinct of loyalty implies trust in the constancy of its object. This peculiarly German virtue, illustrated by stories of Penelope, Gudrun, Griselda, etc., may
be exercised toward law, profession, party, customs, or country as well as toward individuals. It is also expressed in
the covenant by which the Jews were bound to Jehovah
and the Christian to Christ; but a vow, oath, or promise
can be at best only the emphatic expression of a matured
intention which may change. Love, the unity of the preceding elements, is true to its object though false to all
things else. The ego perishes, all conflict and all disagreement are impossible. In perfect love the "all-unity-feeling,

which flickers in pity, burns with a bright and steady flame.'' To it belong all the predicates of the Pauline charity. It suffers long, believes all things, hopes all things, never dies, etc. It is an identity feeling in which all longing and discontent are forever satisfied. But it is apt to remain specific and individual, and even if it be deepened and broadened it is still vague and indefinite, hence the need of an absolute yet explicit imperative sense of duty. This sense, whether opposed to, coinciding, or at-oned with natural desire, is always in itself an inclination, to which it can never, as Kant thought, be absolutely opposed. Yet because there are conflicts, the state of innocency, instead of being morally highest, is lowest, and the ethical consciousness must be developed to the utmost, while the absolute harmony between duty and desire remains an unattained ideal. Moreover, duty is a contentless, merely formal sense of obligation to which knowledge must come to give substance. Like each of the previous principles it has a moral value not by its own right, but only in so far as it unconsciously serves an end. To become, however, truly moral it must be rationalized. Taste and feeling are particular and concrete, and the higher principle of (3) rational morality, which is more general and abstract, is unfolded. Rationality, like all else in consciousness, *e. g.*, taste and feeling, is an instinct emerging from an unconscious background, which, by its own automatic law, it gradually illuminates. As *practical reason* it imposes its imperative form, as yet unreasoned, upon previously alogical thoughts and actions. Yet it is not mere form, as Kant argued, but is itself as much product and material of subjective experience as anything else in consciousness. The field of its application is the understanding, which is the individual element. Moral truth is the practical reason's knowledge of itself, at first erroneous and imperfect. Every action is essentially a logical proposition in the truth or falsity of which lies the rightness or wrongness of the act, and to judge of the latter, the proposition must be explicitly stated as such. To do this, again, is an innate instinct, but it requires courage. Universal falsity, the natural defense of the weak, would destroy all human society, the conventionalities of which, coupled with those of political, mercantile, and religious life, have wrapped the modern world in a network of mutual flattery, hypocrisy, and deceit, which more than offsets the *éclaircissement* of science. This condition, however, is transient. The principle of freedom is negative and, abstractly considered, is not a demand of reason, which is concerned only with the form and degree of each concrete case of constraint. In every department of life, save religion alone, compulsion is necessary. Unlimited freedom is the state of nature and every tendency toward it is retrogression. What all men need is a rational tyranny, if it only hold them to a steady development, according to the laws of their own nature. Progress in the world-process consists in growth in the consciousness of necessity, as an inner law, which must be obeyed, as Hegel said, freely. Again, all development is by differentiation of extensive and intensive inequality.

All the above may also be said of inner freedom, which has no value in itself but only for the ends it makes possible. The *liberum arbitrium indifferentiæ,* like the problems of perpetual motion, or the quadrature of the circle, is practically impossible, and freedom is not a matter of theory or of æsthetics. The "cultus of arbitrariness," best illustrated, *e. g.,* in Schlegel's misuse of the Fichtean principle of the sovereignty of the ego, is the nearest possible approach to indeterminism. "There must be no pathological disturbance of the normal physiological process of the genesis of the act of willing." This gives occasion for an extended discussion on the nature of individual and especially conscious responsibility as affected by insanity, intoxication, vicious habits, and passions, delusions of the senses, the constraint of egoism, external authority, excessive feeling, and even sleepiness, of all, in short, which interferes with self-control. Indeterminism is irreconcilable with any rational conception of the world as governed by law and of moral life as conditioned by duties, instincts, and desires, and is never based on direct subjective experience. The transcendental principle of freedom is negatively independent of the individual character on account of its intrinsic determination, and positively it is the asiety of the individual with respect to his own essence. Kant, and especially Schopenhauer, who held causality to be the universal law of all thought and being, sought to relegate freedom from *operari* to *esse*, the former by the well-known distinction between the intelligible and the empirical character, and the latter by asserting an identity between the thing in itself of individuality and the intelligible character. Hartmann, however, declares that indeterminate freedom is not only irreconcilable with the fundamental conditions of the moral life, but is impossible and logically inconceivable in every phenomenal sphere. It is possible only for the absolute will. Schelling's self-positing of the ego is conceived by him not as a free transcendental act of choice, but as a sort of contradiction. If Divine Grace is accepted by an act of choice, it is all a free and natural development of the individual function. If it is something which takes possession of the soul unbidden, it destroys the possibility of a free act. To determine the rational distribution of non-freedom and non-equality in the world we must introduce the principle of order "as the first distinct tenable form of rational morality." Harmony, which is the law, and custom, which is the product of this new element, make progress possible and safe. Justice is the "later and more specific deposit of custom," and its development is a continuous conflict between what was and what will be rational. Against striving egoism right must appear might, but only for help to dispense with might.

There is no natural right save as an unconscious instinct which cannot be formulated, but is inadequately expressed in codes, constitutions, etc. Schopenhauer held that wrong is positive and right is primitively negative, and its commands are prohibitions. This is, however, only superficial and accidental, due to man's proneness to evil. The essential thing in law, as in duty, is positive, *e. g.*, to pay taxes, educate children, testify in courts, etc. Rightness is made a predicate of actions; and justice, which must always be *de lege lata*, never *de lege ferenda*, is, in turn, a predicate of judicial decision. Yet literal and absolute justice is unjust and must be discreetly tempered with mercy. This is the feminine element, which is always prone to respect persons to the neglect of legality, principle and even honesty. The higher standpoint thus introduced is equity. Recognizing that *summum jus* may be *summa injuria*, it takes account of palliating circumstances. This is the highest of all moral duties—*noblesse oblige*. It is not mere womanly kindness of heart, still less is it indifference to right. This, of course, leads to the discussion of *moral ends*, the ultimate question for all rational morality. This chapter is an earnest plea for the author's familiar teleological conception of the universe which he applies to ethics by urging that the individual is not an end in nature, but is subordinate, relative, and even insignificant, as witness the premature perishing of all but a very few fittest cells, germs, embryos, young animals, etc., in the world. Nor can the sum of individual self-ends collectively be, as Kant thought, the final end of the moral world. Even these are subordinate in the nth degree to the all-embracing but unfathomable ends of the Absolute. Means can never be sanctified by ends, because all things are both ends and means, save that ''far off divine event'' toward which the world is moving, and which is too remote and too inscrutable to be materially served by any of the feeble offices of consciousness. The higher egoism is thus

222

bankrupt and the ethical soul turns to altruistic social ends.

Under (b) the three *Objective Aims or Ends of the Ethico-moral Principle* are considered. First, the aim of social eudæmonism, or of collective well-being, best represented, we are told, by Mill's essay on "Utilitarianism," is discussed. The greatest enjoyment for the greatest number would be increased by the decay of culture, which is the chief enemy of general happiness. If admitted as a principle it would lead to mediocrity, commonplace comforts, belief in whatever was most agreeable or convenient, and, in short, to universal reanimalization. Public and private weal, individual and general happiness, instead of being in any sense the same, are antagonistic at every point, and we are almost encouraged to ask whether Mill was not guilty of a pious fraud in telling us that the happiness of other people is identical with our own. Social democracy, which takes the principle in earnest, is animated by what Hartmann in the "Philosophy of the Unconscious" has designated as the third or materialistic stage of optimistic illusion, viz., the hope of positive ultimate happiness for mankind on this earth. It takes no account of the metaphysical unity of the race. Imaginary satisfaction and real barbarity reconciled by Jesuitism would be the result. The present party conflict in Germany is thus essentially ethical. A higher moral principle is that of the evolution of culture. The quest for happiness now appears as it really is, viz., as a means of developing culture. This is the *raison d'être* of humanity. As individual enjoyment must be often surrendered for the weal of the community, so the happiness of any given society or generation must be subordinated to the future welfare of the race. Upon this new "philosophy of progress," which it is urged is the only solid basis for any ethical system, Hartmann lays great stress. From it the socialist may learn respect for historical continuity while it widens the horizon of the conscience and goes far to elevate it to the rank of a truly philosophical faculty. In fact, every science of nature or of mind has now become only history. True, the culture of a high civilization necessarily produces misery, poverty and vandalism. It tends to the precocious cephalization of children, excuses competition and even war —but this is well, inasmuch as it is only the most vigorous and virtuous, and, above all, the most intelligent who survive and inherit the earth. The best minds are now turned to the highest problem of thought, viz., the philosophy of history, understood in the widest sense as the genesis of things and the apotheosis of the teleological order. Here appears the principle of a moral world order, in which alone social eudæmonism and culture can be to some extent harmonized. Objective moral principles, as the now at last partially known ends of the world, must be made individual motives or they are unconstraining and foreign, and our purposes must be identified with the purpose of the world or they have no significance. Only as we freely surrender private happiness or any lower end for the welfare of higher ends do our acts become *monumenta* in the absolute teleology with which our own essence is now not merely actually, but consciously identical. We not only know but autonomously will to follow non-egoistic absolute ends as essentially our own. Only so far as we accept its unconscious ends as our own, can we develop the full consciousness that our will is but a branch of the all-will, whose life process is the order of cosmic development. Evil is too radical in the world and in man to be either explained or overcome save by the introduction of a transcendent principle. Hence we are brought finally to consider (c).

(C) *The primal and absolute foundations of morality.* These are detailed at length as (1) the monistic principle of essential identity of all individuals, most instinctive in love, most conscious in deliberate self-renunciation; (2) the religious principle of identity with the absolute, where perfect duty and pure religion are seen to be at one; (3) the absolute principle of teleology as our own essence wherein all historic and metaphysico-monistic tendencies are synthesized; and (4) the principle of redemption as negative absolute eudæmonism. Under the last head he urges that if the notion of an Absolute, or of God, is to have any value as an hypothesis, we must conceive him as unhappy before the beginning of things. The final cause of creation was not, as Hegel believed, a self-mirroring of the Absolute. The unfolding of the universe is rather a pathological healing process which goes on within the Absolute. The universe is a "plaster to draw its inner pain outward." The positive transcendental happiness of God before creation is purely mythic. The divine complacency which pronounced all that was made "very good" expressed no positive joy or satisfaction, but only an amelioration of an inner woe. Cultured piety sees that pity, not love, for God is man's highest duty. The emancipation of the Absolute from its transcendent unhappiness may never be complete. New generations, races, worlds may ever perpetuate the immanent torture, nearing only by asymptotic approaches an equilibrium between universal pleasure and pain. But we must never forget that the world and the Absolute must be redeemed, if at all, together. God can redeem the world only by being redeemed by it. Only the phenomenally selfish individual, who seeks pleasure, fancies that he can find release from the duty of universal coöperation in death, which he is too puny-souled to seek. All the elect understand that the supreme duty of redeeming God from pain, or of "ameliorating the negative eudæmonism of the Absolute" is a duty which will end only with the universe itself. The work closes with the sentence: "Real existence is the incarnation of deity; the world process is the passion-history of God made flesh, and at the same time is the way to the redemption of him who was satisfied in the flesh. To be moral is to lend a

225

helping hand in shortening this way of suffering and of redemption.''

This work exhibits a broader and more philosophical plan of treatment than is found in any modern ethical text-book, even if the author's critical and analytical power does not justify its pretentious title. His transitions are often forced and artificial, his spirit is more dogmatic and often scarcely less mystic than in his earlier writings, while the book, though expressly addressed to lay readers, is far less simple in style. It is impossible to escape the conviction, either in perusing his works or in personal intercourse with the man, that his characteristic positions are matters of feeling and temperament even more than with Lotze. The latter expressly says to the reader, ''I offer you my most matured reflections not because I know or can teach you anything, but because I am in ignorance and in doubt like you, and deem it the highest duty of each thoughtful man to do what he can to clear up some doubt, lighten some oppressed heart, and heighten æsthetic pleasure in order that by standing in the nearest and most sacred personal (*i. e.*, speculative) relations to each other we may forget for the time being the oppression of nescience, although we are able to solve no problem—which, indeed, no individual but only an age is in any degree able to do.'' Hartmann, on the other hand, seems to consider his system a letter-patent by which the truth of the universe is made in some sense his monopoly. He elaborates with hyper-subtle refinement minute differentiæ between his system and the views of Kant, Hegel, Schopenhauer, etc., and yet always with a messianic air as though it were praise enough for these men to play the rôle of prophets, dimly and unconsciously heralding the full dispensation of his new gospel. The old philosophic evolutionism is the bottom motive of all his works. In his boyish period (''Philosophy of the Unconscious'') this was uncritically fused with Schelling's philosophy of a world soul. Matter is ''extinct mind,'' ''organic and inorganic nature reciprocally determining each other," "the ideality of conscious and unconscious activity," "history as the self-revelation of the absolute," "matter as the sleeping vegetable and this as sleeping animal life." The organization of the world-being is inner evolution following the law of potencies, all strictly teleological. Each of these conceptions is rehabilitated by simply grouping about each stage a very readable array of biological and other facts. In this work Hegel's immanent logical development is very unsatisfactorily applied to the most complex questions of human life.

We cannot quite agree with Drews, the leader of the Hartmann revival, that his religious work is his best contribution, insightful and stimulating though that is. We should place his developmental history of ethics on a higher plane. This, supplemented as it should be by Sutherland's "Origin and Growth of the Moral Instinct" (London, 1898), represents the advent of geneticism into the domain of ethics. Together they are the highwater mark of scientific thinking along this line and are hardly less epoch-making here than the work of C. F. Baur was for Christianity. Henceforth the moral instinct itself and all theories concerning its nature must be considered as the product of evolution and treated accordingly, rather than by the old way of introspection and dogmatism. Morals will gain far more than it loses by this change of viewpoint.

Hartmann was an avatar of the mighty spirit of German idealism, which, after several decades of oblivion in musty tomes and unfrequented lecture rooms, suddenly reappears in the daylight of modern science and challenges the culture and methods of the present in the name of those of the past. It is often said that only Hartmann's pessimism will survive him, but this we are compelled to consider a gloomy poem by a sensitive æsthetic soul whom fame does not comfort for personal misfortune or even for the ills of life. To answer him one must go up and down throughout the whole intellectual world and tediously tear off the labels, "Unconscious" and "Pessimistic," which he has pasted on most of the prominent facts of history, science, and literature; in other words, one must write several thousand pages, like him. Such a one who has once read him and felt the satisfaction not usually awaiting those who turn the last leaf of a philosophical work, viz., of finishing and understanding all the author thinks through and through, would be least of all disposed to attempt it. He is so superficial and so uncritical, quoting Baumgärtner, who discusses with great array of scientific learning the question whether Adam had a navel, whether the first man lived in water, etc., undiscriminatingly along with Helmholtz and Wundt, that the farther we read the more harmless do his extravaganzas seem. His pessimism calls attention irresistibly to himself. In spite of his sensitive protests, it is impossible at times for a critic, despite the kindliest personal feelings, to regard him otherwise than as a psycho-pathological problem, and to ask what physiological or other reason will explain why an autocratic and vigorous young soldier, suddenly robbed of his career, his associations, his personal comeliness, his fortune and largely, even, of the use of his muscles—those most faithful servants of the will—living in retirement with a wife sensitive, cultivated, and invalid like himself, should find satisfaction in believing and teaching that all happiness is born of ignorance and that the Deity is in need of human pity and help? We have no present wish to discuss this problem, but Herr v. Hartmann should at least not have forgotten, when he told the complacent world that it is miserable in spite of fancied happiness, that it would be apt, before accepting his pessimistic gospel, to ask most searchingly if the unhappiness which he fancied is or should be universal was not really his own?

Hartmann has of late been taken more seriously, especially since his death. Since Descartes consciousness has been accepted as the supreme oracle in philosophy, and when this young unknown outsider challenged its authority and proposed the opposite principle, the Unconscious, for the place consciousness had so long occupied, it seemed like proposing to erect an altar to an unknown god. Professordom was aghast, and no one either accepted or understood it. The Unconscious was derided as a negative adjective used as if it were a positive noun. It was called a metaphysical and poetic fiction, a verbal fetich, at best, as we saw above, a new avatar of Spinoza's substance, Fichte's ego, Hegel's idea, Schopenhauer's will, an apotheosis of the unknowable, etc. Only after his death did Arthur Drews (whose book arguing that no such person as Jesus ever lived lately set the German theological world agog) urge that this first product of Hartmann's genius marked a third epoch in philosophy, one distinctly comparable with those of Plato and Descartes, the founder of the consciousness philosophy. German idealism had identified consciousness and reality. This Hartmann denied and sought to identify reality with unconsciousness, thus making reality unknown and consciousness only phenomenal. All attempts to attain apodeictic knowledge of reality itself are abortive, for reality is forever at bottom essentially uncognizable and unconscious. All so-called certain knowledge of Nature or mind is really only hypothetical. It was the wish for certainty that made rationalism and deduction, and only when we see that such cataleptic conviction as idealism has sought is unattainable is the field for induction open. Now philosophy can call science to its aid and can go beyond it as he expressed in his "Speculative results by inductive natural history methods." On the other hand, science hesitated to respond to his call to use its results as a springboard to a higher appreciation of reality. But if reality does not inhere in us and can never be got from consciousness, there remains the question—does it exist and, if so, where? This he calls the basal problem of epistemology.

229

Whether we regard consciousness as content or form, as individual or absolute, or as consciousness *überhaupt* (Windelband und Rehmke), or as pure experience with Avenarius, it can give us no reality, but always points beyond itself. In later writings (On Kant's Theory of Knowledge and his History of Metaphysics) Hartmann pointed out the absurd propositions, the preposterous methods, nomenclature, and contradictory conclusions of Kant, whom no writer seems to have so bitterly antagonized or so carefully to have studied (Cohen, Veihinger, and the Kant philologues). Only in the last ten to fifteen years, while the Kant cult has so rapidly declined, have the significance and value of this trenchant and destructive criticism of Hartmann's, which fell dead from the press in the day it appeared, been felt. Now the new admirers of Hartmann are saying that he overthrew Kant a quarter of a century ago, and that it was he who put an end to the long Kant-enchantment of Germany, although, like the foes of Cock Robin, others, too, claim to have killed it. To Hartmann, Kant was only an apostle of confusion, the evil genius of modern philosophy, who brought obfuscation and delayed progress and whom he used to speak of in social converse as *der alte Confusionsrath*. Since categories are not functions of consciousness, their applicability beyond experience need not be denied. Now cause is the chief bridge from immanence to transcendence and over it we can reach the *Ding-an-sich*. Thus his system is in this sense transcendental as opposed to both ideal and naïve realism. Kant was really naïve in saying that concepts are objects. Our thoughts, feelings, acts of will as given do not reveal ourselves any more than the senses do the ipsissimal nature of things. They only show us how we appear. Hence no experience can possibly be immediate. That it can be so is a fiction on which Wundt has built his entire psychology and metaphysics. Consciousness is only a set of impressions or even sensations. Knowledge is only a "logicization" of experience by means of unconscious intellectual functions. Consciousness brings only the passive condition for the operation of these functions and is not a real subject functioning apodeictically. The Unconscious is so to itself as well as to us. It is the bearer of consciousness and is, in fact, reality. Things in themselves are the causes of sensation and of consciousness and are the atoms, and the energies of the physiological principles of life, a position which he developed later in his "Views of Physics and of Life."

The energetics of Ostwald and Mach, who hold that the efficiency of nature expresses itself in mechanical, chemical, optical, electrical, and other ways, he rejects, because it makes these qualities, which are merely in consciousness, objective. He prefers the original view of Clausius and Helmholtz and Thompson, that all energies are summations of variously composed mechanical and molecular energies, regarding matter as the center of energies, as a system of central atomic forces. This he calls his dynamism.

As early as 1873, he had urged that life adds no autonomous principle to the mechanics of energies and he took great satisfaction in his later life in having this principle of an inner developmental nisus held as the first expression of neo-Darwinism and neo-vitalism. Force and will are expressions of the same Unconscious, one without and one within. Without will, we can not know force. Feeling is the limitation or inhibition of will and so is commonly painful, and here consciousness arises. Its feeling is directly as its intensity. Nature and consciousness are related as active and passive. So motion and consciousness coincide. Just as atoms are compounded into bodies and cells into plants and animals, so, and by the same unconscious power, atomic feelings are built up into the individual consciousness. The psyche is only one expression of Nature's impulse to organize.

The new psychology was just isolating itself from philosophy and metaphysics and setting up for itself and so becoming purely and solely a consciousness psychology, when Hartmann, like Carus, Fortlage, and J. H. Fichte, insisted that the cause of consciousness lay in the Unconscious. The consciousness psychology that ignores this, according to Hartmann's phrases, is caught in a cage, has castrated itself, cut its own tap-root, is going up a blind alley, etc. No mechanism of the content of consciousness or association, no spiritistic assumption of a real soul *per se* and a Nature neurologically approached can give us the true psyche. Modern psychologism, with its laboratory empiricism called introspection, is essentially bankrupt—if its books were balanced—and impotent. Hartmann's "Modern Psychology" is not even mentioned by Wundt in his *Festschrift* contributions to Kuno Fischer, wherein he prints the titles of all the psychological literature of the preceding twenty years.

Consciousness rests on three kinds of Unconscious: (a) Physiological (molecular dispositions of the nervous system, mediate and reflexes); (b) relative, or psychic processes unknown to the central consciousness but penetrable to a local peripheral consciousness of a lower order; and (c) the absolute Unconscious, or the immaterial like life and soul *per se*. Out of these consciousness is composed. Mœbius' "Hopelessness of Psychology" (1907) also says there is no way out but to recognize the Unconscious, even if it be only dynamic, and that to consider it as metaphysical only adds to the personal hopelessness of it all. The work of Breuer and Freud and his school, which Hartmann did not know, or at least never evaluated, are in his sense and have contributed to the present Hartmann revival. Drews says that he makes consciousness "a passive reflex of the inhibited activation of the Unconscious," and if this is pathological, it is far less so than the results of the Freudian wish-repressions. The will is checked from without or within. Hence our nodes of collisions or acts of will we call sensations, which are not like Fichte's objects or non-egos, to which the feeling subject is posited by the will, but to which the feeling subject is passive. These reaction feelings are synthetized. To them the intellect contributes ever more as we ascend the scale of psychic life where activity increases and passivity declines, and so consciousness grows and accomplishes no less marvels than other views ascribe to it. But conscious soul is not primary but derived, and we must either ignore its relation to the body or accept some such mediation between material and psychic as his synthesis. We must adjust between Lotze's interaction and Fechner's parallelism. Hartmann identified soul and vital principle, and so far is an interactionist, yet the Lotzians, he thought, are wrong in deeming interaction immediate and in giving consciousness the active rôle. The parallelists he. deems right in denying immediate interaction and the activity of consciousness, but wrong in ignoring a third unconscious action on both sides, and in not seeing the mediation involved in all interaction. For him causality works both ways. Consciousness is not passive because it is a product of arrest, but action on being externally checked is only turned inward and may become conscious. All activity is in itself unconscious and consciousness can only determine its time and direction. Drews says that, so long as we identify consciousness and being, parallelism and interaction are matters of taste. If consciousness is a real, active substratum, why deny its power to act on the organism and vice versa, while, if it is only a passive reflex of material functions, how can it have a function of its own? These views Hartmann mediated, somewhat as Kant did between preëstablished harmony and the theory of physical influx.

As for metaphysics, will and concept are one and inseparable, save by abstraction. In the Unconscious both are united. This is the synthesis of pan-logism and pan-thelism, or of Hegel and Schopenhauer. One cares for the *what,* the other for the *that* of existence. This is both monistic and dualistic. Wundt makes the concept inherent in the will and subordinate to it, but for Hartmann it is a step backward to subsume either one or the other, for each can be known only through the other and the logical and the alogical must coincide. The reverse of Wundt's position is the subjection of the will to the concept, as in gnosticism, with which Hartmann has often been charged. To this he has less objection. His metaphysics seek to unite concrete monism and idealism into ideal realism, for will and concept are attributes of the same absolute substance. This makes him the first pantheist who could accept real evolution with beginning, goal, and end. Will can pass through series of stages and return to its original state of potentialities. The end is an act of consciousness, intelligence determining the will, as in the oriental philosophy of renunciation. Consciousness is the highest immanent end of the world, the transcendental absolute goal. When this is attained, will has no more to do. Knowledge is unrest, and when it is accomplished and complete will sinks to peace, for knowledge is adequate. These eschatological views of his youthful first edition were largely modified later, but he is still judged by their crude first form in all the histories of philosophy that mention him.

His theory of categories is called the most unique since Hegel. He classifies them as those of consciousness, of objects, and of metaphysics. Least objected to is his doctrine of worths. Here he deals with pleasure and pain, and is a frank eudæmonologist and not a pessimist. He is generally regarded as a mere disciple of Schopenhauer, but he really far transcends him. He only condemns the shallow affirmation of the will to live. The world is for him neither worse than none, as Schopenhauer thought, nor is it the best of all possible worlds, as with Leibniz. All progress involves a negative judgment concerning both the past and present. Reason and consciousness always say that blind will is improvable. So he seeks to join eudæmonological pessimism with evolutionary optimism. In his later ethical and religious writings pessimism becomes an ever weaker factor. He held to the prepotence of pain over pleasure, but in the interests of morals and of piety. Kant's pessimism was mundane and his optimism transcendent. Hartmann emphasized pain here and abhorred the idea of transcendental pleasures as rewards of virtue. Neither these nor heteronomous authority could produce true morality. Both have their place, but only for childhood. What he sought was to curb individualism with abandon. This meant unbridled and unscrupulous selfishness and self-indulgence. He condemned Sterner's maximization of the ego, and he also feared the principle of the greatest good for the greatest number as leading to social democracy. All these expressions of the irrational will he would check by admitting pain as a large ingredient in the normal lot of man. As opposed to the then current tendency to give morals their own independent basis, he held them to be absolutely dependent upon metaphysical and religious views of the world.

His "Letters on the Christian Religion" appeared during the War of 1870, and under the pseudonym F. H. Miller, and so they attracted little attention until his final revision of them in 1905 under the title of "The Christianity of the New Testament." This was met by a painful conspiracy of silence, for he said that religionists are unable to meet the present crisis. All his bitter polemic was not in hate but in love for the interests of true religion, as we have seen.

In his 800-page "History of German Æthetics since Kant," and in his "Philosophy of the Beautiful" and various essays, Hartmann has developed a somewhat unique viewpoint. Beauty is always phenomenal. It is the appearance of the true *Ding-an-sich*, and has ideal reality immediately behind it. Thus a work of art is the truest of all phenomena, for it best represents metaphysical reality. It must also make an entirely disinterested appeal to the observer. Æsthetic feeling is distinct from ordinary feeling in that it is more generic and less bound down to the concrete and individual. It brings a unique identity between the soul and the noumenal entity it stands for. The illusion transports us to the ideal world of beauty in which the soul delights to bathe and revel, for here supreme pleasure is found and the soul is satisfied, having reached its own true home. Beauty has many grades, and historically for the most part it has progressed up the scale of the æsthetic values. It bottoms upon the logical ideal of purpose in nature and culminates when the Unconscious in the artist utters itself irresistibly and spontaneously, and reveals to the onlooker the highest stages of perfection in the human domain or in Nature when supremely anthropomorphized. The artist thus finishes what the whole evolutionary momentum which is behind him has become and he carries it still higher. His work must be naïve and as unforced as the song of birds. If he plans his effects consciously we are repelled, for we want to see the inmost core of his own soul so as to get the exquisite feeling that human nature, as he reveals it, is sound as well as productive. His production is, in a sense, a superfluity, like the excess of vitality which prompts play. Thus Hartmann has sought a synthesis of the concepts of very diverse writers and schools. From Kant he borrowed disinterestedness; from Hegel, the logical idea of which art is the apotheosis; from Schopenhauer, the identification of subject and object in artistic contemplation; from Groos and Spencer, the play motif. And these elements, which he takes great pains to knit together logically, are further enriched by suggestions from Fechner, Köstien, Fischer, and many others, so that the unity he thinks he attains is not so much that of an immanent development of sequence stages (such as evidently is his ideal in his history of ethical stages) as a finished whole into which all historic factors have been incorporated. A work of art is more generic than actual objects in nature without becoming abstract, for, as it leaves the concrete, it gains more enrichment from the idea it embodies than it loses in departing from actual fact.

While his religious views are now attracting great attention, his æsthetics is still partly unknown even in his own land. Psychological æsthetics is somewhat advancing now in the universities, but his mediation between the speculative classics of idealism and modern empiricism has met with little favor. His view, however, is free and wide, combining Volkelt's "significance for man" and Lipps' "personality in life," yet especially opposing subjectivists and individualists. A work of art embodies a supersensible idea. So far he is with Hegel. For both æsthetics is an integral factor and therefore is of cosmic significance. This principle he carries through in great detail.

Through most of his writings runs a polemic vein, and he has defined his position with about all the chief thinkers of his time in Germany. He is always making more precise the positions of his earlier writings and sometimes modifying them, so that it is sometimes hard to see his final views. His polemic view, however, always has a positive goal, so he is about the very best of the modern philosophical critics. He discusses about every current question, generally with kindness, insight and clearness. His system is the most comprehensive of that of any one since Hegel. He has a clear and consistent *Weltanschauung*. In his countless essays he discusses the widest range of topics, often those of only current interest. Living in great isolation he, perhaps for this reason, had a passion for keeping in touch with all the great movements of his day and for establishing personal relations with the most diverse men and movements. He wished to bring his philosophy to bear, although he partially failed, if, indeed, he did not repel, by abstruse views and expressions not intelligible to the masses. Still Drews says he might have been a leading journalist or *feuilletonist*. He wrote for the weekly and even daily press on education, the Jews, feminism, fashions, spiritism, the German duel, taxes, suffrage, teetotalers, music, drama, social, religious, and political questions. He even reported.

Hartmann's proof of the eccentric, penumbral, peripheral, marginal nature of consciousness makes him a modern Copernicus. The erection of the Unconscious as a world principle marks the great revolution of views since the Renaissance, which was its prelude, in emancipating the world from the views of the past. Not those thinkers who throw over all metaphysics and speculation and base everything upon empiricism, but men like Hartmann, are true representatives of the modern spirit, for he conserves rather than ignores the best in the past. He is too high and too hard for most to read and understand. He is not a stylist, but his words are remarkably fit and adequate for his thought. He is very synthetic, often very technical, and feels free to use foreign words. He scorns to be merely interesting or popular. Neither his learning nor his writings attracted much attention, and he died in comparative obscurity, like Spinoza. Professor Stern at Berno pronounced an eulogy and so did Lasson in the little philosophical club of Berlin, but few academic people attended.

He was a product of the very best tendencies of German philosophic tradition, but lived amid the rank revival of naturalism, materialism, indifference, and skepticism that attended and followed the German War of 1870, when applied science and politics attracted the chief attention. He sought to save philosophy and to perpetuate it, that its traditions of 2,000 years be not lost. He refused a professorship on account of both health and the limitation to freedom, and well he did. Reinke's "Welt als That" is about as near Hartmannism as could anyone's be who did not know him. Modern empirical psychology Hartmann thought sustained by outer power and usefulness, not by its own inner worth and light. If we ever have a new idealism in the world again, it will be somewhat along the lines of Hartmann's Unconscious.

Hartmann's chief significance lies in his advocacy of the Unconscious and his opposition to the "consciousness philosophies," which have been in academic vogue ever since Descartes. He saw more clearly than did even Comte (who rejected psychology in his hierarchy of sciences because of the fallacies inherent in introspection) their fallacies. To him, even more than to Lotze or even Fechner, Kant was the arch sophist, the Protagoras of modern times, because he taught distrust of the senses, which alone can give us true reality. Only observation and induction can supply the foundations of science and of philosophy as well. It was from their action and data that he inferred an unconscious teleology that pervaded all nature. In conformity to this view he sought to reinterpret epistemology, logic, metaphysics, and even æsthetics. If everything that shows design in the world is a product of instinct, and if all progress is measured by intellectualizing all aspects of nature, life and mind in their stages of evolving up to *Für-sich-sein*, until mind becomes adequate to nature, the process, though painful and inevitable, is ameliorative. Noetics and energetics should and will ultimately be equated, because only thus does the world find surcease from pain. Thus, for him the sadness and suffering in the world do not lead to quietism or oriental resignation, but are the chief spur to push on to nature and subdue the blind forces of the world and of the soul. To know is to completely envisage, and the norm for knowledge is the intuition of things as they are in Nature and not the construction of the objective by the subjective. Thus we start from sense and not from consciousness, and the former supplies the norm for the latter and not conversely. The great World-Form, or Autos, does not need eyes or consciousness to always do the one and only right thing. It would be less creative if it had them. Its inherency is due to its unconsciousness, and so with the best things in the life of man. But man is unhappy and out of the travail of his dis-ease-ment the noetic impulse is born and he evolves consciousness and science just as the Absolute did the world in order to ease his inner woe, or as a sinner extradites guilt or a Freudian patient an inner trauma by confession. Noesis is only therapy, but is a necessary, a benign palliative. Measured on an absolute scale, no pleasure is positive, but is only the abatement of pain, conscious or unconscious. Only when we know ourselves, not subjectively and introspectively, but objectively, as we do nature, do we redeem ourselves and with ourselves also the Absolute from pain, and thus alone come infinite truth, rest, and peace. The ceaseless, impelling will will cease its striving. The supreme wish, not only of the human race but of the cosmos, will be attained because it will have found its goal and fulfillment. When knowledge is adequate to and equipollent with will, history will end, for man will be a finished being in some superman, whereas he is now incomplete and in the making; and perhaps the most and best history before he attains his final place and poise in the world is yet to be made and written. The equilibrium which man has now lost will then be not only established but stable. Man and his univere will fit each other just as instinct or atomic forces fit their sphere, and thus generations, one like the other, will succeed one another as long as the present world-order lasts. The goal is still far off but every new discovery and law, every subjection of Nature to man's domain, and every new progress in hygiene, every true moral and religious advance contribute something to bring us nearer to it. Art is now largely idealization, and it enraptures us just because it anticipates this great day when it will be an exact photographic reproduction of man when he has attained his ideal in body and soul by a complete harmony with Nature. It now charms us because it is prophecy and suggests a future possibility, but ultimately its highest present form may be transcended, and when we are beyond it will seem reminiscence.

Schelling's positive Philosophie als Einheit von Hegel und Schopenhauer. 63 p.

Dramatische Dichtungen (Pseudonym Karl Robert), 1871. 237 p.

Ueber die dialektische Methode. 1868. 124 p.

Philosophie des Unbewussten. 1869. 11. Aufl. 3 Bde. 1904. 678 p.

Aphorismen über das Drama. 1870. 46 p.

Das Ding an sich und seine Beschaffenheit. 1871. 126 p.

Gesammelte philosophische Abhandlungen zur Philosophie des Unbewussten. 1872. 132 p.

Erläuterungen zur Metaphysik des Unbewussten mit bes. Rücksicht auf den Panlogismus. 1874. 82 p.

Shakespeare's Romeo und Julia. 1875. 38 p.

J. H. v. Kirchmann's erkenntnistheoretische Realismus, ein kritischer Beitrag zur Begründung des transcendental Realismus. 1875. 633 p.

Die Selbstzersetzung des Christentums und die Religion der Zukunft. 1874. 122 p.

Wahrheit und Irrtum im Darwinismus. 1875. 2 Aufl. in Bd. iii der Philosophie des Unbewussten. 1904. 177 p.

Kritische Grundlegung des transcendent. Realismus. 2. erw. Aufl. v. "Das Ding an sich," etc. 1875. 3 Aufl. 1886 in: Ausgew. W. W. 138 p.

Zur Reform des höheren Schulwesens. 1875. 88 p.

Das Unbewusste vom Standpunkt der Psysiologie und Descendenztheorie, 1872. Anonym. 3. Aufl. in Bd. 3 der Philosophie des Unbewussten. 410 p.

Gesammelte Studien und Aufsätze. 1876. 729 p.

Neukantianismus, Schopenhauerianismus u. Hegelianismus in ihrer Stellung zu den philosophischen Aufgaben der Gegenwart, 2. Aufl. der "Erläuterungen zur Metaphysik des Unbewussten," 1877. 362 p.

Phänomenologie des sittlichen Bewusstseins. 1879. 2. Aufl. 1886, in Ausgewahlte Wohlfiele Werke. 871 p.

Zur Geschichte und Begründung des Pessimismus. 1880. 2. erw. Aufl. 1891. 373 p.

Die Krisis des Christentums in der modernen Theologie. 1880. 115 p.

Das religiöse Bewusstsein der Menschheit. 1881. 627 p. Davon der 2. systematische Teil: Die Religion des Geistes. 1882. 2 Aufl. 1907. 328 p.

Philosophische Fragen der Gegenwart. 1885. 278 p.

Des Spiritismus. 1885. 2. Aufl. 1898. 118 p.

Das Judentum in Gegenwart und Zukunft. 1885. 195 p.

Moderne Probleme. 1886. 250 p.

Die deutsche Aesthetik seit Kant. 1886. 112 p.

Die Philosophie des Schönen. 1887. Beide in Ausgewählte Wohlfiele Werke. 836 p.

Lotzes Philosophie, 1888. 183 p.

Zwei Jahrzehnte deutscher Politik und die gegenwärtige Weltage. 1888. 401 p.

Kritische Wanderungen durch die Philosophie der Gegenwart. 1889. 311 p.

Das Grundproblem der Erkenntnistheorie. 1889 (in Ausgewählte Wohlfiele Werke). 127 p.

Die Geisterhypothese des Spiritismus u. seine Phantome. 1891. 126 p.

Kants Erkenntnistheorie und Metaphysik. 1893. 256 p.

Die sozialen Kernfragen. 1894. 571 p.

Tagesfragen. 1896. 286 p.

Kategorienlehre. 1896. 556 p.

Schelling's philosophisches System. 1897. 224 p.

Ethische Studien. 1898. 241 p.

Geschichte der Metaphysik, 2 Bde. 1899-1900.

Zur Zeitgeschichte. 1900. 172 p.

Die moderne Psychologie. 1901. 474 p.

Die Weltanschauung der modernen Physik. 1902. 233 p.

Das Christentum des neuen Testaments, 2. umgearbeitete Aufl. der Briefe über die christliche Religion. 1905. 316 p.

Das problem des Lebens. Biologische Studien. 1906. 440 p.

Alle Werke sind jetzt durch H. Haacke, Verlag, Sachsa i. H. zu erhalten, nachdem früher der Verlag mehrfach gewechselt hat.

HERMANN L. F. VON HELMHOLTZ
1821–1894

HERMANN L. F. VON HELMHOLTZ

HERMANN L. F. VON HELMHOLTZ

1821-1894

Hermann L. F. von Helmholtz was born in Potsdam, Prussia, in 1821. His mother was a direct descendant of William Penn, his father a German gymnasial teacher, and one grandmother a French Huguenot refugee, so that the best French, German, and English blood mingled in his veins. In his early boyhood he was sickly, and his father taught him at home languages and philosophy. He found the classics hard but memorized poetry with amazing facility and at twelve even read Arabic and Latin a little and learned something of Kant and Fichte. At seventeen he left the Potsdam Gymnasium for the University of Berlin, with extraordinary attainments in mathematics and physics. Here he met his life-long friends, Du Bois Reymond, Brücke, and Virchow, and studied under Gustav Magnus and Johannes Müller, the founder of modern physiology, who left the deepest impression upon him. In his doctor's thesis in Latin at the age of twenty-one he discussed the relation between ganglion cells and nerve fibers. From this point his biography is chiefly comprised in his 217 scientific papers, nearly all of which added to the sum of human knowledge. After graduating in medicine he was made an assistant in chemistry in the *Charité* hospital in 1842 and at the new year was appointed military surgeon. In 1848 he became an instructor in anatomy in the art school; in 1849 was called to Königsberg as professor of physiology; in 1855 took the chair of anatomy and physiology at Bonn, and in 1858 that of physics at Heidelberg. In 1871 he came to Berlin as professor of physics at the head of the new and magnificent "temple of physical science," for years, all things considered, the best of its kind in the world.

In 1887 he organized and became first head of the *Physikalisch-Technische Reichsanstalt* in Potsdam, where physical and chemical science were applied to technology, an institution which Lord Kelvin said had conferred unusual advantages upon Germany. In 1893 he visited the Chicago Exposition and saw much of this country. On the voyage home he fell downstairs on the steamer and never completely recovered, dying in 1894 at what Du Bois Reymond called the early age of seventy-three. He was twice married, first at the age of twenty-eight, to a lady who died ten years later leaving two children, a daughter, who married a geologist, and a son, who is a civil engineer. In 1861 he married again a lady of high social station, who made his home the center of a brilliant group of artistic, scientific and literary people, and where I was occasionally invited on Sunday evenings to attend his musicals. She bore two children, a son, Robert, who gave great promise in his father's lines, from the shock of whose early death at the age of thirty-three Helmholtz never fully recovered, and a daughter, who married the head of the great house of von Siemens, makers of electrical instruments and founder of the Reichsanstalt.

Until he went to Berlin Helmholtz had worked in comparatively cramped quarters, with scant provision for apparatus and assistants, but there he found a new "temple of physics," as it was called at its dedication, with perhaps better facilities at that time than existed anywhere else. It is of interest to the higher academic pedagogy to note that not long before this time there was a strong tendency to make the teaching of the sciences almost spectacular. Czermák [1] at Leipzig devoted much of his wife's wealth to

[1] See my Aspects of German Culture. Boston, James R. Osgood & Co., 1881, pp. 109 et seq.

248

building, equipping, and conducting a "physiological theater" devoted to the exposition of what Pick called "The
highest and most fruitful of the collective sciences," although it was burned soon after his untimely death. Du
Bois Reymond, too, perpetuated in some degree this tradition at Berlin, and the same tendency was shown to some
degree in other magnificently illustrated lectures which I
attended, notably those of Kolbe, in chemistry, whose laboratory bore the inscription, "God made the world according to number, weight, and measure." This was also
seen in Kölliker's biological lecture and to some extent in
that of Hitz in anatomy, and also in botany. Czermák's
theater had hundreds of large charts that could be raised
through the bottom of the stage, let down from the top, and
slid in from each side; magic lanterns; magnified scientific
apparatus of every kind. For the preparation of the lecture of each day, there hung behind the scenes a large
chart designating the equipment and several expert assistants devoted their entire time to its preparation. The purpose was to represent every important experiment which
had been made in physiology on a large scale, so that the
results could be seen by all. For demonstration purposes
hundreds of animals, large and small, were sacrificed, and
in one case even a horse was introduced to show heart
action. The auditorium could be darkened by steel slides
or curtains almost on the instant. There were immense
models of the eye, ear, and nervous system and the raised
metallic keys brought currents of various kinds and of the
required strength to the large table of the lecturer, which
was fitted up with all kinds of baths. There were arrangements of lenses and mirrors to show the spectrum, and
steam engines, carbon pencils, etc. The lectures of course
were entirely experimental. The piers of the table went
deep into the ground without contact with the floor in
order to avoid vibrations. This method of course aided
greatly in the popularization of science, and textbooks

were almost useless, even such as the large book of Hermann, except for review. In each lecture was a description of what was actually done and shown, the lecturer sometimes having to be prompted in his rôle of demonstration by his assistants. It is curious to think of the new possibilities in this direction which X-rays and moving pictures, perhaps the greatest didactic invention since printing, now make possible. Many of the great laboratories of the world have since gone beyond this in experiment, but I doubt if teaching anywhere in any subject is now so richly objective. Indeed, as Irving made something of an epoch in staging the great dramas he acted, so the great teachers of this day gave science a royal setting such as perhaps it has never had before or since. It is interesting to contrast with this the simple equipment of Agassiz at Penikese in 1872 on his lonely island with almost no apparatus save a blackboard and chalk, when on the day that school was opened he said, after a brief talk, "I do not feel like praying before you. I do not feel like asking any of you to pray, but let us spend a few moments in silent prayer!"[1] The Cavendish Laboratory of Cambridge, under J. J. Thompson, of course is far better equipped in its own special lines, as to which perhaps F. L. Moore is right[2] in saying "the work done here is comparable in amount to that of all other great laboratories taken together." Agassiz's was a scientific camp meeting and he held that "a laboratory is a sanctuary which nothing profane should enter." After all, the great teacher makes the school as the lives of men like Jowett, Fichte, and others show.

Helmholtz left all such elaborate demonstration and all introductory work to his assistants and himself taught in a small room to a small group of advanced pupils, rarely using any illustrative apparatus or device, but writ-

[1] Louis Agassiz; his Life and Correspondence, by E. C. Agassiz. Boston, Houghton, Mifflin & Co., 1885, vol. 2, p. 766.
[2] Nature, February, 1907.

ing rapidly upon the board complex equations, often leaving wide gaps in his mathematical deductions for his hearers to work out for themselves, and not infrequently discovering errors in his work which had to be erased after his hearers had it all down in their neat pandeses. Unlike his colleague Kerschoff, of spectroscope fame, whose equations were as clearly written and faultless and regular as works of art, he made no special preparation for each lecture, but impressed one throughout as a man far more gifted in discovery than in teaching. In his laboratory, besides the large rooms where many students could do practice work, repeating the standard experiments, there were many smaller ones for advanced students, and in these one by one Helmholtz used to spend some hours a day with the investigators, suggesting new lines, or modes of experiment, repeating, verifying, or controlling the work already done, or perhaps hastily drawing sketches of new apparatus to be made in the shop, or ordering new instruments. In this work he had a habit of thinking out loud and soliloquizing almost as if no one was present. It was marvelous to see how his eye and ear, perhaps the most cultivated organs in modern times, were able to ''do things,'' the readiness, for instance, with which he would distinguish overtones in a vibrating rod or string.

Helmholtz was not exactly a good *Gesellschafter*. He used often in the afternoon to take long walks in the *Tiergarten* alone, where he might be seen strolling almost aimlessly or sitting on a bench, perhaps making notes. He was an excellent pianist himself, and in youth something of a singer, becoming a convert to Wagnerism, and for a number of springs he held at his home a series of musical evenings where eminent German musicians gathered. He was a favorite with the imperial family, particularly with the Crown Prince Frederick and his wife, who afterward became the Kaiser and Kaiserin. More than any other man, he was the idol of the younger professors of his day.

Helmholtz's scientific productivity has not only been, as every one knows, immense, but it covers an amazingly wide range of subjects. Of his two great works, "Tonempfindungen" and "Physiologische Optik," only the former has been translated into English. An edition of the "Optik" up to date, which had been pronounced impossible on account of the vast mass of literature produced after its publication, has been edited since his death by Gullstrand, von Fries, and Nagel. We shall confine ourselves chiefly to the characterization of the various works bearing on psychology, which it is our endeavor to epitomize in a clear and intelligible form, and which we consider more important for psychology than the contributions of any individual thinker since Kant.

One of his earliest, neatest, and most classic demonstrations was that of nerve time. It had long been thought that this was far too rapid ever to be measured. The iatromathematicians of Montpellier assumed that the rate of motion in hollow tubes was inversely as their size and on this basis figured that, starting with the rate of blood movement in the aorta, the movement of currents in nerve fibrils must be about 600 times as fast as light. Johannes Müller and Du Bois Reymond, the latter as late as 1848 in his great textbook of physiology, concluded that, as the length of the nerve fibrils is so small, even in the largest animals, and the motions so rapid, we could never measure nerve time. Yet two years later Helmholtz did this accurately (condensing in a two-leaf monograph in a characteristic way the results of many months of pruning), stating that a nerve impulse travels along the motor nerve of a frog at the rate of about 90 feet per second, or nearly one-eleventh that of sound. Soon after, by stimulating alternately the toe and the thigh of a man and requiring the subject to press a key (or by registering his movement upon the myograph, which Helmholtz invented and which led to the invention of the kymograph by Ludwig) the instant the stimulus was felt, he found that the velocity of the sensory impulse is between 160 and 200 feet per second in man and later that that of the motor impulse is about the same, also that heat accelerates and cold retards this ráte. This opened the way to all the volumes of time measurements, reaction times, association times, etc., which have since played so large a rôle in physiology and in laboratory psychology, a form of which Jung now uses as a basis of psychoanalysis, for the detection of crime and submerged psychic complexes and constellations.

The so-called theory of knowledge (*Erkenntnisstheorie*) in the form in which it was first elaborated in Kant's "Transcendental Æsthetics," which Fichte made the central problem of philosophy, and upon which the subsequent systems of German idealism were built, asserts that time and space are a priori intuitions in us as color and sound are, and do not exist independently of us in the external world. In his phrase, they are transcendentally ideal and we can know nothing of the *Ding-an-sich*—at least beyond the mere fact of its existence. All knowledge which comes through sense must take on the universal forms of time and space. Johannes Müller, the father of German physiology, who, Helmholtz declares, exerted as his teacher an inspiring and guiding influence over all his intellectual development, formulated the parallel but more scientific principle known as that of specific energy of the nerves. The optic nerve, *e. g.*, may be pinched, heated, irritated by acid or electricity or light, but responds always only by the one sensation of light, and so every nerve responds in its own specific way to all forms of excitation. Developments of this thought have now become almost the entire philosophy of many German physiologists, who arrange their experiments with a view perhaps of finding new central seats or peripheral nerves for specific functions, such as thermal reactions or the contraction and dilation of blood vessels, or perhaps of formulating the indispensable conditions, electrical, thermal, chemical, etc., or the necessary forms—rhythmic, intermittent, inhibitory, tensive, etc.—under which all or certain nerves must act.[1] This development, coupled with the growing discontent with absolute idealism, was the motive for the cry of "back to Kant" which for a time made his "Kritique" the Bible of philosophical orthodoxy, and about which there sprang up a new, vast, and curious literature, exegetical, dogmatical, and polemic, descending often to scholastic subtleties and detailed verbal criticism which, when it is remembered how rapidly and awkwardly he put his conceptions into words, is nothing less than nonsense.

Meanwhile Herbart, who rejected all the post-Kantian philosophy, attempted to lay the foundations for a new departure. Kant, he said, has told us that time and space are in us, but he has not told us how they arise in us; he has divided, not explained, the fact. From his work, undeveloped beyond a propadeutic stage, came dualism, which ignores the psychological problem that underlies the theory of knowledge. Ancient dualism divided the universe into a here and a yonder, and from the intellectual tension its modern form has caused came Schopenhauer, who conceived the will as a *Ding-an-sich* which breaks in upon consciousness at a certain point. Science, however, must have one organic conception of nature. Again, from Kant has come the modern habit of speaking of *simple* ideas. Countless ontological and metaphysical inferences are based upon an assumed simplicity of perceptive acts or of intuition, whereas, on the opposite side, psychologic science now assumes that there is nothing whatever in consciousness which is not indefinitely compound and composite. The analysis of the simplest acts of perception into more intimate elementary processes, which are not expressable in words, the existence of which was undreamed

[1] See A. Riehl, Helmholtz in seinen Verhaltniss zu Kant, 1904, p. 78.

of in Kant's time, and which must remain unknown to philosophy so long as it busies itself only with verbal or logical knowledge, Helmholtz regards as the "most essential progress of the present time."[1] To him belongs a large share of the merit of taking Kant's problem into the laboratory and, in an age when ideal aims are too often suspected or disparaged, of directing science with its more laborious method and more tangible results "toward the same ideal goal which German philosophy fondly thought it had reached before." This he feels should be done with piety toward the old systems (especially Kant's), even when the new results cannot be fitted into them, but postulating a larger ulterior synthesis.

McKendrick says that no physiological principle influenced Helmholtz so much as that of the specific energy of nerves. To him, this showed that there is no correspondence between the sensation and the physical nature of the stimulus arousing it, seeing that the latter may be varied while the former remains unchanged. This, in his study of the senses, controlled and directed his psychological work as did the idea of the conservation of energy his physical work. He was interested in the senses because he was in a modified way a follower of Locke, who held that the mind was a *tabula rasa,* and that everything in it came through the senses. Sensations are signs and symbols, not copies of external things, and are no more like the real things than words are like the ideas they stand for. Helmholtz repeatedly expressed his general agreement with Darwin and Lamarck, and was prone to stress a gradual accumulation of experiences through generations as accounting for the origin of what seems a priori. Such ideas seem universal because the element of experience in their formation is overlooked, and he would have subscribed to Spencer's view that what is innate in the individual is acquired by the race. He was not ready to ac-

[1] Thatsachen in Wahrnehmung. Berlin, 1879, p. 42.

cept Kant's view that space or geometric axioms are a priori, and thought this view refuted by the study of the horopter, in which the two different sensations from the same object on each retina are blended together without any known anatomical function, but mentally and as a product of experience. Indeed, he thought the results of experience mixed up even with the three basal concepts of geometry, (1) that there can be only one shortest straight line drawn between two points; (2) through any three points of space not in a straight line a plane may be drawn; and (3) a point lying without a straight line, only one straight line can be drawn parallel to it. Creatures living in a two or one-dimensional space could develop a geometry all their own in which the axioms would be like ours or Euclid's, but such beings, if living on a spherical surface, would develop another, a spherical, geometry, so that Kant was wrong in thinking axioms a priori. He also held that this belief was not necessary, and was useless for explanation, and in his article in the Zeller *Festschrift* in 1888 he best summed up his conclusions in this field.

There was to him perhaps no more fundamental question in psychology than the origin and nature of our notion of space. The most radical side of Helmholtz's empiricism is to be found in his abstruse and largely mathematical discussions respecting the nature of the Euclidian axioms, to which for twelve or fourteen years he repeatedly turned. Professor Gauss, of Göttingen, had declared, near the end of the eighteenth century, that the axiom that parallel lines might be infinitely prolonged without meeting was an assumption which could not be demonstrated, though so many mathematicians had tried to prove it, and that it was unnecessary and impaired the strictness and certainty of geometry. During most of the first half of the nineteenth century he frequently recurred to the subject in conversation and in letters, although he never attempted to complete a non-Euclidian system. We can conceive, he says, of beings which are conscious of only two dimensions of space, and others which stand above us may likewise look down upon our knowledge of three. He declared that he had laid aside certain problems with the design of treating them geometrically in a higher state.[1] It was his merit to first treat surfaces as independent space forms with one dimension infinitely small, and to distinguish between even, conical, and cylindrical surfaces (each of which may be produced by bending the other), and all forms of spherical surfaces. He then proceeded to develop the fruitful idea of the measure of curvature.[2] He also first gave an unambiguous expression for the shortest, straightest, or thread lines which lie at the bottom of all measurement, and therefore of all geometry. His analysis showed that the plane, cone, and cylinder have no curvature. Because their measure of curvature is constantly null, their surfaces are congruent, *i. e.*, each part can take the place of every other equal part; while for the same reason the conception of the straight line or shortest way between two points is valid alike for all, although the curvature-relation of a straight line (the notion of

[1] See Erdmann, Die Axiome der Geometrie, 1878, p. 22.

[2] ''The measure of curvature'' of a surface at a point is the *limiting value* of the quotient that arises when the total curvature of an element of the surface that includes the point is divided by the area of the element *as the element shrinks up to the point*. But the ''total curvature'' of a portion of the surface was defined by Gauss before it was possible for him to define the ''measure of curvature at a point.'' The notion of a geodetic line has nothing whatever to do with curvature,—is, in fact, a far more elementary notion; a geodetic line is, within certain limits, the shortest distance on the surface between two of its points, but by no means necessarily the *straightest* line between such points. The surfaces of *no* curvature are the only ones on which a geodetic line measures the shortest distance throughout its whole extent. Geodetic lines on any surface are geodetic lines on every surface obtained from it by bending without stretching. W. E. Story.

which must be somewhat enlarged) is the same for a cone as for a plane.[1]

For spherical surfaces, as is evident, the measure of curvature has a constant positive value. From its constancy results congruence as before, but because its value is positive the straightest possible lines are also the arcs of the greatest circles. On such a surface, between any two poles or from opposite ends of diameters, any number of straightest possible lines can be drawn. There can also be no parallels. Several Euclidian laws lose their validity in such surfaces. The sum of the angles of a triangle is always more than two right angles, unless the radius be infinitely large, and similarity between great and small figures loses its necessity and its meaning.

With the analytical method already developed it was natural that the residual question should arise as to what sort of surface would be produced if the measure of curvature be constantly negative. In this saddle-shaped pseudospheric surface, constructed in 1868 by Beltrami, the law of congruence of figures and the law that one geodetic line only is possible between two points are as valid as for the plane, but many lines can be drawn through a point without a straightest line, which will never meet it if infinitely produced, and the sum of the angles of a triangle is always smaller than two right angles, unless the figures be infinitely small. Thus again plane geometry is subsumed as a special case.

Other classes of surfaces are moreover possible, and the measure of curvature need not be constant, e. g., in the case of ellipsoidal or egg-shaped surfaces. For all such the law of congruence is not applicable. With change of direction surfaces stretch and figures change their form, while the equivalent of the conception of the straightest and of parallel lines becomes extremely complex. There may even be as many sorts or standards of measurement

[1] Erdmann, p. 52 et seq.

as there are different values of the measure of curvature, save in the case of infinitely small line elements. But singular measurement is only one kind if we admit the possibility of turning all the way around a point or line.

From papers printed since his death, and especially his habilitation address on the hypotheses which underlie geometry, which created great discussion when it was published in 1867, thirteen years after its delivery, B. Riemann, of Göttingen, appears to have been led to this problem, not merely by the study of Gauss, upon whose work his deductions are largely based, but also by Herbart, and by the doctrine of the persistence of force. Rejecting Herbart's metaphysical and natural philosophy, as most of his school have since done, he saw, no doubt, the shortcomings of the mathematical method when applied to the indefinite complexity of psychic processes, wherein, contrary to the Herbartian hypothesis, disparate perceptions as well as those of the same continuum must inhibit each other, where clearness and intensity are not coincident and where intension has suggested to scores of philosophers a rubric distinct from every form of tridimensional extension.

Riemann first explains how the general properties of space, its continuity, and the manifoldness of its relations may be analytically expressed by reminding us that its every element or point is determined by measuring an indefinite number of variable magnitudes or coördinates. If n of these are necessary, the manifoldness may be said to have n dimensions. Thus, e. g., we may fancy a chemical compound of many elements, the nature of the whole variable with the quantity of any one or more of its elements. We can thus reach a generic conception and formula of manifoldly extended greatness.[1]

Every color may be produced, Helmholtz held, by mixing the three ground colors, and every tone is compounded

[1] Abhandlungen der Göttingen Gesellschaft der Wissenschaft, Bd. 13, S. 134.

259

of pitch, intensity, and timbre. Color and sound are thus, like space, tridimensional manifolds, and the mathematical expression of the relations of their respective elements is to some extent the same. On the other hand, however, the saturation and the shade of color, the pitch, and the intensity of tone are practically incommensurate, while we can measure distance in each dimension of space with the same footrule, or, as Riemann next postulates, every lineal element of space is comparable in magnitude with every other.

This is simple and leads us to Riemann's chief problem, viz., to determine the nature of the relation of the "length element of a line" to the corresponding differentials of the coördinates. This he does by the hypothesis that the length element equals the square root of a homogeneous function of their differentials of the second degree, or, in other words, by identifying it with the familiar Pythagorean theorem. This assumption he justifies as the simplest, and upon it all his deductions are based, although he admits that a higher root of a polynomial of higher degree is also possible. This hypothesis, however, is unnecessarily broad, and it is valid for any system of measurement whatever.[1]

Recurring now to the special case of two dimensions, Gauss had already shown that the formula for the length element must be found in a surface of our actual space to which the ordinary laws of analytical geometry are applicable, and, as we have seen that figures can be moved and turned in all directions in it without change of the measurements of their lines or angles, such a surface must have a constant measure of curvature. These formulæ, Riemann shows, are applicable to any number of dimensions, and he explains how the measure of curvature may be determined in each case.

[1] For a recent expression of this hypothesis see Elemente der Absolute Geometrie, von Prof. Frischauf, S. 121, Leipzig, 1876; also, Heidelburger Jahrbuch, 1868, S. 734-5; Göttingen Nachrichten, 1868, S. 194 et seq.

Thus his general problem is solved, and it only remains to specialize it by postulating congruence for an n-fold extended finite figure. This brings him to our actual space where these conditions are fulfilled. Thus far, however, it is not proven, and indeed cannot be from these data, that space is infinitely extended as represented in ordinary geometry, and the axiom respecting parallels is far from being logically necessary. Only when the measure of curvature is zero can we have our infinite space, which, to distinguish it from other species of space, we may call plane.

Helmholtz meanwhile, feeling the same necessity of a more careful examination of the axiomatic attributes of space than that upon which the Euclidian geometry rests, had been led to inquire how many of its fundamental principles have an objectively valid sense, and how many are mere definitions or consequences of definition, and had reached quite similar conclusions without being acquainted with the work of either Riemann or Gauss. He was specifically led to the subject by trying to explain how we come to localize and measure objects in the field of vision and by investigating the methods of spatially representing his color system, where it is required to compare two tridimensional forms. His method was thus very different from that of Riemann—almost its converse, in fact. Instead of trying to deduce all geometrical laws from one general principle Helmholtz makes principles out of the simplest presuppositions, from which he develops Riemann's fundamental hypothesis, as above stated, although perhaps he was anticipated by Bolyai. Helmholtz's independent but consillient argumentation and the influence of his name however first attracted general attention to the subject.

He starts by assuming that in our space figures or bodies of constant form can be freely moved, and that all original measurements of space rest upon the empirical observation that bodies can be brought into congruence. The conditions of congruence, which he makes his first problem, he finds to be the familiar law of determination of position by coördinates, the definition of a firm but movable body, and finally that, after one revolution about a fixed axis, such a body must revert to the same position as at first. A geometry is possible where the latter would not be the case, and thus would not be included in Riemann's deductions, but the ordinary geometry silently assumes its truth in treating the circle as a closed line, just as it assumes the existence of bodies firm in themselves and freely movable in the postulate of congruences, and again as it presupposes the continuity and the number of dimensions of space. If now the number of dimensions be taken as three and the infinite extension of space be postulated, no other geometry than that of Euclid may seem to be possible. Yet all of Helmholtz's assumptions hold for hyperbolic space (the non-Euclidian or imaginary geometry of Labatschewsky) as well as for parabolic. In this way Helmholtz shows analytically that there is a homogeneous expression of the second degree of differentials which remains unchanged by every motion of two firmly connected points infinitely near each other,[1] and thus Riemann's hypothesis is proven. It is, in a word, equivalent to saying that space is monodromic and that infinitely small elements of space are congruent apart from any considerations of their boundaries or their place.

Labatschewsky[2] had deduced an absolute geometry, based upon the assumption that the sum of the angles of a triangle is less than two right angles. He, however, expressly called this an imaginary geometry and ascribed to it a differential character under which the geometry of Euclid became a special case when the lines are infinitely small. He insisted that the results are not analytically absurd, declared that whether it be true or not only actual

[1] See Göttingen Nachrichter, 1868, S. 202 et seq.
[2] See his Pangeometrie, 1855.

measurement could decide, and admitted that thus far the largest astronomic as well as the smallest triangles conform, within the limits of error, to the rule of Euclid. Yet any triangles that it is possible for man to measure must be so small in comparison with all space that no measurement can possibly determine whether our space is actually of the one or the other of the three kinds of space (elliptic, hyperbolic, or parabolic).

Thus far the question had been mainly abstract and logico-mathematical. It was high time however to remember that analytic equations were devised only to abbreviate and summarize complex, perceptive operations, and that Descartes' process must be reversed if results of any sort of serviceability were to be obtained. Descartes' geometric algebra was really intuitive. Descartes invented analytic geometry (as it is now called) to solve algebraical problems by geometry and not geometrical problems by algebra, as we do now. In attempting this Prof. E. Beltrami [1] devised a method by which meta-mathematical spaces might be perspectively represented in a sphere of Euclidian space, and proved that this pseudo-spheric was nothing other than the imaginary space of Labatschewsky. A general geometry which assumes only constancy of curvature is possible, which may be ideally still further generalized by introducing extension of n-dimensions (Caley had written on this subject in 1845). Thus, says Erdmann, the bold conception of a supreme geometry which Kant conceived in his first published treatise is realized.[2]

[1] Annali di Math., Ser. II, 1868.

[2] Prof. W. E. Story remarks: ''From the mathematician's point of view, it is not of any consequence whether any particular theory affirms or contradicts ideas that mankind, or any individual, has assumed as justified by experience, but it is only of importance and interest to determine what we really *know*, that is what is *essential* to a consistent comprehension of the phenomena that affect us. Absolute truth is beyond our powers to determine. The real objection to Euclid's geometry is not that it is inconsistent with our experi-

Professor Lipschitz, of Bonn, investigated and demonstrated the applicability of the above abstract results [1] to the general principles of mechanics. Helmholtz made the yet more hazardous attempt [2] to describe the sensuous impressions that would be produced in such hypothetical space, and finally Erdmann and Wundt [3] and a score of others less intelligible have attempted to estimate the philosophical results of the discussion; while Houel in France, Clifford in England, and Tilly in Belgium have introduced and advocated the new doctrine of space in their respective countries.

On the other hand the whole question has been described as "superlative nonsense impossible outside of Germany." Even Lotze calls it "logical jugglery," or "a grimace of science to intimidate ordinary consciousness by useless paradoxes." Dühring thought that mechanics and geometric axioms together were in danger of being undermined, and ironically congratulated metaphysicians that they had lived to see "fruit which was all of their own planting ripen on the soil of mathematics." Lange saw in it only the conceivability of a more generic notion of space and thought no philosophical consequences could be drawn from it; and even Drobisch thinks Herbart's distinction

ence, but that it assumes more than is necessary or useful for our comprehension of form and magnitude. The same principles that lie at the foundation of measurement of space of three dimensions lie also at the foundation of the measurement of one dimensional time. There is no more or less reason why time should be finite or infinite than why space should be so, and the one may be finite while the other is infinite. Again, for aught we know, space may have a fourth dimension, which is imperceptible to us solely because we have no sense capable of receiving impressions from it,—or perhaps we have."

[1] Crelles Journal für Math., Bd. 71, S. 71; Bd. 72, S. 1; Bd. 74, S. 116.

[2] Pop. Wiss. Vorträge, Heft. III, S. 24, also Thatsachen in Wahrnehmung.

[3] Logik, 1880, S. 441 et seq.

between intelligible and sensuous space somewhat endangered.[1] On the other hand the most surprising deductions have been made by those who have no less uncritically and precipitately accepted all the above results. Professor Zöllner, the eminent Leipzig astronomer, *e. g.*, argued from the conditions of the stability of the aggregate of bodies composed of fluid drops that space must have at least an infinitesimal positive measure of curvature. All matter, even the most solid, he said, must slowly suffer volatilization if its temperature is above the absolute zero point. Infinite time having already elapsed, he continued, since the origin of the world, all bodies would have vanished if space were infinite. He not only believed, as Riemann seemed to, that the Newtonian conception of the universe must be revolutionized, but that the above deductions are of immediate and paramount importance and application for the knowledge and understanding of natural phenomena.[2] If the number of heat and light-diffusing bodies or fixed stars were actually infinite then the whole arch of heaven would, but for absorption, dispense light and heat, as now the disc of the sun does. But this last Zöllner attempts to refute, and finally resorts to the physical fact of the vaporization of ice and the smell of metals and minerals. He quite forgets moreover that it is by no means certain that all parts of the universe are above the temperature of absolute zero and that there are forces which act against volatilization. These omissions seem fatal to the strict logical consistency of his theory.

Later a curious turn was given to the discussion by the conversion of Professor Zöllner and the partial conversion of two colleagues, Professors Weber and Fechner, to spiritism mainly by the performances of the American prestidigitator and self-styled medium, Slade, whose tricks

[1] Erdmann, op. cit., p. 10.
[2] Ueber die Natur der Cometen, von F. Zöllner, Leipzig, 1872.

by the way were afterward purchasable in Berlin, and which the writer has seen performed at evening parties there by a young docent in physics. In four large volumes of rambling discussions Zöllner explains that spirits exist, and all sorts of physically impossible things may be done "in the fourth dimension," and thus a phrase of recent scientific origin has been made to play a very prominent part in the development of spiritism in Germany. A spiritistic journal was started in Leipzig by a disciple of Reichenbach, and a number of students became ardent disciples of Professor Zöllner, who continued to lecture and write with vigor despite the ridicule, remonstrance, and predictions of insanity, etc., on the part of his fellow professors.

Extravagant condemnation of Helmholtz for causing a "scientific scandal" and encouraging "mathematical mysticism" was one of the many violations of collegiate decorum for which poor, blind Professor Dühring was, although no doubt with justice, dismissed from his chair in Berlin. But violent as were Zöllner's denunciations of Helmholtz for rejecting his conclusions and more and more insane as he unquestionably was in his universal aspersion, none of his less-abused colleagues wished him removed from his chair, but preferred that he should remain as a conspicuous monument of the principle, almost universal in Germany, that a professorship is for life. We cannot however entirely acquit Professor Helmholtz from the charge of making an indiscreet appeal to the scientific imagination. His vivid characterization of intelligent beings of two dimensions, whose life is confined to a surface, and who can conceive nothing outside it, whose geometry, if they developed one, would be planimetric, who could know no more of a third dimension than a person color-blind from birth could know of tints and hues, and whose sense impressions could not be fully characterized, etc.,[1]

[1] Pop. Wiss. Vorträge, Drittes Heft, 1878, S. 27 et seq.

tickles the popular consciousness to which it is expressly
addressed by the cunning of its pseudo-conceivability to
fancy tridimensional space as the middle term of a syllogism, and to say that as the knowledge or life in two is
to that in three so is the latter to a conceivable state of
existence in four dimensions. That the shades of error thus
suggested have filtered far down among lower intelligences
is seen in the reported statement of a laborer at a Leipzig
socialistic gathering that a great scholar in Berlin claimed
to have discovered heaven; while even an eminent philosophical critic has proposed—we know not with how much
of humor—that the term ''spirit world'' be substituted for
''fourth dimension'' in all future discussions on the subject. However it would have been in Plato's own time, we
fancy that from a true republic of science every seer
who tells us we are still sitting in the cave with our back
to the real world, studying its ghostly shadows of inadequate dimensions, would be excluded along with far falser
prophets as dangerously mythopœic. It is irrelevant and
misleading to conceive of a world, like the image in a convex mirror, wherein a mirrored surveyor with a mirrored
chain measures off as many rods in a mirrored acre as
in the actual world, because all would be diminished and
foreshortened in the same ratio. A world in Pflücker's
lines, Beltrami's sphere, or seen through convex prismatic
glasses is no less irrelevant even though we could adapt
ourselves to such a world and should have to unlearn our
impressions in coming back to our own. We have no fear
that science will be seriously discredited but we do fear
there is some truth in the oft-repeated charge of their ri-
vals in other universities that the Berlin professors,
through the rapidly increasing seductions of society in the
great *Hauptstadt,* and through the perhaps too cordial
personal patronage of the Court, are constantly, though
perhaps gently and unconsciously, tempted to produce popular and striking novelties, a trifle perhaps after the fash-

ion of the professors in the *Ecole Normale* in Paris. This may seem an unscientific and illiberal criticism to some, but it applies here only to Helmholtz's attempt to make a fourth dimension conceivably perceptible, and every unprejudiced mind must admit that more recently in his argument that space may be transcendental, while all the geometric axioms must be regarded as of empirical origin,[1] he came as near to a confession of error as can perhaps be reasonably expected of a great professor in Germany with his important "record" and his strange reputation for infallibility at stake.

Admitting thus the mathematics or logic of the fourth dimension and denying its conceivability, we must, as is so rarely safe, seek the truth in the middle. It is no real argument to say with Wundt that we might as well conceive of time of other species than present, past, and future; nor is it fair to say there might as well be several contradictions to one and the same proposition as a fourth dimension to space, although even this may be only a necessity of language rather than of logic in its purer sense. Neither is it wise to compare the whole matter to the question whether this is the best world possible, nor to struggle to conceive what a "cross section of magnitude of four dimensions" would be like; nor to measure Nobert's infinitesimal lines and astronomic distances to see if there is any indication that parallels do meet after all if they are infinitely near or long; nor to seek for proof that all things do or do not regularly change in form with every degree of translocalization.

Following Erdmann's rubric we will add briefly, first, that the logical consequences of the discussion thus far are very important. Space, every one admits, has never been adequately defined. Its notion cannot be called distinctly that of a genus or a species. Whether it is purely the

[1] Der Thatsache in der Wahrnehmung, von H. Helmholtz, Berlin, 1879.

result of perception or of reason, or of both, has been long disputed. If it were only a part of the content of the sensory, logic ought to do something toward defining it; were it a necessary determination of being it should be subsumed under being as its genus as was done by Hegel. Even if the discussion does not succeed in raising the notion of magnitude to the rank of a genus including space, we must yet protest against Wundt's assertion that there can be here no question whatever about genus and species, and that all manifolds must forever refer back to space. We would rather urge that conceivably new and suggestive points of specific relationship with other magnitudes have been brought to light, which make our ordinary space idea somewhat less absolutely unique and peculiar in the world of conscious thought than before, and which already suggest the reflection that its uniqueness, as well as its prominence, may be due in part to the constancy with which it is inwrought into every expression of our unique and peculiar organism from its earliest beginning upward. Moreover the separation of the question of the origin of axioms from that respecting the origin of space itself as abstract extension we regard as one of the most sagacious and valuable distinctions yet made in all the voluminous literature on space, although it seems to have been an afterthought with Helmholtz.

The bearings of the question upon the theory of knowledge have been greatly discussed in Germany. Hartmann, *e. g.*, laboriously and curiously argues that if we assume that the world without us is made up of manifold objects we must infer a continuous form of existence through which motion is possible, a form which need have but three and cannot have less than three dimensions; and that it is "highly probable" in the absence of all proof to the contrary that this form of existence is identical with our space. We have no room to epitomize the discussion, but there seems now to be a growing consensus that these speculations do not necessarily affect the question of idealism or realism.

Although the psychological question is so closely connected with the others it will be affected far more than they by the final verdict. Geometric facts have not only been distinguished from color and sound and secondary qualities as quite independent of our bodily organism, but geometric axioms have long been cited as the most important cases of innate a priori truths preceding and independent of all experience, as in short transcendental. Assuming rather than arguing the validity of the notion of local signs as a physiological basis, Helmholtz urges at some length [1] that the hypothesis of an intuitive knowledge of axioms apart from experience, is unproven, is unnecessary, because it explains nothing not equally well explained otherwise, and is irrelevant, since axioms can be applied to the objective world only after they have been otherwise proven to be objectively true, and that thus there at least exists a geometry the general principles of which rest on experience.

As early as 1874 Helmholtz briefly declared the law of the persistence of natural forces and stated that kinetic was inversely as potential energy—a law which with but a few modifications has since become almost axiomatic in German science. He was one of the first to study the chemical and thermal changes in muscles at work. The invention and application of the modern method of accurately measuring the rapidity of nerve currents, and also of the simplest case of reflex action, which is now divided into as many as eight or more distinct periods, are both due to him. In 1851 he invented the ophthalmoscope, which marked an era in both physiological optics and in clinical practice, while in anatomy he was one of the first to see the now universally admitted connection between cells and fibers.

[1] See Mind, April, 1878, pp. 212 et seq. Also Thatsachen in Beilage, III.

In 1854 he laid down the law of summated or superposed muscle curves and ten years later demonstrated and determined muscular tonicity, neither of which has been essentially modified since. Into these important points we have here no space to enter, but this enumeration will show what initiative influence and what conclusiveness his scientific observations have had and how commonly his philosophic instinct has drawn him to central and fundamental questions.

A few of his popular lectures should be mentioned here, although many of them have appeared in English. In one he inquires whether the unity of the sciences, if merely a survival of a medieval ideal, should not be broken, and whether the organs of science, the universities, should not dissolve into various special and professional schools; or whether on the other hand there is an organic or logical connection between all branches of learning sufficient to justify the name University of arts, sciences, and letters. This very popular theme for a rectoral inaugural in Germany he argues in favor of the latter alternative. First, he says, there is the unity of lexicons, indexes, catalogs, reports, etc., wherein facts when they become too numerous for memory are grouped, in lieu of a better system, on the principle of accessibility in the order of the alphabet or of time. This work is in most cases a necessary preliminary to all others. Next comes the method of inductive classification according to genus and species. Thus the method of natural sciences requires ever severer schooling in the general laws of thought, for as facts accumulate more and more general laws by which they are ordered should be educed from them. Hence comes the application of mathematics, developing the mechanical side of nature, and hence, too, the fact that inductive science has done so much more for logic than have professed philosophers. In the ordering of genus and species, in a preëminent sense knowledge is power. In the third place there is the unity of artistic induction. Characteristic marks or attributes are selected and grouped. Tact and a fine feeling for analysis play an important part even in scientific discovery. Once more there are the unities of grammar, law, and theology, imposing illustrations of fine logical completeness and self-consistency, perfected by ages of observation and ratiocination, and hence, though founded inductively upon facts, now presenting themselves to the student's mind with the sanction of external authority. Thus men of science constitute an organized army. Each must feel his organic connection with the whole and make it a supreme end that his work be incorporate with the growing body of contemporary science by choosing timely themes, presenting his results in brief, clear, and accessible form, and seeking by self-criticism to avoid overestimating himself or his work. This latter the scholar is sure to do if self-culture is made a supreme end. He who seeks knowledge for the satisfaction it brings to himself is on the road to that pessimistic self-pity which complains of lack of recognition, and he will probably fail in life, however gifted he may be. The scientific man is never more unscientific than when he looks for immediate practical utility. Would he succeed he must work for the sake of science itself. Most of the discoveries by which science has revolutionized the modern world were made by those who least sought the results they obtained. Moreover a modern investigator must work not merely with books. He must detect the imperfections of instruments, devise new ones, and measure their errors, must know organisms and their various conditions at various times, must spend perhaps more than half his time in bringing a stubborn bit of glass or tin into shape and position, must be a smith, a tinker, a chemist, a draftsman, and a musician by turns. He must whittle, saw, and hammer, must be a toxicologist, a microscopist, and possibly a vivisector, as well as a psychologist and a logician. He must train his eye, ear, nose, hand, and must control all details of his experiments, and then perhaps fail, and begin again. He must, in short, spend most of his time in preparation, and in determining what problems are ripe for investigation, and what must be left to the future. This is especially the case with the physiologist, who must borrow aid from all branches of natural science. The more limited and special, however, one is compelled to make his field of work, the greater is the mental need he feels of not losing sight of the whole to which he contributes his mite. Facts or isolated observations have no value, theoretical or practical. Things are truly discovered only when their laws are known.

In his famous discourse on academic freedom in 1877 Helmholtz asserted that at that moment "the extremest consequences of materialistic metaphysics, the most daring speculations on the basis of Darwin's evolutionary theory, and the extremest deification of papal infallibility" could be taught unhindered in the German universities. In the Middle Ages every doctor could teach in the university, and now, save the added examination, every one who can pass it is moderately sure of a professional academic career. The university is the home of the freedom which threw off the yoke of the church, which is guarded so carefully and with a strong corporate sense by teacher and student. With a few needful restrictions any person can teach and any student can hear anything in Germany. The English universities he admits take more pains to cultivate a fine sense of language, so neglected in Germany; the physical well-being of the student is better cared for and he is restrained more within the customs of good society than in Germany, but on the other hand the best scientists—Davy, Faraday, Darwin—are not professors, so that the stimulus of being brought into contact with original minds is lost. In the older English institutions almost no deviation from the established orthodoxy is allowed on the part of teacher or student, while party and personal feelings influence the choice of professors and the fellows do little because they are not brought into any close connection with the spirit of investigation.

In another address [1] he sketches some of the delusions which have pervaded the science and practice of medicine and which in Germany culminated in the doctrine of vitalism. Physicians had come to believe that in treating disease they had to do with a kind of psychic existence whose symptoms and reactions were to be understood by a sort of philosophic intuition and controlled by spurring, pushing, mollifying, etc. The noble old Hippocratic maxim, "Godlike is the physician who is also a philosopher," had been so perverted that their artificial pathology had, till Lotze's annihilating critique in 1842, come to be considered as the very finest fruit of medical science and experience. Thus Helmholtz himself admits that at the time when he entered upon the field convalescent from a fever in the *Charité* hospital, but the fortunate possessor of a microscope bought with the proceeds of his slender income (which had been continued during an illness which cost him nothing because he was an assistant there), he had a wide and fruitful virgin soil before him wherein every stroke of the pickaxe disclosed new treasures, and behind him the motives of a profession which should spur men on to a knowledge of nature's laws more strongly and incessantly than any other. To be sure, the old doctors shook their heads; they said auscultation and percussion were too coarsely mechanical means of investigation, disparaging to the dignity of the patient, and unnecessary for a physician with a clear mental insight, while ophthalmoscopes, measurements of temperature, etc., were decidedly not in good taste. Medicine became a science with the establishment of the law of specific energy of nerves, which is compared to the discovery of the Newtonian law of gravity, while vivisection "made accessible an abundance of

[1] Das Denken in der Medicin von H. Helmholtz, 1879.

deep-lying problems which even to this generation seemed quite hopeless.'' Now with physiology as its fundamental science the practice of medicine is rapidly becoming more exact in all its methods and the laws of the human body are coming to seem more and more exact and mechanical. True philosophy—which is related to metaphysics as astronomy to astrology—must be first of all experimental. All the wisdom of the world lies in the type boxes of the printer, all that is needed being to arrange them rightly; so perhaps all the details of all true scientific hypotheses already exist in the countless speculations about ultimate questions which are evolved with such facility from metaphysical minds, but which until proved and confirmed are worse than useless for the progress of true and certain knowledge. Physicians have ever been, and will long remain, the true *Aufklärer*. As the microscopist, when he reaches the limits of visibility, must turn all his attention to the improvement of his instruments, so now must they, with scientific specialists in so many departments, turn a great part of their attention to the chief instrument with which they work, and study the nature and laws of the human mind. The truest and the highest science is now grounded on a knowledge of the laws of psychic processes.

We come now to speak briefly of Helmholtz's most complete and epoch-making work on ''Tonempfindungen,'' long since translated into English. Let us first, with Helmholtz, suppose ourselves in a ballroom with all its sounds assailing our ears at once. A piano is emitting sound waves of from thirty-two feet to six inches in length, and at the rate of from thirty to nearly four thousand per second. The voices of the gentlemen are composed of waves of from three to six feet long. Those of the ladies cause waves of from two to four feet in length, while the rustle of their silk dresses gives rise to perhaps as many as thirty or forty thousand waves per second. All these and many other sounds are proceeding from different centers and their concentric waves now strengthen, now weaken, and perhaps strike others which they meet at all angles and in all directions. This may be illustrated by what takes place on a fluid surface of two dimensions, as, *e. g.,* on the surface of the sea. There is first the long ground swell, crossed by the smaller waves thrown up by a passing steamer, these again transversed by yet smaller waves from a skiff, these again by those from a stone, and all ruffled by a light passing breeze, and so on indefinitely. Now it had been proven by a French savant that every conceivable form of pendular oscillation, no matter what angles and curves it contains, provided only that they are regularly recurrent, can be analyzed into a number of simple oscillations, one, two, three, etc., times as rapid as the given form of oscillation. Another investigator had found that every motion of the air, corresponding to any composite mass of sound, can be analyzed into a sum of simple pendular vibrations and that the ear perceives a tone for every such series of vibrations. Such pure tones, however, are very rare in nature or even in music. The sound of the simple German *U* is about the purest sound of the human voice, but neither this nor the soft, hollow, colorless tone produced by blowing into a round-bellied flask, or even by a resonator before a tuning fork, is unaccompanied by one or more soft higher notes, the octave, third, fifth, etc., above, which are called overtones and which, according to their number, intensity, and proportion, make notes sharp, shrill, full, hollow, rich, clear, etc. In vibrating strings these overtones are given by each half, third, quarter, etc., of the string separated by nodes, each vibrating slightly by itself two, three, or four times faster than the string as a whole, with which they sympathetically vibrate like fine ripples on a dancing wave. A large or stiff string will of course have fewer nodes than a small one of flexible material, and hence Pythagoras had noticed this law of monochords, and now piano makers have learned empirically of how great importance it is for the tone-color, not only where but how the hammer strikes the string. If it strikes, *e. g.*, in the middle there is no octave overtone and the sound seems hard, and almost nasal. If the hammer remains resting more than the time of half a vibration against the string the ground tone is impaired, and even a far shorter time damps the higher overtones, which with a quick stroke of a thin metallic hammer would almost pain the ear. In bells, vibrating rods, etc., the overtones are sometimes still stronger and in vibrating columns of air like organ pipes they are commonly too few, so that mixed registers are used with agreeable effect.

It is a remarkable fact that we distinguish these overtones only with great difficulty and generally only after considerable practice, although they are often much louder than the ground tone itself, and although a familiar sound, with the overtones eliminated, seems strangely low in pitch. It is far harder to recognize the overtones in the human voice than in an instrument although they are strung and fall largely in an octave where the ear is peculiarly sensitive. This is because the sensation persists in developing into perception and apperception, or prefers from long habit or otherwise to be interpreted rather than to be simply felt. When we hear a voice in ordinary conversational inflections, above us in clear air at a distance where we cannot distinguish the words, we are struck by the richness of the ''speech music,'' and can sometimes almost realize what a different sort of resonator the mouth cavity becomes with different vowels. The difficulty of understanding words which are sung, however plainly articulated, is another fact belonging to the same category. Every one who has made observations in this field has experienced a periodic oscillation between perception and sensation. Now the words were understood and the speech music grew clear, and now only vocables were heard, with rich and melodious cadences; now the full, rich note was heard, now it dissolved into the sweetest harmony of three, four, or even five or six, overtones.

Helmholtz has shown how the analysis can be made with ease, in rare cases as far as the sixteenth partial overtone, by an application of the principle of sympathetic vibration. This is familiarly illustrated by the example of a small boy ringing a large church bell. This he can soon do with ease if he pulls the rope every time precisely when the bell is swinging in the direction in which he adds his weight; otherwise he may be lifted off his feet. So if of two pendulums very near to each other, of precisely the same oscillation time, one be set in motion and the other remain at rest the slight pressure of air caused by each beat of the one in motion will very slowly set the other in motion until at last both move with about the same amplitude of vibration. Now, all sound whatever being objectively composed of just such pendular vibrations as those we have instanced, only more frequent, we see how any tremulous object of nearly the same vibration time as the sounding body is sure to be set in sympathetic vibration by it. Helmholtz resonators are a series of such sympathetically vibrating bodies, each responding only to its own note. By arranging these near to various sounding bodies, as strings, flutes, organs, the human voice, etc., and causing one after another of these instruments to sound, he observed not only that the resonator corresponding to the ground tone and that giving the octave above, the higher third, fifth, etc., were also set in tuneful vibration, but also that a harp string for instance caused more of these higher-tuned resonators to sound, and also made them sound louder than an organ pipe tuned to the same pitch. In this way he was able to demonstrate that timbre or *sound-color* is due to the number-relations and the intensity of overtones, and by reversing the experiment and setting the proper resonators in vibration with the right relative intensity he even succeeded in *composing* tones in different timbres. He then repeated his observations on the different vowel sounds sung one after another on the same pitch and found that the difference between them also is due to differences in the strength and number of overtones, and by reversing the process he was able to compose a distinct *A, O, U*, etc., sound. In this case the overtones are produced by sympathetic vibration within the cavities of the mouth, throat, etc., the walls of the chest acting in some sense as a sounding board. Thus the proof that the simplest tone is a complex of an indefinite number of yet simpler elements is complete, just as a taste which at first seems simple is found to be composed of salt, pepper, mustard, etc., and just as the sensation of wetness may be made up of the sensations of coldness and smoothness.

But *how* then does the ear, which cannot apprehend the long sound waves as a whole, as they may be graphically represented to the eye, but perceives them sectionally, as it were through a long, narrow tube, distinguish these subtle qualities? If we raise the damper from the strings of a piano and sing or sound an instrument near it we shall notice that the strings actually make this analysis. That string which corresponds to the ground tone sounds most loudly and those corresponding to the respective overtones sound each with its own relative degree of intensity. Now, if we imagine a distinct nerve fiber attached to each string and running to our brain, we shall have a good idea of the anatomy of the ear, which contains just such a series of responsive strings from each of which nerve fibers proceed to the brain. In the ear, however, instead of eighty-four, as on the seven-octave piano, there are over four thousand such strings, making thus nearly fifty steps between each half tone. It has since been observed that one-fifth of a half tone is about the finest distinction which the most cultivated ear can make. Although we can hear tones of nearly forty thousand vibrations in a second, we can distinguish pitch very imperfectly above five or six thousand vibrations.[1]

The second part of the "Tonempfindungen" treats of the phenomena which arise when two tones are sounded together. If one string vibrates at the rate, *e. g.*, of four hundred times in a second and another at the rate of five hundred, producing thus the chord of the major third, it is evident that some particles of air will be set in motion by both strings at the same time, and others will vibrate only once while the strings are passing from one rhythmic phase to the next. Of these, which are called combination tones, the first or summation tone will have nine hundred; the latter or difference tones, which are far more distinct, will have only one hundred vibrations in a second. The former were first observed by Helmholtz. Both grow in strength in much more rapid ratio than the two ground tones. Of course, toward the upper end of an ordinary piano keyboard the summation tones are lost among the higher sounds, the pitch of which—depending, as Helmholtz conjectures it may, upon a less elastic apparatus, the Corti arches—is very imperfectly determined, while the difference tones of the lower notes are inaudible. These combination tones may be produced between a ground tone and an overtone, between ground tones and combination tones, or between overtones and combination tones. All of these, though recognizable, are very weak, especially the latter. Helmholtz is convinced that most of the strength of combination tones arises in the ear itself, and is due to the rattling of the two external ear bones against each other. The objective sound waves are so weak, especially if the two tones are separated, and the structure of the tympanum and the position of these bones is so loose as to

[1] Helmholtz later conjectured that shrilling, squeaking sensations may be perceived through the means of the vibrating hairs of the sac and not by the Corti arches or the fibers of the tympanic membrane.

make this a priori probable, and finally he has been able to distinguish this rattling sound in his own ear, and thinks any one may, when two clear sopranos sing test passages.

The essence of discord consists of beats or the interference of sound waves, by which the waves alternately strengthen and cancel each other. Here again, with the aid of his perfected apparatus, Helmholtz's researches were most fruitful. It had been supposed since the treatise of Thomas Young that when a series of beats was caused to grow more and more rapid they passed into a combination tone, when they numbered more than about thirty per second. This Helmholtz disproved by showing that beats occurred only when the ground tones were so near together as to be perceived through the same fiber of Corti, and by observing that as many as 132 beats could be distinguished by a good ear, and that however numerous they became they never caused the sensation of sound, but only that of discord, while ten irritations per second are sufficient to keep a muscle in constant contraction, and while forty electric sparks a second cause a continuous sensation of light in the eye, which cannot distinguish at one-twenty-fourth of a second interval whether two sparks coincide or not. The ear, which is eminently the organ for fine distinctions in time, makes the latter distinction for intervals of one hundredth of a second, and can detect beats of 1-132 of a second. Discord therefore is unpleasant as is a flickering light, because it causes intermittent periods of rest during which the organ grows more sensitive, only to be thrown into sudden and violent action again.

It is very difficult to determine the deepest audible tones. They have been estimated by different writers at from fifteen to forty vibrations per second. This difficulty is due to the fact that tones grow feeble as they become low and the overtones become proportionately louder, so that, it being difficult to distinguish with any degree of accuracy the pitch of the fundamentals, an overtone is often mistaken for a ground tone. The tone must there-fore be strong, composed of only simple pendular vibra-tions and the result controlled afterward by counting the beats when it is sounded with another adjacent tone of known pitch. The number of oscillations per second which produce a tone with any sensation of pitch seems to vary with different persons, with practice, and with the degree of attention. There is a degree of frequency where a strange oscillation occurs between the impression of distinct vibrations and that of tone, nothing varying but the at-tention.

The subject becomes most complex when we reflect that overtones also produce beats. These however are all exactly reckoned out and the consonant intervals deter-mined throughout the scale, and laid off in one of the most instructive plates of curves the graphic method has ever produced. Accords which are very pleasant on instru-ments of few or weak overtones become sometimes almost unendurable if produced with highly colored tones. The overtones of the higher tones fall above the region of clear-est sensation and hence two high tones are often accordant when, if the same tones are sounded two or three octaves lower, they throb with painful discord. In ancient Greece, where our scale was developed, and in most Oriental lands, music was mostly made by men's voices, which fall usually in a low octave peculiarly rich in overtones. Hence prob-ably it was that even the tertz was pronounced discordant by the Greek ear, and that no taste for harmony was de-veloped till instruments and higher notes were introduced to a normal ear. Nothing is more horrible than a flute con-cert, yet simple flute melody was the acme of antique mu-sical art.

It now only remained to determine the beats of combi-nation tones with others and with overtones, to ascertain what intervals were best adapted to different instruments and sound colors and finally to determine the degrees of harmony or dissonance when three, four, or more notes were to be sounded at the same time, always bearing in mind the simple note rule that consonance is a continuous, and dissonance a discontinuous, sensation of tone.

This concludes the original and more strictly scientific part of the work. The third part, which is confessedly mainly a compilation, is occupied with the history of music and the divisions of the octave into the various scales, and is of great interest to the general reader, as well as of great convenience for every musician. We shall mention but a few points in it. Scales and keys are by no means fixed in the nature of things, any more than is the Gothic arch, but were developed by an instinct mainly correct but in every essential respect undergoing changes even now. In the first or homophonic period nothing was known of key notes or of harmony, nor was music independent of words. This form of music was indicated by twenty-five signs for cadence and melodic phrases (found in old Hebrew manuscripts), and was used in odes, tragic choruses, and still survives in the Catholic intonations, Italian declamation in recitative passages, and perhaps in accents and "speech music." Polyphonic music, extending roughly from the tenth to the seventeenth century, was mainly a weaving together of melodies in such a way as to avoid bad discords but without much regard for the value of harmony *per se* and with little unity save that of time. With Protestants the choir became the congregation and out of individualities it was sought to develop the wholeness of the community. Repetitions and fuguings were sometimes, especially in the Netherlands, as complicated and fanciful as the illuminated devices of an old missal. Church music was, at first, undeveloped, and old madrigals and other tunes were very clumsily fugued together till early in the sixteenth century accord with a fundamental bass, the adaptation of the Ionic as a major scale, and the transformation of the other five ancient scales to our minor scale prepared the way for modern music. The harmonic period of music began perhaps with Luther and his simple chorals, and was broadened, enriched, and established by the foundation of the modern opera—which attempted to produce the old tragedy and found great variety of tone-color and even dissonance necessary for strong expressions.

The fundamental postulate of all European tonic systems is that the entire body of tones and harmonies must always stand in close and distinct connection with a freely chosen keynote. The material of music is more abundant and more plastic than that of the other arts, and is used with greater freedom. The finest changes in consciousness are reflected and revealed as by no other kind of physical movement. Music is, in Vischer's language, a sort of "mechanics of the movements of the *Gemüth*" rather than of the feelings (as Helmholtz defends Hanslich for saying). Its effects upon and articulation of the states and changes in consciousness are more generic than is articulate speech. Melodic changes of pitch are graded and not continuous in all known ages and races for the same psychological reason that rhythm is universal. We are in the habit of measuring movement in space by our steps, hence rhythm. A scale is like a yardstick, with feet and inches, to measure changes in pitch. If there is no exact standard of measurement, as in the untonality of the whistling of the wind, or in arabesque ornamentation in architecture, if no system or unity is manifest, the effect is unpleasant. The æsthetic impression of music is like that of waves of water, and is described as a restful sense of a mighty but beautifully symmetrical life. It had been urged by Rameau that the ancient composers of homophonic melody had harmony in thought more or less consciously in composing harmonic accompaniments, at least of bass, long before the period of harmony began. This Helmholtz doubts. Oriental musicians cannot tolerate harmony now. At the same time he grants that for ears acute enough to detect overtones the higher octave and even the third, when heard in accompaniments, would be nothing new. Two tones are closely related if they have two overtones in common. The stronger the latter are as compared to all the rest the closer is the relationship and the more easily will singers and hearers recognize it. It must thus vary with the tone-color of different instruments. With instruments like the flute, which have few and feeble overtones, the intervals of the most common chords are perceived if at all in memory or not immediately, and hence when sounded seem new and strange. But if the ear is used to song and instruments with more colored tones in melody, the chords of the more common intervals seem already familiar, and are soon tolerated even if played on flutes. Now, a practiced musician, in hearing a melody or even reading its notes, can call up in mind a full harmonic accompaniment. The old five-note scale without half tones, in which Chinese and Gaelic music is written, is of course less harmonic than ours. It still maintains its own against the modern twelve-note scale, adapts melodies from which the notes it does not contain can be omitted, and tends to make up for few notes by greater compass. Hence the clearness and liveliness of the old Scotch melodies. There are five of these scales, and with the aid of transposition all the music written in them can be played on the black keys alone of a piano. The Greek scales were developed from the enharmonic chromatic diatonic tetrachord, to which many liturgic melodies of the Roman church are still limited, and till Pythagoras added an eighth they consisted of seven notes. For the various forms of expression which we effect by harmony and modulation the Greeks, whose music was homophonic, could use finer and more manifold gradations of their species of scale, while we have left but two, the major and minor, which are very easily distinguished. The greater fineness of the Greek as compared with the modern ear is thus vindicated. By natural construction, taking account of the first and second degrees only (whole and half notes), the five melodic scales of antiquity are reproduced according to acoustic principles. So far as homophonic song is concerned all are equally correct. With the gradual reference of all tones to one fundamental keynote the sense of a catenal relation of all tones to each other was gradually lost and the modern conception of tonality was unfolded.

Chords may be said simply to emphasize tone-color. The harmonious sequence of the popular major scale restricts all tones to their nearest relationship. The major is more purely diatonic, simpler, clearer, more consequent in both melody and harmony, than the minor scale. The latter best expresses what is indistinct, desolate, dreadful, mystic, savage, unæsthetic. The great musicians have not only made frequent use of this but sometimes even of the ancient, discarded scales.

In modulating or changing from one major key into another, several effects are secured. The change itself is agreeable, like the alternation of consonance and dissonance, and has in a sense taken the place of the more effective old Greek modulation from one species of scale to another. If an instrument with fixed and uniform tones is so tuned that all its half notes are equidistant, Helmholtz finds no reason why a distinctive absolute character should inhere in the different scales. They have a different character as usually played on a piano because the player's touch is unavoidably different for the black keys, and because the open unfingered strings have a distinctive tone. Corresponding differences exist also in wind instruments; the note and the overtones to which the cavity of the ear sympathetically responds may also have a peculiar character. It is these external accidents which enable us to distinguish the different scales.

This, however, is not the case with pure or natural, as distinguished from tempered, scales. The absolute char-

acter of the former, especially in the higher octaves is
quite distinct, and modulation becomes more striking and
effective by the use of tempered scales (introduced chiefly
by the piano, although within the compass of the voice the
beats are so infrequent that very few are heard before the
tone declines). These scales have lessened the accuracy
of the ear and the voice. In the natural system the tone
of a given key would vary a little according as it was consonant with a tertz or a quint. Helmholtz made the important observation that highly cultivated performers on
stringed instruments, and singers who habitually sing with
other voices or without accompaniment, actually use the
natural scale. But the mechanism of instruments and
mere convenience domineer over the natural necessity of
the ear and threaten the supremacy of the tonic note and
its chords, which is the fundamental principle of modern
music. They have even affected composition by making
modulation too easy and ineffective, so that the more drastic means of sharp dissonance and unnatural modulations
become necessary. The "tonic solfa associations" in England sing with enharmonic organs with sixty-five keys to
the octave, by the natural method, and the effect of this
music is most pleasing. Even children there, it is said,
find the piano wrong and think they sing the "real notes"
of the natural scale more easily. It was by this practical
application of his discoveries that Helmholtz, soon after the
first edition of the work we are describing, found himself
at the head of a strong party in the musical world and
the center of a controversy which has by no means yet
ceased.

Dissonances are means of contrast and of expression.
They excite a sense of impulsion forward, and are generally used just before endings to suspend the anticipation
of final accord already excited. Thus they have no independent right of existence. Those in use are carefully
enumerated and classified.

Sequent tones may be connected by a direct or an indirect relationship of the tones. In the former case they are separated by a consonant interval—the major sext and tertz being the most beautiful steps; in the latter, by movement along the scale in whole or half notes. Tones may also be brought into musical connection by adjacency of pitch, as where looped together by intersecting chromatic passages or transition notes. In the seventeenth century the feeling for catenal sequence of accord was developed—this, however, is manifestly possible with far less freedom for harmony than for homophonic melody. Thorough bass, according to Helmholtz, is made up of those tones which alone or chiefly are produced by the tones of successive accords. It thus comes to pass that each of its notes is followed by another nearly related to it and most commonly the octaves, quint, or tertz, above or below, as required by the famous rule of Rameau.

In this great work, in fine, Helmholtz has shown that harmonic overtones have always played an essential rôle in musical culture, not only for harmony, but also for melody. All the intervals of the scale might have been made equally distinguishable. Fechner's psycho-physic law has shown that such a gradation is possible for all our sensations, and it is almost universal in musical rhythms. Its analogue is the chromatic scale of the piano. But in none of the known scales of history has melody ever moved over uniform tone intervals. They are all constructed upon another principle, viz., that of the varying degrees of relationship in tones, which has become the foundation of modern melody and particularly of harmony. Scales and harmonies are thus a product of artistic invention and are by no means, as has usually been supposed, immediately given in the structure or properties of the human ear. They are rather the stories which art has used in the construction of our musical system, which to its very foundation must be judged according to æsthetic laws.

The work concludes with Helmholtz's famous æsthetic theory. Beauty he premises must conform to the laws and rules inherent in the nature of the human reason. No indication of consciousness or purposiveness should ever be apparent in a work of art. It must be judged and created conformably to laws and purposes not distinctly defined in the artist's consciousness, although the more rationality and symmetry the observer can discern by critical study the greater his interest and enjoyment become. It is the characteristic of great works of art that we see more intelligibility in them every time they are presented to us, and yet the most immediate and uncritical judgment recognizes æsthetic beauty without thinking of laws or reason, etc. Making allowance for national and individual variations of taste and for the undoubted enhancement of æsthetic pleasure which comes by education and practice, we expect and demand of every other sound mind the same recognition of beauty which we ourselves give it. This shows that we do not regard beauty as casual or individual. This recognition of lawfulness by intuition is a most essential element and is the most difficult to explain. When we recognize manifold traces of order without grasping the law, a feeling of rationality which is unlimited arises. We credit the artist with a tact or thought superior to our own power to analyze or even fully to recognize. In a great artist we revere a genius with a spark of divine creativeness which far transcends our slower-paced thought, and yet we know that he is a man, with the same faculties as we, although purer, clearer, and better poised, so that we feel that we, too, have part in all his powers. Our trust in the bottom soundness of the human soul, bringing home to us a sense of unusual exaltation, our faith in the possibilities of our own nature, and our belief that the world is rational to its core thus are strengthened.

It has been seen how musicians have very gradually found out the analogous relationships between tones and chords, first in melody, then and more particularly in harmony. The entire system of rules which constitute the theory of thorough bass has been derived from the attempt to make this relation in the series of tones which constitute a piece of music clear and sensible. This sense of relationship, it has been shown, is grounded in the sensation of partial tones, the distinct existence of which can be proven, but which are generally perceived only in the aggregate by consciousness. The æsthetic problem is thus reduced to explaining a peculiarity common to all our sensuous perceptions, viz., the recognition of competing aggregates of sensations as sensuous symbols of apparently simple external objects without analyzing them. Our attention is so restricted to external objects that we are quite unpracticed in bringing peculiarities of our sensations as such to consciousness. We have only learned to know them as expressions for distinct things or processes. The similarity between an accord and its elementary tones is like a resemblance between two faces which is everywhere detected, while yet no one can point out any particular features which are alike, or specify wherein its resemblance consists. If father and daughter, he says, have noses or mouths alike it is readily observed but does not interest us, as where the resemblance is more indefinable. The latter case would constitute the chief beauty of painting and would show that the artist had an unusually fine feeling for the significance of features. So the octave is a clear, unattractive interval, while the great tertz and sext which are near the limit of intelligible intervals, requiring as they do for complete comprehension that the five partial tones should be audible, are most attractive for either melody or harmony. Again it is an essential characteristic of space that like bodies and like movements can be in every part of it. All that can occur in one part can also occur in every other part. So in the scale every phrase or chord can be executed at any pitch. So great is this analogy that we speak of the movement upward and downward of the voice. Hence it becomes possible that musical movement like that in space expresses the peculiar characteristics with impelling force, in fact, presents us with an image of powers and impulses that lie behind it. Hence may it be in the power of music to express and affect moods and dispositions. Nor is this inconsistent with the opinion that music originated in imitation of the instinctive modulations of the voice, rhythm, and accentuation, which express the liveliness and violence of psychic impulses, exertion raising the pitch, etc. The attempt to make recitation richer and more expressive may have led our ancestors to invent musical movements and cadences. But the scale makes musical imitation imperfect in the same way that embroidery on tapestry, canvas, or cardboard perforated in squares, with graded colors, gives imperfect representations of nature, while the introduction of tone-colored instruments makes music still more unlike the natural human voice. Thus music now has attained a far more general significance than instinctive vocal sounds could ever have.

The subject of visual perception had been zealously studied in Germany for several decades and a mass of most interesting physiological and psychological observations had been made when the first part of Helmholtz's "Physiologische Optik" appeared in 1856. Many experimenters, before they had attained the skill needful in studying subjective visual phenomena and in controlling the movements of the eyes, had injured their own vision more or less seriously. Not only had confirmation of contrary peripheral hypotheses been found in the results, but the play of individual peculiarities in ascertaining what the facts really were seemed greater than in any other chapter of physiology. To give some account of all the copious literature upon the subject, particularly the more modern, to verify in and to his own eye every observation of any importance or which had ever been made, and to bring order into the department by critically sifting all this chaotic material and introducing the empirical theory as the one by which the facts could be most consistently arranged and explained—this was the vast plan Helmholtz proposed to himself. The "Optics" is thus less an individual creation than the "Acoustics," but represents no less or less valuable scientific labor, while its importance for psychologists is even greater than the "Acoustics," greater perhaps with one exception than that of any book since Kant's "Kritique." In the space at our command any adequate résumé or digest of it is quite impossible. The chief psychological elements cannot be sifted out as we have attempted to do to some slight extent for the "Acoustics," but it is safe to say that no teacher of the laws and phenomena of mind can afford to be ignorant of a paragraph of it. We shall only attempt to give to those who have never read it some idea of its scope.

The comparative anatomy of the various structures of the eyeball, its curvature, diameter in various directions, the orthoscope by which the iris can be seen nearly at its true distance behind the cornea, the ophthalmometer which Helmholtz invented to determine the curvature of its cornea, which is about the same for eyes of all sizes, are described in the introductory sections. The grand divisions of the work are: (I) Dioptrics, or the course of the rays of light in the eye; (II) Visual Sensation; (III) Visual Perception. The first division is devoted to refraction by means of lenses, to methods of obtaining optical constants, and the cardinal points of the eye, to accommodation and the optometer, the colored edges of the retinal image caused by dispersion, astigmatism, or monochromatic aberration, the manifold entoptic phenomena, and the ophthalmoscope. The second division is occupied with the various methods of stimulating the retina and optic nerve, with simple and compound colors, the intensity and duration of sensations of light, with changes of irritability and after-images, contrast, and subjective phenomena. The third division treats perception in general and optical illusions, the movements of the eye-ball, the monocular field of vision, the innervation feelings of the muscles of the eye-ball, the perception of depth, binocular vision, and the rivalry of the fields of vision, with a criticism of theories.

We must restrict ourselves principally to the more specifically philosophical third part. Down to the seventeenth and eighteenth centuries the history of the theories of vision is comprised in the history of philosophy. From Democritus and Epicurus to Cartesius comparatively little was added to our knowledge of sight. The latter distinguished between the subjective qualities of sensation and the objective quantitative relations, and with Leibniz later established a consequent system of innate ideas. Berkeley, Locke, Hume, and Kant, as is well known, made the question of the existence of these ideas central in philosophy. The a priori theory was adopted from Kant by Johannes Müller, and, indeed, by most scientific men, before the publication of Helmholtz's work, and is now known as nativism. Müller assumed that the retina feels itself as extended in space by virtue of an innate capacity to do so, and that the sensations of both retinas are combined by the same sort of capacity. He urged that not only space and time, as Kant had said, but that the special localization of every impression immediately given in sensuous intuition is innate in the anatomical structure of the eye. It follows, necessarily, from this, that the soul knows immediately what points in the retina of one eye give the same localization as those in that of the other. Aubert believed that these congruous points (*Deckstellen*) were identical in the sense that it made no difference with our perception of space whether an image fell upon one retina or upon the corresponding point of the other. Professor Hering of Leipzig, the ablest living exponent of nativism, holds that in the perception of distance the sensations excited by the congruous points in the two retinas are innately different. This Helmholtz also admits. But Hering concludes that these sensations have from the first different spatial character, or distance, and gives the well known perceptive powers of a newly hatched chicken as a practical refutation of the empirical view. Helmholtz holds that the sensations excited in the right eye have an unknown quality which distinguishes them from sensations of corresponding points of the left, a quality which, like simple sensations themselves, has no spatial character whatever, but is used by the mind, which learns to create out of it perceptions and conceptions of space. The notion of space is thus not a pure intuition, or, in Kantian phrase, an a priori form of the external sense, but is inferred or induced from unspatial sensuous data, as, indeed, must be assumed by all logical believers in a fourth dimension. For nearly a score of years the subject of binocular vision has been the chief battleground between empiricists and a priorists in Germany. Since Wheatstone's invention of the stereoscope and the publication of the studies of Helmholtz, most of the best studies of optical phenomena, Nagel, Wundt, H. Meyer, Donders, Volkmann, Fick, Classen, and nearly all younger scientific men hold in some form with more or less reservation the empirical theory. The fundamental proposition of empiricism, according to Helmholtz, is that for our consciousness sensations are *symbols,* the meaning of which it is left to our understanding to find out. For the eye, these symbols differ in intensity and in color. There is also a place-mark or local sign which is different for every point of the retina. We feel, also, the degree of innervation which passes to the muscles of the eyeball. Experience teaches us what other sensations arise if the object is contemplated from different sides. The aggregate of all these manifold sensations—qualitative, quantitative, local, muscular, and also those possible from a different standpoint—gathered into one collective notion we call the perception of an object, so long as it is supported by present sensations, or an image of memory, if it is not thus supported. These elements make up the actual and only content of our notion of a seen object. The only psychic activity involved in this process is the regularly recurring association of two or more notions or impressions which have been often connected. These associations are, of course, more fixed and compulsive the more often the constituent elements have been repeated together. Indeed, the psychic processes involved not only in perception, but in many associations of ideas, are so compactly welded together that they have ceased to be permeable or analyzable by pure consciousness, or controllable, except indirectly, by the will. Hence it comes that the results of such compacted associations seem given to the mind from without as something quite foreign to it, as by an objective force of nature. When results of previous psychic processes thus attach themselves to present sensations, the former seem given like the latter, instead of having once been freely thought out. If any one prefers to say that these processes of association and the natural flux of concepts are due to the properties of nervous substance rather than to psychic activity, *i. e.*, to experience, Helmholtz has no objection, provided that innate neural mechanism is not made to produce ready-made spatial concepts when certain nerve fibers are stimulated. Such a mechanism must be admitted just as far and no farther to account for the association between the sensations and the conceptions of spatial forms, as it would be, *e. g.*, to account for the associations between the letters, the sound, and the meaning of a word, which are admittedly due to practice, experience, and custom, and could be unlearned as they have been learned.

The law according to which visual perceptions arise when impressions are made upon the retina is that we always conceive such objects as before us in the field of vision as must be there to make the same retinal impression when the eye is used under normal conditions. If, *e. g.*, the outer edge of the cornea is mechanically pressed, we think we see a ray of light coming from near the bridge of the nose. This is, in short, the principle by which optical illusions are to be explained. The psychic activities here involved may be designated as unconscious necessary analogical inferences; necessary because the impressions produced cannot be canceled by any degree of understanding of the real cause of the illusion; analogical because the cases where the spontaneous interpretations of the impression are correct so manifoldly outnumber the exceptions; inferences because from the observed effect upon a sense-organ the mind produces a conception of a cause of this effect. In designating these processes as unconscious, it is admitted that the psychic activity in the two kinds of inference may be different, but the similarity of results in both cases is assumed.

The second general characteristic of our sense perceptions is that we attend to them with ease and accuracy only so far as we can utilize them in knowing external objects that we understand, and we ignore all those parts of sensations that have no significance for outer objects. Some men, like Purkinje, Volkmann, and Fechner, seem to have a special talent for observing the latter, but the phenomena of the blind spot in the eye and the existence of summative tones had to be first discovered theoretically. Many persons can see even after-images and floating specks in the vitreous humor only casually or after considerable practice. A similar difficulty arises when composite sensations are to be resolved into their elements. The perception of bodies of three dimensions of space, which depends on the existence of a different perspective in the two eyes, and the apparently simple quality of luster, which depends on different colors, or brightness, of the two retinal images, may serve as examples of many cases in which a composite aggregate of sensations is used as a whole for a sign of a single object. The colors of a landscape, *e. g.*, look brighter and more like a flat picture without the perspective which it should have, if we view it with inverted head, because we are accustomed in a normal position to interpret the modifications in the tones of sky, foliage, etc., as a sign of distance. With inverted head, the half of the retina which is more used to seeing sky and cloud where color is perceived in itself more than as a sign of distance, receives the colored images of hills or trees and interprets these relatively unusual sensations not as signs, but, according to its wont, at their own worth. So, too, the sensation of wetness one sometimes experiences in touching a cold, smooth piece of metal shows that this sensation is composed of coolness and smoothness. We are thus well practiced in inferring the objective qualities of objects from our sensation, but we are entirely unpracticed in bringing our pure sensations themselves to consciousness. The same is true of our perception of spatial relations. We have to look at a walking man through a telescope which gives inverted images in order to be conscious of the manifold springings, twistings, and swingings of the body which are combined in the ordinary perception of a man walking.

The great difficulty is, of course, to find a criterion by which to distinguish between what is immediately given as sensation and what comes by experience and practice. This Helmholtz attempts to lighten by assuming that no element in perception can be admitted to be sensorial which can be suppressed or reversed by movements which experience has demonstrably given. What experience can overcome must be a product of experience. The sensation of light, *e. g.*, which is caused by pressure upon the eye-ball, cannot be obviated or eliminated by any amount of explanation or understanding of it. The attention may be diverted, but whenever we attend, the sensation is there, as usual, as if caused by an outer object. According to this rule, only the qualities of sensation can be regarded as pure sensation, and all else, spatial or temporal, as products of experience. Of course, experience does not teach only facts and experience may confront experience with illusions that are produced by experience, and may long prevail against better knowledge and new experience. If we fixate on an object with only one eye, if we see it only in indirect vision, with the head held obliquely, or, in case it is near, with eyeballs rolled up or down, certain illusions are caused which do not occur if both eyes are used normally. Thus we are not equally practiced in interpreting visual sensations in all positions or directions of the eye, but are best practiced for those which follow the most accurate and accordant perceptions. What we have learned under these conditions of normal use we apply to all cases. A similarity of sensations which are caused under such unusual conditions as the above with those which arise in normal vision is not so striking that inferences from the former to the latter are infallible or uniform. Hence the different interpretations of different observers and even of the same observers at different times, which have occasioned so much strife in physiological optics and cause good observers to be so often misled by individual peculiarities in other natural sciences.

In designating sensations as *symbols* of things, as above, Helmholtz denies all likeness or similarity between the two. The great historical question is whether sensations agree with things, *i. e.*, whether they are true or false. Not only a preëstablished harmony but even an identity between them has, as is well known, been asserted as the basis of imposing systems of philosophy, with which, indeed, the nativistic theory is thus far in accord. The English associationists, on the other hand, denied a correspondence between them and regarded our perceptions, therefore, as illusions and all real knowledge of any object as impossible. Premising that all our intuition and perception are

298

effects of intuited and conceived objects upon our nervous system and in consciousness, that every effect depends upon the nature of its cause and also upon the nature of that on which it works, Helmholtz urges that to require a conception to reproduce the nature of the thing conceived with absolute truth and without reference to the nature of the senses, nerves, and consciousness is absurd. Helmholtz continues in a noteworthy passage that it is senseless to speak of any other than a practical truth in perception. Our notions of things must be symbols for regulating movements and actions. When we have learned to read these symbols correctly we are able with their help so to direct our actions that the desired result, *i. e.*, the expected new sensations, shall follow. Every other comparison between things and thoughts is not only unreal, but inconceivable. To ask whether the notions which I have of a table, its form, density, color, weight, are true in and for themselves and accordant with actual things apart from the practical use that can be made of these notions is as absurd as to ask whether a tone is red or yellow. Things and our conceptions of them belong to two entirely different worlds, as incommensurate as color and tone, or as the letters and the sound of a word. Even a perspective projection of a table in the brain would not be a notion of the table, but a second physical object to be perceived like the first.

Properties of things are only the effects which they exert upon us or upon other things. They are not inherent in objects in and for themselves, but always relate to other objects or to our senses. The only respect in which there is a real accordance between our perception and reality is in time. The sequence of external changes and our perception of them are, with slight qualifications, the same. Of space we have correct images at most of but two dimensions. The conception of a table, again, comprises a multitude of single visual impressions of its different sides and distances, another series of tactual impressions received by moving the hand over different parts of its surface, etc. This collective conception is in fact already an idea (*Begriff*) in the same sense as the generic "table" is. This conception is correct, accurate, true, if I can infer from it exactly what sensations will come by moving hand and eye in various ways and over various parts. There is no other sort of similarity between an object and a conception, which is its mental sign, not arbitrarily determined like speech and writing, but compulsory from the nature of sense and mind. This concept may be valid and sure, since our idea of things may be true without being like things, and yet it is imperfect as is, *e. g.*, every normal eye—with bits of solid and opaque matter floating in its fluids, with a lens imperfectly transparent at the seams of its structure, without the power to unite rays which proceed from one point and converge in a point again, able to react upon ether vibrations within only limited variations of wave lengths, seeing well only in direct vision and within certain distances. But the eye is nevertheless the most practical and serviceable of organs.

As to the nature of inference, Helmholtz declares himself in accord with John Stuart Mill, that the major premise is a product of experience and that the conclusion teaches us nothing new. Unlike Mill, however, he believes that the law of casuality, instead of being a product of experience, is a law of thought which precedes experience. The inference by which we are impelled to pass from the world of sensations to the notion of an external world, and, in fact, most instances of cause in organic as distinct from inorganic nature, are cases in which the causal connection between natural processes cannot be rigorously proven, but is nevertheless firmly believed to exist. Were it a product of experience, the degree of its validity would be at best about the same as that of rules for the changes of weather and fluctuations of the wind, and the vitalistic physiologists who assert that its scope is very limited in organic nature

could not be disputed. The natural instinct to believe in
freedom of the will also presents a wide field, in which it
is impossible to prove the causal law with any rigor, however firmly reason may believe in its existence. Again, the
application of the law that everything must have a cause
has less to do with experience than with our understanding
of it, for from cases of error we infer not the falsity of
the law, but our own ignorance of all the complex of
sequences. The final term of every causal train of reasoning is that masses exist, move, and act on each other in
space. But matter and force are abstract ideas, and how
can we make these, which are not proven by experience,
the sufficient grounds of natural phenomena? Natural
laws are simply general ideas derived from changes in
nature. But since as generic ideas they pertain in the first
place only to our thought, yet must be held to be solid and
operative apart from it, we call them causes and forces.
The law of sufficient ground is thus simply an instinct of
our understanding to subject all its perceptions to its own
control, rather than to a law of nature. Our understanding is the faculty of forming general ideas, of seeking
causes and tracing out causal connections. This is comprehending, and hence what we cannot comprehend cannot be
thought of as existing.[1]

What Helmholtz thought on religious themes no one
seems to have known, for he was strangely silent upon such
subjects. His work, however, was penetrated with the
spirit of reverence. He knew and needed no double housekeeping, and apparently had never experienced any conflict
between the head and the heart, which, as we have seen,
was the mainspring of very much that Lotze and Fechner,
like so many others, have done. He was content to think
God's thoughts after him in Nature, the first great revela-

[1] The above psychological paragraphs are epitomized statements
of § 26 and § 33, of the Physiolog. Optik and what is criticized in
same.

tion, and perhaps understood this so well and found it so satisfying that he felt no need of any other.

He was probably the greatest master of experimental physical science of the nineteenth century. He paid no heed to the boundaries that separate the sciences and took no interest in surveying boundaries, as one would infer is often the chief interest of Wundt. During his life he taught anatomy, including its applications to art, surgery, physiology, physics, and mathematics, and added greatly to the world's knowledge of psychology, of meteorology, and of chemical theory. In his work on the eye and the ear it is often hard to say whether he is more anatomist, physiologist, or mathematician, so freely, constantly, and unconsciously does he modulate from one to the other in quest of his theme. Had he not been an expert in all these domains and had he had greater respect for fences and less love of cross-country excursions, he could not have accomplished his great work. He felt it a duty and a pleasure to give popular lectures (of which we now have two volumes in English) in order to explain in non-technical terms to intelligent laymen what his work and what science meant, and in this he was hardly behind Du Bois Reymond, Huxley, or Tyndall. Some of this work, like so much else that he did, is a model of its kind. When he heard of the telephone and wireless telegraphy, he only remarked that they were to be expected and were inevitable results of what he and the most brilliant of his pupils, Hertz, who was cut off at the early age of thirty-three, to Helmholtz's profound grief, had discovered. He was too dignified and economical of his time and energy to engage in polemics, and perhaps his Quaker ancestry contributed to make him a man of peace. His lectures were never thronged by students, for not very many could understand him. He taught sometimes subjects far from those which he was at the time most intent upon, but later in life he had one of the supreme satisfactions of a professor's life, perhaps

to a higher degree than any academic teacher, save in the
field of metaphysics, ever enjoyed, viz., that of teaching
chiefly what he himself had discovered and wrought out,
with the reporting at second-hand on others' views reduced
to its minimum. This first-hand teaching has an inspiration all its own to both teacher and taught. The range of
topics to which he had made important contributions became so wide that, if this plan had been exclusively ad-
hered to, he would have had to omit but very few topics
in the field he covered. Thus his teaching, though to the
few, illustrated the very highest academic ideal. His best
work, too, was done in small, plain quarters, with but little,
cheap, and largely self-devised and constructed apparatus.
For one, I believe that his "Optics" and his "Accoustics"
are and will long remain by far the greatest and most original masterpieces in experimental psychology, the study of
which should be felt supremely incumbent upon all who
specialize in this field. Again, most who cover so many
fields as Helmholtz did (and it is a peculiar affectation of
philosophical and even psychological thinkers to affect this)
are usually regarded by experts in each branch as superficial amateurs, but the best mathematicians of his day could
hardly bestow too much praise upon Helmholtz's work in
their field; physiologists recognized that he added more,
perhaps, to their domain than any other man of his day,
while for physicists he was by general acclaim the man of
the century. I should place him, in addition, as, *facile
princeps,* the leader and model to all experimental psychologists. Save Hering's rival color theory, hardly anything
he did has ever been questioned, and in almost no respect
have we yet gone beyond him in the themes he treated.

Once more, his temper, bearing, manner, and whole
diathesis are hardly less ideal than his work. His form,
face, and head were commanding. Hansemann, after his
death, found his brain among the largest of all, and the
sulci, especially in the region which Flechsig assigns to

association and originality, were deep and many. His eye and ear were remarkable organs and had seen, heard, and done more, perhaps, than those of any other man, and he also had the hygienic sense not to impair even his eye, as Volkmann, Purkinje, Fechner, and others had done in optical investigations. That these and his brain were not more minutely and comparatively studied is a misfortune to science.

Perhaps he comes nearer than any other man (although possibly some might except Darwin, despite the fact that his type of mind is so different that comparisons are idle) to deserving the highest compliment ever paid to a man, which was given him by a colleague after his death, viz., that from maturity his every serious thought had added something to the sum of human knowledge and expanded its boundaries. Certain it is that, in all the titles, degrees, medals, and other honors conferred upon him by his countrymen and in other lands, the paintings hung, the busts set up, and the large statue in bronze erected on the initiative of the Kaiser in the yard of the University, Germany has honored herself no less than she has honored him. Could eugenics ever teach us how to breed such men, the progress of mankind toward penetrating the boundless secrets of Nature would be incalculably accelerated.

No brief sketch can do justice to a man like this. To my thinking, he more than Wundt is the ideal laboratory psychologist, fittest of all to set fashions and point the way to experimentalists in this field. He kept with great tact and discretion to problems that were solvable and practically every result he reached still remains unquestioned. Progress will, of course, in time, transcend but will never invalidate his conclusions. His methods, too, no one impugns. He always subordinated them to the subject matter, and, accurate as they were, they were never more exact or complex than was absolutely necessary for the theme. Always the theme stood out. So far was he from being a method pedant or a tinkerer that he always kept methods and apparatus severely in their place as means, never as ends. In his model studies of the ear and the eye he repeated every experiment of his predecessors and more often simplified than intricated their ways of doing things. Little cared he for definitions or demarcations. He wasted no energy in laying out or building fences between the different departments of knowledge, as Wundt has done, until some of his pupils are prone to lose sight of or ignore the natural bonds between them. He had no respect for such artificial partitions, but followed his theme across or over them all. When investigating the eye and the ear, nothing pertaining to their structure, evolution, natural or culture history, physics, psychology, æsthetics, philosophical or epistemological relations was foreign to his interests. These disciplines were all kits of tools from which must be taken those that helped to make the finished work better. Mere classification or taxonomy is necessary, but it may well be left to narrower minds merely to discriminate methods, domains, and results. Again, he never wrote himself out or published prematurely. He waited till all was finished, clear, unitary, and then set forth the results as succintly and plainly as he could. His scientific writings are, therefore, less often prolix than liable to contain omissions, or are perplexing because of their condensation. He seems never to have felt that he had made a subject thoroughly his own until he had stated it in its simplest terms and made it accessible to the common sense of the mind. This instinct, which is responsible for the three large volumes of his popular papers, seems a product of two factors: first, to get a clearer grip of the subject itself, for he felt that nothing was completely understood until it could be stated so that a very elemental and uninformed mind could grasp it; and secondly, his deep and unique conviction as to the duty of savants to popularize their results not only for the benefit of universities and the winning of confidence in research, but as no small factor in the advancement of civilization. In the choice of problems, too, which he made with such remarkable sagacity and opportuneness, if not inevitableness, the same motive is apparent, so that his mind seems almost an oracle of the scientific consciousness of his age. His style, also, is plain and clear and perhaps was more or less modeled on English patterns. He is sometimes terse and crisp, and his sentences are never involuted, contorted, ambiguous, or hazy. He seems to have had an æsthetic instinct that made him feel the charm of the easiest way. For these reasons, it seems possible that, just as after the great speculative age of German philosophy, it was found by general consent necessary to slight his successors and go back to Kant to start over again, so, when those tendencies have spent their forces that have irradiated from the Leipzig cult, in which the proportion of method to matter has been constantly increasing of late, experimental psychology will go back to Helmholtz if it is to remain truly scientific and to make sure progress along experimental lines.

BIBLIOGRAPHY

Engelmann, T. W., and others. Beiträge zur Psychologie und Physiologie der Sinnesorgane: Hermann von Helmholtz als Festgruss zu seinem siebsigsten Geburtstag, gesamm. u. hrsg. von A. König. Hamburg, Voss, 1891. 388 pp.

Rohr, Moritz. Abhandlungen zur Geschichte des Stereoskops von Wheatstone, Brewster, Riddell, Helmholtz, Wenham, d'Almeida und Harmer, hrsg. von M. von Rohr. Leipzig, W. Engelmann, 1908. 129 pp.

Koenigsberger, Leo. Hermann von Helmholtz. Braunschweig, F. Vieweg & Sohn, 1902. 3 vols. Tr. by Frances A. Welby, with a preface by Lord Kelvin. Oxford, Clarendon Press, 1906. 440 pp.

McKendrick, John Gray.—Hermann Ludwig Ferdinand von Helmholtz. London, T. Fisher Unwin, 1909. 300 pp.

HERMANN L. F. VON HELMHOLTZ

Ueber die Methoden, kleinste Zeittheile zu messen, und ihre Anwendung für physiologische Zwecke. König. naturwissen. Unterhaltungen, Bd. 2, Heft 2, 1851. 190 p.

Handbuch der physiologischen Optik, ergänzt und hrsg. in Gemeinshaft mit A. Gullstrand, J. von Fries und W. Nagel. 3rd ed. Leipzig, L. Voss. Bd. 1, 1909, 376 p. Bd. 2, 1911, 391 p.; Bd. 3, 1910, 564 p. (First issued in Allge. Encyklop. der Physik, v. 11, 1867, pp. 433-875.)

Helmholtz und G. von Pietrowski. Ueber Reibtung tropbarer Flüssigkeiten. (Aus den Sitzungsbericht, 1860, der K. Akad. der Wissensch.) Wien, Gerold in Comm., 1860, 54 p.

Die Lehre von den Tonempfindungen als physiologische Grundlage für der Theorie des Musik. 3rd rev. ed. Braunschweig, F. Vieweg & Sohn, 1870. 639 p. Tr. by Alexander J. Ellis from the 4th ed. London, Longmans, 1877. 576 p. (First ed., 1863. 600 p.)

Populäre wissenschaftliche Vorträge. Braunschweig, 1865-76. 3 Hfte. In dritter Auflage (1884) erweitert in 2 Bänden u. d. T. "Vorträge und Reden" (5th Aufl., 1903, 2 Bde.) Tr. by E. Atkinson with an introduction by Professor Tyndall. N. Y., Longmans, Green & Co., 1904. 2 vols., with an autobiography of the author.

Wissenschaftliche Abhandlungen. Leipzig, J. A. Barth, 1882-95. Vol. 1, 1882, 938 p.; Vol. 2, 1883, 1021 p.; Vol. 3, 1895, 654 p.

Goethe's Vorahnungen kommender naturwissenschaftlicher Ideen. Berlin, Gebr. Paetel, 1892. 55 p.

Zwei hydrodynamische Abhandlungen. Ostwald's Klassiker der exakten Wissenschaften. hrsg. von A. Wangerin, Nr. 79, 1889.

Vorlesungen über theoretische Physik. 1897-1903.

    Vol. 1. Einleitung zu den Vorlesungen über theoretische Physik, hrsg. von Arthur König und Carl Runge. Leipzig, J. A. Barth, 1903, 50 p. und Vorlesungen über die dynamik discreter Massenpunkte, hrsg. von Otto Krigar-Menzel. Leipzig, J. A. Barth, 1898. 380 p.

    Vol. 2. Dynamik continuirlich verbreiteter Massen, hrsg. von Otto Krigar-Menzel, 1902. Leipzig, J. A. Barth, 1902. 247 p.

    Vol. 3. Vorlesungen über die mathematischen Principien der Akustik, hrsg. von Arthur König und Carl Runge. Leipzig, J. A. Barth, 1898. 256 p.

    Vol. 4. Vorlesungen über Elektrodynamik und Theorie des Magnetismus, hrsg. von Otto Krigar-Menzel und Max Laue. Leipzig, J. A. Barth, 1907. 406 p.

    Vol. 5. Vorlesungen über die elektromagnetische Theorie des Lichts, hrsg. von Arthur König und Carl Runge. Leipzig, L. Voss, 1897. 370 p.

    Vol. 6. Vorlesungen über Theorie der Warme hrsg. von Franz Richarz. Leipzig, Barth, 1903. 419 p.

Sur les mouvements atmospheriques. (In Brillouin, L. M. ed. Mémoires originaux sur la circulation générale de l'atmosphére. 1900, p. 132-61.)

Festschrift zur Feier des 70 Geburtstages von Hermann von Helmholtz. Hamburg, L. Voss, 1893. 91 p.

Ausprachen und Rede gehalten der am. 2 November, 1891, zu Ehren von Hermann von Helmholtz veranstalteten. Feier. Berlin, A. Hirschwald, 1892. 63 p.

WILHELM WUNDT
1832–

WILHELM WUNDT

WILHELM WUNDT

1832–

Wundt was born in 1832 and will be eighty next August, an event which his many pupils and admirers in Germany, this country, and elsewhere ought to commemorate. Of his early life and parentage I find no record, though I am told that a few records have appeared in the German press. He attained the degrees of M. D. and of Ph. D. and habilitated as Docent in Physiology at Heidelberg, where he became for a time an assistant of Helmholtz, who later desiring a helper more accomplished in mathematics and physics, sought another in his place. When Helmholtz went to Berlin, Wundt's friends proposed his name for the chair of Physiology left vacant, but Kühne won the appointment. In 1873 Wundt went to Zurich as Professor of Philosophy, and in the following year was called to Leipzig, where he has been ever since. From the first he was a hard worker, but won scant recognition until the first edition of his "Physiological Psychology" appeared in 1874. One of his competitors for the Leipzig position was Horwicz, the analyst of feeling, but the scale was turned in Wundt's favor by the Herbartians, whose stronghold was in this university. Here Wundt has been from the first one of the most popular and influential and of late the leading professor in the philosophical department, and has served one term as Rector. The very term "psychophysics" designated something which was in good repute at Leipzig, as was the idea of applying mathematics to the studies of the human soul, which Fechner as well as Herbart had

21   311

advocated and promoted. Thus, no place in Germany was so favorable for the reception of the new mode of applying the exact methods of physical science to psychology, because the succession to Wundtism from the doctrines of Herbart and Fechner was both legitimate and direct. Here Wundt developed the first experimental laboratory of psychology, and here in the early eighties I heard his lectures and took part as a Versuchs-thier in several experimental studies, most of my time being absorbed by physiological work with Ludwig, where I investigated the summation of muscular stimuli and also printed another small joint monograph on retinal stimulation with von Kries, attending other rather miscellaneous scientific courses.

In this circle, Wundt was then regarded not without some disparagement. He was married shortly after leaving Heidelberg and is the father of a son, Max, and a daughter, the former first a philologist and now a philosopher who has written on Greek Ethics. He is a man of modest and rather unimpressive personality, of simple tastes and life, and untraveled, having, I think, never visited even England, reading but not speaking English with ease. In 1900 and again in 1910 the institution with which I am connected made earnest efforts to induce him to visit this country, but he was unable to accept, pleading none too vigorous health and the pressure of work. He has never been induced to attend any congress and avoids all public functions. In his laboratory and at his home he is courteous and helpful, and talks very freely with his students though he is often a little preoccupied, and is by nature not *gemüthlich*. In his laboratory, when I knew it, he was suggestive and assiduous, but he has lately depended more and more upon assistants for details of technique and practical manipulation. Perhaps not his interest but his personal attention to laboratory work, although always maintained relatively, has declined as he has become more absorbed in literary and philosophic activities.

Wundt is a superb academic lecturer and to this he owes much. He was the first professor in the philosophic field to experiment before his classes, as he used to do when the laboratory was a small private venture of his own. He has always had a talent for making philosophical and psychological topics interesting and popular for students of medicine, theology and even law and his service in stemming the tide of specialization by attracting attention to the most humanistic of all fields has been very great. As an expositor of opinion, Wundt has nearly every quality of effectiveness. Some have thought he simplified too much before his large academic audiences and made topics too easy by passing lightly over difficulties. Certain it is that most of his lectures are more elementary than his texts and indeed only a German special student in that country where the lecture method is so potent a tradition would be likely to attend, as they do, courses on topics on which the lecturer has already printed a book. It is a curious illustration of the different academic temper of that country that students will crowd long courses which they could get up for themselves from the lecturer's text with great saving of time and effort. Outside his own classroom, Wundt has never been a popular lecturer. He has no gifts such as Du Bois-Reymond, Huxley and even Helmholtz had, to simplify his own ideas for the general public or perhaps it should rather be said that he has no taste for this sort of work. So far as he has attempted to make propaganda of his own views, it has been within academic walls by elementarizing what he has written in greater detail.

Wundt has the great natural advantage of having chosen a life course of work that is in harmony with the progressive stages of adult development. In the docent years of apprenticeship, he was in hot pursuit of the problems of physiology, the modern development of which is one of the great achievements of German science and which has lifted medicine throughout the world to a higher plane. Physiology brings various other sciences to a focus. To know it has well been called a liberal education as well as an excellent practical discipline in logic and in manipulation. The science is so new as still to be invested with some of the glory of its dawn. It rests upon the great ideal of applying physics, the most exact of all sciences, and more recently chemistry, to the study of the functions of living tissue and of the human body. This suggests a further conquest of nature quite in line with all Baconian ideals and opens endless vistas of substituting definite and well assured in the place of vague knowledge in realms both practical and theoretical which had hitherto been invested more or less with speculative and traditional ideas. Thus, to apply these methods to the senses and to the elementary intellectual processes was the inevitable next step and behind it was all the momentum of the physiological Renaissance which was itself of great culture significance. With biology Wundt has had little, perhaps too little, to do. When he began experimental psychology there was little save the psychophysic law, reaction times, the experimental physiology of the senses and the early studies in brain localization. Now, we have a vast body of organized methods and results requiring in a novice several hundred standard experiments with apparatus, under experts who spend most of their time in the laboratory, employing new methods of observation and introspection. From all these sources has come a Renaissance of interest in the studies of the human soul, which had long been discredited by exuberant and unsubstantial speculation. Of this movement for nearly fifty years Wundt has been the center and more and more the leader and to him more than any one else is due the fact that instead of being despised and rejected of science, the studies of the mind, the highest thing in the highest creature, are rapidly winning a place of such influence and importance as to suggest to some a revival of

314

the old sovereignty of studies in this field over other departments which was exerted by the philosophers of the
great romantic age that ended with Hegel. Not a few
of Wundt's pupils—Titchener, Kraepelin, Müller, Cattell,
Meumann, the Würzburgers and others—have gone distinctly beyond Wundt. Some of them are turning out
works that rival the productiveness of the mother laboratory, have opened new fields and even challenged and
transcended and occasionally refuted a number of the cherished positions of the leader who has sometimes been
stirred to polemics against the very pupils whom he has
inspired, although he has never indulged in the extrava-
gance or violence that was characteristic of the philosophic
intermezzo which for a generation preceded his entrance
upon the stage. The psychological laboratory has constantly changed and is a very different thing from what
it was in the early eighties when I was enabled to found
the first Wundtian laboratory in this country at the Johns
Hopkins University, to be followed in a few years by those
of Cattell at Philadelphia and Columbia, Titchener at Cor-
nell, Münsterberg at Harvard and many more. All the surface mining has been done and the technique of methods
(which at its best is an admirable and new school of logic, a
logic which however has never been written) is a more effective engine for exploiting the field and has a larger
future than was at first realized, even though some of the
followers of the Wundtian movement seem to me in danger
of forgetting the grand old Aristotelian precept which
should be written upon the walls of every psychological
laboratory to the effect that it is only pedantry to apply
in any fields methods more exact than those of which the
subject admits. Beginning in the small and more accessible
field of sensations, experimental methods have steadily
moved on and up toward the more complex problems of
association, attention, will, voluntary movement, the higher
thought processes and even feeling, so that to reach the

frontier and establish really new facts now requires a rather elaborate panoply of knowledge, experiment, ingenuity and skill. Wundtian methods are also now to some extent applied in the study of insanity, as witness the new laboratories in fifteen of our progressive asylums. It is also to some extent to Wundt's pupils, although far more to his spirit, that we owe the new enthusiasm and the recent improvements in controlled observational methods in the study of animal instinct from tropisms up to the tests of the intelligence and training of dogs, monkeys and the rest, although Wundt himself has done little or nothing in this field. In experimental æsthetics, his contributions have been of minor importance and to others must be ascribed the more significant initiations, although this too has not escaped the influence of his work. He somewhere says substantially that everyone who studies philosophy, ethics, psychology or related branches should always have on hand some experimental work as a tonic. For many years Wundt conducted a weekly philosophic club or seminary of students to each of whom he assigned topics and references beforehand and who read their essays in turn. These are, or at least were in my day, mainly digests of larger works or monographs or topics traced through the history of thought and reported for mutual benefit. Here he was the most diligent and assiduous of note-takers and thus used the work of others as an instrument for foraging, so that this has doubtless been of great and legitimate service to him in the preparation of his various books, some one or more of which he seems also to feel that every real scholar should always have on hand. Unlike Lotze, who also began as a medical psychophysiologist, he has never lost his anchorage to scientific methods although he occasionally drifts out into the shoreless ocean of metaphysical speculation. He is not, however, a great scientific genius like Helmholtz, nor is he always exact enough to avoid error or escape just criticism, although precision of phraseology is almost an obsession with him. But after fifty years of hard honest intellectual work, taking into account quantity, quality and range, there are probably few men of our day or his own who deserve a place above him. His work requires vast information in various diverse fields, breadth of sympathy, and critical acumen to sift out those errors which abound in studies of the mind perhaps as nowhere else, and a moderation and temperance of inference in sifting and judging which is one of the rarest virtues in those who deal with philosophic problems. He has traversed the long and often dreary field of theory concerning the relations between the body and the brain and nature in general, now suggesting further research, now brushing away many carefully woven fabrics of cobwebs, making on the whole remarkably few blunders and misjudgments, and, in fine, doing much to vindicate perhaps his deepest feeling that psychology in the large sense, including the other mental disciplines, ought to be the queen of all the sciences.

Among his earliest works was his theory of muscular movements,[1] dedicated to Du Bois-Reymond, which is expressly based upon the author's own investigations begun in the summer of 1857 in Berlin at Reymond's suggestion and stimulated by the work of Eduard Weber. The young investigator here experiments upon the elasticity of muscles at rest and the influence of the nervous system upon them, the effect of blood and its occlusion, and of heat and chemical agents. He studied also muscular death, and relaxation. In the second part he experimented upon elasticity during action and showed the effect of tetanus upon cohesion; he also tested the effect of the constant galvanic current, applied mechanical, thermal and chemical stimuli, and tried to observe spontaneous irritability, and measure fatigue.

[1] Die Lehre von der Muskelbewegung, 1858, p. 241.

Wundt's first book,[1] published in 1862, when he was privat docent at Heidelberg, based upon papers that had been printed in Henle's *Zeitschrift* since 1858, bore Leibniz's motto, *nihil est in intellectu quod non fuerit in sensu, excipe nisi ipse intellectus.* Here he discusses briefly the history of the theory of vision, then describes vision, monocular and binocular, discusses luster, contrast, rivalry, the horopter, eye movements, the development of the field of vision, accommodation, etc., with minor sections on perception, touch, muscle sense, etc. He expresses the general conclusion that the soul is something that develops from itself and acts according to logical laws. He is much impressed with visual paradoxes and anomalies. We have here a number of the cuts which have appeared in successive editions of his psychology, and still more of the matter. He was here attempting with some enthusiasm to make experimental observations upon vision with the aid of certain physical apparatus. This meritorious little work has never reached a second edition and should be regarded as having chiefly historical value, as showing an early stage of the development of the author's interest in experiment.

Wundt's general point of view and both the problem and standpoint of his life work are probably best expressed in the long and important introduction to this work. It is so significant as a key to his own general position that it should be briefly résuméd here as follows: He premises that the progress of natural sciences is bound up with progress in the methods of investigation. Every important new apparatus or instrument like the ophthalmoscope, laryngoscope, etc., is followed by a series of new discoveries, and modern science itself originated in a revolution of methods in the hands of Bacon, Galileo, etc. Assuming psychology to be a natural science, it is the only one which had not felt the impulse of new empirical meth-

[1] Beiträge zur Theorie der Sinneswahrnenmung, 1862, p. 451.

ods. Hence it had advanced not one essential step since Aristotle. Questions concerning the constitution, essence, seat, origin, and future state of the soul, which have hitherto been the leading themes of psychological investigation, belong only to metaphysics. They are problems which stand behind psychology and have a sort of justification only after all its specific questions are answered. To put them first is as if physics instead of confining itself to the phenomena and laws of light, heat, sound, electricity, should occupy itself in discussing the ultimate constitution of matter and the nature of force. Why does psychology, he asks, insist on beginning where it should only end, especially as there are so many psychological questions which admit of an independent solution? In proportion as it has been more and more clearly seen that philosophy, like other sciences, must take experience as its point of departure, it has received more attention and acquired more significance till "it is scarcely too much to say that all our philosophy is at present psychology." It has made so little progress because there is no scientific field so crowded with presuppositions and prejudices. Most psychologists still seek for new standpoints and ideas which they hope may shed a sudden light or bring sudden order into the dark chaos of miscellaneous facts. Here as everywhere the most complex problems are most readily seen and the simplest must be sought by painstaking analysis. The development of the soul of the human infant, the comparative study of animal instinct and of savage races he declares are among the most important and promising fields, although great improvement of method is needed before work here will have real value.

The methods of psychology, he continues, have hitherto been principally two: first, self-observation, and, second, the derivation of psychic phenomena from metaphysical hypotheses. The first can never get beyond the facts of consciousness to their causes or their elements in unconsciousness. For this reason the so-called empirical psychology can at best consist of only a disordered grouping of a few conscious facts. Because this method can give even the meager array of facts which it has at its command no continuity and no organic connection, empirical psychology has cultivated the vicious habit of representing the various forms of psychic activity as due to distinct powers or faculties. This extremity of psychology gave to the great philosophic systems an inviting opportunity to construe psychic phenomena according to metaphysical hypotheses. Because the stones in this psychological structure were not cemented but only loosely tumbled together, they were easily built each into its distinct place in vast and tediously compacted metaphysical systems only to fall with them if a single stone was anywhere loosened. Hence came the deductive metaphysical psychology, while the inductive, empirical branch of it gave very few facts because it used but few of the methods of induction. Hence psychology stands in no such relation to metaphysics as does mechanics to geometry or sociology to psychology. Metaphysics should confessedly, as it does really, rest upon psychology instead of conversely. Aristotle, and, after him, still more sharply, Wolff, divided psychology into two parts—one deductive in which the essence of the soul was developed from ideas, and the other inductive in which its properties given by experience are investigated, but even this distinction between rational and empirical psychology was lost in the idealistic systems of Fichte, Schelling and Hegel. These assigned to psychology a very subordinate position. In attempting to give the commonplace empirical psychic facts a factitious ideal or logical unity, their real genetic connection, given in experience, was destroyed.

After it had been attempted to deduce the whole domain of experience from metaphysical hypotheses, nothing was more natural than that psychology should be subjected to mathematical treatment, such as Herbart attempted, who thought it could be so treated with as great certainty as physical science. This, although it added little to fact and was mistaken in method, had the great and signal merit of having first recognized a unity if not of the soul, at least of psychic phenomena, with science. It regarded the soul life as a whole. The principles from which Herbart took his departure in his deductions were not developed from psychology, though they were dependent upon it, but were taken from another department and adapted to facts in this. Concepts were regarded as if they were physical masses acting upon and causing motions in each other in space, and so could be treated statistically and mechanically. Since Leibniz, who devoted so much of his life to mental science, discovered the differential calculus which is continually passing over to functions which cannot be spatially represented, it has now become clear that for pure thought there is no limitation to three dimensions, and so the application of mathematics to the phenomena of mind cannot be pronounced impossible. Previous methods are to be improved in two ways: first by statistics, by which history is raised to the natural history of man and human society as we see, for instance, where this has been applied to the causes of suicide, and which help us to determine the effects of age, sex, nationality, occupation, season, climate, etc. Statistics alone, he avers, have taught more psychology than all the philosophers since Aristotle, and what they teach is practical and not merely theoretical. The second new method is experimentation. Fechner's psycho-physic law, which, be it remembered, despite its too comprehensive name, tells us nothing of how sensation arises from physical impressions upon peripheral sense organs, nor even hints at the law of the reaction of consciousness upon the external world, is valid of extensive or spatial as well as of intensive stimuli. Hence if space is constructed by psychic processes from sensations, it follows that the relation of perception to these follows the same law as the relation between sensations and the physical stimulus. This granted, we have a law that if two psychic functions are immediately dependent the one upon the other, the dependent function increases as the logarithm of the one upon which it depends. So, too, the true measurement of simple and relatively pure psychic processes, experimentally determined in so many cases, is an inductive method of great use in establishing distinct psychic constants.

The volume from which the above is the condensed introduction seeks to determine the law of the logical development of the soul or of one psychic function from another by a detailed study of the genesis of perception by touch and sight. The book has not a few immature and paradoxical statements, *e. g.*, ''Abstraction is exactly the same as what in the German language we call thought''; ''Thought consists alone in the process of conclusion''; ''Thinking and time are the same thing''; ''Time is man''; ''Experience is space''; ''Mechanism and logic are identical.'' The book was thought by some to display an exaggerated and often extravagant tone of hope and confidence in the nearness of vast results. Drobitsch,[1] the chief pupil of Herbart, the venerable Dean of the philosophical faculty at Leipzig, attempted to refute Wundt's strictures on Herbart and remarks in this book signs of too hasty or non-exhaustive reading of the great philosophers. It owed much of its inspiration to Weber's classic experiments on the sense of touch which were wrought over by the author for nearly a quarter of a century and printed in both Latin and German, one of the most stimulating papers in the history of science, which experimental psychology might almost call its Magna Charta. In this publication Wundt began a movement which in Lotze's ''Med-

[1] Über den neusten Versuch die Psychologie naturwissenschaftlich zu begründen. In Herbartian Zeitschrift f. exacte Philosophie, IV, p. 347.

ical Psychology" had practically failed. The best books he could refer his students to when he began were Drobitsch, Lindner, Volkmar, Waitz, Lazarus and Steinthal; also in English the two Mills, Bain and Tylor.

Illustrative, too, of his early enthusiasm are his views of neurology as expressed in the first edition of his "Psychology." After calling the nervous system the master tissue and showing how it increases in relative importance up the animal scale and becomes supreme in the adult human vertebrate, he declares in substance that all the secrets of the universe are contained in it; that it is the focus of all the results of experience; that in terms of its structure and function can already be stated more of value about the soul than is contained in all the old philosophies, although he is judicious enough to urge that tremors, molecular vibrations, negative variations, chemical changes and all the rest are not as such the essence of thought, and that the whole question of whether idealism or materialism be correct, or whether the brain is the essence, the medium or the substratum of mental life is all a matter of belief and not of knowledge, although beliefs in themselves should be respected as having real value.

In 1865 Wundt published a "Lehrbuch der Physiologie des Menschens" designed to introduce beginners to the subject and to assist those further advanced. This begins with a general section treating the composition and structure of the organism, its functions and elements, and then digestion, absorption, circulation, respiration, animal heat, function of nerves, muscles and senses, including at the end the physiology of procreation and development. This work reached a fourth edition which had grown to 851 pages in 1878. There were many other textbooks in the field and it was soon superseded. It is especially full upon the senses and nervous elements and treats rather hastily the chemical side of the subject.

In 1867 Wundt, who was then a professor in Heidelberg,

surprised his friends by publishing a voluminous "Medicinische Physik" of 555 pages. Here he treats first natural phenomena and laws in general, with sections on the laws of the composition of matter, movement, pendular vibrations, gravity, ideas of body, fluidity, force and pressure, molecular activities, currents, etc. After treating gravity he passes to sound, then to sight, heat and electricity, with which the volume ends. The purpose of the work appears to be to collect and describe all the more exact physical methods by which medical procedures could be determined or controlled. This work lays no claim to originality, but it was designed to be a useful compilation, as it doubtless was. It never reached a second edition.

Probably his own most belabored experimental venture is recorded in a work on the mechanics of the nerves and their centers,[1] the first part of which was printed in 1871 (pp. 278), and the second part in 1876 (pp. 144). This was the time when Du Bois-Reymond and his successors were subjecting both nerve and muscle to manifold electrical tests and were exploring the effect of testing with the interrupted current each point between the positive and negative poles of a constant current. This allowed manifold conditions—cathodic, anodic, extra- and intra-polar opening and closing currents, short and prolonged shocks, varying temperatures, etc. The results were always recorded by a muscle writing upon a pendulum myograph. In the second part of this work Wundt passed from the study of direct to that of reflex response and also studied the effect of various toxic agents and interference, and concluded with a very interesting and ingenious theory of the nature of reflex excitement and of central innervation. This it is impossible to do justice to, but it may perhaps be roughly indicated by saying that he held that most of the reflex phenomena could be explained by assuming an afferent disturbance upon the periphery of

[1] Untersuchungen zur Mechanik der Nerven und Nervencentren.

a motor cell, the surface of which was easily excitable, but that resistance to the molecular lability increased as the disturbance approximated the center of the cell. From this center the efferent reflex discharge must always take place. Wundt's theory held that the first result of initial or subthalamic stimulation was to cause the development of higher metabolism, in which molecules were made more compound and unstable, but that as the strength of the stimulus increased a certain point of complexity was reached which could not be transcended and where sudden lability of the parts of the molecule caused a discharge and their relations sank to a lower and more stable equilibrium. Clever as this was and admirably as it fadged with the experimental data, it has almost no demonstrable validity, and electrical stimulation has now a vast body of facts which this assumption cannot explain. This work of Wundt's we have always regarded as perhaps on the whole having a higher scientific quality than any he has ever done, despite the fact that his hypothesis was not validated and that he does not quote it with great approval in his later works. It was a thoroughly painstaking and ingenious effort to control as many as possible of the very subtle and manifold conditions under which currents pass along bundles of nerve fibers and are generated reflexly from motor cells. Many had studied the myographical phenomena involved, but all these he ignored, making a bold and praiseworthy effort to penetrate to the secrets of what took place in the axis cylinder of the fibers and the nucleus of the nerve cells. Wundt has often been censured and perhaps his rating with contemporary physiologists has not been improved by this work, but it certainly, in the writer's opinion, deserves to be ranked as the boldest and most interesting hypothesis ever offered to explain quite a large group of facts in a domain where we still have no adequate theory, for Sherrington's conjectures are less comprehensive.

In his inaugural as *Extraordinarius* at Leipzig [1] Wundt emphasized the contributions of science to philosophy, while in his address the next year on assuming the full chair, he emphasized the influence of philosophy upon the special departments of academic work and urged that it is now affirming "its old influence upon the empirical sciences." [2] He refers with satisfaction to the great influence which Kant, Schelling, Hegel, and even Schopenhauer had in the past and proceeds to insist that now in a new sense logic, epistemology, metaphysics and the exact study of such philosophical concepts as cause, purpose, matter, space, atoms and the nature of knowledge itself should be inculcated by philosophers in students of all the various departments of the university, thus indicating the rehabilitation of the ancient hegemony of this department. These utterances as he made his début in the field of philosophy were significant, for they assume for it a supreme position over all the other sciences by one who also proposed to advance psychology to an independent position among the sciences. The achievement of this twofold ambition in modern times is characteristic of Wundt's lifelong endeavor.

In 1880 Wundt published the first part of his "Logik" entitled "The Theory of Knowledge" (585 p.). Here in the first section he discusses the development of thought, beginning with associative connections and concepts; then perceptive relations; and thirdly, the development of logical norms. In the next section he discusses ideas, their general properties, their species, relations, connections. The third treats of judgment, its essence, forms, predication, relationships, the transformation of judgments and algorithm. The fourth section is devoted to inference,

[1] Ueber die Aufgabe der Philosophie in die Gegenwart. Leipzig, Engelmann, 1874, 21 p.

[2] Ueber die Einfluss der Philosophie auf die Erfahrungswissenschaft. Leipzig, Engelmann, 1876, 27 p.

treating its essence, forms, etc. The fifth discusses the
fundamental ideas of knowledge, the general concept of
experience, intuition, ideas of substance, etc. Next follows a section upon the laws of knowledge, logical and
mathematical, including axioms, causation, and finally
the principle of purpose.

In 1889 Wundt published a "System of Philosophy"
which has never been translated, containing 669 pages. In
the introduction he discusses the problems of philosophy,
its relations to religion and sciences. He then presents a
theory of thought, including judgments and ideas and
their transformation and connection, negation and inference. He then takes up the discussion of knowledge, beginning with perception and passing to understanding and
reason. In the third section he treats of the concepts of
the understanding, which he divides into fundamental;
formal concepts such as number and function; reality concepts (substance, cause, purpose). In the fourth section
he discusses transcendental concepts, cosmological, psychological and ontological. In the fifth the chief points of
natural philosophy are taken up, viz., the concepts of matter, principles of mechanics, problems of cosmology and
biology. In the last section he presents the outlines of a
philosophy of mind, treating of *Geist* and nature, the individual soul, the forms of development of the collective
soul, and historical development, including morality, religion and æsthetics.

The historic perspective was at this time roughly as
follows:

Like the positivists, Lass and others, Wundt considers
Plato the founder of the modern idealistic philosophy,
and Aristotle as the father of the philosophy and especially
the psychology of Christology. The modern, Christian
form of the notion of immortality is based directly upon
the Aristotelian conception of the nature of the soul.
Souls have their natural, historic genesis, and the compre-

hensive idea of development including plants, animals and man originated with the great Stagirite. So too did the doctrine of the powers or faculties of the soul. Instead of the dependence of the material upon the ideal, Cartesius first affirmed and established modern dualism. This, to some extent, took the place of the Platonic idealism, and is now profoundly rooted in the popular consciousness. So exhaustive and radically dichotomous was the dualism of Cartesius that even animals, because they could not reach his famous form of postulatory consciousness, must be held to be machines. Locke, the founder of modern empiricism, if not materialism, attempted to explain the ideal from the real by asserting subjective and objective experience as the origin of all notions. His work was too one-sidedly in the interest of the question of the theory of knowledge, and is, in a sense, supplemented by Berkeley. The chief influence of Leibniz on psychology was to increase the disposition to besoul the physical world and the great importance ascribed to unconscious processes. Wolff emphasized dualism and gave the notion of the powers of the soul the shape in which the great idealistic systems took it up. Hegel made sensation immediate and certain. Perception regulates sensations; the concept unites them. His psychology is of little value. Some of Schelling's pupils, Schubert, Carus, Eschenmayer and others, inclined to psychology. To them, however, it meant the mystic, night side of the soul's life—sleep, dreams, somnambulism and animal magnetism. With Herbart began a reaction against the notion of distinct faculties; a notion also opposed by Banta, who was less accurate and less exact. The aim of psychologists now must be to widen experience and to multiply methods by specialized monographs rather than by speculative work, the time for which is not yet ripe.

Wundt has also written an "Introduction to Philosophy" which in 1909 reached a fifth edition (471 p.).

The problems of philosophy he states to be the definition of it, its relations to science and religion, and the doctrine of goods or values. Next comes the classification of sciences with a historical survey of the chief efforts to classify from Plato down. The three domains of science he finds to be mathematics, nature and spirit. The classification of the individual sciences may be made as formal or real, or as nature and soul, or as practical and theoretical, etc. The divisions of philosophy are closely connected with this and here he discusses its relations, especially to psychology. In the second section he passes to the historical development of philosophy, beginning with that of the Greeks, devoting some sixteen pages to the pre-Socratics, ten pages each to Plato and Aristotle, twenty-five pages to Christian philosophy ending with scholasticism, and then passing on to Herbart and Positivism. In the third general section he discusses the chief tendencies in philosophy and the three fundamental problems: First, the epistemological section where naïve, reflective and pure empiricism are treated. Here, too, belongs rationalism in the three forms of apriorism, ontologism, and panlogism; also a criticism in the negative or skeptical, and the positive or essential form. The second general tendency is metaphysical, and here first materialism is treated as dualistic or monistic; then idealism as objective, subjective or transcendental; realism as dualistic or monistic. Third come the ethical tendencies, which are heteronomous, transcendent or immanent.

In his "Human and Animal Psychology"[1] the author refers to his earlier work on the same subject, printed thirty years before, as "wild oats," but yet retains much of it unaltered because of its youthful freshness. This work has probably injured more than helped his reputa-

[1] Wilhelm Wundt: Lectures on Human and Animal Psychology. Tr. fr. 2nd ed. by J. E. Creighton & E. B. Titchener. London, 1894. 454 p.

tion. He complains in the preface to the second edition that the crude youthful views expressed in the first had often been mistaken for maturer opinions, to his embarrassment, and intimates that this was one reason which impelled him with some reluctance to prepare a new edition. It is not easy to see why Creighton and Titchener selected this, especially if they had Wundt's approval in doing so, to introduce his psychological views to English readers. The two greatest defects of this book are the following: First, he repeats essentially, but in very fragmentary form, matter already much better worked out in his "Psychology." A condensed abridgment of the latter would have been well, but this professes to be made up only of certain special themes selected very arbitrarily from his psychology. It contains supplementary topics that strictly belong to psychology, but the treatment of which had up to that time been omitted in the successive editions of his "Psychology." Why, for instance, does he serve up here Fechner's right and wrong cases as the only scientific method, when he elsewhere admits it to be the worst? The second greatest defect in this work is that it is perhaps the most anthropomorphic treatment of animal psychology ever undertaken by a modern writer. He assumes that the processes of perception, apperception, association, the senses in animals not only follow the precise laws that have been determined for them in man, but that they can only be understood from the standpoint of human psychology. Here again Wundt is following his favorite occupation of interpreting into his rubrics. Not a single systematic attempt is made to study animal life at first hand, no effort even to make a careful survey of the literature, but the work as a whole gives the impression of a kind of propaganda of his own psychological ideas in the domain of animal psychology. It resembles the crude and now happily passing colonization methods in which it was assumed that precisely those forms of government, education, justice, industry that had been found best for white civilized men were also best for the aborigines and so were imposed upon them. Surely a great teacher of psychology ought to know the precious scores of elaborate studies upon the spider, wasp, ant, bee; the controversies between the tropistic and the psychic theories of the lower organisms; the educational and other studies that have been made of higher forms of life; but of nearly all these things Wundt betrays hardly a sign of knowledge. Those whose knowledge of human and animal psychology is based upon this work would assume that the two were controlled by the same rubrics and that if experimental methods could be applied to dogs, horses, etc., they would show similar laws as essential for animal as for human life. This revised edition cannot possibly have been done by the author *con amore*, and the new part of it especially bears traces of reluctant and therefore of hasty and even superficial work.

In his "Facts of Moral Life"[1] the author does excellent work by using the best that was in English Utilitarianism, yet with a clear insight of its limitations, by concisely summarizing the views of the great German idealists, but not ignoring their successors, and by giving us a very concise but luminous sketch of the history of ethical opinion. Here the author had an excellent opportunity. There was no good history of ethical theory and pragmatism had never been completely applied to the facts of moral life, so that when Wundt based his treatment upon the subordination of metaphysical conceptions of right and wrong to actual moral experience and practice, valuable new combinations were possible. In this work, to our thinking, the best quality that appears, however, is not scholarship or research, but robust common sense in a field

---

[1] Wilhelm Wundt: The Facts of the Moral Life. Tr. by Julia Gulliver and E. B. Titchener. London, 1897, 339 p. See Miss Washburn's translation from the 2nd edition, "Ethical Systems," 1897, 196 p.

spun over with cobwebs, rutted with conventionalities, haunted with fears, and, in most minds, not yet entirely divorced from religion. For the average reader, not an expert, perhaps none of Wundt's writings is calculated to do more good.

Nevertheless, here again he goes so far and is so good that it is easy to be dissatisfied that his merit is not grown in a field where it might easily be made greater. Morality is not so purely based on custom in the sense in which he discusses that word, but it is an affair of daily life and habits, and these, as L. V. Schmidt has shown,[1] really do condition all philosophic and literary ideas. So, too, Wundt has some words of praise for evolution and the evolutionary ethics, but he is quite as far from realizing all that this is and means in the sense of a writer like Sutherland as he is from understanding its relations to the homely matters of eating, sleeping, exercise, and sex, in which all morality begins and has its root. What shall we say of a treatise on ethics which fails to discuss the chief and most insidious temptations of youth and manhood, that sees no psychological problem in the temptations to debauchery, lying, dishonesty, infractions of the sense of honor, the ideals of daily conduct, etc.? Ethics remains for him a theory, for he is a German and at root a philosopher, and thus does not and probably cannot come into too close contact with life, hot and red-blooded as it is actually lived out in the world. His theories are mainly right as far as they go and mark a great and wholesome advance, but they remain academic abstractions.

In 1896 Judd translated Wundt's "Grundriss der Psychologie" with the author's coöperation. It was designed by the author as a manual for his own students and follows in general the principles of the large "Psychology." After the introduction, treating problems, theories, methods and survey, psychical elements are discussed. These

[1] Die Ethik der alten Greichen, 1882. 2 vols. in 1.

are the pure sensations and the simple feelings. Then the
psychic compounds, including all ideas concerned with
space or time, such as space touch and space sight, location,
etc.; also temporal ideas, composite feelings, emotions and
volitional processes. The third part treats of consciousness, attention, association, complications, memory, apperception, psychic states generally. The fourth deals with
psychic development in the child and in communities and
with speech, myth and custom. The fifth, entitled "Psychic Causality and its Laws," deals with the concepts of
mind, the laws of relation, and then of development. This
handbook is well translated and has done good service in
this country. It is all the more needed since his "Psychology" has grown so large and complex. Not the latter, but
this handbook, more nearly represents the standpoint,
method and scope of the author's academic lectures.

His "Grundzüge der physiologischen Psychologie,"[1]
first published in one modest volume in 1874, has in the
sixth edition (1908-11) expanded to three stately volumes,
to which is appended a voluminous analytic index of 133
pages by W. Wirth. This work is Wundt's masterpiece,
and upon this perhaps as much as or even more than all
his other works combined his lasting reputation will rest.
Into it have gone most of the best results not only of the
works published previous to the first edition, but by
amplification, not a few of the best insights developed in
the other works published during the thirty-seven years
between the first and last editions. It contains also antici-
pations of his subsequent publications on language and
myth and indeed furnishes the apperception point from
which an expert might in a sense predict his viewpoints
on many if not most of the problems discussed in these
later works. In the successive editions of the "Psychology" he has not merely added, but eliminated, revised, con-

[1] E. B. Titchener translated the first part of the fifth edition,
Principles of Physiological Psychology. London, 1904, 347 p.

densed, and also in the 399 illustrations has incorporated most of the best of the various forms of apparatus used, modified, or in some cases devised in his laboratory.

It is no part of our purpose to attempt a criticism of this monumental work, the *vade mecum* of the scores of psychological laboratories in this country and elsewhere, the material out of which many courses are conducted, and the staple of the department. We shall only make a few remarks. First, to our thinking, the author has laid too much relative stress upon the works turned out of his own laboratory. These have been copious and voluminous, usually of a high quality, and in view of the many volumes of the *Studien,* now everywhere accessible, and of their unnecessary prolixity and absence of summaries, this was necessary and has been beneficent. The temptation was no doubt strong to give these studies the first place, and the fact that this was done can hardly be severely criticized, but it is to be regretted that so much good work elsewhere, especially in this country, has not also been more completely recognized. Wundt has here many followers, not a few of whom have done excellent work, the average of the best of them almost equaling that done in his own laboratory. He should have given them more space, whether from the motives of courtesy, good policy or scientific completeness. But in fact, not a few of the best of these are entirely ignored and others arc treated with only scanty mention. This, no doubt, is partly due to the fact that the American studies have been scattered and are not all or even a majority of them accessible in any one serial publication.

Another fault, to our thinking, is here again the excessive and often arbitrary schematization. Why, for instance, should it be necessary, in order to get a connected idea of the psycho-physics of touch, to look in so many different places, according as the author thinks touch to be a sensation, a perception or an apperception, according as it comes under the psycho-physic law or as a matter of brain localization, etc.? Again, the writer of this article happens to have made an extensive study of this particular subject, of which he is perhaps better able to speak than of any other in the book, and finds, on reading carefully what Wundt has to say upon the subject, much that would have been better otherwise. Epoch-making studies, like those of von Frey, Goldscheider and others, are very inadequately described in either their methods or results. Judgments might differ and it is not forgotten that this is not an encyclopædia or history, but such investigations should have been more fully characterized, even if the space devoted to their criticism had to be reduced. This can be said of at least a dozen experimenters. Again the author too rarely goes outside the laboratory, where many of the most interesting and vital facts upon this sense are to be found. We ought not, perhaps, to criticize his omission throughout the work to utilize, except inadequately and incidentally, the results of abnormal psychology, although these are very fertile here, because this work professes to deal essentially with normal phenomena. Nevertheless, we cannot forget that one of the great desiderata of psychology to-day is an exhaustive memoir which shall collate *all* the ascertained facts upon touch, which is so fundamental to all the others and is basal for not a few of the most vital theories of psychology generally. The writer who would undertake this would soon find himself far beyond Wundt. And yet again this criticism ought to be held in reserve by the consideration that perhaps on the author's plan of treatment it has its full proportion of space. What should have been done, to our thinking, is that more facts and methods should be stated in a far more condensed style with the discussive element reduced.

In general the author in this book seeks to survey the main features of the psychologic domain and adjudicate between different theories. Very rarely indeed does he originate a point of view, but selects, and wisely, most of his positions from others and amplifies them. His is eminently a judicious mind and his decisions are usually sound, a quality which in a founder and creator (for such he will always deserve to be called) is a most fortunate one. There are no great luminous and inspiring ideas such as have lately so often reanimated other sciences, few important discoveries, but endless determinations, formulæ, better definitions, directive hints. Indeed the dominant quality of the author's mind might be described by the word "mechanical" if that word were stripped of all its lower and well invested with all its higher meanings. The impulsion of his life has been to bring exact physiological methods to bear upon the study of the psychic life. This was a great desideratum and has marked a great step in advance. But this book demonstrates the fact that an inordinate appetite for work, amounting to talent, can exist without a spark of genius. Wundt's great power as a writer consists in bringing different facts and viewpoints together into fruitful relations with each other, comparing and grading them and making his brain a clearing-house for all kinds of special activities over a very wide domain. It is praise enough to have been able to do this. But Wundt will not long dominate the psychology of even the near future, though he will remain a great landmark. Indeed, those who have been with him have in many respects already gone beyond him and some of the best of them have shown the tendency to turn upon their master with effective criticism. It may be that he has been animated with the encyclopædic tradition of the heroic age of German philosophy, when the influence of great thinkers like Kant and Hegel was projected into successive generations and dominated even sciences that were more or less remote from those they treated, because they gave animating formulæ and inspired new impulsions and insights and ambitions. There is none of this power in Wundt. No doubt he has brought as much mentation to bear and certainly he commands a far vaster information than ever Kant or Hegel attained, but he lacks the formative, creative, artistic power of suggestiveness and to use a greatly abused word, inspiration. The world of science is too large to be dominated again by any one man, but Wundt has done so much and so well that we cannot but wish he had done better to the extent, at least in the field of normal psychology, of having given us one or more great unifying ideals or set up lofty goals in the far future or supplied motivations or made wider and more significant correlations.

To epitomize: In beginning his psychology, Wundt postulates that the nervous system is the chief, characteristic feature of animal life. Wherever organs or parts of a living body function together for a common purpose, they do so through a nervous mechanism. The relative importance of this system increases all the way up the scale of animal life, and in the adult vertebrate becomes supreme. The nervous system is of course developed, together with the skin, muscles, and organs of sense, from the outer layer of the embryo, in distinction from the organs of nutrition and reproduction, which are formed from the inner layer. All the processes of development of the animal body are directly or indirectly under the influence of the nervous system. It is one of the first parts to be differentiated in the embryological structure. In short, all the secrets of the soul and, therefore, from the position which Wundt assigns psychology we may infer he believes of the universe are wrapped up in nerve cells and fibers.

It may be worth while as his large psychology has never been translated to give below a very condensed epitome of the next few hundred pages showing his general mode of treatment, his point of view and his remarkable pedagogic quality. Pure sensations are never given in consciousness but are products of abstraction, and possess only intensity and quality without spatial or temporal elements. There is no reference to a without or a within, and they differ from the so-called sensuous feelings which reflect our somatic condition, only in being differently related to developed consciousness. These elements, out of which all other elements of consciousness proceed, are often accompanied—even those from which sight and hearing are developed—by a characteristic tone of sensuous feeling, besides intensity and quality. The causes of sensations are stimuli, which may be external or internal. Even in the popularly distinguished five senses, immediately accessible to external stimuli, the effects of internal stimuli are often felt. Internal organs, however, are accessible only to internal stimuli, which give rise to what are called generic feelings (*Gemeingefühle*). These comprise, first, hunger, thirst, want of breath—feelings which regulate vegetative processes; second, innervation feelings of the muscles, which play an important part in our movements and in the development of our senses; third, those due to the irritation of sensory centers, a frequent cause of dreams, hallucinations, etc. Stimuli are movements, four forms of which can cause sensations in each of the five organs of sense, viz., pressure, electricity, heat, and chemical action. These act not so much on the peripheral sense organs, by which the specific senses are differentiated, as upon all nerves. All these four generic forms of stimulation cause sensations like those which would be caused if the peripheral organ was excited normally by its own peculiar stimulus, *e. g.*, the same electric current causes a sensation of taste if applied to the tongue; of light if applied to the retina; of sound if sent through the cochlea, etc. This is expressed by saying that each nerve and organ of sense has its own specific energy.

The intensity of sensations, next to be considered, does not increase in the same ratio as the intensity of the stimulus. Below a certain degree of intensity, the stimulus causes no sensation; and above a certain point, increase in the intensity of the stimulus causes no increase in the intensity of the sensation. The first limit may be explained by assuming a certain inertia in the nerves which must be overcome, and the second merely by postulating that the supply of accumulated energy may be exhausted. Back of these physical, however, other psychic limits may be assumed, and sensation may be said to occur only when nerve action has reached a certain intensity and to stop increasing at a certain point, even though nerve action continues to increase indefinitely as the logarithm of its stimulus intensity, or the materialist can still postulate a second, more centrally seated scale or series of neural activities and affirm if he will its identity with sensation. For sensory nerves it is impossible to determine the relation between the strength of the stimulus and the intensity of the resultant nerve action. The psycho-physic law is known to be valid only of the relation between the stimulus and the intensity of sensation. From the effect of stimulating motor nerves in connection with muscles, it seems probable that there is a direct proportionality between the stimulus and the nerve action; so that we may henceforth speak of the relation between the nerve action and the sensation, instead of between stimulus and sensation.

The great question is whether the psycho-physic law is reliable as giving us an accurate measure of the intensity of *sensations*. If so, psychology becomes so far an exact science. But in the first place it is hard to exclude all other stimuli and begin with a zero of sensation. Intraocular pressure upon the retina, and the manifoldness of Nature's noises, keep the eye and ear almost always above the threshold at which sensation begins, despite the manifold precautions of the experimenter. The sensitiveness of the organs is changeable, and thereby it is so exquisite that errors in the objective method of determination are very hard to eliminate. A piece of cork, *e. g.*, weighing one milligram and falling one millimeter can be heard 91 millimeters away; and we can have the sensation of touch, if an object presses upon the skin of the forefinger only enough to depress it one two-thousandth of its thickness. The sensitiveness of the ear and eye is greatest nearer the upper than the lower end of the scale of notes or colors. Up to a certain point, sensitiveness increases with the extent of the surface irritated. It is still harder to determine the maximal than the threshold value of stimulation.

There are three methods of experimentation. The first is, after deriving a uniform scale of external stimuli, to determine by minimal variations the just observable difference between two sensations. This difference threshold is a psychic value of apparently constant magnitude. This is done for touch, *e g.*, when one person applies to any given point of the skin within two compass points, gradually diminishing or increasing the distance between them, a successive application until a difference of interval is perceived. This difference is measured and recorded many times and at last averaged. The eyes of the person experimented upon must, of course, be blindfolded or diverted. The second method seeks to determine how great a constant difference of interval between two successive applications of the points there can be without being perceived. This is called the method of average error. By the third method, the compass points are applied successively at two constant intervals, which are not clearly distinguished, and the person experimented upon must determine each time which interval on the whole seems the greater. Then the number of right will preponderate over the number of wrong judgments according as the interval approximates a clearly discernible magnitude, and with the sensibility of the part to which they are applied. This is called the method of right and wrong cases. By the first method, the upper; by the second, the lower; by the third the intermediate, threshold value of sensation is best attained. The first method was derived and wrought out by E. H. Weber, and his results are among the most perfect in the history of psychological science. Not only the psycho-physic law but the inference that each nerve fiber is irritated all the way from the periphery to the central seat of consciousness is based upon these experiments. Fechner's experiments by the other two methods devised by him have confirmed and established the psycho-physic law which may be fully formulated as follows: The difference between any two stimuli is perceived as constant if the relation between the two is constant; or, if the intensity of a sensation is to be increased by a certain amount, the relative increase in the strength of the stimulus must be constant; or again the intensity of the sensation is proportional to the logarithm of the stimulus. This law may be illustrated graphically by dividing a horizontal line or abscissa into equal intervals. These, counted from left to right, represent the constant increase of sensation. If at each of these points of division, perpendicular lines or ordinates be erected, increasing in length not by equal intervals but by a constant multiple, the curve connecting the tops of these ordinates will represent the concomitant increase in the strength of stimulus required to cause the constant increase of sensation. The latter, in other words, is measured by the distance between, the former by the length of the ordinates.

This law is approximately valid not only for touch but for pressure, light, heat, sound and even for taste and smell, and perhaps for muscular sense; in short, wherever psychic and physical functions are immediately connected. It is the most generic law of the relation between outer and inner conditions. It is possible that we even learn to distinguish the qualities of sensation to an unknown extent after and by means of quantitative distinctions. It may have important bearings upon apperceptive reproduction and the higher mental processes. At the same time from much detailed, experimental study lately devoted to this law, it is apparent that it is only approximately true and that it is most applicable to intermediate values in the various scales of sensation. It is truer, *e. g.*, of temperatures near that of the blood where we can distinguish slighter differences, than of those much above or below it; it is truest of notes neither very high nor low; of light not very strong nor dim, etc. Wundt's treatment of this law in the first edition of his psychology was the most inadequate part of it; when, considering the important rôle he assigns to internal sensations, *e. g.*, muscular, especially innervation feelings, it should have been very thorough.

Over against those sensations which are distinguishable only in quantity, like the organic, general, muscular, and innervation feelings, essentially uniform in kind and variable only in intensity, are those of the special senses, where qualities as well as intensities are graded and measured. Qualities are distinguished probably more by means of the terminal apparatus which transmits the stimuli to the nerves than by differences in the central nervous substance, although the law of specific energy teaches us that this too cannot be ignored. Wundt is fond of analogizing the central with the peripheral "sense surfaces." The sensory nerve has at one end ganglion nerve cells; at the other end, other cells adapted to receive impressions from without, all of which are, in Meynert's phrase, projected upon the cortical surface of the brain; these form the retina upon the anterior; these form the cochlea upon the temporal part of this surface, etc. Central cells, however, appear to be quite uniform, while those of the periphery are much differentiated, although probably all, genetically construed, are modifications of those of tactile surfaces. At the same time, Wundt rejects the hypothesis of Weber

342

and Müller that the order of the peripheral corresponds
to that of the central nerve ends in such a way that the
form and extent of the central surfaces, excited by a given
impression, are the same as the form and extent of the skin
or retina excited by the object which causes the impression. Great generic, qualitative differences between groups
of sensations we designate as the five sense organs. These
differences, however, are indefinitely manifold. According
to Lotze's theory of local signs, every sensory circle (*Emp-
findungs-Kreis*) is, figuratively speaking, a sense by itself.
Indeed different sensations can be perceived even within
one and the same sensory circle. The fact of discrimination of tactile peripheral sensibility, which in a normal
person varies from about 68 mm. between the shoulders
behind to .0005 mm. on the *fovea centralis* of the eye, shows
us that the special senses might be conceived as rough
groups of many far more minute and special senses, each
with its own qualitative character, and the nerves of each
having their own specific energy. What the peculiar local
"color" of each is, whether indeed it does not at bottom
consist of purely quantitative or intensive differences, it
seems now impossible to ascertain. Wundt with all now,
except the Nativists, holds that we localize sensations by
means of an inference from their quality. Perception, he
says, cannot separate in space sensations which are qualitatively identical.

After an anatomical characterization of the sense organs and after distinguishing the senses as either chemical
or mechanical, Wundt attacks the extreme form of the
doctrine of specific energy of nerves.

Sensory cells are no more unlike than peripheral fibers,
and there is as much reason to assume functional indifference for the former as the latter. If, according to the
Young-Helmholtz hypothesis, three sorts of retinal fibers
for red, green, and violet respectively be assumed, it is
hard to explain how it is that we can perceive a point of

23   343

white light, which on the theory requires the presence of all the specific fibers, quite as small as a point of red, green, or violet light, where the action of but one fiber is involved. So, too, special nerves for heat, cold, pressure, touch, must be assumed. The doctrine of specific energy everywhere multiplies the number of required nerve fibers to an incredible extent. Hence, Wundt prefers to assume that either the molecular processes in the nerves are always of the same nature, while the periods of intensive increase or decrease change in frequency; or, as may be assumed in the case of stimulus through a second nerve inserted into the circuit, the form of nerve action and of stimulation being here in a sense the same; or else there may be no periodicity but the nature of the molecular process may change with the kind of stimulus, as may be assumed from the chemical senses. It may even be assumed that, in both cases, the molecular process is unchanged from the periphery into the central seats where they affect consciousness. The fact that every form of stimulus excites the peculiar quality of the given sensation Wundt accounts for by the "extraordinary capacity of the nerve substance to adapt itself to the stimulus." How, he asks, can the theory account for the fact that those born blind and deaf, but with perfect nerve fibers and central organs, have absolutely no visual or auditory impressions, in spite of the forms of automatic central stimulation, which are so common that they may be assumed to exist. The facts of color-blindness, too, he thinks cannot be explained according to this hypothesis. He regards the theory in short as an unjustifiable, physiological inference from Kant's conception of the subject's condition of knowledge, and thinks that many facts which seem to support it are due to the great preponderance of red, green and blue in nature. We think every competent reader must admit that Wundt's molecular hypothesis of the way in which the specific energy of the nerves operates may be taken as a further explanation rather than as a rival, supplanting theory, and that his arguments against it readily admit of other explanation, into which space and our plan of work forbid us to enter here.

After discussing tone-sensations without attempting to add anything of importance to the work of Helmholtz, Wundt passes to the law for mixing colors, and to the form and properties of the color table. Hering had rehabilitated Goethe's ideas by regarding white and black as two colors like those of the spectrum. Wundt, however, holds the opposite view and asserts that intensity and coloration or hue are relatively independent variables. A hue can remain unmodified by greater or less intensity of light; not so white and black or gray, which they compose. Here every change is toward one extreme of light or dark. All colors may with more propriety be distinguished as darkish or lightish, or as saturated or unsaturated, and saturation therefore is a third variable. Even complementary after-images may be spoken of as positive or negative, according as they are of the same or of less intensity than the original impression. Geiger's theory that Homer knew only red and blue, which Noiré and Gladstone have popularized, Wundt thinks extremely improbable. Even if he had no words to designate it, he may still have perceived the color as we do. Yet the colors most abundant in nature were probably first distinguished, and the power of making fine distinctions may have come later.

The different times required to perceive different colors in their highest intensity and for their respective impressions to fade out as after-images show that the maximum of excitation does not occur for all colors at the same instant. But the cognate phenomenon of the flickering of a color-top with white and black sectors Wundt prefers to explain quite differently from Helmholtz, as due to contrast. With the most rapid rotation which admits of any of the phenomena of color, the white sectors appear reddish, the black bluish. This, however, does not prove that red stimulates the optic nerve more quickly than do other colors. As the course of a light stimulus excited by a white sector would be interrupted by the appearance of the black sector in the field of vision the more rapidly the top revolved, the color of the black sector would approach the earliest stages of stimulation. Green and violet must reach their maximum sooner than red, since the black sector with the most rapid rotation has a blue color composed out of green and violet. If the disk rotates slowly, the entire stadium of increase of stimulus may fall within the time occupied by the passage of the white sector before the eyes. Then the black sectors appear slightly colored at their margins, and the white sectors seem blue upon their first half, and red upon the last. Hence, color sensations increase to their greatest intensity in the same order as they fade away. In one instantaneous stadium of stimulus by white light, blue is at one point of the retina the predominant color perceived; but at the same instant, at another retinal point, the white light has excited another stadium of perception, so that here, by the law of contrast, a red coloration is predominant.

A color seems more intense if the retina is previously fatigued from the complementary color, or if two complementary colors are seen side by side. By combining the methods of successive and simultaneous contrast, colors appear most intense. Not only do complementary colors thus modify or, in Brücke's terminology, induce each other, but the tone of every color is changed by another adjacent to it more or less toward the nearest complementary color. These phenomena are most marked within certain degrees of intensity and saturation, which must be experimentally determined. Our determinations of degrees of illumination here are far from being absolute, but are affected by all adjacent and by preceding sensations. Certain colors, still thought by many to be real, as *e. g.*, those long ascribed to shadows, are more likely to be purely subjective effects of contrast. If a piece of gray paper is pasted on a larger, colored paper, the former is not seen in contrast so long as the boundaries between the two are clearly seen. This is one of many illustrations of the law that if the two impressions can be referred to separated objects the contrast effect is much less recognizable. This can be explained only by assuming that the degree to which a retinal sensation may be affected by impressions made upon other parts of the retina is, to some extent, determined by previous impressions. Hence, Helmholtz and others have explained contrast as an illusion of judgment as if these were correct sensations which were here perverted. Wundt, on the other hand, holds that the manifold studies of contrast show that all sensations of light are relative to others. The character of the present sensation is always first, while the reproduction of other past impressions which constitutes judgment is later and secondary. Contrast then, is strongest where sensations are loosened from all their relations to distinct objects. If objects instead of colors for their own sake are suggested, *i. e.*, if memory is active, the effects of contrast vanish. Pure color sensations reciprocally induce each other. Contrast phenomena have no objective, physiological cause, as Fechner's refutation of the idea of colored shadows shows. Neither can it be well explained why different parts of the retina should lose this reciprocity of action the instant the conception of separated objects arises. The theory of an illusion of judgment is so far right as it points to a psychologic explanation. Contrast phenomena are in short just as psychological as sensations themselves and no more so. Absolute brightness can be varied within wide limits without affecting the distinctness of the contrast. Hence, we see that the difference between the sensations remains the same so long as the relative brightness of the light stimulus remains constant, so that we have only a special form

347

of the psycho-physic law, which is now seen to be applicable to quality as well as intensity of sensations.

With every sensation, a certain sense-feeling of pleasure or pain is connected, like tone-color to every musical tone. There are many sensations the sense-feeling of which is so weak as rarely to depart far from the indifference point, where neither pleasure nor pain is felt; and others call up invariably very strong feelings. Sense-feelings may vary with either intensity or quality of sensation, or may change and the latter remain unchanged. They are analyzed but little and often falsely by language. Even the designations "pleasure and pain," "joy group," etc., belong to too high and intellectualized a sphere to be applicable to such rudimentary feelings. It is no explanation of its nature when Lotze defines pain as a contradiction of the stimulus with the condition of excitability, for it is only ulterior reflection that suggests that pain is connected with injurious stimulus and pleasure with that which is salutary. They are all related to consciousness, which is an empirical, rather than to the soul, which is a metaphysical motive. Herbart, who had in mind chiefly the more complex forms of feeling, held that all feelings resulted from the reciprocal relation of concepts (or ideas), conflict and opposition between them causing pain; their coöperation causing pleasure. But his theory gives the simplest and most elemental forms of sense-feeling. The horizon of consciousness at any given moment is very narrow, and reproduction of past impressions is a law of its nature. This may occur by the law of relationship of association. According to the first, every sensation as seen above is perceived only as relative to other disposable, homogeneous sensations; according to the second, concepts are connected in such a way that, if one appears in consciousness, the other strives to do the same. The results of the former law are more uniform and common for all persons than those of the latter. The intensifying effects

348

of contrast may be observed in all feelings and their rapid
alternation constitutes the charm of play. The analogy
common between disparate sensations, *e. g.*, darkness and
a low tone, rests upon the likeness of their accompanying
sense-feelings. Their quality varies with their intensity.
Pleasant sensations, those, *e. g.*, of tickling, moderate muscular effort, or fatigue, are of very moderate intensity;
while very intense sensations are painful. The weaker,
unconscious, or, as graphically represented, negative sensations have no sense-feeling, and are therefore pure. When
sensations cross the threshold into consciousness, the pleasurable sense-feeling is at first very faint, but rises rapidly
with increasing intensity to a maximum, only to sink no
less rapidly below the indifference point into pain which,
if extreme, is the same for all senses, with no qualitative
difference. The maximum of pleasurable sense-feeling is
obtained at about that degree of intensity of sensation
which is most favorable for distinguishing external stimuli. So, too, as sense-feeling soon diminishes, even if the
stimulus remains moderate and constant, it is probable
that that degree of strength of stimuli which is most favorable for change of sensations occasions the greatest sense
of pleasure. Even of complex sentiments, the psycho-
physic law seems valid. To one who possesses one hundred
dollars the addition of one dollar causes the same amount
of pleasure that the addition of ten causes to the possessor
of one thousand dollars. But, for appreciating the minor
fluctuations of fortune, the most favorable condition is
that in which happiness is directly proportional to the increase of goods. Below this limit the absolute value of
the latter is too small; above it, ordinary fluctuations are
too insignificant to cause the highest satisfaction. This is
in accordance with the experience of all times that a moderate amount of external blessings is most favorable for
the feeling of happiness.

In organic sensations and those of taste, smell, and

even touch, the sense-feeling so preponderates over and absorbs the other elements of sensation that they are primarily and popularly classed as either pleasant or unpleasant, although no quality of sensation is absolutely so. A very slight intensity, *e. g.*, of bitter, is sufficient to carry the sense-feeling beyond the indifference point over to pain; while other sensations, *e. g.*, sweet, must become intense or protracted before they become unpleasant. For many organic sensations, the indifference point seems almost to coincide with the threshold of sensation; and almost as soon as the latter is felt, pain is also felt. This is no indication that there is no pleasure connected with these sensations. They are normally so weak that the pleasure elements can hardly be recognized, yet together they constitute the feeling of health and well-being which is most positive and pleasurable.

The feelings connected with tones are very complex and manifold. Low notes excite feelings of dignity and seriousness; high notes those of merriment and sport. A ground tone with few overtones, as of flute or organ, seems serious, while rich tone-color as of stringed instruments seems merry or passionate. Hence, low, highly colored tones and high, uncolored tones excite contrary sentiments, bringing a feeling of distraction. A mass of shrilling overtones as in the trumpet rouses a sense of force and energy; but if the fundamental tone preponderates as in the horn, calmness and repose are inspired. These feelings are modified by intensity or rapid changes of tone. The unrest caused by discords only ranges with their intensity from a feeling of soft melancholic distraction to one of strong energy. Harmony or satisfaction, which is the ulterior object of every æsthetic effect, is a high, complex feeling, while dissonance is only a pure sense-feeling.

Respecting the æsthetic effects of light and color, Wundt agrees substantially with Goethe, and gives an interesting comparative analysis of the feelings excited by lights and tones. These, in contrast with those of the lower senses, have a quality of their own which is relatively independent of sensuous pleasure and pain; hence, their æsthetic effects. Pleasure and pain seem dependent only upon the intensity of sensations; while æsthetic qualities, although analogous, belong to a different category.

Sense-feeling is affected very largely by associations. Black suggests funerals; bells, church service; trumpets, war, etc. Our civilized stage of development is poor in originality of feeling, and perhaps associations give to our feelings that natural emphasis which primitive man found in his sensations alone. If, however, there was an ancient emphasis given by feeling to sensation, the association reveals a remarkable harmony between our sensations and external nature. This by no means warrants us in inferring that the qualities of feeling can be derived and developed from the conditions of irritability with which they are related only as sensations are. Feelings are also strengthened by analogies between disparate sensations as, *e. g.*, when we speak of *warm* colors, *sharp* sounds, etc. It is very important for life as well as for æsthetics that moods can be thus strengthened by the amalgamation of different sensations with the same tone of feeling.

Sense-feeling is a far more variable element of sensation than is intensity or quality. Especially has the development of self-consciousness affected it profoundly. Indeed there is no reason to think that in primitive consciousness there was any difference between the sensations of the several senses, in and for themselves, and the intensity of their sense-feeling. As soon, however, as the ego was distinguished from the external world, very different values would come to be attached to different sensations, according as they were caused by stimuli without or within our own body. Sight becomes the most objective sense and through it and hearing our own feelings are objectified and reflected from without, thus causing æsthetic effects. The organic feelings are more subjective, more restricted to simple pleasure and pain, and more uniform in quality, and their element of sense-feeling outranks that of sensation. All of these together constitute in consciousness, as it were, a background, or mood (*Stimmung*), and even temperament. Upon them depend the characterizations of intensity and calm certainty or of relaxation, restlessness or mobility. It is a fundamental characteristic of all feeling that it moves between extremes from one toward the other. It is a bottom peculiarity of consciousness that all feelings tend to raise certain states into it or to expel others from it, giving rise in the former case to pleasure, in the latter to pain, which tends to monopolize consciousness to the exclusion of other feelings, while pleasure allows or even aids others to enter freely by reproduction or otherwise. So of the objective feelings; black excludes sensations of light. Deeper notes are composed of slower vibrations and require longer time for perception; hence their somber tone. The ear is preëminently the time-measuring sense, and the sequence of musical tones imitates the inner movement of ideas, so that music more than color depicts the feelings in their inmost nature. All the tendencies of sensation, according to intensity and quality, to exalt other sensations or ideas into or to expel them from consciousness, are given or continued immediately in consciousness, so that no intermediate process is required to explain the origin of feelings. All else that has been thought to inhere in the nature of feeling, as utility, or danger, etc., is secondary and due to subsequent reflection, which may perhaps invigorate subjective sensations and give them significance for our entire psychic state.

The chapter on feelings is the darkest in psychology. Wundt groups into three classes the many theories concerning the nature of feelings. They have been regarded

(1) as a special activity of the cognitive power; (2) as neither sensations nor ideas but as originating in the reciprocal action of ideas; (3) as the state into which the soul is brought by sensations and ideas. The first view is represented by Locke, Leibniz, Spencer, Bain, where the natural history of the feelings and emotions is considered, and in antiquity by the Stoics, who made the mood depend upon belief in a future or present good or evil. Leibniz, who introduced the infinitely small and the unconscious into modern philosophy, said that after enjoying the profit without the disadvantage of evil by infinitely small sensations of pain, pleasure arises by overcoming these, which become small or dark. Hegel's conception of feeling as obscure knowledge; Wolff's notion that it is an intuitive knowledge of perfection or imperfection; Lotze's idea that feeling rests upon an unconscious judgment of increased or diminished harmony in vital functions; the view of many physiologists that organic feeling is the most generic form of feeling, or a little of many sensations crowding into consciousness, or a sum of many slight sensations —all these show how the explanation of feeling has been influenced by the theory of knowledge.

The second or Herbartian theory which makes sensations elementary ideas first emphasized the influence which the movement of ideas in consciousness exercised upon the *Gemüth,* and the significance of the æsthetic effect of sensations and ideas on each other. Joy, sudden hope, etc., however, can never be explained as merely formal feelings independent of the qualitative content of ideas. It is arbitrary to say that sense-feelings arise from the relations of partial ideas; and some of Herbart's own disciples have accordingly identified them with sensations as the "tone of sensation." Benecke, who called feeling the measuring of psychic activities, the one with the other, also sees that single sensations and ideas, so far as their content indicates distinct knowledge, bring no motive from feeling; but does not explain why their relation is apprehended as pleasure or pain, nor see that feeling is conditioned by the relation of ideas, not to each other, but to consciousness.

The third view, which regards feeling as the subjective complement of sensations and ideas is related to the first view so far as it assumes that feeling is not merely a condition of the soul but an apprehension of its condition. It is more truly Kantian while rejecting the metaphysical implication of the substantiality of the soul, to substitute consciousness in its place. In so doing, however, an element of conscious knowledge again appears. This was Wundt's assumption throughout his work on animal instinct. But feeling belongs to the most primitive of subjective experiences, while self-consciousness is developed relatively late. This Horwicz had in view in his theory that feeling has an important influence on the development of consciousness. However this may be (and Wundt has since disputed the primacy of feeling in this sense) as soon as consciousness is developed, the reference to it is there.

Leaving sensations, we come in the third division of the psychology to ideas (*Vorstellungen*[1]). These constitute the world as we know it. Ideas, according to Wundt's terminology, include both products of imagination and fantasy, dreams, hallucinations, and percepts or intuitions; the latter originating in peripheral, the former in central stimulation. Primitive man or the child does not distinguish between these nor even with reflection and experience determine what is objective and what is subjective in origin. Ideas are composed, according to psychic laws, from several or many simple, indiscerptible sensations, the latter being developed in either a successive temporal or spatial order. Indeed all ideas take a position in space and

[1] Usage now rather generally translates *Vorstellung* into idea, though the English word, "idea" does not ordinarily include percepts. It seems, however, to be our nearest equivalent term since "concept" is now generally limited to the class-idea.

in time. The ear is preëminently the time sense, and the eye the space sense. Ideas of touch and movement combine both. Every movement is apprehended as having temporal succession and as through space; hence this class constitutes the foundation of all other sense ideas. The other senses are called special with peculiar propriety, since they are developed from the generic sense of touch. The sensation of movement is of central origin since it is immediately accompanied by motor innervation; hence the working of the will upon the motor nerves and the muscles is the foundation of our intuition of space and time. This is supplemented by the organ of touch, by which the entire surface of the body is accessible to external stimuli. Ideas are called complex if composed of sensations from disparate senses. The elements of such ideas are in general more loosely united than the elements of more simple sense ideas. We think, e. g., in visual images, and into many trains of thought other ideas may or may not enter. Still more loosely compacted and analyzable are ideas composed of sensations and other ideas of the imagination. If the relation of the conceiving subject to an object remains unchanged, the number and character of the sensations comprising the idea of the object remain constant. Other ideas are variable, in relation to certain components, while others remain fixed, or else their entire content changes so that only an empty form remains, as, e. g., in the general ideas of space and time. The variable ideas never exist as distinct acts; only the constant ones are actually existent in consciousness. Ideas, like sensations, enter into relation with consciousness, as qualities secondary to the spatial and temporal forms, giving rise to æsthetic feelings, based principally upon spatial and temporal relations. This use of the word "æsthetic," although including its most important artistic effects, ignores those complicated intellectual and ethical meanings popularly attached to it.

After an excellent account of the experimental investigations of touch, Wundt passes to the question of the origin of the tactual spatial order. Nativism thinks that because the conditions of space perception are innate the perception must be; and, on the other hand, empiricism cannot prove, great as has been the influence of experience, that it gives more than the occasion for the spatial idea. Movement must be taken as a co-factor with touch in solving the problem. It is proved that at least generally speaking the fineness of tactual discrimination of a part increases with its mobility. With touch, innervation feelings must be combined, as indeed they are by pressure and tension when we move our limbs. This is probably of prime significance for the first stages of spatial perception. The two sensations are united when we touch our own organs of touch, and especially when we move the latter along an object under such conditions as to receive one tactual impression of innervation feelings with different degrees of intensity. Thus we gain our first spatial knowledge, which is of the different parts of our own body. Those parts seem to be first distinguished in space which are most mobile, one against the other. The local color of sensation varies for every part of the body, changing gradually from one part to another, forming a continuum of two dimensions but not identical for opposite halves of the body. The spatial order is thus a new product of psychic synthesis from two series of sensations, one qualitative and one intensive. The organs of this synthesis may be supposed to be the complex, reflex centers of the optic lobes. Only innervation feelings can be conceived as an absolute and qualitatively uniform, graded measure of intensity, independent of the changing conditions of peripheral stimulation. It is by their aid that we learn not to measure the distance between two distinguishable points of stimulation by the muscles but somewhat according to the diameter of the intervening sensory circles. That as concerns our own movements the amount of effort put forth is measured by innervation feelings is proved by paresis, where the sense of effort is not followed by the usual muscular contraction. The content of the innervation feelings is by no means Trendelenburg's original consciousness of motion, although it is granted that the idea of motion is the simplest and probably the primitive form in which the temporal and spatial orders coëxist.

Nativism is the standpoint of the naïve, unschooled consciousness. Locke made the first important attempt to overcome it and gave the impulse to the empirico-genetical movement of Berkeley and Condillac which, on account of Kant, did not reach Germany. J. Müller thought we had a primitive idea of our own body, because it was permeated by nerves, every peripheral end of which was represented in consciousness as a point in space. Weber thought that within the smallest interval at which two points could be distinguished, one or more sensory circles must be supposed in order to account for the impression of an interval, and that with practice the number of intermediate circles necessary to produce this impression decreased. Czermak substituted interfering circles. Experiences being thus granted to be of influence, various genetic theories, two purely psychological and two psychophysical, arose and are characterized as follows: (1) (Waitz). The space-idea arises from the indivisible, simple nature of the soul, which prevents the fusing of several sensations arising at the same instant into an intensive idea and compels them to group themselves side by side. But impressions of disparate senses, e. g., ear and eye, may coincide in time without producing the spatial qualities. (2) (Herbart). The space-idea originates in a succession of sensations, so arranged that their order can be inverted. But this is to be done confessedly by reversing movement and it is this latter, according to Wundt, rather than succession which is the real vehicle of the space-idea. We can play a musical scale upward and downward and no idea of space arises. Herbart gives a description of objective space, rather than the subjective process of spacial intuition. (3) (Lotze). All sensations are purely intensive; where a spatial order arises, it is by means of an additional, neural process which serves as a sign by which it can be related to a distinct point in space. These local signs may be different for different senses, but must be members of an ordered series, and do not, like sensations, change with the nature of the stimulus. This theory is in the right, physiological way, but is insufficient. Such signs might aid localization, but presuppose the space-idea, which cannot arise from mere qualities. (4) (Berkeley, Bain, Wundt.) The space-idea originates from our own movements, as above described.

Unless the tensor muscle accommodates the tympanum to pitch and teaches and aids us in judging of direction —all of which is uncertain—the ear, unlike other sense organs, has no way of adapting itself to, or even of escaping, the rich but uniform stimulus. This organ develops for us the time-idea, which the motion-idea gave. After discussing the various degrees of relationship between consonant tones, it becomes apparent that no analysis of them can be made unless they are also sequent. The simplest form of rhythmic articulation, with its inevitable reference to future and past, arsis and thesis, contains already the whole time-idea. Most closely related to the change of intensity in sound is the corresponding change in innervation which accompanies motion, e. g., in the rhythm of dancing, and preëminently of walking. It has also been shown that in reproducing intervals of time after a pause we tend to overestimate those which are somewhat more frequent than ordinary steps in walking, and to underestimate those that are longer. More than three degrees of arsis or accent are unknown in the rhythm of either poetry, where they are grouped into feet and strophes, or in music, where they are grouped as measures and phrases.

Melody is simply change in quality combined with change in intensity. We can form even tolerable ideas of the lapse of time only by the aid of some sort of rhythmic form. According to modern metrical laws, the arsis must fall on an accented, the thesis on an unaccented syllable, while periods and clauses are determined only by the sense. Rhythm would be thus impoverished but for sounds of constant relationship, rhythmic occurrence, etc., to mark the beginning or end of lines. Classic rhythm, by distinguishing between long and short syllables, was not only a more accurate measure of time, but gained thereby great freedom of movement within the single feet, thus more resembling melody. The shortest duration allowed to a single note is estimated at about one-tenth of a second, or about the same as the shortest perception-time. Within the free movement of sounds in time, melody is determined entirely by the varying relationships of tones. By filling them with melodic content, time-intervals are well apprehended, for there is a certain limit beyond which clearly distinguished degrees of intensity cannot aid us, and where the principle of tone-relationship comes to greatly widen and perfect the rhythm-sense. Here harmony began to be developed from melody; and rhythm, the sense of which was never so perfect as among the Greeks, ceased to be an end in itself alone. Harmony cannot, as Euler thought, be caused by our direct perception of the integral proportion between the number of vibrations of the accordant notes, for this perception is at any rate unconscious. The theory of Rameau and d'Alembert that tones are harmonious if they have partial tones in common, which Oettingen has assumed in his ingenious argument that the tones of the major chord belong to a single ground tone, and that those of the minor chord agree in a single overtone, distinguishing thus the principle of tonality or indirect relationship from that of phonality, or direct relationship of tones, must be supplemented by the theory of Helmholtz that harmony is due to the absence of beats or roughness, and dissonance to their presence. Helmholtz gives only a negative explanation of harmony, Wundt urges, and does not account for the contrast between major and minor.

We come next to visual ideas. The eye is an imperfect organ: remains of prenatal, opaque structures float in its fluids; the lens is regularly traversed by seams between the structural elements; and the light which passes through it suffers both spherical and chromatic aberration. There is not only the blind spot near the center of the retina, where the nerve leaves the eyeball on the way to the brain, but there is a network of more or less opaque blood-vessels just in front of the retina, the shadows of which may be clearly seen by sending a ray of light sideways through the cornea instead of through the pupil. The eyeball is not round and its movements are not schematically exact, and vision is subject to illusions from many other senses; a subjective retinal image is perhaps less perfect than the objective image. It is, however, precisely these slight imperfections which have been highly instrumental in directing science to the vast mass of detailed but somewhat unordered knowledge now recorded about the eye. Indeed, all the range of topics which constitute psychology might be exhaustively treated by a thorough and comprehensive presentation of the problems and phenomena of vision. Full and fundamental as his treatment is, Wundt does not attempt this, and we must be brief even with him.

In indirect vision, especially along the vertical meridian of the retina, we distinguish objects far less acutely than in direct vision; yet distances are not proportionately underestimated, as might be inferred from the fact that the rods and cones are farther apart than in the *fovea centralis*. The intervals between them are not perceived as gaps, but the sensation arising from each rod or cone seems to be spread out between them just as the blind spot is filled up in consciousness. If three-fourths of a circle is drawn, and the gap where the other fourth belongs falls in the blind spot, we seem to see a complete circle. Hence, our sensation of light cannot immediately possess the spatial form. The form of the field of vision in the eye is fixed; and so are the relative distinctness of vision in each direction from the point of direct vision, the number of degrees through which the eyeball can be moved in each direction, and the action of each of the six muscles independently. Everyone can easily determine for his own eye Listing's law, that, if the eyeball moves from a primary to a secondary position, it moves on a fixed axis, while when it moves from one secondary position to another, or rotates slightly at the same time, the direction and amount of this rotation are the same for every position, however reached. The impressions which we gain from the motions of the eye we use in our judgments of the field of vision when the eye is at rest. We infer the form of objects seen indirectly, not from the impressions they make at the time upon the peripheral zones of the retina, but from those we believe they would make if seen directly. If one eye-muscle is lamed and we try to move the eye in its direction, objects seem to move the same way, probably because the patient infers from the innervation feeling that the eye has moved, and this inference is for the instant too strong for the retinal sensation. Vertical distances seem greater than horizontal, perhaps because the muscles are so arranged that more effort is required to move the eyes up and down than laterally. By looking at the letter S or the figure 8, first upright, then inverted, we may see how prone we are to overestimate the upper half of the field of vision. If we attempt to divide a horizontal line, seen with one eye only, in the middle, the outer half is made smaller than the inner, because the cross-section of the internal muscle is larger than that of the external. Regarded with one eye, a line crossing a horizontal one seems perpendicular only when the upper end is a little inclined outward, because the muscles are so arranged that the axes of the eyes naturally converge if lowered, and diverge if raised. If a space between two points is filled out by other points, it seems greater than if empty; the same is true of angles divided by other smaller angles; hence the curious phenomena of Zöllner's famous figure. In these cases, the movement of the eye, instead of, as usual, increasing the accuracy of perception, gives rise to illusion. To explain this phenomenon Hering argues that the eye measures the distance between the two points by the direct distance between their retinal images; i. e., according to the chord which could be drawn between them, this chord being smaller in comparison to the retinal arc it subtends the greater the distance between the two images. Wundt objects to this that, even with very small intervals, the difference between the real and the estimated distance is too great to be accounted for in this way; and it is impossible to understand how we come to base the estimate upon the chord, even if an intimate knowledge of the retina be assumed. Helmholtz thinks that the error in judging the angles may perhaps be due to a sort of contrast between direction of lines and distances. If this were so, objects Wundt, the smaller of two distances or figures ought to seem relatively too small instead of too large, as it does. Helmholtz thinks that vertical seem greater than horizontal distances, because we are in the habit of looking below the level of the eyes, so that vertical lines seem perspectively shortened. Wundt objects that a square drawn with free hand does not seem the less a square if we tip the surface on which it is drawn. Helmholtz explains the fact that we cannot divide a horizontal line without constant error, with one eye closed, by assuming that we are wont to see the right half of such a line with the right, the left half with the left, eye. The same objection, says Wundt, holds here. If visual objects move, or if our body is passively moved in riding, or even voluntarily, as in walking, whirling around, etc., judgments are

362

more difficult and complex. After we have followed moving objects a while, the eyes move more and more involuntarily until we lose the power to fixate objects at rest; the eye moves on, but unconsciously, so that the objects seem to move in the opposite direction. Helmholtz thinks that the reason we cease to be conscious of movement in one direction is that, being accustomed to fixate objects at rest, we come to regard the volitional effort required to see moving objects as natural for fixation. Wundt objects that perfect fixation in such cases is impossible. The eye is turned toward one side while the constant but fruitless innervation in the other affects consciousness. If two objects change their relative position in space, the one which the eye does not follow seems to move, and the object fixated to remain at rest. Other things being equal, the smaller object is more apt to appear in motion, as, e. g., in the case of clouds passing across the face of the moon.

The form of the field of vision which we attain with the aid of movements and feelings of innervation Wundt calls the subjective, in distinction from the objective, field, or the actual form of surfaces presented to the eye. Hence, he is able to assert, as the law of binocular vision, that we see things singly as soon as and as far as the objective coincides with the subjective field of vision; while those points of the objective field of vision which are not placed in the subjective field seem double. The difficulties of correctly apprehending the objective field are formulated by saying that the excitation of such retinal points as in the great majority of cases correspond to agreeing objective points, gives rise to a simple idea more easily than does the excitation of such retinal points as do not so generally correspond to agreeing objective points. This is made extremely probable from the phenomenon of concomitant squinting, when the angle which the lines of vision of the two eyes make with each other remains constant. In most such cases, objects are fixated alternately by one eye and then by the other, and yet are commonly seen singly and not doubly. Hence, the retinal center of one eye appears to be coördinated in a constant manner with that point of the other retina upon which the same objective point is imaged; while the other coördinate retinal points are transposed accordingly. The horopter Wundt then comes to define not as the aggregate of all those points in space which are seen singly, but as the aggregate of all those points in space the images of which fall upon corresponding points of both retinas. In the stereoscopic phenomena of rivalry, when different objects are presented to the eyes, he lays down the law that that image is given precedence the contours of which run in the same direction as the accidentally or designedly chosen movements of the eye. With the stimulation of any and every retinal point there is connected a feeling of movement which suggests the direction and amount of movement required to follow contours, etc., without the movement being actually made.

From what has already been said, it may be readily inferred in relation to the question of space-perception, that Wundt is not exactly an empiricist, because, as he says, perception as the foundation of experience cannot itself rest on experience. His "synthetic" theory that we come to know space as an inference from an intensive and a qualitative series is admittedly more or less nativistic, because it presupposes an innate constitution of the peripheral and central sensory apparatus and of the centers of motor innervation. Neither of themselves, as Helmholtz believes, can mediate the perception of space; nor can the local signs, as he also thinks, be arranged in any conceivable order over the retina instead of being regularly and constantly variable, without presupposing a spatial element already contained in sensation. The synthesis here proposed is a strictly logical one, and, indeed, illustrates again Wundt's fundamental conception that, as all the manifold objects and phenomena of the organic world may be grouped and studied in the history of the cell, so all the manifold psychic phenomena, from the unconscious ordering of the elements of sensation to the formation of abstract ideas and systems, are expressions of a few fundamental and inextricably connected logical laws.

In the chapter on imaged ideas (*Vorstellungen*) Wundt assumes that the laws of association are universal. It is because, when various sorts of indistinct feeling are vehicles of reproduction, the train of association is indistinct, and because the latter may attach to any of the many elements of sensation or conception, that images seem to arise in the mind without occasion or antecedent. Phantasy images are due to psychical more manifestly than to physiological stimuli; but even in this case, the latter must follow the former as the effect, because the imagined image has the same color, only paler, as perception itself. The mild sensations which participate in ordinary perception are more adequately reproducible than extensive ones like pain. This is the physiological cause for the oft-observed fact that the freshest memories of our past lives are the pleasant ones. The latter are not irradiated from the central to the peripheral sense-surface, as hallucinations often are; and, unlike the latter, they are independent of the movement of the eye. Phantasy occupies itself especially with the future, especially the maturing dreams of youth. These and the play of children should be so directed by educators as to develop individual action and guide it toward practical ends. Hallucinations, although accompanied by peripheral activities in the organs of sense, probably originate in cortical hyperæmia or anæmia. Accumulated products of decomposition not only increase irritability, but become themselves active irritants. Hallucinations are most commonly visual or auditory,—particularly so when recorded of painters or musicians—less often tactual, and very rarely olfactory or gustatory, and are best observed just before going to sleep. Long isolation in darkness or silence predisposes, if it does not cause, hallucinations of sight and hearing. Feeble visions are best seen with closed eyes. Their constant change of form or color shows how independent of the will they are. The feeble stimuli to which eye and ear are constantly exposed seem often to be plastic material for such imaged ideas. The automatic cerebral stimulation must be strong to cause hallucinations in broad daylight, or amid the noises of the street. Illusions are caused by sensory impressions wrongly perceived or judged. Physiological illusion is the mingling of images of memory with perception, which really gives us only an approximate scheme of objects; as, *e. g.*, in the common failure to detect type errors in a printed page, which sometimes escape even an experienced proofreader. In this case the impression acts as a psychic stimulus, calling up the common idea by association. If the central sensory center is very irritable and the perceptive factor becomes relatively very small, illusion is called phantastic. Clouds, rocks, trees, take more or less human forms; in the dark a stump becomes a ghost. Illusions of hypochondriacs that they are in the bellies of animals, that their bodies are glass, etc., show that hallucination may extend not only to sight and hearing, but even to touch and somatic feeling. Far more commonly than is supposed, dreams of seeing large numbers of birds, fishes, pearls, flowers, Wundt thinks due to the retinal stimulation known as light-chaos, or dust. Dreams of being half clad in public are caused by the bedclothes having fallen off. An uncomfortable position excites dreams of seeking for something lost, climbing in a perilous situation, etc. The general character or drift of ideas in these cases is determined by present sensations, while their more specific content is due to the reproduction, commonly of very strong or recent impressions, or else of those of childhood. The motor centers are not so often or strongly excited in sleep. The hands and arms are most commonly moved, and complex actions are rare. The judgment is so narrow and imperfect that we often fancy, *e. g.*, that we speak unknown languages fluently, and perhaps wake with the last phrase in our ear, to find that there was neither sense nor real words in our utterances. Or we make a quick discovery, or write a speech or poem which seemed most admirable, which turns out to be utterly absurd. Conscience, like judgment, is a comprehensive activity of the soul, and hence cannot be fully active during sleep.

Most of our *Vorstellungen* are complex, *i. e.*, they rest upon the perceptions of different senses. Visual and tactual impressions are perhaps most fixedly cemented in this way. If we see an injury, we seem to feel the very touch of it ourselves; so that there is a sensuous source of our sympathy for the pain and danger of others. Sense-impressions may also be connected with our movements. Pantomime and mimetic, facial or manual gestures are the subjective reflexes of distinct ideas. The association between certain ideas and the expressive movements they excite often becomes almost indissoluble. Language is only a form of gesture, and is developed, like pantomime, partly from feeling or passion, and partly as imitative movement. Both the sound and the sensation of movement must at the beginning of language have stood in some relation of internal affinity with the idea and have formed together a complex of related ideas. But the objects to which the ideas correspond are, for the most part, complex, with disparate qualities and attributes, and language and gesture must select and match themselves to only such of these as are in some way related to sound or movement. This relationship is very close for language, amounting, indeed, in Herbart's quaint terminology, to passion, if the permanent attribute of an object is auditory. If the idea belongs to another sense, the analogies of sensation come in, making possible, *e. g.*, the translation of the most diversified sense-impressions into auditory sensations. The fact that these analogies originate in sensuous feeling explains, on the one hand, the origin of the indistinctness of the relationship between vocal sounds (*Sprechlaut*) and ideas; and, on the other, the close connection of language-making with feeling and passion. In losing the primitive and sensuous significance of its sounds, and becoming a concrete symbol of ideas, just as letters have developed from pictures to arbitrary signs, language has lost much virility but has become a medium for the expression of abstract and generic concepts. The former could not exist before or without verbal expression.

The origin of the most important abstract ideas, Wundt describes as follows: *Thing* was first distinguished from *idea,* or *being* from *thought.* The idea of being naturally passes to its abstract opposite, *not-being.* As images come and go, the concepts of *becoming, passing away, persistence,* and *change,* or *substantial* and *accidental* arise. One image is followed by another, hence the concepts of *means* and *end, cause* and *effect.* If two ideas are not connected in objects, but are in us, their connection is a product of our voluntary movement. We can see the inner reciprocal connection between them, where intentionally by our own act we can cause one to pass over into the other. Hence, means and end are applicable to external objects only so far as we imagine in them, really or symbolically, similar, intentional action to that which we find in ourselves, as the animism of children and primitive men really does. Only when this standpoint is abandoned do we reach abstract ideas of necessity and chance. The most comprehensive of the above abstract ideas are commonly called categories, because they are the most general expressions of consciousness about things. The motive of logically coördinating these into a system or scheme, as Kant attempted, has no psychological significance save in the admitted fact that every abstract idea, when it comes into consciousness, is indissolubly accompanied by its correlative ideas. Abstract ideas are not psychic structures. Therefore, and because they are inconceivable postulates for which a symbol is substituted, idealism asserted their a priority. The categories may be regarded, with Kant, as purely subjective forms of knowledge, or, with Hegel, as subjective determinations of being. The element of necessity is said especially to distinguish them from every empirical synthesis. Especially Schopenhauer singled out the idea of cause in trying to establish necessity, and Kant made necessity itself a category. It is upon this idea that all proofs of idealism must rest. And yet it is itself, according to Wundt, of psychologic origin, so that the conception of a priori ideas is superfluous. The psychologic motives for the origin of the idea of causal necessity are found in every purposive action. The end in view or the object to be attained comes first and represents the cause. The act itself, which in normal conditions always follows the volitional impulse, seems a necessary result or effect. Here we have a definite and predeterminable sequence, where the consequent can always be anticipated from the antecedent, and this sequence is what analysis gives as the fundamental element of causal necessity. From this stage of teleological causality, which characterizes the child and earlier scientific motives, etc., external or mechanical causality is developed. In making this transition, the motif of a purpose in the cause is dropped, and that of necessity (which springs from inner causality, rather than, as Hume said, from the regularity of the sequences, although after it is once adopted this is its chief support) is retained. The motif of subjective necessity thus arises from regarding a single act, first conceived, then executed; while the motif of freedom, its complement, arises from comparing this act with other purposes, all equally conceivable.

This brings us to general *practical* ideas, which may be æsthetic or ethical. These ideas also are in pairs of opposites, as good and bad, beautiful and ugly, etc. Religious ideas proceed from a peculiar combination of theoretical and practical ideas. Just as a first cause is postulated, which is not an effect, and a final purpose, which cannot be a means, so is an absolute reality or substance, with its correlative ideas of negation or accedence postulated. In this absolute reality, an idea to which all others belong, and which only absolute substance can possess, the analogously formed, practical ideas of good, beautiful, sublime, etc., must inhere, so that at last all absolute ideas come to be regarded as components of an absolute sublime. Polytheism occurs because the unification of the manifold practical ideas is so difficult. Instead of being designated by words, practical ideas may be exemplified in images. This, indeed, is probably their original form. We represent, *e. g.*, the idea *think,* and indeed all possibility of thought, with great difficulty as an image; but the idea *goodness, sublimity,* and all those postulated of action, suggest readily a good act, a lofty dome, etc. Indeed, before goodness and beauty were named, men had imaged them as gods. The feelings which clung at first to practical images came later to be excited by the words alone. All moral and religious, as well as æsthetic, ideas are accompanied by feelings so nearly identical that they may be, as by the Greeks they were, called æsthetic. Theoretical ideas, like concepts of objects, excite no particular tone of feeling unless perhaps a shade of satisfaction accompanies the act of positing reality, or substance, and of dissatisfaction in positing their correlates, negation, accident, etc., If so, general ideas and feelings agree in a sort of dialectic sequence between opposites or contradictories—a peculiarity which belongs to no other psychic production. After abstract ideas have once come into existence, they enter into manifold, reciprocal combinations not only with each other, but with empirical ideas, which it belongs to ethics, æsthetics, and the philosophy of religion to trace out.

Like abstract ideas, time and space are postulates, but, unlike such ideas, can never be represented in consciousness by a mere sign without evoking the notion of a particular time or place. It is for this reason that common sense, as well as many philosophers, regards time and space as existing outside ourselves, comprehending all things. Then it was said that they were at the same time subjective and objective forms. As soon as Kant demonstrated their subjective nature, the psychologic problem of explaining them was presented. Every idea, after it has given place to another in the mind, leaves an after-effect behind, and this gives rise to the "idea that ideas can be reproduced," or made disposable to consciousness; and from this perspective the notion of time is developed. But a series of faint and vivid ideas at one given instant is not a true series. A succession of ideas is not an idea of succession. A series of sense-impressions is the indispensable condition of the notion of time. The first beat of a pendulum, e. g., marks a beginning; the second beat marks an end, and the time between is a mere phantasy image. The ending of the first with the advent of the second represents an extent. The instant the second beat is heard, all three elements acting together produce the idea of time. In it, thus, there is not even a succession of ideas. Not only the abstract idea of number, but the four elementary methods of arithmetic, and even the ideas of power and root, are implicit in the idea of a complex period of rhythm, because time is discrete and not like a line, continuous. The abstract idea of time is alike in every moment which proceeds outside our psychic processes; the sense of time, even in the timeless states of sleep, etc., has no reality, but is a product of abstraction. Yet this abstract idea leads to that of continuous, spacial, non-discrete magnitudes, which is quite apart from the magnitudes of number.

Space magnitudes are entirely independent of numbers. Because the latter are discrete, they become irrational when applied to continuous space. Even discrete objects occupy continuous space and their enumeration requires time. In the domain of time, magnitude arises from number; in the domain of space, number arises from magnitude. Irrational numbers, though robbed of discreteness, have one dimension left, but only one. They can increase or decrease in only one direction. Let imaginary numbers be applied and the product arising from these new unities and the previous single unity is represented by a plane surface of two dimensions. So, too, the product of three imaginary unities with ordinary unity, called quaternions, gives any curved surface or space of three dimensions. The difficulties which arise from complex and imaginary numbers are due to the psychological fact that number originates in time, is essentially only discrete or rational, and has only one dimension or form of unity. Space, as conceived above, is only a complex, imaginary, *temporal* structure of three dimensions; and, as this may be substituted for true space, so we may substitute still other properties which transcend our actual intuition of space, as those have done who have attempted to demonstrate a space of more than three dimensions. Again, space is plane and continuous because it can be represented by three straight lines alike in all but direction. Geometrically speaking, any given continuum may be distinguished in several ways. Firstly, single dimensions are not indifferent and interchangeable, as are those of space; tone, *e. g.*, is a continuum determined by pitch, intensity, and duration. Secondly, the number of dimensions may be more or less than three, as a geometrical surface, color tone, saturation, intensity, duration of light. Thirdly, the continuum may not be plane, *e. g.*, the dimensions may be represented by curved instead of by straight lines, and hence be determinable by the measure of curvature. This third determination of a continuum is clearly connected with the second. A plane space of three dimensions is readily conceived as a curved surface, *i. e.*, we can conceive the first two dimensions of a continuum, the measure of curvature of which is not zero, but we are not able, even in thought, to add to this not plane continuum a third dimension of our plane space. Indeed, if the first dimension were represented by a visible curvature only, it would be conceivable. Thus for every not plane continuum we can substitute a plane continuum of more dimensions. Colored light, *e. g.*, cannot be graphically represented in space of three dimensions. The geometrical representation of systems of sensation is a process extremely like that by which the notion of space is formed. The single dimensions of the sensations given as conditions of consciousness have, then, spatial distinctness.

Thus, although there are continuums, like color, which cannot be constructed in our ordinary space, there is no justification for such speculations as that the world may exist in a space the measure of curvature of which is not plane. It is idle to assert that things *must* be conceived in a manner in which we *cannot* conceive them. The conceivable can never be derived from the inconceivable.

The fourth section of Wundt's psychology is devoted to consciousness and the changes and reactions of ideas. Consciousness is the condition of all man's experience; it consists in the fact that we find states and processes in us. All attempts, therefore, to define it are either tautological, like Herbart's definition that it is the sum of all real or coexistent present ideas, or else lead to determination of the activities perceived in consciousness, like the definition of it as the activity of distinguishing and contrasting subject and object. As this latter conception does not distinguish between consciousness and self-consciousness, it is plainly suggested by the idealism of Fichte and Schelling. Although we must and may postulate that unconscious processes, though not differentiated into premises and conclusions, are logical after the analogy of consciousness, this by no means justifies us in conceiving, like Schopenhauer, of an unconscious will. The two processes which are characteristic of consciousness, are the formation of ideas and percepts out of sensuous impressions, and the going and coming of reproduced ideas, pure sensation being an abstraction unknown to consciousness. The latter is the act of synthesis, which brings sensation into the forms of time and space, and like this process may be of various grades. As soon as a previous idea is not reproduced, it exists only as a disposition to reproduction. To ascribe to such unconscious ideas a real existence, apart from the physiological disposition of the central organs, helps nothing, and, on account of their vast number, is entirely improbable. They must be excited by inner, as new ideas must by outer, stimuli. Such associations, therefore, must occur in consciousness, which may be additionally defined as an ordered connection of ideas. The synthesis of sensations presupposes a certain physical organization. Where sense-impressions can be united, the nervous irritability accompanying a certain grade of consciousness cannot be denied. It by no means follows, however, from the fact that in the lower animals a rudimentary consciousness may be assumed to coexist with even single nerve-centers that in man or the higher vertebrates, along with the central consciousness, lower grades of consciousness are seated in the basal ganglia of the brain, the spinal cord, or the sympathetic nerves. The unity of the nervous system is the physiological basis of the unity of consciousness. Although the latter is more intimately connected with a certain part of the nervous system, this must by no means be assumed to be the organ of consciousness in the current sense. If lower nerve-centers are conscious when severed from higher, this is not a residual, but a newly developed consciousness, by a process perhaps the converse of the centralization and cephalization in growth and along the ascending scale of animal life. The unity of consciousness is expressed in the fact that several contemporaneous ideas are united in one, and that present ideas are connected to those which precede and follow. But there is also a distinguishing activity of consciousness by which ideas disunite. *Vorstellungen,* which follow one another in the mind according to the laws of association, are first distinguished from those imposed upon consciousness by the constraint of external impressions. One class of external impressions is connected with the conditions of our own body, and is thus more constant, more subjective, and more distinguished from the more changeable impressions which arise from external objects. Chief among the former are the sensations of movement, depending upon voluntary motor nerves. These and the somatic feelings are the foundation of self-consciousness. From these the conception of those internal processes, which in higher human development are the central part of consciousness, suggests the notion of a soul as an essence and causes us to contrast our ego with the external world. But the idea of our ideas in which self-consciousness is noted is really an idea assumed and labeled; or else we have only a second consciousness making the first its object; and we may even, with Herbart, speak of an idea of an idea of an idea, etc. In fine, consciousness is both synthesis and analysis, but primarily the first.

To explain attention, Wundt, under the figure of consciousness as an inner eye, distinguishes the field of vision from the center of vision. The entrance of an object into the former is perception; into the latter, apperception. But the center of internal vision cannot only be directed to any point in the field, but may be enlarged and narrowed. The narrower and brighter it is the darker the peripheral field of vision becomes. Sometimes attention can be directed toward objects seen only in indirect vision; and then those at the center become indistinct. If several ideas,

25   **375**

even from disparate senses, enter the focal point of attention at the same instant, they always become components of a complex idea. The fact, *e. g.*, that attention may be called to a single weak overtone among a multitude of others by sounding it beforehand alone, shows that the degree of apperception depends upon subjective attention and not upon the strength of the external impression. If a picture be illuminated by weak electric sparks, with intervals of several seconds between, at first very little is seen, but with each successive spark more outlines and colors appear until at last all is seen. We see it at last by the aid of impressions accumulated in memory. We also perceive a familiar object sooner and more perfectly than a new one. Ideas also require a certain time to come into the focal point of apperception, and if an object is intensely and momentarily expected, we can feel, so to speak, the tension of attention, as sensuous feeling is probably due to the innervation of voluntary muscles. In an attentive state, again, we are very conscious of our own activity, and it commonly seems subject to the will, but is the same when it is and when it is not. Attention must be accommodated to the quality as well as the intensity of the impression, or else an unpleasant sense of surprise is felt. Upon the accuracy of this accommodation and not at all upon the strength of sensation or idea depends the acuteness of apperception. The act of innervation which thus adapts both the eye or ear and the cerebral cortex to external impressions is one and the same. Every stimulus, we may thus conceive, whether external or internal, excites first a perceived or imagined idea which lies at first in the periphery of consciousness. Sensory stimuli, however, pass at once to the central domain of voluntary innervation, whence the process thus occasioned may pass back again to the sensory domain, thereby strengthening the idea; or it may cause the muscles which mediate the feeling of attention to contract. Attention is thus distinguished from voluntary motion chiefly by the fact that in the former case the reaction from the stimulated center is chiefly to the sensory parts, and in the latter it is chiefly to the muscles. The fact that volitional effort can excite very vivid images and that, with the attention thoroughly aroused and properly directed, impressions are perceived in much less than the normal time, indicates that voluntary concentration of attention immediately affects sense-perception. Impressions of unknown intensity, as well as those which cannot be united and those for which the tension of consciousness is inadequate, are unpleasant. Those for which the level of attention can be adjusted beforehand, and those which, like rhythm, symmetry, harmony, etc., alternately intensify and satisfy expectant attention, are pleasant. Feelings arise as effects of sensation and ideas upon consciousness, since attention, which makes the former accessible to internal observation, is a sensuous feeling of innervation; yet there is a sense in which consciousness rests on feeling. When we speak of affecting consciousness, we mean simply that all psychic elements are measured in terms of that inner tension which is active wherever impressions are apprehended or reproduced. Consciousness is, then, not coincident with attention, but more comprehensive.

Perhaps the most original and valuable of Wundt's experimental work in psychology is recorded in the chapter on the succession and association of ideas (*Vorstellungen*). Attention has hitherto by most psychologists been regarded as the expression of an instinct by which the mind pushes on from one idea to another, waking successive elements of psychic life by a native, spontaneous impulse of growth and development. The dependence of the flow of ideas upon sensuous impressions, meanwhile, has been neglected, upon the assumption that the sequence of perceptions repeated immediately and without change the temporal sequence of external impressions. This, however, is not the case. The way in which external events are received in the mind depends upon the peculiarities of consciousness and attention. To demonstrate this the relation of the origin and sequence of impressions to the external stimuli which cause them must be first experimentally investigated. If eye, ear, or skin is stimulated, e. g., by an electric shock, and if, as soon as the stimulus is felt, a single movement is made, the time which intervenes between stimulus and movement, small as it is, is composed of several smaller periods. Of these, two—viz., the time required for conducting the stimulus along the nerve inward to the seat of consciousness, and that occupied by the passage of the corresponding motor impulses outward—may be eliminated here as mere physiological constants. There remain, (1) the time required for the entrance of the impression into the field of consciousness, called the perception time; and (2), the time required for the generation of the volitional element. The time occupied by these processes is called the reaction time and exceeds that occupied by the former two, conductive processes, which are less variable. The first and last of them undoubtedly record the time required for the excitation of the sensory and motor centers; and hence may be regarded as psychophysic. Even apperception seems not purely psychological when we remember by what manifest physiological reactions attention is manifested and attended. All of these five processes into which the personal equation is divided, especially the last three, are experimentally inseparable; but, by altering the conditions, certain variations in the net result can be ascribed with great probability, now to one, now to another, of these elements. In one series of experiments, the observer reacts upon an impression of predetermined quality and strength, the exact time of the occurrence being unknown. In the second and easiest series, this latter is known. In the third and most difficult series, either the occurrence of an impression at all is

378

uncertain, or its nature is unknown, or else the kind of reaction depends upon and must therefore be determined after the nature of the stimulus is known. The stronger the stimulus, the quicker is the reaction. But, save in the case of minimal stimuli but just above the threshold of consciousness, it is impossible to compare their strength when acting upon different senses. Hence, it is possible that reactions from sound are not in themselves quicker, nor those from light slower than touch, as most experimental results with moderately strong stimuli indicate. Wundt even ventures the assertion that, with just recognizable stimuli, the time of perception and reaction is the same for all senses, assuming, we question how justifiably, a relatively constant threshold and suggesting important effects of different intensities. By using as a stimulus the noise caused by the fall of a ball from different and exactly measurable heights upon a resonant plate of wood, the effects of varying degrees of auditory excitation upon the time of reaction are found to be quite constant, as already observed in the case of a simple nerve-muscle preparation, although small compared with the involuntary variations in the degrees of attention. The latter does not oscillate about a center of equilibrium, but the center itself seems to change somewhat uncontrollably, however long the series of experiments averaged in the result. The attention is apt to accommodate itself involuntarily for a stimulus of greater than threshold intensity; hence, often after a minimal but distinct stimulus is received in consciousness or is perceived, an instant is sometimes lost in hesitation. Yet, as a rule, it is hard to see why, once perceived, the reaction should be quicker for a strong than for a weak stimulus. When in these experiments we tense the mind in expectation of the stimulus, it often happens that another than the awaited stimulus is given—a sound, *e. g.*, when we expect a flash of light. In such a case, we react upon or register the false signal involuntarily, knowing even the instant we do so that it is wrong. This Wundt explains by assuming that the attention develops, along with itself, a preparatory innervation of the motor-centers, so that the latter are discharged by the slightest impulse from whatever sense. This explains how the volitional time may be an almost vanishing quantity.

If the stimulus is preceded by a signal, the time of reaction is greatly diminished up to a certain point in proportion to the interval between the signal and stimulus, and may even be reduced nearly or quite to zero, by the preparatory "tension of attention," which may thus accommodate itself to the stimulus in time. In these cases, the three central processes may be conceived to coincide in time. The physiological time sometimes seems to vanish or even to become a minus quantity; and the impression is perceived sooner by the time of motor conductivity than it actually occurs. This is because we instinctively seek so to register that the sensations of touch innervation resulting from the movement of reaction shall coincide with the impression. If the coincidence in time of two different stimuli is very unlike in strength, we can do this with marvelous accuracy.

If neither the time nor the strength of the stimulus is predetermined, the time is longer and more variable. The reaction time is here increased. At the apex of apperception if the stimulus is strong enough to cause fright, delay is occasioned, because attention cannot accommodate itself to more than a certain degree of intensity. The time is still further increased if the observer does not know beforehand what sense is to be stimulated, and especially if the stimulus is entirely unexpected; and still more if the kind of movement or the kind to be used by the reactor is not predetermined but made to depend on the nature of the stimulus. If, *e. g.*, the observer reacts or registers with the foot of the same side as the hand stimulated, not knowing beforehand which hand it will be; or, if the stimulus is a vocal sound and the reaction is its repetition, reflex associations preëxist or are readily established, which is different from the case where he reacts arbitrarily, e. g., with the left hand for a red, with the right for a white light. This perhaps explains in part the fact that it requires nearly twice the time to register with the voice, a written as it does a spoken vocal sign. The measure of the time of perception in the latter case cannot explain this, but we wait because the connection between written and spoken words is not so fixed and solidary as between heard and spoken words. It is probable that impressions are perceived in the same time whether known beforehand or not, and that the delay in the latter case is in apperception; but when the kind of reaction is not predetermined, the delay is chiefly in the volitional time required to choose between two movements of registration, and this depends on the physiological connection between the central sense domain and the reactionary motor apparatus.

In Donders' experiments, the reactions of the first series (a) were upon known, of the second series (b) upon unknown, vocal sounds. In a third series (c) the position of the mouth was fixed for a distinct vowel, which was sounded, however, only at irregular intervals and between others, but upon which alone the observer was to react. The difference between (c) and (a) reactions, which was found to be about one-twenty-fifth of a second, Donders thought to be the time occupied in forming the idea. Wundt, however, objects that in the (c) series the time of volition is not entirely eliminated, and that the conditions of apperception in the (a) and (c) series are alike.

If, at the same time with these experiments, other constant stimulations occur, Wundt found that when these distractions occurred in disparate senses, the time of reaction was more delayed than when they occurred in the same sense. From this he infers that if, e. g., when we are reacting upon sounds, we are distracted by flashes of light, the innervation of attention is different, perhaps because proceeding from different central localities, from what it is when we are distracted by other sounds. Or, again, the other stimulus may also be momentary, either just before or after or coincident with the main stimulus. By these experiments the remarkable result is attained that the succession of our perceptions is not always the same as that of the stimuli, but the last may be perceived first, as, *e. g.*, when the attention is accommodated for a sound, but the sound preceded by an induction spark, the latter comes latest to consciousness. The greater the attention the greater the interval which may be thus inverted. If the disturbing sound occurs after the sound upon which the reaction is to be made, it is often unheard and does not affect the physiological time; but, if it occurs before, the time is invariably increased. If the distracting stimulus is disparate, the two are within wide limits perceived synchronously. When successively perceived, Wundt found a habit to be established by one series of observations, which made it hard in distracting to invert their order. The delay caused by interference is set mainly to the account of apperception. As in these experiments there is no choice between different forms of reaction, we see again how intimately apperception and volition are connected. Again, reaction and volitional time may be eliminated and the shortest time during which the stimulus must act in order to produce an impression can then be sought. This, however, is very hard to determine because we can perceive almost instantaneous stimuli by means of their physiological after-effects, so that the time required is not identical with the shortest perceptible interval. If, *e. g.*, an after-image is eliminated by a subsequent flash of light, the first flash must last longer to be perceived by itself. In general, the time of perception decreases arithmetically as the intensity or extension increases geometrically.

If a more complex image, *e. g.*, three letters, be thrown

upon the retina followed by another "extinguishing" image, the interval between the two can be made just great enough for distinct perception. As, without the second image, an instantaneous illumination of the first is sufficient for perception, we may infer that the above interval is the time of apperception, which is estimated at about one-eighteenth of a second. The second image must, however, be quite vivid in order to completely arrest the development of the idea. Not only the complexity of the figure and its vividness, but also its size is of influence. Large letters require less time because the accommodation, which occupies relatively more time, need not be so sharply adapted. The position of the object on the retina relative to the center makes a difference because the most sensitive or the most sharply perceptive part of the retina is at the center. In the preceding observations, there is no objective interval between the impressions, for when the second occurs the first is not extinct; and yet an interval is always noticed in which neither of the two impressions is distinctly apprehended—another illustration of the discreteness of time. So, too, ideas are discrete when the impressions which give rise to them are constant in their succession. Only when the latter change in quality, strength, or place, instead of from one to another kind of impression, is no trace of such an interval observable. The attention needs time to pass from one to another impression. Two impressions, *e. g.*, a particular sight of spurting blood and pain of the knife, seem exactly contemporaneous impressions only if the attention is equally directed to both at the same time. Indeed, all impressions which reach attention at the same time appear in consciousness as one more or less united idea, but if this union does not occur, even contemporary impressions appear successive. This is important for the movement of attention. When the eye passes from one point to another, images of intermediate points and objects must be formed on the retina. But when consciousness attends to successive objects, it is first, as it were, diffused over a considerable part of the subjective field, and it is concentrated upon the second object after emerging from a momentary twilight of more generic consciousness.

Wundt devised an ingenious apparatus, which consists of a long pointer moving at a constant rate before a semicircular numbered scale, and a device by which a small bell can be struck while the moving finger is at any point of the scale. The observer must determine in a series of experiments just where the pointer is when the bell sounds, with the design of ascertaining how an impression is combined with another regular series of ideas. If the sound is apperceived later than it really occurs, the translocation is positive; and if conversely, as is far more commonly the case, it is negative. The first time the location is very indefinite, but as the observation is several times repeated the judgment grows quite specific. Casual combinations of attention are also frequent. By arbitrarily choosing a distinct position of the figures, or by covering the same at a single point of the passage, intervals of more than a fourth of a second can be figured. We will consider first the sense of the translocation. This was found to be positive if the finger moved with more than a certain rapidity, and negative if it moved with less. There is a tendency while the rapidity increases to a negative, while it decreases to a positive, translocation. This is, moreover, greatest with slight rapidities and slight changes in rapidity. So, too, in recording the time of the passage of a star across the vertical thread of a telescope, if the star is moving fast, *i. e.*, is near the celestial equator positive, but if near the pole negative, translocation is to be expected. When differences in the personal equation amount to only a few hundredths of a second, the translocation of the two astronomers compared is probably with the same sense; where it is very large, amounting as it sometimes does to a full second, the translocation is with different senses. Another reason why the personal equation is so great is because there are two records during the passage of the star, so that individual peculiarities are doubled, and perhaps also because attention is more or less exhausted during the second record.

Attention, then, always requires a certain accommodation time in order to bring impressions into the focus of consciousness, but this may be done beforehand if any elements of the stimulus are foreknown. In this way the time between perception and apperception can be shortened to nearly or quite zero. So, too, the kind of voluntary attention may be predetermined and even practiced, or it may be left indeterminate, to depend upon the nature of the stimulus. In the first case, the volitional time coincides with that of apperception. This can only be explained by supposing that the preparatory concentration of attention is identical with a process of innervation which manifests itself at the same time as the augmenting volitional energy. Attention is a voluntary process. The physiological side of apperception is an increment of motor innervation, which can discharge itself indifferently upon motor organs or a central sensory domain. The subjective feeling of attention changes with the quality and strength of the repeated impression and with the form of the intended motion. Either of these conditions can be left more or less indistinct. If the kind of external impression is unknown, the motor tension is sufficient but the innervation is distributed to different senses. With the feeling of unrest peculiar to this case, the time of apperception increases, but that of volitional reaction coincides with it. From all this it may be inferred that apperception and volitional reaction are essentially the same process, the physiological origin of which is from the centers of motor innervation. Apperception and voluntary motion are indeed only different forms of the excitation of will. This result has an independent confirmation in the phenomena of the voluntary reproduction of ideas, and throws new light upon the fact that, while the cortical centers of sensation are seated in the back part of the brain, those of voluntary movement are in the front part, which is generally thought to be also the seat of intelligence.

If attention is withdrawn from external objects, the mind is mainly occupied with an internal train of ideas, originating in previous sense perceptions. The questions which arise here are: First, how remembered are related to actual impressions in time; and second, how the two are related as to content.

I leave here the original text and base for a few paragraphs upon the admirable and concise epitome of Eisler, supplemented at points by that of König. Wundt holds that consciousness is not a unique independent activity, nor is it something outside of psychic experiences, nor yet a property of the latter, which may be absent. In fact, it is only an expression for psychic experience in general in some particular relation. We find states and processes in us and these states cannot be separated from these inner processes. This is consciousness. It is not a theater stage, for it changes constantly with experience, nor is it one psychic process beside another, but it is an expression of the fact that we have inner experiences. To have an idea and to have it in consciousness are one and the same thing. The only reality that corresponds to an elevation above the threshold of consciousness is the fact that something occurs that had not occurred before. Again, consciousness consists not in the mere sum of psychic processes, but in the inclusive connection of coexistent and sequent happenings. The collective consciousness proceeds from the connection of the individual conscious images.

Consciousness has various degrees, the highest being the clearness of apperception, while the lowest consists in the absence of all psychic coherence in the unconscious. To call a psychic process unconscious means only the possibility of its reëntering the connections of experience. But unconscious ideas as real psychic structures are contradictions. We can, in such cases, only speak of the functional dispositions of ideas and this consists only in easement of reproduction. This can be proved both directly and by inference. For psychology, the unconscious is something transcendental with which it never can have occasion to occupy itself, since it is only concerned with immediate psychic experience. It is therefore fruitless for psychology to make assumptions concerning the state of the unconscious or of any unconscious process that may be presumed to occur beside the experience given in consciousness. All that is *geistig* is therefore conscious efficiency and unconscious *Geist* is a *geistig* efficiency of which it can at the same time be said that it is inefficient.

Consciousness is not an aggregate of psychic elements, but a unitary experience that only abstraction separates into components and momenta, and hence it cannot exist alone. We thus distinguish some of these parts as images of outer objects or ideas, others as reactions of our ego or feelings, and still others as reactions of consciousness itself. Now one and now another of these components becomes clearer. Thus we cannot speak of faculties or powers of the soul, nor of simple psychic processes the apperception of which constitutes the content of consciousness. Ideas thus express the immediate action of consciousness on the outer world. In the movements of the *Gemüth* we see mirrored the way in which consciousness, by means of the states of the *Gemüth*, accepts this reciprocity, while in will the subject immediately grasps its own inner actions.

Ideas are memory images as well as percepts in so far as both arise from sensations. In ideas we bring a content into relation with an object without us. Ideas are products of psychic synthesis. They appear as something new over against or above their components, which latter do not give the form or order of these elements. It is clear, according to this theory of actuality, that ideas are not persistent objects or states, but events.

The elements of ideas are sensations, which appear empirically only as parts of ideas connected with simple feelings. Pure sensations are therefore products of isolating abstraction or states of consciousness not further analyzable. Besides a feeling tone, every sensation has its quality and its intensity. Each sensation is an intensive *quale,* the connection of which with other similar sensations is outwardly occasioned by certain coexistent or sequent stimuli-activities, but is not in any strict sense caused by them. Hence Wundt does not fully accept the old doctrine of specific sense energies. To him differences of sensory qualities are conditioned by the processes of stimulation that arise in the sense organs and the latter are first dependent upon the composition of the physical sense stimulus, and in the second place are due to the peculiarity of the receptive apparatus that develops from adaptation to these stimuli. There is thus no primary tuning of the cortical endings of nerves, but a functional indifference.

Originally idea and feeling are a unity, but abstraction separates them into objective and subjective references and then into feeling and will. The simple feelings are subjective elements of inner experience. The manifoldness of feeling-qualities, Wundt, in distinction from other psychologists, makes very great, but all are of three chief classes, each representing a direction of opposite determinants. In reference to the conceptive side of feeling, pleasure and pain are qualitative directions; excitement and quieting are the intensity directions; and tension and relaxation are the temporal directions of feelings. These directions depend upon the course or flow of psychic qualities. Composite feelings arise from the composition of simple feelings. In these are partial feelings and total feeling, which is something new over against and above its components.

All feelings have this in common, that they are related to a state of the subject itself or to the passivity or activity of the ego. Feeling is not a mere function of knowing or sensing, nor is it a product of ideas (Herbart), nor is it a by-product of sensory stimuli; but it is a central psychic product with parallel psychic phenomena. Sensory feeling is made of reactions of apperception upon sense stimulation. The subjective or psychic side of the more central process of apperception is added to the central stimulus when the activity of consciousness turns to it. Feeling is the reaction of consciousness to the ideas that enter it, or the way and manner in which ideas are received by the ego.

The relation of feeling to apperceptive processes shows their close connections with the will. In fact, only a willing being can have feeling states and, conversely, there is no feelingless will. Willing is the most perfect product of consciousness. Feelings partly originate and partly accompany willing. They are volitional directions which may pass over into actual willing. Feeling and willing are partial phenomena of one and the same process, which begins in the excitation of feeling and ends in the act of will and we have to distinguish them because the latter process may fail while the initial feeling element is present. Desiring and resisting, by which consciousness reacts on ideas, are the conditions of all pleasure and pain. If the subjective state pauses at the stage of pleasure- or pain-tone (which is connected with the varying course of excitation or tranquilization), we speak of feelings proper. If the direction manifest in distinct feelings of tension passes on to a new sequence, we call the inner process a striving or impulse (*Trieb*). The unity of the feeling state (*Lage*), which in any moment can form only a total feeling, depends upon the unity of the will.

Since feeling appears as a reaction of will or as potential will, an act of will is the end moment of the course of feeling of an *Affekt*. The latter Wundt defines as any process of feeling in which a temporal sequence of feelings combines to a coherent course that stands out as peculiar from preëxisting or subsequent processes, and which affects the subject more intensely than a single feeling. The *Affekt* always begins with an initial feeling that originates in the idea; then follows a series of ideas with their accompanying feelings; and finally comes an end feeling which may eventually introduce a new *Affekt*. There are also mimetic and pantomimic physical accompaniments which, on account of their sympathetic significance, may be called expressive movements.

The end of an *Affekt* may be one of two things: It may give place to a normal course of feeling, or, secondly, it may lead to a sudden change of consciousness which momentarily conditions the *Affekt*, in which case the *Affekt*, together with the terminal result, is a process of will of which the act is a part, *e. g.*, when it ends in a pantomimic movement which produces another effect that terminates or sublates the *Affekt*. Contrast of feeling is the fundamental condition of acts of will. Although not all feelings or *Affekte* issue in acts of will, all are connected members of one process, which, when perfect, is a full volition. In this sense, feeling may equally well be regarded as the beginning of the process of willing, or, conversely, will may be conceived as a composite process of feeling and *Affekt*, or as the transition between the two.

Will Wundt makes neither a simple unconscious quality, like Schopenhauer and Göring, nor the action of ideas on the sum total of muscle sensation, like Herbart and the associationists. There is no abstract will, but only concrete willing, which never occurs without other conscious content. Nor is will divorced from consciousness, but is no less primordial than it. There is no consciousness without inner will-activity, and on the latter all connection of ideas rests. Hence will is a very composite yet very typical process characterized by a feeling of activity and a feeling of success or failure. It is the ability to turn to the object we prefer and to flee from the one we abhor. It is the power of the subject to work independently upon his ideas. Wundt's theory is autogenetic and not heterogenetic. Will is the original energy of consciousness. Acts of will cannot arise out of willess reflex movements which gradually become voluntary. Either will is primordial and *need* not be derived, or it is not and then it *cannot* be derived. If, as the soul in this case must know, the movements of its own body are subject to a will that does not exist, that fact cannot be found out. Heterogenetic theories of will assume that there are unconscious activities of the will. Wundt postulates that movement of will, impulse (*Trieb*) and reflexes, all evolve from one form of movement which bears the marks of will and reflexes at the same time. But we must distinguish a primary impulsive from a reproductive apperception of movement ideas. There may be inner without outer, but never outer without previous inner acts of will.

We come, finally, to the question, what general theory we can frame concerning subjective experience. First, the theory of knowledge must determine the relation between internal and external experience. The former has immediate, while objects have only mediate reality. In this nothing is implied respecting the nature of the soul, while an idealism is established which, however, need not deny the external world, but necessitates a critical discrimination of those elements of the knowledge of objects which originate in the functioning of the subject from those which are to be presupposed as truly objective. Hence the only critical realism is an ideal-realism, which does not deny reality but seeks to show the relation of the ideal principle to objective reality, just as the laws of thought are also the laws of the object of thought. It is idle to attempt to resolve either into the other. Instead of the general idea of the thing, science has substituted that of substance, which is defined as that idea of an object which remains as objective after the elimination of the subjective elements of our knowledge and of the contradictions of the original idea of things. This general idea is both metaphysical and hypothetical. Its cause is the mediate reality of our experience of the external world. Immediate internal experience gives no occasion to form or apply the idea of substance. Regarded as mere psychical processes, our conceptions, feelings, and volitions never give rise to such contradictions as to require the assertion of an inner being, different from themselves. The psychological application of the idea of substance, such as is seen in the hypotheses of psychophysics, has only one main defect—it cannot reach the problem of being, but it can hope to develop and further the hypotheses which natural science has begun to unfold. Not only will psychology be thereby advanced in that the all-pervading reciprocity between psychical and physical processes is made manifest, but the idea of physical substance will be enriched for the purposes of the natural sciences. But the organic cannot be explained merely from the properties of matter which physics presupposes, because all organic development is a psychophysic process. From the psycho-physic standpoint substance in motion must be also the organ or bearer of instinctive impulse and of elementary psychical phenomena. The latter involve directly motion or elementary physical phenomena. From the psycho-physic standpoint their every movement may be conceived as an expressive inevitable impulse, *i. e.*, as a process which corresponds in the external world to the sensation which accompanies and varies in its nature with the movement. Even in atoms and their simpler combinations, the most elementary forms of instinctive impulse are preformed. Although we can see only the external side, we may infer an inner state, which, under favorable conditions, can become instinctive impulse. There are lacking only the inner continuity and connection of states, which we must regard as the condition of consciousness proper. The conditions presupposed everywhere in substance may thus be described as the unconscious or unconnected elements of instinctive impulse, and we may see what Leibniz meant by designating bodies as animated by spirits. For us isolated psychic states do not survive the moment of their existence and are inconceivable although necessary preconditions of consciousness. Primitive instinct contains movement, first as sensations of movements, then as conception of motion. Real and perceived motion are distinguished late in the history of consciousness; hence the power of the will over bodily movements is from the first an integral part of inner experience. Instinctive movements pass over into automatic or reflex movements, so that the physical is the effect of the psychical development. In the light of Darwinism the soul may again be conceived as the first entelechy of the living body. From this standpoint the purposiveness of life is manifest. Not only are voluntary acts, which make up one part of the phenomena of life, purposive, but another part is solidified from residua of purposive volitions. Even vegetative life seems not entirely without a psychic element.

From the psycho-physic standpoint it is assumed that nothing occurs in our consciousness without a foundation of definite physical processes. The question here is, can the idea of physical substance be so extended as to include the phenomena of psychic life and its substrate, the brain, which is the most complex of all substances? Substance thus or even otherwise conceived is, of course, hypothetical, mediate, inferential, and all parallelism between the two is transcended as soon as we pass beyond the psycho-physic standpoint. Yet the dualistic antithesis between outer and inner is so old and persistent that the problem is too important to be ignored or disparaged by the old truism that objects are only ideas or products of thought. Any theory of the soul is due partly to an unjustifiable transference of this idea from outer to inner experience and partly from the need of explaining the connection of internal with attendant physical processes.

From the psychological standpoint it is plain that inner experience depends very largely upon causal sequences which do not originate in it. The physical train of events is complete in itself and cannot break in upon the psychical train. To determine the connection of inner experiences is the first and chief object of psychology, and the discussion of psycho-physic presuppositions is rather metaphysical than psychological. Psychology starts from simple facts of inner experience. As these are immediate, it is the only science which need make no metaphysical or hypothetical presupposition. Psychology therefore grows more purely experimental while physics becomes less so. Complex states must be analyzed to find fundamental indissoluble phenomena in order to make a future synthesis possible. Their analysis is made, however, inductively. The primitive psychical activity is not feeling or will but impulse (*Trieb*). This is apparent from the development of the race and the individual. Psychic elements are manifest in animals and consciousness begins in them in impulsive movements. The latter also are constant elements in the psychic synthesis of sensations. From their connection springs also the spatial and temporal ordering of ideas. Apperception is first dissociated from movements. The internal and external acts of will are separated when the external factor is inhibited and apperception is left independent and alone. Psychic development consists largely in the disintegration of an impulsive act of will into various elements which develop and combine with others independently. The establishment of the independence of the process of apperception gives the impulse to all intellectual development. The only problems of psychology are the complexity of the psychical combinations, their duration, and their psychical connections. These were ignored by the hypothesis of monads. There is a remarkable parallelism between those connections of inner consciousness which we have called the condition of its existence, and the complex chemical molecule from which the removal of one atom changes the nature of the whole. This latter is explained by assuming an equilibrium of the oscillatory movements in the molecules, which are more labile the more complex they are. This disturbance of equilibrium may be propagated to adjacent molecules. If the movement of even a single element of substance is a psycho-physic phenomenon, then these elements are compounded so that the external states of movement and the internal conditions are continuous. Whether the nervous system is by nature such a connection need not be determined here. The consciousness of its outermost parts is manifest, but from the psychological standpoint, the condition of many parts of even the central nervous system does not reach consciousness. We may postulate a complex unity, but for the development of consciousness it is necessary that all parts must once have possessed a substantial unity. This fact of our development from a single cell makes Leibniz's designation of an organic body as *unum per se* as opposed to an inorganic body, or *unum per accidens,* intelligible. What we call soul is just the inner being of the same unity which we regard externally as the body belonging to it. This solution of the problem of reciprocity implies that psychic being is the reality of things and that its most essential property is development from a less to a greater differentiation of which human consciousness is the apex, the focus in which nature reflects itself. Not as simple being in the sense of Leibniz, but as the most complex and developed product of countless elements is the human soul a mirror of the world.

Wundt started as a sensationalist and an associationist, accepting Helmholtz's *unbewusste Schluss,* and on this basis he developed in the successive editions of his "Psychologie" his doctrine of apperception on the analogy of the fovea, making apperception directive and volitional and finally something in a sense above and controlling the course of association and disposing of it as it would. Here, then, we find his ego, which is focal far more than marginal. It does its work where consciousness is raised to its highest potentiality. Mind for him is not so much all that happens in consciousness, as what goes on at its center. This at least is his norm. Foveal and marginal sensations result in eye movements in order to bring preferred images to the center of sharpest vision. This is his dominant analogy and when in his later revisions he urges the importance of the conative or outgoing phase of the process and stresses kinesthetic (especially verbal) feelings, he does so hardly enough to compensate for his primary visual bent. In his last reply to the Würzburgers he intimates that one of their cardinal errors is in judging psychology from the very highest, *i. e.,* logical activities of mind, but, if so, it was he who started this trend. At bottom, too, his feeling elements are felted sensations, fused and impacted, their relations to each other are too like those of sensations among themselves, and he is always more intent upon their synthesis than upon their bifurcation or differentiation, just as he is with sensations, and for the same reason, viz., because of his lack of genetic perspective.

Among the topics which for some forty years have been most central in Wundt's interest is his quest for pure elemental sensations and feelings, which, in his mind, are not without analogies in their all-conditioning value with chemical elements. His views upon this subject have undergone much transformation and development, but they may be very roughly summarized from his "Psychologie" and with the aid of Miss Washburn [1] and E. H. Hollands,[2] somewhat as follows. For elementary sensations he does not look to observations of the primitive manifestations of life in the simplest organisms but to analyses of adult cultivated minds on the basis of introspection. Such sensations must be absolutely simple and unanalyzable and independently variable if not discoverable by themselves and attended to separately. They must have reference to objects, although they must be regarded by psychology as independent of all epistemological results. They must of course have a certain intensity and quality if not clearness, duration and extension. Although such pure sensations are abstractions and are never found isolated in consciousness, we must presuppose them and assume that the actually accessible representations of the outer world may be analyzed into them. Their intensity and quality at least are independently variable.

Feelings are unlike sensations in that they are not referred to objects, and they may vary independently of sensations. Introspection can never observe conscious processes while they are evolving, but only their after-traces in memory. This is especially true of feelings, in which we attend to the inner process itself rather than to its outer cause as in sensations. About all sensations have some feeling tone, although some may be without it, but there can be no feelings without sensations. Feeling is a mode of reaction of the apperceptive activity upon sense excitation. It depends upon how perceptions are taken into consciousness. The feelings are also related to ideas referring to objects. Simple feelings are also primitive facts of consciousness and are never separated from ideas or volition in apperception. As feeling ''does not refer to an object, it cannot be isolated as an object of attention, but it can be particularized by its connection with a sensational

[1] Philosophical Review, Vol. XI., pp. 445-62 and XIV, pp. 21-26.
[2] Amer. Jour. of Psychol., Oct., 1905, and April, 1906.

substrate.'' Ideas are facts of inner experience with objective reference and the subjective differences are emotions if they affect ideas; otherwise they are feelings, which latter are therefore simpler. Hence emotions have more connections with psychological processes. Feelings are the ultimate elements of emotional activities. All the contents of the soul, sensations, ideas and the total state of consciousness affect emotions so that they are extremely variable and manifold, so much indeed that meager words designating them are entirely inadequate. We can describe them only by reference to the above accompaniments. It is the unity of apperception that makes them seem simple. Ideas are related to value determinations. It is a merely popular idea to hold that these putative products of analysis can be made unassociated objects of attention. Finally, sensations change along a scale of difference from zero to a maximum, while feelings change along a scale of opposites. Sensations are more separable, while all feelings have some general relation to all other feelings and so are more unitary. They tend to fuse into a single system. Their modality is not marked off by a reference to outer stimuli. They depend upon sensations and the disposition and union of feelings may be so complete as to give perfect unity. Then come Wundt's famous three dimensions of feeling—pleasure-pain, excitement-depression, strain-relaxation, some feelings having all three and some only one pair of determinations.

Titchener [1] criticizes Wundt's tridimensionalism by saying that pleasure is not the absence of pain but the one is as positive as the other. There is no opposition between excitation and depression but these are only extreme points on a qualitatively like scale of intensity. Absolute depression or rest is only the zero point of excitement. There is no counter excitement on the opposite side of this zero. The same is true of strain or tension and relaxation. Sense

[1] Zeitschrift für Psy., Vol. 19, p. 321.

feeling of active inhibition is identical in quality with felt relaxation. Wundt tries, on the one hand, to be true to a logical schema, feeling and counter feeling, and on the other, to the facts of inner observation. But he wanders very far from the latter and is perhaps constitutionally predisposed to decide with the former. When he adds that pleasure and pain are qualitative, excitement and depression intensive, and tension and relaxation temporal, it is hard to square this with his exposition in the "Grundriss" that pleasure and pain represent present states or modifications of consciousness; excitement and depression a future; and strain and relaxation, a past state. How are these temporal categories harmonized with the above quality, intensity, and duration? Again, why have we not quite as much ground to add to this hyperschematic system a spacial direction, e. g., expansion and contraction, and perhaps a feeling of abandonment and restraint or control? Vogt suggests activity-feelings related to the will; but feelings to him are not types of direction, but are simple and indecomposable. Indeed, Gurwitsche has proposed a fourth dimension, viz., striving and counter-striving. Such pairs of ideas do not indicate any such intrinsic elements of feeling as pleasure and pain, and their functions must be regarded as partly sensory, partly logical; at any rate, not as fundamental dimensions of feeling proper.

To Titchener's brief criticism Wundt replies at much length reproducing, though somewhat imperfectly, six pulse curves from Lehmann's atlas of them, and interpreting them very differently from their author, to illustrate his three pairs of feelings. Certainly the pulse curves he chooses seem quite distinct, one from the other, and he deems these differences characteristic. This he does to escape the charge that his tridimensionalism is based not on introspection but on general reasoning. Although the last two pairs may not be opposites, he answers that they are, nevertheless, facts of introspection. Feelings are at the same time related to the three sensory attributes, on the one hand, and to the three temporal moments on the other. Two feelings may be located in so far as they are connected with sensation. Lehmann thought that all his compound curves (those not representing mere pleasure-pain) were algedonic states plus strained states of the attention; and therefore were purely sensory with no feeling elements. But Wundt found in his large collection of curves some that agree very well with his logical, pre-elaborated scheme. And so he concludes that [1] P, E and R go with intensified pulse; P retards its rate, E does not change it, R accelerates it. S, D and U weaken; S retards, D does not change, U accelerates.[2] That these curves do not bear out the construction here put upon them Stevens has pointed out with considerable detail.[3]

Along the lines of this rough thumbnail sketch Wundt has wrought out a set of clear coherent concepts which he thinks describe the elements of the mind. In doing so he was doubtless influenced to some extent by the analogy of chemical elements, atoms or ions as constituents of matter. His schemata are alluring because of their simplicity and consistency and are probably more nearly correct than any other. But can such a scheme be as complete or final as he thinks? Elements, to be generally accepted, should be anywhere demonstrable under prescribed conditions. How many sensations that are undecomposable and otherwise conformable to his conception can be, I will not say isolated and demonstrated, but even defined? Or suppose

[1] P—U=pleasantness—unpleasantness (Lust—Unlust); E—D= excitement—depression (Erregung—Beruhigung); S—R=strain—relaxation (Spannung—Lösung) (Wundt's "Psychologie," sixth edition, Vol. 2, p. 298).

[2] Studien, XV, p. 149.

[3] See his Plethysmographic Evidence for the Tri-dimensional Theory of the Feelings, in an article résuméing and criticizing Wundt, in Amer. Jour. of Psych., Jan., 1903.

a few could be, *e. g.*, in the domain of light, color or hearing, with which his experimental studies have been chiefly occupied. What about reaching elements by the analysis of lower and more obscure sensations such as thermal, somatic, tickling, etc.? Suppose we could isolate and stimulate a single light-, color-, or tone-mediating nerve. Would the resulting sensation be a true psychic element or should we not also have to isolate the effects of the brain or other centers and determine how much of what went on there was thus caused, or define a uniform state in both? Even this would not be an elemental but a developmental result, for it would define only a certain evanescent stage in an instantaneous, ever-changing and never exactly repeated process. This can be said without too much stressing any Bergsonian ideas of creative evolution.

But again, suppose we grant Wundt's doctrine of elements, how did or do they synthetize so that it is so hard and rare an achievement to isolate them that most of them must be considered like those chemical elements that have such strong affinities that they will not remain pure or can never be isolated? How do they come to combine? Surely not by logic or any process of inference or consciousness, as Wundt intimates, but spontaneously and unconsciously as by some blind affinity. Some were probably compacted and integrated by the ordinary processes of growth. They fused because the cells that mediated them made connection. Other junctions remained from the differentiation from a more homogeneous, perhaps protoplasmic psychophysic basis and never were entirely separate. To say, as Wundt does, that these junctions are the product of a more primitive consciousness that has now lapsed is going beyond accessible data just as certainly as any panpsychist does. It is interpreting the lower by the higher rather than the higher by the lower, as evolution is perhaps prone to do. Instead of forcing the rubrics of consciousness speculatively beyond its possible limits, we should here modulate over to the only method science can admit in such a case, that of objective observation, and get the most and the best we can out of it by watching children, animals, tropisms, etc., not ignoring the processes of ontogenetic and phyletic development of both structures and functions wherever they shed a ray of light. Otherwise we shall be in constant danger of psychological anthropomorphism or reading into brute souls, as Wundt does, logical and epistemological processes which the actual facts in these fields less and less justify us in doing. Each species of animal life represents a type of soul life as unique and as different from ours as is its body, and we must sedulously lay off our culture and humanity, if not in a sense psychically decapitate ourselves, before we can reach the lowest forms of psychic life. We must abandon ourselves to new orientations and cultivate new *Einfühlungen* to catch the long-lost chords of primordial mentation. Only then can we cut out the individual organism from its prehistoric sense of solidarity with all its environment. Each species that became extinct took out of the world with it its own unique type of soul life. Beyond the mountain ranges that bound human consciousness are also psyches where the solipsism of idealism is *Bornirtheit*. Even if we can never feel their consciousness, we can infer something concerning it.

Feelings are among the most aboriginal elements of the soul. When they are strong they specially point him who would explore them backward to the early history of animal life, and while we may agree with Wundt in rejecting the Lange-James theory, we do not do so for the same reason he does, that if it were true we could best study feelings by objective observation. Indeed there is truth enough in this view to vindicate for this method an important place in this field. So the question how different feelings fuse into perfect unity is still more unsatisfactorily answered by Wundt, who thinks that consciousness isolates them until they are welded into a true continuum. But many of them, too, have differentiated from more homogeneous processes and by no scheme of bifurcation which logic can supply. Besides, Wundt overrubricates feeling processes.

Psychology proper for Wundt, we may summarize from Eisler, deals with consciousness and its analysis and the central thing in it is will. The soul is not object, nor substance, but subject. Its persistence does not depend on any inner being, but on the statedness of its changes and this is due to the activity of apperception. His parallelism does not involve a metaphysical principle and is not universal as it was with Spinoza and Fechner, but holds only of that content of experience that can be at the same time the object of natural science and psychology. We may say that the psychic effects of physical causes are psychic processes or conversely, that the physical effects of psychic causes are physical processes. The soul is the entelechy of the body. Hence we cannot derive psychic from physical processes, but they have a causality all their own. To call the psychic noncausal and to say that psychic coherence is mediated by material processes as Münsterberg does, or to say that psychic causality is unconscious, as Hartmann does, are alike wrong. There are not two causalities in any dualistic sense, but only one, which may be regarded almost independently from either point of view. Association cannot explain the structure of the soul. It may make assimilative and complicative or fusional compounds, but association is more passive than active and above it and more positive and spontaneous, representing the activity of the ego, is apperception. Both it and attention are at bottom activities of the will. They bring clearness, check other rival impressions, give sensations of attention and co-energize other associations. If the apperception processes involve changes of sensory content, we may assume a parallel physiological process with possibly its center in the forebrain. The function of apperception is clarification. It is a function of the inner will. Passive apperception is instinctive and active apperception involves choice. Its synthetic and analytic activities always involve some arrest of ordinary associations and its activities are thus of the ego as a whole. Apperception can thus give us whole ideas and the forms of coherent thinking, agglutinative if loose, or synthetic if the components are lost in their union, and, finally, the *Begriff*. On this basis, he proceeds to explain fancy and judgment. Thus in his theory of the world he assumes an original, ontogenetic energy of consciousness, although it unfolds from reflexes and instinct. The will is always psychologically determined. To act without constraint is not to act at all, but freedom is impulsion from within instead of from without. To act freely, to choose, is to act from within with "a consciousness of the significance which the motives and purposes involved have for the willer." The controversy concerning free will is due to the antinomy between the moral and the religious feelings and is solved by the fact that the former rest on the empirical sense of freedom and the latter on the transcendental ground of all things. There is nothing in or out of us which we can call completely our own except the will. Hence the ego is not merely a bundle of ideas as associationists say, but a total living actuality. It is not outside of consciousness, but it unfolds only in and with it and self-consciousness rests on a series of psychic processes, is their resultant rather than their basis. It depends too on the continuity of psychic events.

The problem of the essence of the soul is transcendental, for the facts of inner experience do not need any such hypothesis. The problem is that of an ultimate ground. This alone can make the future of the existence of these causally connected events intelligible. Is this ground individual or universal? We cannot assume an absolute simplicity and independence of the soul for this would contradict the facts of the reciprocity of consciousness with other beings, while experience teaches us nothing of the persistence of the soul. In place, therefore, of the useless idea of the soul as substance, we must for metaphysics substitute the idea of psychic activity and remember that will is the core of the psyche and that feelings are active or passive will tendencies. Ideas are given and in entertaining them we are active because we are conscious. Thus activity is our ego. Pure will is apperception and this is transcendental, as Kant said, but empirical psychology has nothing to do with this metaphysical idea of the soul. Thus pure will is implied unless we suppose conditions precedent which if progress is unitary must again be called will, and thus we come to a psychic totality in Spinoza's substance which is purely intellect, and in Hegel's absolute which is only the pure will to think. Uniting Plato, Kant and Schopenhauer, Wundt calls will the ultimate ground of all that happens psychically. But this will cannot be unconscious if there is no true will without ideas. Schopenhauer's will is not volition but the basis of it. It is a universal and collective will, the idea of which is progressive humanity. Here morality roots and God is a moral postulate who may be conceived as the transcendental unity of mind and of nature. The problem of natural science is to know nature objectively and independently of the subject. Only from their relations to a subject, however, can the objective relations of things to each other be inferred. Apart from their relations, things cannot be specific objects. All their true relations are temporal and spatial, based at bottom upon motion and hence mechanical just as science postulates. The presupposed properties of matter which condition intuition are (1) that the elements of substance are simple; (2) that substances are efficient as known only by their effects; and (3) that they persist. Continuity and atomism may be harmonized by saying that space is full of the effects of matter acting on other matter at a distance, and so does not demand contact or impenetrability. There is no absolutely empty space, and atoms are the points upon which analysis rests. Matter is an abstract idea and unrepresentable, but physics must find approximate symbols for it. Matter has for physics only outer properties. The connection between things and their properties does not need the substance idea, which is only ancillary at best. Causality is enough. To Ostwald's demand that we give up the idea of matter as superfluous and substitute energy Wundt replies that we cannot drop the substance idea if we try, for the subjectivity of certain properties compels us to believe in a substrate presentable only in thought. Again, energies must have their loci, foci or seats. Logically too we cannot drop the mechanical view, for analyses of light, heat, electricity, etc., show at bottom something moving. Still, his causality idea makes matter dynamic and science kinematic. His four principles are gravity, centrality of energy, reciprocity and composition of forces. Energetics cannot supplant mechanism, for it depends upon it. The indestructibility of matter and the persistence of energy are super-empirical hypotheses which lead to the question of the universality or the oneness of nature. The indifference of matter and the universality of mechanism— to these must come purpose before we can have a true cosmos and thus we reach the idea of development. In organisms causality and finality work together and nature becomes "a means for the development of spiritual ends." Cosmic evolution is not unpsychic but it is not to be taken in Fechner's "fantastic" hylozoistic sense, for the psychic (*geistig*) is always the result of development from the lower, while at the same time all true evolution is at bottom psychic.

The principle of the stability of evolution for the universe is seen in biology in the constancy of species. Wundt doubts the possibility of abiogenesis under modern controlled conditions but makes the strange suggestion that the origin of chlorophyll-bearing organisms is to be found in a process of composition that appeared when primo-genesis was becoming extinct. He denies Weissmann's immortality of the germ plasm, for reproduction goes back to chemical division (*Spaltung*) and thus involves an al-ternation of organizing with disorganizing forces, and so the tiny link between parent and offspring is chiefly made by an up and down wave of metabolism and so of contrac-tion and expansion. He postulates a "holoplasm" (which he prefers to Nägeli's ideoplasm) to connect cell groups chemically as well as biologically.

To Darwin, he objects that selection and the struggle for survival may explain the increase or reduction but never the origin of traits. Outer influences cannot modify organs that do not function. We must be careful in in-ferring from ontogeny to phylogeny and remember too that there are always inner as well as outer conditions for, while psycho-physical functions are developed in plants and in animals, outer conditions are still more subordi-nated to these and are in fact only provocative agencies for complete functional practice. The nervous system brings unity and will. The latter advances to control more and more what is within and without the body. For Wundt, as for Schopenhauer, the body is for the most part an objectivization of the will which begins as impulse and instinct and slowly comes to unify all the heterogenic principles into supreme ends. As opposed to the idea of chance adaptations and variations, he thinks the chief spur to both perfection and differentiation of functions is their exercise and he believes in the direct inheritance of the ef-fects of practice (versus Weissmann). Heredity must bot-tom on chemical continuity. We are constantly mechaniz-ing acts of will originally done with full consciousness. In this all progress consists—so consciousness which origi-nally accompanied all acts of will is being constantly elim-inated. Animals are thus in a sense machines which it took long and very much lapsed consciousness to make. Indeed consciousness is always abdicating in favor of the will.

Geist or mind is conscious and to speak of unconscious *Geist* is a contradiction. Consciousness is actual and effective inner experience. Knowledge and self-consciousness are products of development, but consciousness (*i. e.,* true psychic inner experience or *Für-sich-sein*) can never arise out of any other psychic content not in itself conscious. Thus there can be no unconscious psychic processes. Psyche and consciousness are one and inseparable, in fact identical. Consciousness has, however, degrees of clearness and these are measured by the duration of their processes as observed in the possibility of recall (or remembering) or their continuity. Dimly conscious elements (*e. g.,* local signs) are still conscious or they could not effect psychic syntheses. All here resolves itself to the point of momentary consciousness and this may be further resolved to a Leibnizian infinitesimal degree. This "temporal point" must be assumed as being over against a spatial or atomic point, for continuity demands that where matter begins the psyche must also begin. Only thus "is nature the self-development of *Geist*" which latter arises out of it, nature being only its prestadium. Now to be sure it seems outer, yet all its forms must have psychic content. So the psyche is the highest developmental form and the body is the tool it has made with which to realize its own purposes. The individual soul in reciprocal relation with its immediate substratum, body, effects the immediate unity of simultaneous and successive states and this well represents this continuum of activities. Here first association is effected. Then comes perceptive unity. As instinct, it unites idea, feeling and will, and to instinct mechanism ever tends to lapse. There is psychic and physical causality and hence parallelism is the only reasonable standpoint, although metaphysically we may speak of interaction between soul and body only so far as "body is in its essential being itself psychic," and its components contend as lower conscious unities subject to one higher consciousness and affecting and being affected by it. Mechanization means retreat of the higher consciousness that is always being dismissed or recalled in the process of development. Elemental organisms, such as plants, have but a faint and gappy and lack a central consciousness. The instinctive reactions of lower centers may affect consciousness without its knowing it. Only self-consciousness is possible in an organism. "The for-us unconscious reflexes or instincts are in fact utterly unintelligent and their apparent purposiveness is due to the fact that they developed from former acts of will of a higher sort and may still be at its call."

For most metaphysical substance theorists, the individual is first and the community lacks true reality. For Wundt, on the contrary, the individual does not exist at all in isolation and the community is aboriginal and its consciousness is supremely real. The collective mind is more worthful, comprehensive and durable if we apply the principle "actuality is as reality." Shaped as he is by society, the individual is not—as Hegel thought—a merely passive agent of the world-will, but only relatively an independent member of an organism. Thus Wundt is not far from Schaefle or Lilienfeld. Although part of a collectivity, the individual is yet free. When we analyze personality, however, we cannot apply all its attributes directly to society, but the resemblance is close as in the stirp, race, state, etc.

The philosophy of history is always seeking inner connections and should be the same as universal history. It has no transcendent ideas and this leads to his ethics, for there are norms for objective worth. His evolutionistic universalism would more and more subordinate the individual to the whole. Heterogeneous purposes play here a great rôle, as, *e. g.,* the development of morality from religion. Happiness is not the goal but a by-product of morality which must generate new psychic contents for life and help to greater concord of wills. All that agrees with the collective will is good and all that opposes it is bad. Science and art are good if they objectively generate psychic worths, and subjectively what springs from a good disposition is good. As to motives, we must seek the good for its own sake and yet as opposed to Kant duty may be done with inclination.

As to freedom Wundt is neither an absolute indifferentist nor a mechanical determinist, but bases his views on the consciousness of freedom which forever makes fatalism impossible. Self-activity seems causeless. Freedom and choice involve acting with a consciousness of the significance which our motives and purposes have for our character. The effects of old activities are determined by inner causes but are not contained in them. The sense of freedom arises in active apperception and so is nearest to our immanent thought activities. Statistics only show that social considerations among others influence the will. There is always a personal factor, the motivation of which springs from character and this psychic causality goes back to heredity, which we can not analyze because psychic development is endless. Here the religious point of view has its place. Hence while the moral viewpoint is empirical, there is always another that goes back to the ground of all things. Thus, empirically, the will is free but transcendentally or metaphysically, it is determined. He thus exactly reverses the position of Schopenhauer and Kant.

Self-consciousness is a product of many components, some ideative and others volitional and emotional. At first, it is gappy and confused, but gradually learns to distinguish itself from other things. Among the objectivities, the body is one of the first to stand out and at length the inner ego emerges and finally the self is identified with will

410

and apperception. The ego is the feeling of the connection
of will processes or tensions. This gives constancy and
unity without need of any absolute persistence. There is
no pure, empty ego and also there is nothing else within or
without that is absolutely our own. Hence the self is neither a substance nor a bundle of ideas. It is a vital actuality, and self-consciousness is thus a process and not
merely the basis of a process resting on the continuity
of psychic events. This view of Wundt's concerning the
ego, while it seems to us in a general way sound, is certainly very inadequate and does not sufficiently take into
account or explain or afford a good basis for explaining the
facts of multiple personality or of the genesis of the idea
of self.[1]

With all Wundt's efforts to keep psychology on empirical or even experimental lines, his philosophic proclivities
have had their effect upon both his own work and that of
a number of his followers, viz., to tempt them to take into
the laboratory certain problems which even Wundt thinks
cannot be solved there in the present state of science. This
has resulted in conclusions that are partial and hence have
provoked discussion or contradiction not only between
Wundt's former pupils but between the master and his pupils and others to a degree that is not entirely creditable
to experimental psychology. Wundt has always insisted
on a close reciprocity between philosophy and psychology,
but whatever advantages this makes possible are offset by
dangers. The question, e. g., of parallelism versus interaction is not a problem that can be determined by controlled conditions, but is a modern form of the old speculative theme of the relations between the soul and the body.
Wundt is a partisan in a question on which many think it
not imperative upon them to choose sides at all. The question involves so many speculative and metaphysical ele-

[1] See my own attempt to derive the self genetically, Amer. Jour.
of Psych., Vol. 9, No. 3, pp. 351-395.

ments that it is open to grave question whether its injection into scientific psychology has done more harm or good. Another inheritance of scientific psychology from older modes of theorization is the question of consciousness, for which Wundt is a partisan and polemizes against practically every form of the unconscious as such. All admit that consciousness is a matter of degrees and fades out into twilight in dreamy revery states and may become indefinitely reduced. What difference does it make whether these states are better called conscious, unconscious or co-conscious, especially so long as there is no definition of consciousness which any two people ever accepted? Wundt's position, that all psychic processes are conscious, is unscientific, to say nothing of its being impolitic. To him, psychology is the science of consciousness. To Pillsbury, Thorndike and others, it is the science of behavior; to Hartmann and Drews, it is a science of the Unconscious, but there is no criterion or standard by which to determine who is right, and therefore it is unscientific to grow hot in such a controversy. Closely related with this is the regard Wundt has for his faculty of apperception-will. In the development of his point of view here, he seems to us to have been unduly influenced by the analogy he makes so much of between the center and periphery of the field of vision, until one almost conceives the mind in the image of a great eye the motion of which we call changes of attention. Perhaps he and even James in his great stress upon the differences between focal and marginal, his discussion of fringes versus the center have made the distinction between the two too great till it has amounted almost to a contrast. In this doctrine perhaps Wundt's interest is deepest and this point too has been the center of the greatest stimulus that has gone out from him to others who are now investigating *Einstellung, Aufgabe,* dominating tendency and *Anlage* and the nature and motive power of thought processes. The master's severe condemnations of some of these lines of investigation which go beyond although they are motivated by him are as unworthy as they are unfortunate. The most interesting problem of laboratory psychology for the moment is why and by what motivation attention moves from point to point and what are all the processes involved in what we call thought, a problem to which controlled experimentation can contribute much but can never of itself solve. To the present writer's thinking, this is simply tunneling into the genetic process from the other side of the mountain, if we only assume that every movement of attention due to inner stimulation is an end result of the very same evolutionary nisus that was given at impregnation. But really, if Verworn and others are right, who would taboo the use of the word cause (because everything is so interrelated as to be at once cause and effect in a constellation of factors each of which is vital), the whole problem here is far larger than any one has yet dreamed it to be.

The drift toward the applications of experiment to problems which it cannot solve may unfortunately tend to make us oblivious of nonexperimental data even where these are the most important and the best available, so that we become almost distrustful of sound insightful common sense in fields where this muse will always be an oracle and where the demonstration of the obvious not only becomes superfluous but discreditable.

Again, the great problems of feeling are at the door and it is no disparagement to the valuable results of experimentation here to say that there are other sources which for the present at least must be seriously if not chiefly taken account of before knowledge can make much advance. Wundt's tridimensionality is another dogma which experimentation will never confirm or disprove. Again, perhaps this is not the place to express my own great regret as a student of the psychology of education that Wundt has contributed so little that can be of use in this

413

field to it; but perhaps a still greater misfortune of his system of thinking is that now, when psychiatry is so generally turning to and feeling the need of psychological principles, it is forced to realize as its representatives are now so frequently saying that Wundt has little to offer them. To this Wundtians might reply that he did not attempt to supply either of these needs, but sought only by esoteric and strictly academic methods to explore the normal adult human soul, particularly that of academic male teachers and students; that his psychology is essentially that of this group and that he did not wish to be pragmatic but only scientific. Only a few would reply that he has laid the basis for these or other applications, and in view of the number of partial successes and repeated failures to establish psychological laboratories for the utilization of his devices in asylums, this answer can be no longer accepted, at least in this practical country. These limitations must in the lapse of time work against the valuable influence of his work. Other qualities also limit his power in America. American thinkers demand more or less clearness and directness of expression. James' snappy, catchy, sparkling, often Nietzsche-like style has made the toilsome reading of Wundt's ponderous tomes very hard by contrast. We need a psychology that is usable, that is dietetic, efficient for thinking, living and working, and although Wundtian thoughts are now so successfully cultivated in academic gardens, they can never be acclimated here, as they are antipathetic to the American spirit and temper. However scientific its principles may be, a doctrine of the soul of man can never entirely escape the verdict of the *Zeit und Volksgeist*. We must at the very least have everything said as clearly and simply as possible and one of our pet abominations is to have simple and naturally comprehensible things made needlessly hard, intricate, technical or prolix. And yet despite all and even if all our misgivings and criticisms are true and more than true

and even if there are more defects, we have to conclude
in a collapsing way that after and despite all, psychology
owes to Wundt a debt far greater than to any other man
living or dead, and the more we know and understand him,
the more this sense of obligation to him will increase.

A careful computation of all the contents of the last
fifteen volumes of Wundt's *Studien,* omitting only the
first ten of the first series and ending with and including
the volume of 1910, also excluding the two volumes of the
"Festschrift," shows that the study of optical phenomena
has during all these years led all other themes with 46
articles and 1,775 pages, of which less than one-fifth were
devoted to color. Next comes audition with 21 articles
and 1,294 pages, besides 7 other articles and nearly 400
pages comparing or involving these two senses, not to speak
of 9 articles with 585 pages on rhythmic phenomena (in
which a study of these senses is often involved), a topic
which in the earlier series of studies was better represented
but which hardly appears in the later series, although
Wundt's new "Primer" would have elementary psychology
begin with rhythm. There are also 3 articles and 168
pages on reaction time. But the Wundtians only just
began to try out association times and left Jung and others
to see and develop their psychoanalytic value. Touch and
temperature phenomena come next with 11 articles and 468
pages. Taste has 3 articles and 107 pages, and smell none.
The feelings have 5 articles and 377 pages; memory has
3 articles and 575 pages; attention, apperception, higher
mental processes and clearness, 1 each, 119 pages; the muscles and psychophysics, 1 each, with 48 pages; while 30
articles with 1,392 pages are miscellaneous and unclassi-
fiable. Many of the latter in the later, and still more in
the first series of studies, were devoted to philosophy and
method and extra-laboratory themes. The first series of
studies began in 1883, nine years after the first modest
one-volume edition of his "Psychology," and the material

for the great and repeated enlargements of it has to no small extent been quarried out of the *Studien,* the character of which is in some sense suggested by the above rude statistics.

The foregoing shows that the two higher senses, which Helmholtz had studied so carefully, have been the staple theme of Wundt's laboratory ever since the *Studien* began. They were also of central interest to Wundt in his earlier experimental studies. The lower senses have had little representation. The higher mental processes have had almost no representation here, and feelings and motor processes have had only a modest one. From this it would not be strange if his theories, so far as they rest upon an experimental basis, are to no small extent eye- and ear-made. Although he has personally done but little laboratory work for many years, Wundt's inductive thinking has rested very largely upon these studies in the now nearly thirty years of their existence in which their content has grown more and more exclusively experimental. Thus the significant fact appears that so far as his thought is based on scientific experimentation, it was shaped by the phenomena of the two higher senses of adult, cultivated males who have been trained to observe subjective experiences connected with these functions, and as his thought departs from this ground it becomes increasingly theoretical. On a basis of at least induced eye- and ear-mindedness he has compensated by a system which naturally stresses the apperceptional and volitional side, and neglects less focal processes. Perhaps the psychoanalysis of the future may be able to trace out the subtle though it may be more or less constrained forces that are here involved. It may be natural that the distinctions between peripheral and central retinal apperception should have been the paradigm or supplied the analogy on which he built his conception of attention and apperception, and the prompt response of the eye by movements or tendencies to move may have suggested his theory of will. His space theory, too, owes more to the eye than to touch, its mother, and optical imagery and experience seem to play the leading rôle in his idea of association, while his persistent formal tridimensionality of feelings may be found to owe more than is yet apparent to his eye-mindedness or eye studies. His ear-mindedness may be somehow connected with his gifts of expression, but the chief conclusion that stands out from these data is that only a predominant familiarity with the clear sensations of light, color and tone could have suggested an ideal of sensory *elements,* which seem vastly more possible from the standpoint of these than from that of the lower and especially the inner or somatic sensations.

Wundt is a great repeater, not in the sense of quoting himself, but of reiterating the same ideas in different connections, now in condensed, now in expanded, form. The "Human and Animal Psychology" and the "Outlines" cover much of the same ground and most of both is found again in the "Psychology," to which these, particularly the latter, are in a sense introductions. The large "Psychology" too contains much in brief that is found more fully stated in the "Völkerpsychologie." The "Essays" and both volumes of the "Kleine Schriften" are newly edited material that has appeared elsewhere. These two books are as close to his own inner convictions as anything, although much that they contain has already found expression in his "Logic" and "Metaphysics." The results of many of the studies are of course restated in his "Psychology." Indeed, most of his best and characteristic views are expressed over and over again, not to speak of the repeated enlargements of successive editions. He must love to amplify and to reiterate his opinions. If one were to undertake the gigantic task of preparing one final statement of all his most typical opinions in their best and fullest form and omit the first and undeveloped statements and all epitomes and introductions, the bulk of his work would be much reduced. Again, if one collated all his epitomized statements elsewhere expanded, a better and fuller introduction to all he has said could be compiled than yet exists. Finally, some of his earlier works should be left to oblivion for they either have been superseded by other books by other writers or they contain matter that time has proven wrong. Hollands in tracing as he did in a masterly way the genesis of Wundt's doctrine of psychic analysis and elements [1] found that his views on this fundamental theme had passed through five distinct phases and had to be traced through a round dozen of his works which must be compiled in this quest. So on other topics he is constantly changing, dropping, adding, modifying, intent only on being always faithful to his latest insights.

Wundt is the greatest definer who ever wrote in the field of psychology. Sensations, percepts, concepts, ideas, memory, reproduction, association, impulse, instinct, will, striving, desire, feeling, wishing, self, choice, motive, cause, freedom, reflex action, attention, apperception, reason and indeed every characteristic act and process and almost the entire vocabulary in the domain of logic, ethics, metaphysics, history of philosophy, mythology, religion, æsthetics, as well as psychology—all are defined, not according to the logic of the schools, but often descriptively and always in carefully weighed phrases meant to be exact to the limit. He is very fond of collecting and repeating the definitions of other writers and of pointing out the shades of differences and agreements between these views and his own. Indeed, his views could probably be most compactly stated in a dictionary of terms with his definitions and descriptions appended. He is fond, too, of defining negatively and telling us that his subject is not this, that or the other, or that it acts so and not so and so, and this often may go on to quite a list of negative specifications. This involves

[1] Amer. Jour. of Psych., October, 1905, and April, 1906. See especially Vol. 16, pp. 503 et seq.

great taste for and love of drawing distinctions and dif-
ferentiations of manifold degrees and kinds, making classes
and subclasses. Thus he is perpetually legislating for all
kinds of normal psychic activity, codifying his legislation
for others, sifting, amending, analyzing, synthetizing, re-
viewing, discussing and often seeming to decree, in his efforts to give us a complete picture, true to the original,
of the life of the soul. With this end in view, we can
perhaps understand why he never says either a brilliant
or a foolish thing, while his style is hard and heavy, with
hardly a passage anywhere that any one would quote for
literary effectiveness. This and the unique indigenousness
of German terms common in this field (*e. g., Trieb, Vorstellung, Einstellung, Gemüth, Geist, Begriff, Anschauung,
Stimmung, Anlage* and a host more), concerning the meaning of which in English there is so much difference of opinion and which indeed can never be translated without more
or less distortion and miscarriage of meaning or connotation,
make him peculiarly untranslatable. He eschews tropes,
illustrations and analogies and never documents his individuality but writes as if with a constant sense of impersonal finality almost as if he strove to show how dry
the light of the mind can be. Perhaps no one ever criticized so many of others' views or was more impatient of
criticism or apparently so jealous of those who advanced
along his own lines as he. To the reader also it sometimes
seems as though no one was so generally right in criticizing those who preceded or were contemporaneous with him
or so generally wrong in criticizing his critics and his more
independent pupils. He is not content with being a great
founder and stimulator, but almost seems to wish to be the
last in fields where he was the first, instead of taking pleasure in seeing successors arise who advance his lines still
further. Perhaps this is the Nemesis of the type of senes-
cense that takes more pleasure in closing than in opening,
in finishing than in originating. Perhaps this is the in-

firmity of speculative philosophy rather than of the true man of science who can rejoice in the work of those he has inspired quite as much as in his own. It is sad to imagine what psychology would have been and done without him, and, indeed, it would be idle to try to do so. But the time may not be far distant when he will be even more prized for what he has impelled others to do than for all he has himself accomplished. In this thought, which ought to be very precious and consoling in the declining years of a great teacher, he seems to take little comfort. This we must ascribe in part at least to his lack of that deep sense of evolution which sees all things, even one's own work, by anticipation in its true historic perspective. Such almost titanic ambition as has impelled him to do so much so well and the retrospect of which must give him satisfaction, perhaps naturally tends later to lessen faith in the infinite progress which the future has in store. But if so, this is again the infirmity of theoretic rather than of experimental talent and Wundt is not primarily an experimenter but a scholar and thinker and a great contributor, orderer, systematizer and critic far greater than any one else in the field where he is strong. He is a great taxonomist of the mind, a marvelous compiler, digester, epitomizer, the prince of map and guidebook makers and not a creator of original, transforming ideas or points of view. He has vastly accelerated progress, but he marks no cardinal turning point, and his best work is so in the very center of the current of tendencies that he is all the sooner to be transcended by the very momentum he has imparted. Thus he will stand in history as marking not an epoch but a splendid acceleration along lines which the *Zeitgeist* had already laid down as inevitable. Had he not lived, others would in time have done his work. Successors indeed are already arising who promise to carry it far beyond his utmost ken. Alas for him that he does not see this, and, seeing it, rejoice!

It is not impossible that experimental psychologists may fall back from Wundt to Helmholtz, as speculative philosophers did from Schleiermacher, Fichte and Hegel to Kant, and that much of the ground that Wundt has covered will have to be worked over again by more efficient and simpler methods, with a number of the problems he attacked restated in order to be solved in a way which all can accept as becomes true science. Something like this I believe will happen. But if Wundt is to suffer eclipse or fall away from the fovea to the indirect field or even the blind spot of attention, it can surely be but for a time, and when his successors shall have reached certainty and agreement on the main questions he experimented on, and when they shall have seen a little more clearly what can and what cannot be done in the laboratory, then Wundt will "come back," as some of the post-Kantian speculators are now doing, and from that higher, clearer viewpoint of the future it will be seen that he smoothed the way to vast new territories and that despite his shortcomings he really builded better than he knew. He has somewhere expressed the conviction that all psychological, not to say philosophical, problems are susceptible to experimental, if not laboratory, tests if not solutions. We may well believe that this new department is in its infancy, that the best by far is yet to come, and even that it has a future so splendid that we can now hardly trust ourselves to dream of it. But till we can control all the conditions of life, from love, conception, birth, and infancy, to old age and death, and also the conditions that underlie primitive races, civilized societies and mental health and disease, there will always remain a wide domain of problems that we can only solve by watching, recording, tabulating the great age-long and world-wide experiments Nature has always made and will make wherein control disturbs the conditions of normal happenings and where we can only observe and interpret data which we had no hand in making but which are given to us.

Of child-study Wundt has small respect and small knowledge. Long ago one of his pupils, H. Eber,[1] criticized the then recent literature on the subject, especially Preyer and Baldwin, and found their method, viewpoint and idea of what went on in the child's mind and how, its psychic elements, association processes, inferences concerning its memory, will and perception all mistaken and suggested how this work might be improved by applying true Wundtian principles, although this could never be more than a subdepartment of folk-psychology. In Wundt's "Outlines" he gives one chapter of fifteen pages to the psychic development of the child, which, like the chapter that precedes it on animal psychology, consists chiefly in applying some of his well-known rubrics or modes of interpreting observations. In his "Psychology" he touches lightly on the topics of childish association and fancy and thinks that certain dreams are the recurrence of memories of childhood. In the "Völkerpsychologie," in discussing language, he argues that children never invent words and that what seem their creations are the results of their efforts at imitation, which are distorted beyond the recognition of adults (a point which observers in this field have always had carefully in mind and which is against the trend of their opinion, as witness nearly one hundred words that, after all eliminations due to this or other sources, are thought to be sporadic but real creations by the child). He has elsewhere a few paragraphs on childish speech, imagination and drawing, but even in his discussion of childish speech where he comes closest to the subject, he shows only a very limited acquaintance with the voluminous literature upon it, and has nothing new to suggest.

His knowledge of comparative or animal psychology seems to be essentially confined to the early works of Romanes and Lubbock. In this domain, also, he is interested chiefly in the fate of the applicability of certain of his own

[1] Philosophische Studien. Bd. XI, 1896, pp. 586-628.

few rubrics and has never done or had in his laboratory
or elsewhere any work or observation upon animals. Here
then are two great slighted fields. Research here must not
disturb the circles of his logical and method-revering mind.
But why, we ask, should this able anatomist and physiologist of one special type of the adult male mind, *homo
academicus,* be so indisposed to recognize psychic embryology and comparative psychic anatomy and physiology?
Why, instead of seeing their promise and potency, does he
use the whole weight of his influence to disparage instead
of develop them? In the same frosty way as he treats
them, his own early endeavors were treated by the physiologists and physicists who were in their prime when he was
young. But he has made good, and those representing
these newer lines which he slights or despises are rapidly
doing the same. I cannot think that any student of animal
instinct or of children could with the best disposition to
do so find a single helpful suggestion in any of his pages.
His entrance in this field is essentially for the sake of his
own methods and to preserve his own fences. The remarkable developments in the field of child-study and instinct in recent years have been entirely independent
of him, and his own work would have been richer and
sounder had he profited by this material. Excusable as
this may be in him at his age and with the great service
we all owe him, its saddest aspect is that some of his
younger followers have imbibed his spirit in this respect,
absorbed as they are in the hard task of understanding,
teaching, and amplifying his work. In them he has what
to-day is a misfortune for true scientific progress, a real
school of the old-fashioned type, cherishing only its own
insights and more or less closed to the things without.

Again, so unbiologically minded and so unread is he
in a domain so cognate with physiology (that some have
advocated that instead of physiological psychology we speak
of biological philosophy), that the phenomena of sex and

all its wider and higher irradiations are hardly mentioned in his pages and that at a time when the sentiments that spring from this root are coming to be understood almost as the dominant forces of life in their sublimation into morals, art, religion, etc., so that to discuss feelings and emotions without these is only a few degrees less absurd than to play "Hamlet" with Hamlet left out. Save for a few minor references to phallicism in his treatment of religion in the "Völkerpsychologie," and a few other sporadic and passing mentions, no one would suspect from his pages that this emotion-instinct had any special psychological significance. In nearly all departments of this subject, then, he is silent or formal, and the very word "adolescence" is hardly in his vocabulary, while "heredity" and "love" fare little better, and the very names of Mendel and Weissmann are each mentioned but once in his "Psychologie." [1]

Perhaps nothing Wundt ever wrote has caused so many of his admirers and would-be followers more grief and pain than his articles disparaging the applications of psychology.[2] That Meumann, one of his most gifted pupils, who had previously made at least three important contributions to pure, should have turned to educational psychology seemed to the master almost apostasy. So he praises his earlier and points out the dangers of his later pedagogical studies, and calls upon him almost pathetically to return from his wanderings to the true fold. Perhaps had Meumann remained true to his first love he might have been Wundt's natural successor, whose earnestness in all this matter would be personally more explicable. Wundt points as his ideal to Röntgen and his rays, which were

[1] The sanest and most competent and conservative critical estimate of what it now seems that psychology must accept here is found in R. Bleuler's Psycho-analyse Freud's Verteidigung und kritische Bemerkungen, Leipzig, 1911, 110 pp.

[2] See Ueber rein und angewandte Psychologie. Psychologische Studien, Bd. 5, 1910, pp. 1-47.

discovered by purely scientific studies with no thought of
the wide range which their practical applications have
since been found to have and to which their discoverer has
remained in academic aloofness and superiority. Of the
philosophers from Plato to Hegel not a few of them have
conscientiously tried to apply their ideas to education.
Although Wundt seems to almost condone Kraepelin for
applying psychology to psychiatry, of which he has made
the most important reconstruction, he finds little to com-
mend and much to criticize in Stern's *Ausfrage* method
and results, and despite the contributions thus made to
psychology and to legal testimony, makes the remarkable
statement that this "can teach us nothing concerning the
illusions of sense and memory or the variations of attention." Nor, he adds, can it tell us anything of importance
concerning normal memory. Child-study, too, and psychogenesis, he refuses to acknowledge as true psychology because the conditions of study cannot be controlled or the
problems isolated enough to make them exact. The way of
orthodox psychology to him is hard, straight and narrow.
To know the soul scientifically we must work in the laboratory with apparatus and technical methods and the crying
needs of the world and the great experiments that life and
disease are making on so vast a scale around us the true
psychologist, he thinks, should allow to go on with their
precious data unutilized.

Yet there is one domain of psychologizing afield which
is permissible, viz., *Völkerpsychologie*. Here psychology
may respond to the call of the world and come out from
the laboratory into the open. It is where he enters this
domain and here alone that Wundt, to our thinking, has
kept himself young and growing, but it is hard to understand why all his labored justification of this kind of work
does not apply with equal force to the others above that
he taboos. Yet here those he has trained and inspired in
the experimental field have shown hitherto but little dispo-

sition to follow him, while the vigorous children whom he repudiates will hardly fail to protest that they are after all his most legitimate progeny. Many of these who have made the most and best contributions to folk psychology had no more training than the best of those who answer questionnaires on childhood. Both have put down in their own unskilled but truthful way facts they saw which were often new and strange, and although we often wish they were more expert, the scientific world is accepting most of their reports with and sometimes without much critical sifting. In Wundt's treatment of the topics of children's language, gesture and imagination, he has made such use as served his purpose of just such data and used them as Darwin used the letters and observations of breeders and observers the world over who were often unknown to him. Finally even pragmatism he condemns,[1] as we should expect, from three motives. First, that much of the philosophy that he reveres and has treated would be disallowed by the pragmatist; secondly, his academic ideals of pure science lead him to undervalue practicalities generally; lastly, it certainly does not chime with his theory of will.

Most drastic of all are his criticism and repudiation of the Würzburgers, who have for now nearly twelve years attracted growing attention. Having little apparatus in their new laboratory, they made a virtue of necessity and boldly attacked the highest problems by what Wundt dubs the *Ausfrage* method. After reacting to certain problems involving an act of reflection and responding by a word or gesture meaning that it was or was not understood, the subjects were afterward questioned by the investigator concerning everything that went on in their minds in the process of responding to the invocation to think. This whole procedure Wundt deems illegitimate.[2] He lays down

[1] Kleine Schriften. Band 2, 1911, p. 324.
[2] Kleine Schriften. Band 2, 1911, pp. 249 et seq.

the following four rules to which all proper psychological experiments must conform: (1) The observer must if possible be in a position to determine himself beforehand the entrance of the process to be observed. (2) He must as far as possible grasp the phenomenon in a state of strained attention and follow its course. (3) Every observation must, in order to make the results certain, be capable of being repeated several times under the same conditions. (4) The conditions under which the phenomena appear must be found out by the variation of the attendant circumstances and when this is done the various coherent experiments must be varied according to a plan, partly by eliminating certain stimuli entirely and partly by grading their strength or quality. On the basis of these rules he formulates his objections to the *Ausfrage* methods somewhat as follows: (1) They are no real experiments but self-observations under difficulties or with hindrances. Not one of the above conditions for psychological experiments is met but all are violated. (2) Of all the forms of self-observations these are the most incomplete. They occupy the mind of the observer with unexpected, more or less difficult problems, and demand of him that he also observe the conditions of his own consciousness. (3) In both forms of their application they are to be rejected. The questions before the experiment place self-observation under the unfavorable influence of examination pressure and the questions afterward open wide the door to the disturbing influence of suggestion. Both forms act against self-observation in the most exquisite way, for they put the subject, who must observe himself, under the control of another person while he himself is supposed to do it. (4) The question method violates the venerable rule that in order to solve complex problems one must first be familiar with the solution of simple ones. As a result the attention changes with consciousness and the observer falls a victim to the popular error of believing that all that goes on in consciousness can be directly followed by self-observation.[1] To this Bühler replied with some acerbity.[2] Into the controversy thus inaugurated we cannot enter here save to insert the following note:

Introspection is as old and as broad as self-consciousness, and to some degree is involved in consciousness itself. As applied to the higher thought processes, it goes back of Descartes to at least Plato's epistemological dialogues. Hence, there is nothing essentially new in the procedure of the Würzburgers except in their close ranged and morselizing method of focusing and reporting upon these processes. Wundt had repeatedly and strongly insisted that exact experimental methods could not be applied here because of the complexity of this type of mentation. His conservative attitude was no doubt connected with the fact that the output of his own laboratory showed a constantly increasing predominance of method over matter. Indeed, not a few of his disciples here and elsewhere were growing discouraged, some consciously and some no doubt unconsciously, concerning the prospects of their own department. Some were a trifle weary of its limitations. Hence when the Würzburgers broke away from these dicta of the master and actually began to study little actlets of reason under more or less controlled laboratory conditions, carefully recording a vast body of multifarious, incipient and accompanying processes that had usually been regarded as waste by-products, experimentation almost discovered a new world, and great was the joy of those who were coming to feel themselves shut in to the study of the lower processes. Indeed, it was an epoch so suddenly to find a field where there was matter so abundant and easily accessible and so little method necessary, and the contrast of this with the

[1] Ueber Ausfrage Experimente u. über die Methoden der Psychol. des Denkens von W. Wundt, Psychol. Studien, Bd. 3, 1907, pp. 301-360.

[2] Archiv f. d. Gesämte Psychologie, 1908, Vol. XI, pp. 445-459. See also an excellent report upon the work of the individuals who originated the Würzburg School by P. Bovet, L'étude expérimentale de jugement et de la pensée. Archiv d. Psychologie, 1908-9, Vol. 8, pp. 9-48.

preceding status where method was approaching its maximum and matter its minimum was almost dizzying. Wundtianism, which had not only promised but done so great and memorable a service, was probably, on the whole, in the early stages of a decline, if not in the numbers of its disciples at least in the value of its output, so that the Würzburgers brought a new dispensation in which logic and metaphysics if not epistemology itself were opened to experimental methods by Marbe, Messer, Ach, Ort, Bühler, Watt and many others. The end of an old thus became the beginning of a new period.

The new introspection is probably in its infancy, and there are many and new methods yet to be developed and protocols even vaster than those already accessible will be forthcoming. On the one hand, it would seem that the observation of psychic processes can furnish empirical data for the study of the intimate behavior of our own minds by not a few of the same canons that we follow in collecting objective data in the study of conduct in men and animals—of which indeed thought is a part. But there are important differences. A subject who performs a task when his mind is pervaded by a sense that he must remember and report upon all his states and processes and catch all of even those factors which naturally tend to fade beyond recall in a few seconds works in a manner essentially artificial, for most of the problems that life sets us are of a radically different nature. Such a subject must simply describe, we are told, and ignore meanings, although others tell us that thought in its very nature is pragmatic. Communication, too, is a very different matter on which introspection has as yet almost nothing to say. While we are performing the task set we are told that we must forget the coming hold-up and report later what occurred by the perseveration tendencies we find after we turn the mental eye inward to tell us how we saw. This is in fact as hard, if not as impossible, as to forget an impending examination when we are cramming for it. The point is that in such types of introspection there is always a second *Aufgabe*, the first being the instructions and the second the unformulated demand to report. I do not find that the obsession of the forthcoming report has ever been adequately studied, although it may be no less all-pervading than the *Aufgabe* itself.

Again, in reporting new processes, we find that some things stand out clearly and others less so. Then come yet others that are still more hazy, and so on until auto-suggestion must play a very important rôle. Here we need more introspection of the act of introspection itself, of which we know little, except its results. We feel at the end of a conscientiously performed introspection that there are yet many further probable and, back of them, many possible factors, and then if there is an *Ausfrage* it is extremely provocative of sources of error, as the Stern experiments have shown. As Dilling says, recollection is metamorphosis. However vivid and with however florid details the protocol is worked out, and however glibly it is reported, one can hardly escape the conviction in the first stage of catching the vanishing engrammes that there is a mass of residue not exhausted in the report. Indeed there is often the feeling that a quite different system of stresses and elements in the constellations of imagery and ideas would have been about as accurate a story of what occurred as the story actually given. At the best, there is no such control as in observing outer objects and processes, for only the introspector can see his own inner states. For him their *esse* is their *percipi* and he unconsciously gravitates toward a kind of epistemological solipsism just as truly as a hysterical patient evolves systems that are of profound interest to a physician. So the too introverted introspector learns to bring to light a fascinating account of the uncontrolled happenings within his soul, which are often marvelously unique and fascinating. Of course no one would for an instant suspect the trained and eminent men who have introspected for our benefit of anything but the most absolute honesty and sincerity, but one cannot help asking what is the psychological effect upon human nature of this habit of self-envisagement of auto-suggestive happenings within that no one else can by any possibility know as we do? How and how far then can others use these delectable self-revelations? Shall we take everything at its face value? Are there any criteria by which we could eliminate the returns of some far gone theorist or roguish wag, who might set out to be entertaining by inventions on purpose to impose upon the investigator? Are there no new and as yet undetected sources of error in all this new and unexplored field? Surely with all the possible methods of introspection, no one has a right to say to any one else, as certain Freudians do, "You must get our results by our methods or you are no true introspector." Divergences so far vastly outnumber agreements. My own imagery, *e. g.*, for "meaning" is a bright nucleus shining up through a darker and less clearly outlined mass, while Professor Titchener's is the glint of a colored dipper handle. Yet we mean approximately the same thing by "meaning," enough so at least to understand each other, although there is nothing in common in our imagery. From this it would seem to follow that the thought we use in communication is either imageless or else that we have not really got at its true imagery.

In my own introspections of two hundred abstract words, I find much of the data to be simply infantilism or imageries of unequivocally childish origin. Many of them are also as irrelevant as are etymologies to sentence meanings. Even on themes I have most elaborated I often find a fugitive Puck-like imagery that seems to be a kind of rudimentary or vestigial organ related to real thought perhaps about as such vestiges are to the adult body and its functions. It is possible that they may serve as a loosely attached tag or label of our imageless thought. The hold-up type of introspection ought to suddenly catch a very real and intense type of mentation and make it stand and deliver what is in it. The act introspected should not be trivial, nor without an end save only itself. Such a hold-up would be almost a shock and the report can not be entirely unlike the recalling of elusive dreams upon waking or the effort to coerce memory to deliver up its contents to recollection, in which process we are often prone to think hypothetically or in phrases perhaps sometimes actually muttered sotto voce, "such as," "as if," "somehow like," "either," "or," "perhaps," "was it," so that a certain Freudian *Entstellung* or secondary *Bearbeitung* is sometimes almost inevitable. The protocol may be given while we are in a state not unlike that in which dreams are coaxed to develop into the waking consciousness. Again, the danger, trifling though it be in most subjects, of *Entstellung* is hard to obviate and often a *censur* motive may be detected, especially with reference to painful or discreditable or betraying thoughts, while the question of a tendency of the introspective habit toward a new, even though very mild, type of paranoiac *Grübelzwang* must be at least considered. We surely should not become hypochondriacal about our thought symptoms. In a way there will be no organon in this field until we have a psychology of introspection which shall clear up these difficulties and give us criteria and better control.

Of course the words with which we must communicate the findings of our introspections are rough, general, too few, and ingrowing consciousness can at best only furnish certain specific data so that its rôle as a muse or oracle must not be magnified. Introspection in a sense inverts apperception which has a volitional or outward reference. It studies mental processes by their after-images, which are more defects than perfections of vision. If we are "watching out" inward, then one part of the mind is set off against another part, while in the most efficient thinking the soul acts as a unit and there is little left to look on and report. Again, if consciousness is in its nature remedial or therapeutic, introspection is not the high level of healthful mentation, but might easily become a psychosis. Our mental processes when functioning at their best are like the sun, which, though it casts all shadows, can never see any of them, and indeed we should learn little of the sun by their study, nor shall we from introspections if they are really confined to marginal processes. Hence it is those who believe that the ipsissimal nature of all thought is imaginal and can be got at by introspection that magnify this function, while it is quite possible on the other hand that these scrappy flotsam-jetsam images and innervations that accompany them are its defects rather than its perfections, as they certainly are vastly more individual and variable and therefore of course less generic than the thought-function itself. A good many of such data are like exuviæ or casts, the gill-slits and dew-claws of thought, the fossils or hard parts from which we infer conclusions concerning the thought itself. In the new introspection there is always a certain partition of the psyche into active and passive. Skilled and patient introversion may very likely make contributions of far greater value than all the patient study of after-images did, but the dangers and limitations of both have some analogy with each other. That they will have high genetic value, shedding light not only on the individual, but on the phyletic developmental history of thought, I for one am quite convinced, although psychology is really now in the stage of collecting. Its attitude is not entirely unlike that of the enterprising pilgrims of early crusading days who first found fossils of sea life upon the Alps and explained their presence theologically because they could no more foresee geology and paleontology than the modern introspector can foresee what genetic psychology is to become. It is well to take account of the survival value and power of the past in our word-dominated thinking, but the real process of thought is too perfectly evolved to leave many banal images in consciousness. Possibly they tend to bring, keep or recall into the conscious state processes which can become perfect only when consciousness is sloughed off or transcended so that my own conclusion at any rate, from studies elsewhere to be reported, is that the most intimate and efficient mentation is the most inaccessible to introspection.

This movement marks one very significant and wholesome change of attitude in modern psychology. All the dispositions, *Einstellungen,* determining tendencies, attitudes, *Anlagen,* facilitizations, the problem of imageless thought itself, etc., invite psychology to a deeper and less conscious stratum of the soul. They take us a most significant step nearer the underlying evolutionary nisus or push-up or will-to-live and will compel certain correlations with the Freudian psychology with its doctrines of wish and the great *Einstellung* of sex love. For instance, a few years ago, revisiting a farm that I had not seen since I was thirteen or fourteen, and coming across a wild rose-bush, to my amazement I experienced something very like a sob in the throat and tears in the eyes. I could evoke at first no intellectual experience or even memory, but upon the heels of these challenging physiological phenomena came an image of my mother in the front door in the distance, as she used to stand many years ago, although even the house is gone. Then came an image of her singing "The Last Rose of Summer," and finally a suggestion that I had associated this, to me in childhood, very pathetic song with this particular rosebush. Very likely the constellation contained other factors, for prettier roses grew about the house, and my mother greatly loved flowers in general, and perhaps I

433

may have felt juvenile pathos that so beautiful a flower should grow wild among the brakes of a pasture, and I may have had some thought of transplanting it. This, of course, is very far from the Würzburg type of introspection. Still it falls very well within the genus and illustrates certain dangers. Had I been able to recall nothing of these reminiscences about the wild rose, even though a psycho-analyzer had brought me to a more or less hypnoidal state so that revery might play freely, or if no *Ausfrage* had evoked anything further, or if I had been neurotic or degenerate, or if my throat feelings had been the result of some psychic trauma and there had been no escape into memory, then this whole constellation might have come to express itself as a hysterical globus or perhaps as sobs of a clonic and controlled kind. But in point of fact, although during that same summer and several since I have revisited this scene, there has been no trace of such symptoms, but only a kind of introspection. Now, the vague and voluminous feelings which I had toward that rosebush were probably closely paralleled by the intense and fetichistic sensations of Harnold at the first sight of the toe-poised foot of Gradiva.[1] Those who have read this story, which Freud thinks more typical than almost any real case, will remember that for this young woman-hating archæologist, who was so fascinated by the cast of this unique foot and went to Pompeii and elsewhere to parallel and explain it, this experience was the nucleus of a very complicated but quite submerged love experience with a girl whom he had known all the years of his childhood, but had so ignored and forgotten that when he first met his old acquaintance he mistook her for a Pompeiian come to life, and she cured him by falling into his moods at first and recalling step by step their old acquaintance.

We must realize, however, how large the field of introspection is and not become esoteric and raise the cry of amateurishness against psychologists who attempt new ways. This was the attitude long affected by Hegelians, a club of whom, for instance, many years ago in Boston insisted that James did not understand Hegel because he could not agree with him, so that he felt

[1] Der Wahn und die Träume in W. Jessen's Gradiva by S. Freud, Leipzig, 1908, 81 p.

compelled to react by his brilliant paper entitled "Some Hegelisms." It is illustrated also to my mind by Jung's and Ernest Jones' recent insistence that Morton Prince did not understand Freud truly because he did not find that his last remarkable case confirmed the Freudian rubrics, when in fact it was one which I can testify from personal acquaintance showed various types of multiple personality for which Freud has not provided. Indeed, Jones almost intimates that he has studied so many more cases than Prince that he (Jones) is therefore justified in assuming, without seeing Prince's patient, what the latter did or should find in her. So too it does not follow that, because one psychologist has made so many thousand introspections or evolved, matured and refined his own methods, others may not suddenly reach other results by other methods, which indeed may be more valuable and attained by simpler ways. The taxonomists of the thought process tell us that we must forever distinguish between true psychological introspection and logic, epistemology, metaphysics, physiology, meaning, communication. We might well, from this point of view and that of their results to date, apply here the Faustian phrase addressed to alchemy "Zwar ihr Bart ist graus, doch hebt ihr nicht die Riegel." (Your key is very complex, yet it does not turn the lock.) We have yet to see what professional introspection can do, which I believe promises to be very much indeed. But surely we must not forget that there is a little of the same difference here that there is between private thinking or writing for one's own personal edification and writing for publication, that some of the results of introspection are perfectly clear and others extremely uncertain, that the mind fairly oozes with after-thoughts, that questions—as Stern's work has shown—are exceedingly fruitful in suggestions and in causing errors. What do habituation and expertness in introspection consist of? Are they not in part the ability to act thinking as if it were real thinking, to think in a falsetto way so nearly like the natural register that it cannot be distinguished, as singers often try to add a few notes to their upper register? School children often complain that they can perform and understand, *e. g.*, sums aright, provided only they are not explained by or to them, for then they are paralyzed, just as children first learning to walk often fall when they suddenly realize what they are doing. The process to be introspected is, at any rate at first, far easier as well as briefer than the introspection. Processes that tend to lapse to the unconscious are dragged into more focal regions of apperception or into a searchlight to which they are not accustomed. This gives them a certain artificiality. It would seem that a process which we are just beginning to acquire, e. g., typewriting, would furnish the best material for introspection, and that completed processes would furnish the least, so that the more perfectly the mind worked the less we could tell about it. The artificial laboratory conditions not only often provoke actual sleepiness, but give the processes experimented on another goal than the natural, namely their own envisagement, and this renders them a little mimetic and scenic instead of natural. We are actor and audience by turns. Probably genuine introspection of a more or less perfected process necessarily involves dehabituation. It is in the direction of dissection and analysis. We tend a little to revert to the trial and error stage. Facility means obscuration and obliteration and impossibility or difficulty of introspection. As we acquire facility, we are less and less able to give an account of it. At any rate, expertness in introspection must involve a readjustment between effective mentation and the description of it. Facility in the one tends to be inversely as that of the other or, in Aristotelian terms, the enthymeme in its highest embodiment should be least of all explicable by introspection.

Perhaps, as Betts thinks, thought tends to become imageless in proportion as it becomes unconscious and vice versa, while at a certain point, as it sinks from the neo- to the paleo-pallium (or, as Ferrari [1] thinks, to the sympathetic system), it perhaps actually becomes feeling, so that instead of seeing with what we have seen, thinking with what we have thought, etc., we, in fact, feel with all that we have thought, felt, willed or sensed combined, feeling being the accumulated deposit of experience. At some point down this scale, though perhaps not a fixed one, the individual inherits as innate what was acquired in his forebears. Or again, as Baldwin and Dewey hold, concepts may be

[1] Ferrari, G. C.: "Le emozioni e la vita del subconscientie." Rivista di Psicologia, Vol. 8, No. Mazo Aprile, 1912, pp. 93-118.

generalized forms of motor response, the reduction to motor patterns tending to unify the manifoldness of experience. Thus the various motor patterns which often manifest themselves in the kinetic accompaniments of ideas may often shed light upon their genesis. Feeling is probably the next great theme looming up before psychology, our present knowledge of which is confusing almost to the verge of bankruptcy. Here introspection may contribute a little, but it must, from its very nature, be solved mainly by objective not to say observational methods.

Thus Wundt has tended to isolate himself from his natural allies and successors. But so technical and elaborate had his laboratory methods grown and so out of proportion to the importance of his results, so limited had his field become and, we must add, so efficient and so rich had been the previous output of the mines he had more or less exhausted that a break to newer fields, even if it did involve cruder, simpler and more superficial methods, was inevitable. Many of his followers were growing a little anxious for the future of the standard eye, ear and other half-physiological work, but these new departures have brought new zests and promise and had Wundt been a seer as well as a psychologist he would have made the dreams of these younger men the inspiring visions of his old age.[1]

[1] On the other hand, as Professor Titchener suggests to me, it should not be forgotten that when Wundt brought Meumann to Leipzig, it was left undecided whether the two laboratories, one devoted to pure and one to applied psychology, should be ultimately united or kept distinct; also that there were other reasons than the above and unconnected with his relations to Wundt, why Meumann accepted the call to Hamburg; also that Wundt has not opposed the laboratory of the Leipzig *Lehrerverein*. Professor Titchener also informs me that Kraepelin preferred to be a psychologist and that Wundt advised him to turn to psychiatry and to that degree is responsible for his signal achievements in that field. Wundt also gave Heller to psychiatry and Otto Fischer to physiology. Professor Titchener justly points to Wundt's *Festschrift*, made up of contributions by his students, as showing among them a range of topics such

Although Wundt devotes nearly one thousand pages of the sixth edition of his "Psychologie" to the senses and sensation and their implicates (chiefly to the two higher senses) and gives us at the outset nearly four hundred pages on the nervous system (chiefly a résumé, for he is not a neurologist), the last or seventh section is given up to the discussion of what he terms the principles of natural science, viz., causes, purpose, mechanism, energetics, noetics and parallelism, in which he embodies some of his favorite philosophical ideas. Even his doctrine of feeling and will is attracted by the analogy of his theory of sensations, so that he is really a sensationalist and an associationist, though a reconstructed one, for his superstructure is all built upon these foundations. Feelings associate or fuse much as sensations do, while apperception and will are directors and modifiers of association. His most important contributions lie in the advances he made in precisely this field. The prominence he gives to apperception makes his psychology a focal rather than a marginal one because he assumes that the most characteristic phases of psychic life take place where consciousness is most highly potentialized. Apperception is a perception of perception, and is the light of all his seeing, and so he is not only anthropomorphic but pædeiamorphic (if we may coin a clumsy name for a new thing), or prone to interpret the

as perhaps no other one man in his generation could have inspired in students. Wundt, too, has never misused his influence in academic circles, great as it is, despite the fact that he is averse to public functions and never attends scientific conferences or meetings of any sort, although his success as Rector was brilliant. Professor Titchener notes, too, that his omissions in psychology are only the negative side (which I have magnified) of a tremendous commission; that his differences from the Würzburg School are really only an episode; that I am too antagonistic and that the true verdict of history concerning Wundt's place will lie somewhere between my view and such a one as would be presented by so complete and devoted a Wundtian as Wirth.

lower by the higher, the less by the more conscious processes, the simpler by the more cultivated and trained men-
talities; and yet also he is prone to construe the more elementary sensory, emotive and volitional activities as normative for those higher thought, feeling and conative operations which his psychology does not deal with, being
concerned chiefly with the more rudimentary operations of
the most cultured minds, as evidenced in his relatively few
subjects.

Indeed, so elementary are the processes Wundt chiefly
deals with that his psychology helps neither him in writing nor us so very much in understanding his ''Völkerpsychologie,'' which deals with the highest forms of the psychic
activities of primitive people and moves among the most
long-ranged and intricate processes of the collective mind.
Here none of the conditions can be controlled or limited
in time or space, for we deal with secular activities of
large groups. The viewpoints too are new as well as the
method, and radically different from and opposed to those
with which the laboratory and logic make us familiar.
Wundt however has boldly entered here and his remarkable powers of compiling, ordering, digesting (for here
as also in neurology he has done no first-hand work) have
enabled him, with far more help from his philosophical
than his psychological forestudies, to achieve genuine success.

Wundt's passage to the, for him, new field of *Völkerpsychologie* is itself a fact of great interest to geneticism,
since it is comparable to the developmental changes, often
marking distinct nodes, so well seen in Plato, Kant, Schelling, Fechner, and others, to say nothing of such cases as
Swedenborg and Tolstoi, whose work in middle or later life
took new directions. Most laboratory psychologists, like a
few rare men in other sciences, insist on a frontage that
opens into the broad fields of philosophy. They do this
either from taste or, sometimes, from the necessities, or

for the security of their chairs. But the philosophical register into which he so easily modulates did not satisfy all Wundt's humanistic proclivities, which experimental work so sternly represses. His logical trend too and his rich experience in putting experimental results and thought into words interested him in language, and his reflections on the imagination and *Gemütsbewegungen* pointed him to the psychology of speech, from which he passed to that of myth and religion. Thus we have his remarkable achievement of five stately volumes totaling over 3,000 pages, issued between the years of 1900 and 1909, when the author was 68-77 years of age. This of itself is an achievement perhaps without precedent in the history of philosophy. It shows a conservation of mental energy which, particularly in one who had toiled so hard and unremittingly all his previous life, makes him one of the grandest of grand old men. It suggests many unanswerable questions as to his mode of mental and physical regimen in developing what James called the higher powers of man, how much was due to constitution and heredity and how much to his plan of life and course of work, what his method of preparation and writing really is? It makes us feel that he owes to the world before he dies a confessional autobiography concerning the conditions of his boyhood, his home, his parents, and the other guiding influences of his early life about which Helmholtz did not scorn to give his friends most interesting, if all too brief, intimations. This so impersonal and reserved man owes this to his pupils, friends, and the public, for his importance will compel, if not challenge, posterity to persistently explain him, which Hegel says is the supreme criterion, if it is also at the same time the penalty of greatness. If we regret his lack of hospitality to developments along other lines which he has in part inspired, we should not forget at the same time that in the above work he has shown marvelous capacity to embark on new seas with the enthusiasm of his youth unabated and his faculties undimmed.

For Wundt the problem of language bottoms on gesture and the movements expressive of feeling or affectivity, and so he exploits his views of the relations between feeling and the circulation, and also his tridimensional theory, as somewhat basal, assuming that every psychic movement is accompanied by a physical one. Gestures are classified as pointing, imitating, referring and symbolic, and they have a syntax of their own which he characterizes. Vocal elements which arise in close connection with these as perhaps their matrix are traced in the animal and child world and the imitative and traditional factors are stressed. Rhythm and tempo play an important rôle but language is too complex to have any single origin. Then follows an exposition of phonetic change, analogy, etc., as connected with the laws of association. His position is that changes of sound (e. g., those illustrating Grimm's law) are not at all due to two parallel principles, the one physical and the other psychic, but that the latter dominates. Then come words, their form, their combination in sentences, their changes of meaning, and finally his conclusion concerning the origin of speech, which is in substance that it is a continuous product of very many factors, all of which are still active, so that no specific time or conditions under which it arose can be described. The same forces that made it are still operative. Speech is what it becomes and it is still becoming. In all this to our thinking he has drawn far too little upon the data available from the studies of the language of childhood and has made but slight when he should have made far more extensive use of speech diseases. He has followed too exclusively those philologists who have occupied themselves chiefly with the Aryan languages and has neglected, as they have, the more recent very significant lessons for the psychology of speech to be drawn from the Turanian and Hamitic tongues. He had, too, an opportunity to discuss more fully the vexed problem of the relations between grammar and logic, a theme that to our thinking seems to lie right athwart the way of the further study of the higher mental processes. Perhaps he has been somewhat prone to push into the foreground his own psychological concepts, not so much to urge them upon the consideration of philologists or to give their work new psychological terms and thought forms or trends, as because he overestimates their explanatory power and possibly hopes thus to smooth and straighten the long and hard way from his own stronghold to that of the thinkers in the domain of linguistics and of comparative philology.

On the other hand, experts who read what he says in this field criticize him in the slightly veiled and mildly ironical way which now seems to have supplanted the fashion of the old vituperative criticisms. Delbrück [1] for instance confesses, somewhat as Socrates did of the Sophists, his amazement at Wundt's erudition and the magnificent sweep of his generalizations, but regrets that he has not had time to make himself thoroughly acquainted with the present status of the subject and slyly suggests a relation to it somewhat like that of Gall (whom Bunge has lately sought to bring back to favor) to the later students in brain localization.

The second part of this work on Myth and Religion enters a field common to philology, history, ethnology and theology and begins by a discussion of phantasy, starting from pseudoscopic illusions, space and time phantasies and their relations to the special and to motor sensations. Then

[1] Delbrück, Berth. Grundfragen der Sprachforschung mit Rücksicht auf W. Wundt's Sprach-psychologie erörtert. Strassburg, K. F. Trübner, 1901, 181 p. See also Sütterlin. Das Wesen des sprachlichen Gebilde, 1902. Wundt acknowledges in the third edition (1911) his indebtedness to these authors, but accuses them of a "historicism" which underestimates the psychological point of view.

come the plays and games of children and their imaginative activities as shown in their poems and drawings. Phantasy is further discussed in the development of the different arts and in ornamentation by the use of plant, animal and other forms. Song, poetry, dancing, music and the drama follow, and the first volume ends with the discussion of phantasy as seen in myth, with its theories and modes of interpretation. The entire second volume is occupied with primitive conceptions of the soul, and in discussing this Wundt deals with dreams, visions, ecstasy, the origin of demons, soul cults, animism, magic and fetichism. Under animalism and manism come totemism, animal deities, taboo, lustrations, offerings and sacrifices, ancestral cults and those of ghosts, spirits of vegetation and disease, and protective deities. In the third volume, nearly six hundred pages are given to nature myths, which to our thinking is the best of all, and which ends with the development of conceptions of the *Jenseits*, or transcendency, with the final 173 pages given to the origin of religious cults and their relations to myths and legends, symbols and their changes. The various forms of cult, chthonic and celestial, fire, prayers, sacrifices, purification and the forms of cult legend, especially those of Christ and Buddha, are briefly dwelt on. Finally comes the discussion of the essence of religions, its psychological, metaphysical and ethical aspects and its present and future.

In Wundt's discussion of nature-myths and cults he gives considerable space to those that are founded on the sky and its phenomena and also to those which are connected with vegetation (plants and trees) and animals, but has in some cases little and in others nothing and always far too little to say of other great nature cycles or myth-inspiring themes which deserve almost if not quite equal rank, such as fire, both celestial and earthly, wind, water in its various forms, earth, generation (phallic religions are passed over almost in silence). He appears never to have heard of the important and suggestive studies that have been made on the vital way in which the minds of children and adolescents still respond to these agencies that have done so much both to develop and to mold mind. *Völkerpsychologie* for Wundt is made up of Nature (to which two of his five volumes on the subject are devoted), myth, custom and religion. In this domain, Wundt probably expresses his sense for elements by dealing for the most part only with the lower primitive religions and has very little to say of Brahmanism, Buddhism, Confucianism, Mohammedanism and indeed only a very few general pages at the close on Christianity, from which it would rather seem that he favors a confessionless church, the conservation of the Christ legend and cult, would have a kind of critique of deities and has a very high appreciation of Catholicism, which he calls "an encyclopædia of all religions," containing more or less ordered elements of everything from animism and fetichism up to the very highest things.

Just as Wundt has amplified, revised and rewritten his "Psychologie" over and over so that the sixth is not only three or four times as large as the first edition and almost another book, so this work needs the same amplification to be adequate to its subject. This at least is the writer's impression, based upon those portions of the field to which he has given attention, although he is frankly incompetent to judge all. What Wundt says, for instance, of child-study, of children's language, of dolls, of drawing, animal myths and several groups of the nature myths is little better than platitudinous. Why, too, has he entirely ignored the Freudian interpretation of myth as represented by Abraham, Rink, Riklin, Silberer and others as his "Psychologie" ignores the form of German pragmatism so admirably summed up in Veihinger's "Philosophie des als Ob"? Even if in some parts of this vast domain his work is a little like the first steps in astronomy, which consisted of mapping constellations with no recognition of relative distance and no evolutionary perspective, still he is not like Adam in Eden merely naming everything in sight, for he does classify all that he knows.

Religion Wundt defines as man's "feeling that he and the world around him belong to a supersensuous world in which those ideals that appear to him to be the highest goals of human endeavor are thought to be realized." This at least adds another to the nearly three score definitions of religion which I have gathered. Certain scruples, however, are inevitable, e. g., Is religion all feeling? Must our supreme wishes be thought to be realized, and if so must this be done in the metaphysical world? Myth and religion are to Wundt unique self-revelations of the *Gemüth*. He starts with the "besouling apperception" of animism and traces especially various stages of the soul cult in things, animals and humanity. To these preliminary stages he devotes six hundred pages, ending with the myth and the cult of heroes and finally deities, and hence he does not hold to a primitive monotheism. God is a "late psychic synthesis." And finally in the modern philosophical, critical ideal of Jesus, the old supernatural ideas of deity suffered "entmythization," or lost their mythic form in the image of the ideal man, the embodiment of all moral ends. Myth and cult, however, form a matrix in and under which as their abiding and ineluctable resultant is the belief in the transcendental. This faith abides after the pod in which it grew has gone. Man has an invincible faith in a metaphysical order of things because he once believed in myth and in abiding ethical worths due to his practice of rites, which always stand for ideal conduct. Religion, thus purified, is metaphysical, an eternal creation. As above defined, religion was only implicit in its earlier, cruder forms, but now it is a reverent belief in a world-ground that is moral to the core. The religion of reason which philosophic minds crave must give subjective personal satisfaction and be known to be universally valid, and hence it must transcend experience. It must conceive the world not as static but as evolving toward a goal. Religion, however, must do far more than satisfy reason. A God that is inscrutable and transcendent does not satisfy, because the soul demands a concrete, personal, nonsupernatural embodiment of its moral ideal. "From this viewpoint Christ has a double meaning, viz.: (1) to himself as a moral example (not as God but as a man of the deepest morality, and as such the most eminent witness of his infinity); (2) he must also give a conception of the ground and purpose of the world as necessary and adequate to the moral ideal." Christ to him is thus a symbolic expression of the religious life and has no other supernatural quality, as God is an expression of the idea of the world-ground. The belief in immortality is an expression of the world's purpose. It belongs to the moral world order that we believe that moral values once worked out will never be left to perish, so that our worthy ends somewhere serve other ends, higher and perhaps unattainable to our knowledge. We must value moral traits and acts for themselves and not because they make an ego happy. The lust to survive would not really be satisfied by conceiving the ego as a perdurable substance. The soul de-related to others and to good ideals would have no consciousness and so its mere preservation would be immaterial. The immortality ideal is a mere concept-form which rightly interpreted means the imperishability of good deeds. It brings this thought home to the *Gemüth*. Every soul, too, has its function in the world-process into which we should incorporate our lives. The principle that all spiritual creations have an absolute and imperishable worth leads Wundt to art, in which R. Eisler,[1] I think rightly, makes Wundt's world-scheme culminate.

Wundt's religious views have been variously received

[1] W. Wundt Philosophie und Psychologie. Leipzig, 1902, 210 p.

by theologians. Carl Craig [1] bitterly condemns them along with those of Feuerbach, and Lange, while C. Thieme [2] simply résumés them and expressly refrains from all critical discussion of them.

Wundt is one of the most, perhaps the most voluminous of all authors in any field, living or dead. Taking the last editions of his works, from 1858 to 1911, we find nearly 16,000 pages,[3] together with nearly as many more of which he wrote many in the *Philosophische* and *Psychologische Studien,* including in the former two final volumes of the *Festschrift.* His pages too are not small, and abound in small-type passages. Counting pages alone, we find that Spencer and Darwin each wrote less than 12,000, Hegel less than 11,000, Schelling less than 8,000, Kant about 4,400, while Helmholtz has to his credit about 6,000 pages. Thus it is no easy matter to compass all Wundt has written. It would be interesting to know how many of his leading followers have read much outside his "Physiologische Psychologie," or have even read everything in that. Some of his works have never reached a second edition. His "Essays" and his "Principles of Mechanical Nature" have done so, while his "Logic," "Ethics," part of his "Folk Psychology," have reached a third, his "Introduction to Philosophy" and "Human and Animal Psychology" a fifth, and his "Psychology" a sixth edition.

Varied and voluminous as his work is, it is fortunate that we already have a few helpful and brief digests, finders, or epitomes of his activities which give a bird's-eye view and may serve the beginner as introductions. Of these,

[1] Modernstes Christentum und moderne Religions-psychologie. Freiburg, 1907, 150 p.

[2] Zur Wundt's Religions-psychologie. Leipzig, 1910, 16 p.

[3] The bibliography of Titchener and Geissler (Amer. Jour. of Psych., October, 1908, with the supplements of 1909, 1910, and 1911) totals 18,336 pages.

the first was that by Edmund König.[1] Then came the later and in some respects, on the whole, as it ought to be, more precise *vade mecum* by Rudolf Eisler.[2] Here, too, should be mentioned Julius Wentzel,[3] and, finally, Wundt's own introduction.[4]

Ever since the sway of the great German systems, and especially Hegel's, who lorded it over all the sciences during his own life as no other thinker ever did, every philosopher the world over, and especially in Germany, has cherished at heart, perhaps unconsciously to himself, the fond dream of bringing down from the mount of speculation a table of laws for the special sciences. Each has sought to determine accurately the boundaries between the different sciences, prescribe their methods, explain to them their own fundamental assumptions, criticizing and shepherding them in general somewhat as theology once did, although the reign of reason each sought to inaugurate was milder and less coercive than that of dogma. Of this ideal of the past Wundt is probably to-day the most conspicuous living embodiment. Although it is his avowed ideal even in his Inaugural, it seems to have more and more dominated his work. His rare gifts as a lecturer have enabled him to maintain at Leipzig more than anywhere else in the world the old tradition that students of all faculties should take one or more courses in philosophy, and so his lectures, which are simpler than his books upon the same subject, have always been thronged and his fees from this source perhaps unprecedented. This academic custom is pedagogically sound and perhaps increasingly so in these days of

[1] Wundt; seine Philosophie und Psychologie. Stuttgart, Frommann, 1901, 207 p.

[2] W. Wundt's Philosophie und Psychologie, Leipzig, Barth, 1902, 210 p.

[3] Editor of Wundt's Zur Psychologie und Ethik. Leipzig, Reclam, 1911, 205 p.

[4] Einführung in die Psychologie. Leipzig, Voigtländer, 1911, p. 129.

progressive speculation, when each expert is so prone to lack perspective and see only his own world. All need a broad comparative view such as only one who makes generalizations his specialty can give, even though his material grows ever thinner and more superficial as the domains of knowledge broaden and multiply. But this need is very different from the old philosophic hegemony. Did any modern, up-to-date mathematician ever look to a philosopher to learn the nature of axioms or logical laws of proof? Did any modern chemist ever learn anything from all the modern scholastic speculations concerning atoms and their affinities and repulsions, or a physicist learn of them anything concerning energy, matter, or even magnetism and electricity, which have been almost normative themes with some of them? Did any biologist ever learn of life, any lawyer of the nature of law, and so on of all the rest? Did any discoverer or inventor ever learn a thing from logic, or has he not rather told it something it did not know before? The philosopher may learn of these experts, but he no longer has anything really worth while to teach them. He can talk helpfully to students. He can write in an interesting way to other philosophers who engage in his own business, or perhaps to theologians who still dream of a science of sciences, but the day of philosophic schools recruited from outside philosophy's domain is gone. In fact, philosophy is a department beside and not above the others. In this respect Wundt is to-day even in Germany somewhat of an anachronism, a noble relic of a great age.

How much have students of animal psychology derived from his treatise on that subject, or neurologists from his ''Mechanik der Nerven''? He has no school or following in ethics, logic, epistemology, etc., because his views in these fields contain few salient distinctive traits, but are for the most part only admirable epitomes of and adjustments to the stock philosophical opinions and attitudes. In these several fields, his work shows evidence of amazing reading and careful gathering of data and his conclusions are, on the whole, the embodiments of sound common sense and wise judgment, but, to my thinking, there is not very much more.

On the other hand, certain domains far more contiguous to a true modern psychology, such as biology and evolution, abnormal psychology, and even borderline psychology, hardly exist for him. At any rate they have contributed almost nothing to his opinions, and his works have borne no fruit whatever in these domains. If he does not live in a pre-Darwinian age, he certainly does in a pre-Freudian. If, instead of his excursions into speculative fields, he had brought his genius for unremitting toil to bear here, how different and how far greater would have been the results! On the great subjects of the psychology of sex, psychopathy, psychogenesis, he is almost silent and his hostility to applied psychology even in the field of education, as illustrated by his attitude as shown above toward Menmann and the Würzburgers, is, to say the least, hardly worthy of him, especially as he is so interested in the pedagogy of his own work that he has written an introduction and finally even a primer for beginners. If it be said that he leaves it to others to apply his principles in these domains, the answer is twofold: First, they are all fields where psychology has vastly more to learn than to teach, more to learn even, perhaps, than from the laboratory, so that had he drawn upon these data the plexus of his system, the character of his scheme of things, would have been modified. He has not used all the available data. The other answer is, that, in fact, his own system contains certain features that seem surds and that are positive deterrents to the influence his system might have had in these domains. These handicaps come again from his speculative proclivities, *e. g.*, what does the worker in these adjacent fields care for his tridimensional theory of feeling, his tedious discussions and implications as to parallelism and interaction, and the whole question of the relation of the soul to the body? His theory of apperception has throughout metaphysical implications and the discussions of the theory of knowledge, to which direct and indirect references are so often made in his psychology, are caviar to the scientific attitude of mind.

To my own mind, too, his growing predilection for method, which bulks so large in his later *Studien,* violates the Aristotelian principle that we must never affect to be more exact than the nature of the subject justifies or demands. Some of his voluminous tables and his intricate formulæ are hardly less than methodistic affectations which make things needlessly hard, when science, on the other hand, should make intricate things plain, according to the well-known principle of Avenarius that science consists in thinking the world adequately with the least expenditure of energy, or to secure the very highest economy and efficiency.

Wundt seeks always to be cool, judicial, logical; to approve and weigh all things with conscientious care. He is, however, often dull, dry, involved, and hypermethodical. His is not a *Bahnbrechender* or great original philosophic mind, but he seeks to retain and harmonize the best that is in Leibniz, Kant, Fichte, Hegel, and Schopenhauer, and to combine their sounder speculations with the positivism of modern science.

Gramzow [1] says that Wundt is one of the very few present-day philosophers with polymathic learning. He regards philosophy as the crown of all sciences, bringing them all to a higher unity in which are found the fundamental principles of the world. His speculative system bottoms on all the sciences and leads up to metaphysics. Philosophy to him has two domains, one that treats of the

[1] Geschichte der Philosophie seit Kant, von Otto Granzow. Charlottenburg, Vürkner, 1906, 680 p.

principles of knowledge or epistemology, and the other that treats of the knowledge of the principles that underlie the sciences. The first concerns itself with the origin of knowledge and the last with the axioms, presuppositions, and modes of reasoning in the various special domains. We know by an immediate experience which precedes all understanding and reflection, and this prime noetic function extends both to outer objects and to acts of feeling, conceiving, and willing, and even to their controlling determinants. Subject and object are inseparable and all thought involves elements of conceiving, feeling, and willing. The latter function is basal and distinguishes the ego from the non-ego. It is ever present in the form of peculiar sensations of tension. Nothing but will can be truly called our own. Will brings all our psychic functions into connection and also effects psychic causality. Thus Wundt is a voluntarist as opposed to the intellectualism of Herbart and Beneke.

Will is the absolute actuality; not Schopenhauer's will, first appearing by the principle of individuation in time and space in concrete things, but a totality of individual conscious wills. These are not isolated entities, but acts with vital inner connection. His is not an unconscious will that creates intellect and reason, but the germ of mind which was hidden at first in the natural will, but comes out in society. All will entities are conceptive. Sensation and idea arise from receptionality, action and reaction between the various factors of will, which may be in conflict or may coincide. Will is originally *Trieb* or impulse and instinct.

I, for one, believe profoundly in philosophy as an academic discipline, to be taught historically and enthusiastically, but always as literature and not as dogma, without indoctrination into any school, but in such a way as to give the student sympathy for all views. The speculative romanticizing with thought and the great story of the

categories or nativistic roots in the soul are of high culture interest and value, perhaps are almost the culmination
of liberal humanistic studies. In the long grail quest for
these roots the human soul documents how truly it has been
oriented from the great Greeks down toward the problem
of genetic origins, but how in formulating and making
tables of innate ideas it has set a gate athwart the path
of genetic explanation and has followed the methods of
mathematical deduction to its own great harm in the mea-
sureless domain of mentation, where these methods cannot
apply, save in the simple use of statistics. Systems are
the most refined of methods and are essentially to be
studied as such. Wundt's studies in this latter field should
have mellowed both his method and conclusion in philosophy, the story of which is as interesting and important
for biology, literature, history, politics, as it is for the
sciences, if not more so, but psychology should be no whit
more infiltrated by philosophy than should any of these
others. Wundt's psychology is like Milton's "tawny lion
pawing to get free" from his philosophy, but not yet entirely free. What problem in either field was ever solved
in the other? But to conclude, much as there is in his
thought which we might wish had been otherwise, the one
inevitable fact that stands out above all others is that
none of Wundt's followers or contemporaries in any one,
and far less in all three, of the domains he has wrought
in—psychology, philosophy, and folklore—has begun to
accomplish or at present promises to accomplish work of
anywhere near such magnitude, significance, and solid
worth as his.

Wundt's style is heavy and Teutonic, his sentences involved and loaded with supplementary clauses of every
kind. Perhaps such sentences are nearer to the nature of
thought and perhaps, indeed, German and Greek fit it
more closely than English, as has been claimed by Teutons
and classicists, respectively. In that case, Wundt needs

not merely translation but rather free restatement in order that his thought shall appeal with full force to the Anglo-Saxon mind. He is as far as possible from Schopenhauer's lucidity and studied forcefulness and still farther from Nietzsche's or Bahnsen's scintillating "grasshopper gait," shattered with dashes, parentheses, stars, etc., and no contrast could be greater than between his and James' habit of expression. The Wundtian imperviousness is only partly compensated by his tendency to rubricize or by Wirth's index and he often seems to "write himself clear." In repeating others' views he does not quote, as does James, many chapters of whose psychology are one-third made up of citations. Thus it comes that often if we wish to know exactly the views of others we must look them up, and, indeed, we often need to know more precisely what those he differs from really mean before accepting his conclusions, for he does not himself do justice to those he criticizes, *e. g.*, Horwicz and various French and especially English writers. His style in the main is lusterless as lead and it is as solid. His academic isolation is over-compensated by his vast erudition. Spencer was almost a prodigy of ignorance by comparison, reading little French and less German, and evolving his scheme of things spiderwise from within. Darwin's correspondence was world-wide and his work followed the ant method of collection. Wundt is the true Baconian bee, collecting from without and secreting from within. If Wundt ever did write his autobiography it would doubtless, if as long, be as uninteresting as Spencer's. He is more charmed with books than with human nature at first hand. Huxley was a comparative morphologist who later in life made quite intensive and illuminating studies of Berkeley, Hume, and Descartes. Wundt's knowledge of philosophy is wider and more general, moving rather in the sphere of its ampler historians with no monographic studies of individual thinkers. Spencer was inspired by a subjective oracle and wrought in singular independence of others he should have known until his surprising and unfortunate controversy with Weismann brought an awakening, that must have been painful, to the fact that there was a biology of a very different pattern across the German sea. Like Spencer, Wundt strove to evolve an all-comprehending system, but there could hardly have been two schemes of things so comprehensive with less in common, and while each would have profited greatly by some knowledge of the other, Spencer would have had far more to learn by such mutual acquaintance. Wundt never agonized to solve the great problem of the *Zeitgeist* and sphinx riddle that oppressed his own spirit, either for the benefit of the world, like Kant, or to attain inner personal peace and insight, like Descartes, Lotze, Fechner, and Royce. He is in no sense a philosopher of temperament but is essentially academic. Nor was he ever anxious concerning the postmortem future of his soul, like James. The lay public will, for this reason, always care less for him. If Hegel, the greatest German of speculative a priorism, the greatest of modern scholastics, was platonic in his spirit, Wundt is more Aristotelian. Nor is unity his dominant quest. He is not possessed by one great idea like Spencer and Darwin. He collects, compares, reconstructs judiciously and all with the coolest mind and the soundest common sense. He would rather be commonplace than brilliantly wrong. The future historian of philosophy will find it hard to place him. He is outstripped by experts in all directions, but he has made a memorable contribution to the enlargement and ordering of the human mind. He can hardly be said to have a school and has made no effort to keep in touch with his former pupils, and the word Wundtian will never have any very definite connotations. His views have great length and breadth, but if they sometimes seem to lack depth, it is perhaps partly due to his long apprenticeship to physiology (which, despite embryology, was singularly isolated, at least until Verworn's

time, from general biology), and partly due to his lack
of orientation to evolution. He is a revered master craftsman, but perhaps a trifle lacking in personality and humanism for a philosopher. His work is not a finality and
no doubt even his psychology will be transcended in time
as his physiology long since was. We may well hope that
he will welcome this result. He can never lose historical
significance. For the very impulsion he has given will
carry his followers beyond him. Perhaps the Würzburgers
who have given new life and courage to laboratory workers,
some of whom were growing anxious concerning the future
of their installations, may prove, after all, to be his most
legitimate offspring.

But they have not yet established any such high claim,
and no one has yet appeared who gives promise of being
able to tell us what these vast masses of protocols of introspections really mean, or whither the evermore refined analyses (which the influence of Hüsserl's thought suggests
may prove to be only a new epistemology) really lead.
Neither have we as yet any useful hint as to what *Anlagen*,
determining tendencies, etc., which so far defy analysis,
are; or even whether the problem of imageless thought is
a solvable one, or only a new scholastic puzzle from which
the most and best we can hope is that it may provoke discussion tending to progress, like the Lange-James theory
of emotion. Perhaps what is now needed is another Wundt
with another life as long and as inspired as his has been
by the love of hard, patient work; perhaps it is a bold
synthetic genius who will show us the way out. It would,
indeed, be the irony of fate if it should be found that the
Freudian sympathetic insight or intuition, applied objectively to these very introspective data, treated somewhat as
symptoms for interpretation by the observer, should be next
in order, or, if abnormal psychology should find the clew
of method which the present juncture needs. There are
psychologists who seem to infer from the Würzburg move-

ment the need of indefinite refinement in method, both experimental and logical, who affect esotericism and seem to regard laboratory introspection as a gift of nature and art combined and as the only psychological muse. But these are not creative minds, and indeed, we have had nothing done in this country or in English that measures up to the level of the best Würzburg papers in this entire field. Scholarship, critical acumen, and power of precise definition, we have, and also ability to produce contributions of the doctors' theses order, with minor variations from and combinations of European creations that work out results supplementary to these. It would seem as if laboratory psychology in this country was now sufficiently developed so that it should be less dependent upon new departures made in Germany. The present *impasse* is the most challenging opportunity ever presented to psychologists. In this crisis, our need is a new method, point of view, assortment of topics, and problems. These I believe geneticism is very soon to supply. Meanwhile, we may have, at least for a time, to follow Wirth's call to go back to Wundt.

WILHELM WUNDT

The works in this list are believed to comprise all of the important and certainly all of the larger works of Wundt. They are arranged in order of their first editions, but the number of pages is from the last edition in most cases. For an exhaustive bibliography of all of Wundt's works, including ephemeral papers, see the list compiled by Titchener and Geissler in *American Journal of Psychology*, Vol. 19, 1908, pp. 541-556, together with supplements in Vol. 20, p. 570; Vol. 21, pp. 603-4; Vol. 22, pp. 586-7.

Die Lehre von der Muskelbewegung. 1858, 241 p.

Beiträge zur Theorie der Sinneswahrnehmung. 1862, 451 p.

Vorlesungen über die Menschen und Thierseele (3 vols.).

1863, 955 p. 5th ed., 1911, 558 p. Trans. of 2d ed. by Creighton and Titchener, 454 p.

Lehrbuch der Physiologie des Menschen, 1865. 4th ed., 1878, 851 p.

Die physikalischen Axiome und ihre Beziehung zum Causalprincip; ein Capitel aus einer Philosophie der Naturwissenschaften. 1866, 137 p.

Handbuch der medicinische Physik. 1867, 555 p.

Untersuchungen zur Mechanik der Nerven und Nerven-centren. 2 vols. in one, 1871-1876, 423 p.

Grundzüge der physiologischen Psychologie. 1874. 1st ed. 870 p. 6th ed., 1908-1911, 3 vols., 2317 p.

Logik. 1880-1883. 1st ed., 2 vols., 1205 p. 3d ed., 1908, 3 vols, 1995 p.

Ethik. 1886. 1st ed., 577 p. 3d ed., 1903, 2 vols., 933 p.

System der Philosophie. 1889. 3d ed., 1907, 2 vols., 738 p.

Völkerpsychologie. 1900-1909, 2 vols. in 5. 3161 p. 3d. ed. of Erster Bd., Erster Teil, 1911, 695 p.

Gustav Theodor Fechner: Rede zur Feier seines hundertjahrigen Geburstages. 1901, 92 p.

Sprachgeschichte und Sprachpsychologie, mit Rücksicht auf B. Delbrück's "Grundfragen der Sprachforschung." 1901, 110 p.

Einleitung in der Philosophie. 1902. 2d. ed., 466 p. 5th ed., 1909, 471 p.

Essays. 1906. 2d ed., 440 p.

Festrede zur fünfhundertjahrigen Jubelfeier der Universität Leipzig. 1909, 83 p.

Die Principien der mechanischen Naturlehre. 1910. 2d ed., 217 p.

Kleine Schriften. 1910-1911. 2 vols., 1136 p.

Einführung in die Psychologie. 1911, 129 p.

Probleme der Völkerpsychologie. 1911, 120 p.

Grundriss der Psychologie. 1896. 10th ed., 1911, 414 p. Trans. by Chas. H. Judd.

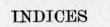

INDICES

INDEX OF AUTHORS

461

INDEX OF AUTHORS

INDEX OF AUTHORS

INDEX OF AUTHORS

INDEX OF SUBJECTS

(1)